Boulogne.

...anoeuvrant sous les yeux de l'Empereur Napoléon.

...rioul, Grand Maréchal du Palais.

...aux bâtiments de la flotille que sa majesté l'Empereur est présent à la manoeuvre.

Explication.

p. Poste établi pour transmettre les Signaux
   de L'amiral à la Flotille en Rade
   ou dans le Port.
q. Plateau de la Barraque de L'amiral.
r. Ruines de fortifications bâties par les Romains
   lors de l'expédition de J. César en
   Angleterre 52 ans avant J. C.
s. Fort en bois bâti sur pilotis pour deffendre
   l'entrée du Port.
t. Balises indiquant le Chenal.
u. Jettée ou musoir de l'est.
v. Fort Napoléon ou jettée de l'ouest.
x. Fort Châtillon.
y. Fort de l'heurt bâti sur un Rocher
   pour deffendre l'une des extrémités
   de la Rade.

We shall fight on the
BEACHES

We shall fight on the
BEACHES
Defying Napoleon & Hitler, 1805 and 1940

Brian Lavery

NAVAL INSTITUTE PRESS
Annapolis, Maryland

First published in Great Britain
in 2009 by Conway, an imprint of Anova Books,
10 Southcombe Street, London W14 0RA
www.anovabooks.com

This edition published and distributed in the
United States of America and Canada
by the Naval Institute Press, 291 Wood Road,
Annapolis, Maryland 21402-5034
www.nip.org

Library of Congress Catalog Card No. 2009937430

ISBN: 978-1-59114-947-7

Edited and designed by DAG Publications Ltd

Printed by CPI Mackays, Chatham, ME5 8TD, UK.

CONTENTS

CONTENTS

MAPS

INTRODUCTION

I first had the idea for this work while helping prepare for the *Nelson and Napoleon* exhibition at the National Maritime Museum. The parallels between the periods seemed striking at the time and, having looked into the subject in detail, now seem even more so – I hope to demonstrate this to the reader in due course. Those of us who were born in the 1940s have never felt very far from World War II. There were air raid shelters and bomb sites, and even in Scotland lines of concrete anti-tank obstacles were to be found on beaches, though thankfully no mines or barbed wire. Later I was in London for the funerals of both Sir Winston Churchill and Princess Diana, and got some idea of the emotion that the burial of a great popular hero like Nelson must have engendered. It is not difficult to identify with the people of the Napoleonic Wars, with their patriotism combined with hedonism – perhaps easier than with the buttoned-up Victorians or the insecure 1930s. Having written extensively on the navies of the age of sail and World War II, it seemed only natural to combine the periods in a single volume. I was not unfamiliar with air force history, ever since the early 1960s when Webster and Frankland's *Strategic Air Offensive against Germany* opened my eyes to the flaws in the original official interpretation. I have had to learn rather more about the army, and I am grateful to Lieutenant-Colonel David Stone, Retd., and Colonel Gerald Napier, RE, Retd., for some comments on this. There is a great wealth of material, especially for 1940, and I have not been able to cover every aspect in detail, or look at every single record. At the same time, as always, there are gaps in our knowledge, as people threw away records of what seemed at the time banal or trivial but might have given us greater insight into the period.

The subject does not lend itself to a linear narrative, for two main reasons. Two distinct periods are covered, and I have arranged the material from each in separate sections, with one major exception, and short linking passages. This gives the reader the chance to follow through one period or the other if he wants to, but also allows him to compare and contrast the two periods through major themes. Secondly, it is not giving much away to reveal that the book has no major denouement in the usual sense of the term. Only in imaginary history can we decide whether an invasion would have succeeded or not, and in what circumstances it might have been successful.

I have tried to keep the work within a tight focus, confined to the period between the beginning of war against Napoleon in May 1803 and his withdrawal from Boulogne two and a half years later; and the real threat of German invasion between June and September 1940. In neither case did the threat disappear – after the British victories at Trafalgar and in the Battle of Britain respectively – but it was no longer 'at the top of the agenda'. Because of the narrow timescale, I have confined myself as far as possible to documents actually produced at the time, particularly for the 1940 period. It is very easy to interpolate backwards from later in the war, but it is worth remembering that the army was disorganized and demoralised after Dunkirk; that the navy was still largely equipped with its pre-war ships and awaiting a large influx of 'hostilities only' seamen; and that the RAF was not the meritocratic force it would become later in the war but was still bound by the class attitudes of the 1930s. Unlike the people of Britain in 1803–5, the civilians, soldiers, sailors and airmen of 1940 had no experience of this kind of war and had to learn very fast. Despite having intelligence services of considerable and growing efficiency, the governments of neither period knew all they needed to know about the enemy and were capable of making mistakes. It is also worth remembering that no one had the benefit of hindsight and that most people in both periods were convinced that an invasion was more than just a possibility – indeed, it was highly likely. In that spirit they prepared to defend their homes and defeat the enemy. Good history should put the reader into the minds of the participants, treat them with sympathy and use hindsight sparingly. I hope I have achieved this.

Thanks are due to many friends and colleagues over the years, including Professors Roger Knight, Nicholas Rodger, Eric Grove and Andrew Lambert; and Chris Ware, Lisa Verity, Simon Stephens, Nigel Rigby, former colleagues at the National Maritime Museum. There seems to have been a tragic death rate among distinguished and relatively young maritime historians in the last ten years or so. I still lament David Lyon and David Syrett, both of whom gave frank advice and combined both the periods of this book in their extensive fund of knowledge. More recently we have had to mourn for Colin White, the greatest expert on Nelson and his period. For editing and correcting many mistakes, I am grateful to John Lee and David Gibbons. Thanks are also due to the staffs of the National Maritime Museum, National Archives, British Library and especially the London Library.

In general I prefer to leave the historical lessons from the periods to the reader's own interpretation. An invasion of Great Britain is almost inconceivable, but there is much to learn about a united country under great stress, which is relevant in all ages and has much to say to the British. The two periods in question also did much to form the British people and gave them a great deal to be proud of.

1

THE THREAT

THE THREAT FROM NAPOLEON

The Napoleonic Wars of 1803–15 and World War II of 1939–45 are far better remembered in Britain than most other wars, partly because each was the last of its kind. The Napoleonic Wars ended a struggle with France that had lasted since 1689 – longer than the gap between 1815 and 1939. World War II was the conclusion of a long conflict with Germany. Technologically, the Napoleonic Wars were the last to be fought using sailing ships and smooth-bore guns, while World War II was the last conventional war of the pre-nuclear age. And both were fought by united countries, able to give full commitment to the struggle, though that meant different things in different ages.

The Napoleonic Wars were on almost as wide a scale as World War II more than a century and a quarter later; they lasted much longer, but they affected the great mass of the population far less. The British of 1940 were conscious of previous invasion attempts, and especially the campaign against Napoleon. In his 'fight on the beaches' speech in June, Churchill referred to earlier 'Continental tyrants'.[1] By 1941 his favourite film was *Lady Hamilton*, aka *That Hamilton Woman*, a rather inaccurate account of Nelson's great love affair. At one stage Nelson addresses his superiors on the Board of Admiralty: 'Napoleon cannot be master of the world until he has smashed us up – and believe me, gentlemen, he means to smash us up. You cannot make peace with dictators. Wipe them out!'[2] Meanwhile the well-known historian Carola Oman published a book called *Britain Against Napoleon*, with topical cover quotes including, 'British volunteers drill to meet the invasion ... the evacuation of families to safe areas is planned ... foreign royalties arrive in flight from their "protector".' And George Orwell wrote of Napoleon, 'By the end of his career this forerunner of Hitler had probably cost Europe about as many lives, relative to population, as the Great War of 1914–18.'[3]

Napoleon Bonaparte was born in 1769 on Corsica, an island that had only just become subject to the French monarchy. Indeed, his father had fought hard for Corsican independence and had to make the agonizing choice, when the island was conquered, between exile and French nationality. Like Hitler after him, Bonaparte was only just a citizen of the country that gave him his power. Like Hitler, he could never understand why the peoples of other nations subject to his rule loved their countries just as much as he did his, and perhaps this transference of nationality had something to do with it. In any case, the young Bonaparte soon became integrated with French society when he was sent off to the military school at Brienne to train as an army officer. He excelled in science and was commissioned as an artillery officer in 1785. A young man of great ability, who could have made a success of almost any profession, he lived in extraordinary times, which catapulted him to the command of armies and leadership of the state by his late twenties.

The French Revolution began in 1789 when the bankrupt French monarchy was obliged to call its first parliament for many years, the National Assembly. Frustrated by the King's refusal to accept change, the Paris mob stormed the Bastille on 14 July and the King was forced to agree to a form of constitutional monarchy, while many of his powers were abolished and the state was reformed. As the Revolution progressed, power tended to pass into more extreme hands, and the King attempted to flee with his queen, Marie Antoinette. They were stopped at Varennes, deposed in 1792 and executed early in 1793. Meanwhile there were riots and revolts, and foreign invasion, which was defeated at the Battle of Valmy. The Jacobin government under Robespierre tried to maintain order by liberal use of the guillotine – the Reign of Terror – until it too was overthrown and its leaders executed. Power lay in the hands of the Paris mob for much of the time, while in other parts of France there were royalist and peasant revolts and the constant threat of foreign invasion. The middle classes, who had benefited from the early stages of the revolution, began to crave stability.

Napoleon had welcomed the Revolution when it broke out, and in 1794, after Toulon had been handed over to the counter-revolutionary coalition forces, he organized the artillery to expel the invaders. His rise was meteoric after that – confronting the Paris mob with cannon (the 'whiff of grapeshot') and being offered the command of the army in Italy at the age of 26. He took over a disorganized, ill-equipped force and restored its morale, going on to defeat the Piedmontese and the Austrians and take control of the region, forcing the Austrians, Britain's most important ally, out of the war. In 1798 he was put in charge of forces for an invasion of England but soon dismissed it as impracticable. Instead, he took charge of a huge sea expedition to Egypt. There he soon defeated the antiquated Mameluk regime, but his battlefleet was destroyed by Nelson at the Battle of the Nile and his army was cut off. Bonaparte himself returned home in August 1799 and found political chaos in France. He seized power in the coup of 18 Brumaire (or 9 November in the traditional calendar) and was set up as First Consul, effectively in control of the government of France at the age of 30. After a decade of revolution and conflict, he brought stability to the country, and the Peace of Amiens in 1802 held out the prospect of reconstruction. But his ambitions were not satisfied, and in 1804, a year after war had resumed, he crowned himself Emperor of the French.

Napoleon lacked moral sense, he was careless of human lives including those of his own conscript soldiers, he had no understanding of the cut and thrust of debate in a parliamentary government – but he was a man of enormous talents. In addition to being one of the great military commanders of history, fighting some fifty battles, he was an administrator of great efficiency who could, for example, reform the government of Malta during a one-week visit. He reformed the laws, banking, education and the system of government in France, and the legacy of his reforms persists far beyond the boundaries of that country. The French occupation of the Netherlands and Italy had nothing of the savagery of the Germans in Eastern Europe or in Crete. And there was no question of him instituting a racial purge of the whole of Europe, with death camps and mass extermination.

In battle, it was popularly believed that Napoleon's tactics depended on the use of skirmishers in front of the main body, and of armies advancing in columns rather than lines as used by more conventional forces. In fact the position was far more complex than that, and the French armies relied on a good deal of tactical flexibility as well as the zeal of the combatants. Certainly it was true that skirmishers or *tirailleurs* were sent out in front of the infantry battalions, in far more open order and with far more initiative than the troops behind them. The infantry itself was usually in 'mixed order', arranged in columns alternating with lines. Any attack was preceded by a heavy artillery assault, for it was not common for the guns of the day to fire over the heads of one's own troops. As well as reconnaissance, cavalry had traditionally been used to protect the flanks of an army, so that there were often separate cavalry battles on each side of the infantry conflict. Napoleon was more likely to use his mounted troops behind the infantry, in support of their attack. All the arms of service worked in the closest cooperation under the direction of the commander. But, more than any specific tactical doctrine, the French army relied on constant innovation, and a general like Napoleon never gave up even against the heaviest odds and in the most difficult situation. At the Battle of Lodi, near Milan, for example, he goaded his troops into attacking across a narrow bridge against all conventional military logic and scored a stunning victory.

The French had built up a vast army through universal conscription, and their resources were not yet under the strain they would be in later years of war. There was little time for formal training of officers, but they were mostly selected from the ranks of the revolutionary army, due to their zeal and leadership, with a number of pre-Revolutionary officers (such as Napoleon himself) at the head. The army of 1803 was beginning to blend a more formal military discipline with the enthusiasm and self-confidence of earlier years, so it was at least as formidable as ever. This was the army that had swept aside the best that the ancien regime could offer – it had defeated the Dutch, the Spanish, the Austrians and the Prussians as well as the Turks in Egypt.

The French Navy was very different. It had spent the last century or so behind the British as the second biggest in the world. It had emerged

16

from the American War of Independence with a good deal of credit, but it was severely disrupted by the Revolution as aristocratic officers were displaced or forced to flee. Unlike the army, the naval officer's profession required a good deal of skill, which in those days could only be learned by long apprenticeship. Petty officers, merchant-ship captains and political commissars between them did not combine the skill, leadership and zeal that a good naval officer needed, and they did not work well together – in the early days, Revolutionary crews demanded the right to veto or displace their officers. In the late 1790s, as order was restored, the navy was on the road to recovery, until Nelson destroyed the Mediterranean Fleet at the Battle of the Nile in 1798. Among those present was Admiral Pierre Villeneuve, who would later command the main fleet in the campaign against Britain. Like many French admirals of the day he lacked tactical confidence against the onslaught of a man like Nelson, and that had not been helped by his experiences at the Nile. The French navy was the opposite of the army, lacking initiative, good leadership and a tradition of victory against the odds.

The French navy had a reputation for building very good ships, though that reflected strategic need rather than any special skill in ship construction. French strategists believed in the doctrine of the 'mission' – that their battlefleet would wait in port until ready for a specific operation, to attack or defend a vital convoy, to capture a colony in India or the West Indies, or to support an invasion of Ireland, Scotland or England. For this they needed fast ships, while the British needed strong ones so that they could wait outside the French harbours for the enemy to emerge. British captains were delighted to be given command of captured French prizes, but dockyard officials who had to maintain them were less happy. And the captains rarely raised the obvious question: if the speed of the ships was so useful, why did so many of them end up in British hands? The French, like all western navies of the age, used heavy 'ships of the line' as the main battle force, each with two or three complete decks of heavy guns. Frigates, with good sailing qualities and a single deck of medium guns, were used for reconnaissance, convoy escort and numerous other tasks, with corvettes as a smaller version. For light inshore craft they

17

tended to favour the lugger rig, with three small masts rigged fore and aft to get closer to the wind, and they would build a fleet of light gunboats and invasion craft in an attempt to control the English Channel and North Sea.

To man their fleet, the French used a system of conscription known as the Inscription Maritime, which on paper was far in advance of British methods. Professional mariners and fishermen were registered and called up to serve for limited periods with the fleet. But in practice the bureaucracy was never as efficient as it needed to be, so press gangs had to be used, and there was a shortage of suitable seamen, so soldiers had to be employed in excessive numbers about the decks.

The Spanish navy could also deploy many good ships, for it tended to take the best of British and French shipbuilding traditions and often employed exiles from these countries. It used the timber resource of Cuba to build the largest warship in the world, *Santisima Trinidad*, which carried 144 guns by this time, on four decks. The Spanish officer corps was far more traditional than the French one, and it had no new ideas. It recruited its seaman from a very small maritime base, using a system of impressment which was just as brutal as the British one. Within these limitations the Spanish seamen were competent and brave.

The Dutch navy had been badly damaged in the last war, especially at the Battle of Camperdown in 1797. What ships remained were scattered, some being blockaded as far away as Ferrol.

In 1803, as in 1940, Britain was fighting against a man who had risen from a relatively humble background to a position of absolute power. The British had occasionally fought against republics – the Dutch in three wars between 1652 and 1674, the French after 1793 and in a sense the American colonies from 1775 to 1783. They were far more used to fighting against kings – Philip II of Spain with his Armada, a succession of Louis in the eighteenth century and Kaiser Wilhelm II in 1914–18. Republics could produce great and sometimes cruel revolutionary enthusiasm, as the French had done in the last war. Kings were expected to be more gentlemanly, but they could still be motivated by religious arrogance like Philip of Spain, or enormous ambition like Louis XIV. But a self-made dictator like Napoleon or Hitler was far more chilling –

a man who was the embodiment of order and triumph to his own people, of ambition and terror to the rest of the world. He and his supporters, military men to the core and uninhibited by morality or traditional practices, could deploy his war machine with devastating and unpredictable effect.

That is not to say that Napoleon and Hitler were morally equivalent. Churchill, with his usual sense of history, put his finger on the difference in May 1941 when he told the House of Commons,

> Some have compared Hitler's conquests with those of Napoleon ... It must be remembered, however, that Napoleon's armies carried with them the fierce, liberating and equalitarian winds of the French Revolution, whereas Hitler's empire has nothing behind it but racial self-assertion, espionage, pillage, corruption and the Prussian boot.[4]

BLITZKREIG

Britain was at peace in Europe for nearly a century after Napoleon was finally defeated in 1815. The only war, apart from numerous ones in the empire, was fought in the Crimea and the Baltic against Russia between 1853 and 1856. There were occasional invasion scares, for example when Napoleon's nephew took power in France as Napoleon III, and when the building of new steam-powered ironclad warships seemed to make Britain's great naval strength out of date. There was a substantial body of 'invasion literature' in the early years of the twentieth century, most notably Erskine Childers' *Riddle of the Sands*, which helped the British to see Germany rather than France as the main enemy. Preparations were made to resist a German invasion during the war of 1914–18, but the enemy had no plans for one. Perhaps because there had been so many false alarms, the nation was not ready when the fall of France and the evacuation from Dunkirk in 1940 revealed a very real threat, the most serious for 135 years. Across the Channel was the great and terrifying German army, and a nation led by a ruthless but strangely successful dictator.

Even Napoleon seems benevolent and moral compared with Hitler, who saw himself as the embodiment of the German people and had no other concern but the furtherance of what he saw as their interests by any means, however brutal, and at the expense of any nation or group that got in the way. These two leaders did have some factors in common. Both had an ability to engage the individual and the mass. Both were great orators in their way. Napoleon relied on ringing phrases. In Egypt he told his soldiers, 'From the summit of these pyramids, forty centuries look down upon you.' He coined memorable phrases such as 'There is only one step from the sublime to the ridiculous', 'An army marches on its stomach' and 'England is a nation of shopkeepers'.[5] Quotes from Hitler are remembered mostly in irony, as broken promises or failed ideas – 'This is the last territorial claim which I have to make in Europe', or 'I go the way that Providence dictates with the assurance of a sleepwalker.'[6] Instead he relied on his oratorical style rather than any gift for words. Somehow the stage management of the occasion, the disciplined enthusiasm of the crowds and Hitler's unfathomable passion and anger struck a chord with his followers. Combined with success in restoring Germany's prestige and self-confidence and unprecedented success in battle, he became an almost god-like figure to the German nation. This was reinforced by an efficient and ruthless propaganda machine and promoted in films such as *The Triumph of the Will* directed by Leni Riefenstahl.

To the British, Hitler was a clown or a demon. He was not cartooned as a prisoner, as Napoleon was, perhaps because he was not expected to lead his army in person, but Frank Richards of *Billy Bunter* fame had no doubt about his comic status:

> Take Hitler, for example, with his swastika, his 'good German sword', his fortifications named after characters from Wagner, his military coat that he will never take off till he marches home victorious: and the rest of his fripperies out of the property-box. In Germany they lap this up like milk, with the most awful seriousness; in England, the play-acting would be laughed out of existence ... The fact that Adolf Hitler is deadly dangerous does not make him any less funny.[7]

There never was a less likely world leader than Adolf Hitler. Undistinguished in appearance, he was uncouth and largely uneducated, and he was not a native of the country he ruled. He had no interest in administration or organization, his own military experience was limited, and he had no obvious talent except mob oratory. He was born in Austria in 1889 but rejected the idea of his father's career as a minor civil servant to become a drop-out in Vienna, sometimes a down and out, sometimes scraping a living by selling paintings based on picture postcards. Having moved to Munich (for he preferred the racial unity of Germany to the polyglot and weak Austro-Hungarian state), he enlisted with great enthusiasm in the German army on the outbreak of war in 1914, though he had avoided military service in his native land. He served well as a battalion runner and was decorated twice for bravery, but in four years he failed to rise above the rank of corporal. He was in hospital in November 1918, partly blinded by gas, when he heard news of the German surrender – and was devastated. As the army and the state disintegrated around him, Hitler became employed as a secret agent among various ultra-nationalist groups, during which time he discovered the National Socialist Democratic Workers Party (NSDAP), as well as his own talent for mob oratory, in the beer halls of Munich. He traded in fierce anti-communism, a rampant nationalism and an irrational hatred of the Jews. Before long he was leader of the Nazi Party, and, as the German economy collapsed under rampant inflation, he and others staged an unsuccessful coup in 1923. He was treated very leniently by the right-wing and nationalist Bavarian establishment and used a short term in prison to write his testament, *Mein Kampf*, but he had no literary talent and, despite heavy editing by his supporters, it was rambling and largely unreadable.

What Hitler had most in common with Napoleon was that both lived in very troubled times. Germany was defeated in war, but many of the people were not prepared to accept that this had been done 'fairly', and the myth of the 'stab in the back' was exploited by the Nazis. In hindsight, the Treaty of Versailles that followed can be seen as both unfair and damaging. The financial crisis of 1923 undermined the confidence of the middle class, and there was more to come, with a world financial crisis – the Nazi Party remained relatively insignificant until the great depression hit Germany after the Wall Street Crash of 1929. The parties of the centre collapsed, and the voters were faced with a stark choice between the Communists and the Nazis. Naturally the middle classes chose the latter, while the industrialists and financiers supported Hitler in the mistaken belief that they could control him. In January 1939 he became Chancellor and, with the parliamentary support of the Centre Party, he took absolute power and the title of Führer, or leader. His opponents (including a wing of his own party) were murdered, put into concentration camps or went into exile. Soon the doubters would be swept up by a tide of Nazi successes, and the dictator's popularity rose through the 1930s to reach very high levels. Hitler took the credit for solving Germany's huge unemployment problem. But he set up a repressive and ruthless state, imprisoning political opponents and openly persecuting Jews and minorities.

The early advances of the Nazi regime might be seen merely as correctives to the grossly unfair provisions of the Treaty of Versailles, and as such they attracted a certain amount of sympathy in Britain. Hitler withdrew from the League of Nations, built submarines and an air force in contravention of the Treaty and introduced conscription with which to build a much larger army than the Treaty permitted. In 1936 he sent his forces to re-occupy the Rhineland, which had been de-militarized by the Treaty, and the British and French failed to react. In 1938 he went further and took over Austria, now a single German-speaking country rather than the great empire in which Hitler had lived as a youth. Later in the year, caught up in the dynamic of expansion, he demanded the Sudetenland, the mountainous, German-speaking borders areas of Czechoslovakia, which formed the country's main defence. This set alarm bells ringing in Western Europe and almost led to war with Britain and France, until they backed down with a promise from Hitler that he planned no further expansion. This was broken early in 1939 when the rest of Czechoslovakia was taken over, and there could be no shadow of doubt about Nazi ruthlessness and unreliability. That summer he negotiated a non-aggression pact with his arch-enemy, the Soviet Union. When he invaded Poland in September, Britain and France declared war.

The British already had the expression 'little Hitler', meaning a petty official, just the kind of person the real Adolf refused to become by not following his father into the civil service. The British also believed that he had an efficient, well-planned and organized state. In fact, the reverse was true. Hitler set up a series of competing agencies which consolidated his power as the only arbiter between them, though access was often denied by his aides and many conflicts were unresolved. It was a system that allowed original ideas to emerge in social Darwinist fashion – successful ones such as the use of tanks in battle, as well as diabolical ones such as deporting and eventually exterminating the Jews. Hitler had the support of the enthusiastic and supremely arrogant membership of the Nazi Party, with Hermann Göring in charge of the Luftwaffe and the German economy, Ribbentrop for foreign affairs, Joseph Goebbels for propaganda (which took on its sinister modern meaning under his charge) and Heinrich Himmler in charge of the SS, the Nazi private army. The country already had an efficient and largely amoral civil service, a strong industrial base and the makings of the best army in the world, founded on the German military tradition. Hitler's system of government, if it can be called that, involved a huge amount of waste but created enormous energy, which was enough to overwhelm his opponents at home and abroad.

Until 1939, Hitler's advances had been made peacefully. The takeovers of the Rhineland, Austria and the Sudetenland had merely been military processions. He had taken the opportunity to test some of his weapons and tactics during the civil war in Spain (1936–9), where the Condor Legion supported the Nationalist rebels under General Franco, and his bombers devastated the town of Guernica to world outrage. Poland was the first real campaign for the new German Army, but it was over in a few weeks, as the Polish army, well-motivated but un-modernized and most famous for its cavalry, failed against the German tanks. In the spring of 1940 the Germans attacked Norway, breaking all the rules of sea power by invading without control of the sea. They took over the country, humiliating the British and French at the cost of heavy losses to their surface navy.

But the war against Britain and France demanded different tactics. Unlike Napoleon's forces, the Germans relied on new technology for their attacks. Tanks, aircraft and parachutes had all been used in the last war but had matured since then. The Nazi regime was fortunate that General Guderian and his colleagues had developed new techniques of tank warfare which had not been adopted in Britain and France; that General Kurt Student followed a Soviet example and built up a parachute force; and that the new Luftwaffe formed under Hermann Göring had inter-service cooperation as its main priority. The German army had expanded very fast from the 100,000 men allowed by Versailles to 3.6 million in 1940. It had built on the national military tradition and appointed its young officers by National Socialist selection methods. It had discarded most of the class discrimination that had dominated the Kaiser's army in 1914, and it trained its officers well. The British had an image of mindless automatons in the ranks, partly based on Frederick the Great's army nearly two centuries ago, and partly on how they imagined Nazi society operated. In fact, even the most junior NCOs were trained to use their initiative, and in that respect the German army was far stronger than the British army.

In Germany artillery was not the primary arm that it was in Britain, though it did produce the famous 88mm gun, which was equally effective as an anti-tank weapon as in its original anti-aircraft role. At the core of its attacking force were the panzer divisions which had led the way in France, though it had expanded from nothing and was very short of effective vehicles. The great majority of tanks were Panzer-kampfwagen I and II, designed in the mid-1930s for training but armed only with machine-guns and cannon. The Panzer III was far more effective, with a 37mm gun, a crew of five and a top speed of 25mph, but its 30mm armour was rather thin. The Panzer IV was intended to give heavy support to the Panzer III, and one platoon of IVs was to form part of each company, alongside several of Panzer IIIs. The Panzer IV mounted a 75mm gun with 50mm armour on later models. During the French campaign the Germans used the effective Czech tanks, which they called the Panzerkampfwagen 38(t) and 35(t). They were also to lay their hands on some good quality French tanks, which might have proved useful against Britain. The Panzer divisions also had wheeled armoured cars for reconnaissance, and the tanks were followed by infantry carried in either half-tracks for movement across country, or trucks for roads. The most advanced infantry elements were in armoured half tracks of the SdKfz 250 series, which could carry a commander, driver, and a ten-man infantry section into battle.

German forces included infantry and panzer divisions that had their origins in the pre-war Nazi Party paramilitary organizations, notably the SS, Schutz Staffelen or Blackshirts. They had originated as Hitler's personal bodyguard and rose in prominence after he eliminated the original fighting wing of the party, the SA (or Brownshirts) during the 'Night of the Long Knives' in 1934. As well as suppressing opposition to the party, the SS took on roles as police and concentration camp guards. From 1934 the Verfügungstruppe, or Special Duty Troops, were formed into military units, parallel to but separate from those of the army. This became the Waffen-SS, with its own ranks and training schools. By the beginning of the war it was being formed into divisions that would fight alongside those of the army. The SS was headed by Heinrich Himmler, one of Hitler's closest associates, and was originally expected to recruit the élite of German youth. But the army clung on to its own conscripts, and by the spring of 1940 the Waffen-SS was beginning to take on young men of Germanic background from the conquered territories. Early on, the force established a reputation for ruthlessness – on the advance to Dunkirk, members of the Leibstandarte Adolf Hitler murdered British prisoners of war at Wormhout in Belgium; the peak of their savagery was still ahead of them.

Not all the German Army was well equipped. For ordinary transport behind the lines it relied very heavily on converted civilian vehicles of many different types, and the maintenance problem was compounded even further by the use of vehicles captured in occupied countries. In the meantime, except for the Panzer divisions, virtually every unit and formation relied heavily on large numbers of horses or mules. Most of the army's field artillery and supply wagons were horse-drawn in 1940.

The German Air Force, the Luftwaffe, had only been revealed to the public in March 1935 though it had been evolving secretly since the 1920s and had built on a good deal of experience in World War I, in which its commander, Hermann Göring, had served as a fighter pilot and had commanded the famous Richthofen Squadron after the death of the famous ace. Göring had no more administrative skill than his Führer, but he employed a series of good staff officers to expand the new force, and as one of the most senior Nazis he had the ear, if not always the trust, of Hitler.

In the 1920s the German armed forces gained experience training secretly in the Soviet Union, and the country pushed the development of civil aviation as far as it could, providing several machines that were easily convertible into bombers. Flying and gliding clubs were encouraged, and the nation was not totally lacking in aerial skills when Hitler announced the setting up of the Luftwaffe as an independent service like its British counterpart the Royal Air Force. Nazi propaganda exaggerated its size for the rest of the decade, and one of the reasons why Chamberlain gave in at Munich was fear of the bombing of British cities. Officially that was only a secondary aim of the Luftwaffe:

> The mission of the Armed Forces in war is to break the will of the enemy.
>
> The will of the nation finds its strongest expression in the nation's military forces. Defeat of the enemy military forces is the primary objective in war.
>
> The mission of the Luftwaffe is to serve this purpose by conducting air warfare as part of the overall pattern for the conduct of the war.
>
> In war victory can only be secured through the combined efforts of all three branches of the armed forces.[8]

German aircraft design was rather hit-or-miss, but it did have some notable successes. Ernst Udet, a famous pilot of the last war, discovered the Curtis Helldiver dive-bomber during a visit to the USA and saw that it could be used against tanks and bridges as well as ships. The concept came to fruition in the Junkers 87, or Stuka. The name was derived from Sturzkampfflugzeug (literally 'plunge-battle aircraft') and was a generic name rather than an individual design; but it became notorious throughout Europe after the campaigns in Poland, Norway and France. Diving almost vertically, it could be aimed with great accuracy and could take account of any last-minute evasions by its prey. With the rapidly changing range, it was very difficult for anti-aircraft gunners to hit. In a coup de théâtre that was characteristic of the Nazi era, it was fitted with a siren to terrify those on the ground, and the very ugliness of the aircraft's design helped foster its fearsome reputation. But that also showed its weakness. It had an old-fashioned fixed undercarriage covered in 'spats' to reduce drag, and its W-shaped 'inverted gull wing' reduced the length of the undercarriage legs to give it its characteristic appearance. The Stuka could rule the ground when fighter opposition was weak, and it was very effective against ships, but at 255mph it was slow, easy prey for British Hurricanes and Spitfires.

The Germans never developed a successful four-engined heavy bomber, but that was not a problem in the short term, for in a land campaign the medium bombers could attack enemy transport and concentrations some way behind the lines. Instead the Luftwaffe had three types of twin-engined medium bombers, all rather lacking in range, bomb load and defensive armament. The Dornier 17 was developed from an airliner, the Heinkel 111 was designed for both commercial and military use, and only the Junkers 88, intended as the standard Luftwaffe bomber, was a purely military design. They had been designed for speed at a time in the late 1930s, when bombers were often faster than fighters and lacked defensive armament; this did not take into account the huge increase in fighter speed later in the decade, and the fitting of single machine-guns in various positions made for an inadequate defence.

The Bf 109 single-seat fighter was the Luftwaffe's biggest trump card. It was popularly known as the Me 109 after its designer, Willi Messerschmitt, who had produced racing machines including one for Hitler's party deputy, Rudolf Hess, but had never worked on a military aircraft before he entered a design competition in 1934. The new fighter was an all-metal monoplane with retractable undercarriage and an enclosed cockpit, and as good as any aircraft of its type in the world. In its developed version, the Bf 109E as used in 1940, its top speed of 357mph was slightly faster than that of the British Spitfire, and its armament of 20mm cannon and machine-guns was superior to the Spitfire's, but the British aircraft performed better above 20,000 feet and was more manoeuvrable at all heights. Perhaps its greatest flaw was its short range – 410 miles. Messerschmitt's other fighter, the Bf 110, known as the Zerstörer (or 'Destroyer'), was intended as a long-range fighter escort, with twin engines and a crew of two. But it was slower and far less manoeuvrable than the fighters opposed to it.

The Luftwaffe owed far more to the Nazi Party than the army, which remained a bastion of conservatism, and perhaps that is why the new force was given responsibility for two arms that would normally have been under army control. The Luftwaffe was responsible for anti-aircraft artillery, both for the defence of cities and for protecting troops in battle; and it had its own private army in the form of paratroopers or Fallschirmjäger, who proved a very effective force in the surprise attacks on Holland and Belgium. The German paratrooper wore a version of the standard steel helmet, cropped to minimise the risk of injury on landing. He was dressed in Luftwaffe blue-grey, with a smock over his equipment, and armed only with a rifle or submachine-gun for the drop. He jumped out of his aircraft, usually a Junkers 52 transport, by diving towards the rear of the wing at a terrifying low low height, which meant that his parachute barely had time to open before he hit the ground. It also meant that the defenders were taken by surprise and had no chance to shoot him as he descended. Once on the ground he was more vulnerable, as he had to get rid of his parachute, take off his smock and wear it under his equipment and then retrieve heavier weapons from cylindrical containers dropped nearby. When he had done that, he became a fearsome fighting machine.

The German navy was a slightly less new creation, dating from the end of the nineteenth century. It was immensely proud that it had taken on the might of the Royal Navy at the Battle of Skaggerak (Jutland to the British) in 1916 and won a tactical victory, inflicting damage on the British though it was forced to retreat. Its U-boat arm had come closer than anything else to winning the war against Britain. For the officer corps that glory was diminished in 1918 when naval mutinies at Kiel and Wilhelmshaven contributed to the downfall of the empire. Honour was restored when the interned High Seas Fleet scuttled itself at Scapa Flow, the first act of resistance to the Versailles Treaty. The Kreigsmarine was a small force under the terms of the Treaty, but its three 'pocket battleships' were built up to and beyond the Treaty limits and gave the Royal Navy some trouble, which was reduced when *Graf Spee* was forced to scuttle herself off Montevideo in December 1939.

The navy was the weakest link in Germany's plans for world domination, not because of any faults in doctrine or personnel, but because it was too small. Under Plan Z of March 1939 it was to have eight battleships and four aircraft carriers,[9] but they would not be ready until 1943. In the meantime it had no modern battleships as the great *Bismarck* and *Tirpitz* were not ready; the battlecruisers *Scharnhorst* and *Gneisenau* were both damaged by torpedoes in June 1940. The cruiser *Admiral Hipper* had been rammed off Norway, and two more were out of action, leaving only three ready for use that summer. The navy had lost ten of its valuable destroyers in the Norwegian campaign and now had only seven in service. The situation was not likely to improve: Hitler expected a short war, and no more were to be built in the near future. The navy was still not strong in U-boats, with only 46 in service in July, reduced to 28 after losses. For inshore work it had developed the Schnellboot, or S-boat, known as the E-boat to the British, which was superior to anything the British had. But German surface naval power was only a fraction of that of Britain.

By 1939 the Germans had evolved the technique of blitzkrieg, or 'lightning war', which fitted their political and economic needs as well as their military ones. The essence was cooperation between all the services and the different branches of the army. An attack might be preceded by sabotage and misleading information by Nazi spies and agents, but the effect of that was grossly exaggerated. Paratroopers and gliders would be used to seize key points as the attack began, and the air force would attack the enemy in detail. The main punch and subsequent breakout would be provided by the armoured, or panzer, units strongly concentrated – unlike their British and French counterparts – and closely supported by infantry and artillery. Dive-bombers were used as highly mobile artillery to seek out enemy formations and destroy them or force them to disperse. All this was carried out with total ruthlessness – the rights of neutral nations were ignored, and terror was part of the process, for refugee columns could help impede enemy troops moving forward in defence. The linear warfare of the Western Front, so familiar to Hitler from the last war, was turned on its head, and concepts of static defence were disastrously outdated.

It was only with the attack on Holland and Belgium, which began on May 10 1940, that the full effectiveness of the German tactics was shown. Ignoring the French fortifications of the Maginot Line to the east and without any warning or declaration of war, the Germans bombed the Dutch city of Rotterdam and glider-borne troops took the Belgian strongpoint of Eben Emael, considered the strongest fort in the world. As the Germans advanced into Belgium, the French high command made its planned move and ordered an advance to save that country, a disastrous policy. The panzers broke through the forested Ardennes, previously considered impassable for tanks, and the British and a large part of the French army were cut off.

A third of a million British and French troops were evacuated from the harbour and beaches of Dunkirk in a triumph of naval organization led by Admiral Bertram Ramsay at Dover. It was sometimes suggested that Hitler deliberately stopped his panzers destroying the British Expeditionary Force to placate the British, but that seems unlikely. He wanted to save his tanks for future operations, and Göring had assured him that he could destroy the British from the air. He, like almost everyone else at the time, believed that a mass evacuation was impossible, and there were better things for his panzers to do, as the rest of France was still unconquered. In any case, the evacuation had the opposite effect. It gave the British a certain amount of self-confidence in defeat and provided them with a core of battle-hardened troops – even if they were demoralized, disorganized and had left nearly all their equipment behind.

As allies the Germans now had Italy, under the original Fascist leader Benito Mussolini, though his declaration of war was purely opportunist and his forces were already proving ineffective.

In 1940, unlike 1803, Britain was taken by surprise by the threat of invasion. Until the fall of France it had been assumed that this war would follow the pattern of the last, with a slow erosion of Germany though trench warfare and naval blockade, or that it would be ended by strategic bombing. But now there was an apparently invincible enemy just over twenty miles away across the Strait of Dover, with the resources of most of Europe at his disposal.

The German armed forces were just as terrifying as the Nazi Party. They had shown boldness and skill in the use of such new weapons as the dive-bomber and the tank. They had used surprising new tactics in the invasion of Norway and France. They had shown no respect for neutrality in their invasion of Belgium, Holland and Luxemburg. There was no knowing where they would strike next, what traitors and fifth columnists they might have recruited, what new weapons or tactics they might have up their sleeves. As the British looked across the narrow seas of the English Channel towards the lands occupied by the most powerful armed forces the world had ever seen, they were naturally fearful – but showed no inclination to give in.

2

THE BRITISH

THE BRITISH AT WAR, 1805

Formally the Scots, Welsh and English had lived in a 'United Kingdom' since the action of Union of 1707, and in 1801 Ireland was brought into this. But such superficial political unity at the top did not necessarily mean that the country was truly united at any other level, even in wartime.

It was rare to find complete national unity in Britain during the wars of the seventeenth and eighteenth centuries. The Civil Wars of 1642–51 were as divisive as their name suggests. The 'Glorious Revolution' of 1688 established parliamentary authority and a Protestant succession to the throne, but it led to Jacobite rebellions during every war for the next sixty years. The Seven Years War of 1756–63 was indeed fought with a unified population, but the American War of 1775–83 was almost a civil war, with many prominent American supporters in Britain. And the war of 1793–1802 against the French revolutionaries had begun with a middle-class opposition movement by means of the Corresponding Societies, with naval mutinies that almost overthrew the state, and with revolt in Ireland.

Unity between Scotland and England had come about in two stages. In 1603 the Scottish King, James VI, inherited the English throne and moved south to London to become James I of the United Kingdom. Scotland retained her own parliament and ruling class, and the partnership was uneasy. Scottish religious and economic interests were very different, and she was excluded from any share in the rich trade of the English overseas empire. The union of the parliaments in 1707 has been described as 'a political necessity for England, a commercial necessity for Scotland'. It gave the Scots a share in the empire, which they would exploit fully over the next two centuries; and it gave England a certain amount of security against a foreign invasion through Scotland. That was not total, however, as another issue arose to divide the nation. The overthrow of the Roman Catholic King James II in 1688 led to a constant threat of revolt by his supporters, the Jacobites, who were particularly strong in the Scottish highlands. The issue was only resolved with the crushing Jacobite defeat at Culloden in 1746. After that the Highland chieftains adopted Lowland ambitions, and the clansmen joined the British army in large numbers. Meanwhile the Scottish merchant classes, especially on Clydeside, became rich through trade with the Caribbean and North America, and the classic industries of the age – cotton, iron and coal – were all growing fast in Scotland. The country's identity had not diminished, but the partnership with England seemed to be working well, and Scots held many leading positions in politics, the army and the navy.

Wales was a different case, integrated both more and less than Scotland. The country had been conquered by England in the twelfth century and integrated in the sixteenth, rather than joining a union as a supposedly equal partner. Its laws were English laws, its religion was subjected to the Church of England, and it was rarely considered as separate from England for any administrative purposes. But Wales had a national language, while in Scotland Gaelic was only used by the Highlanders.

Ireland remained the biggest problem of all. The Roman Catholic religion of the great majority of the people was anathema to most English and Scots, and the poverty of its people accentuated the differences between the kingdoms. The attempt to settle Protestants in the north had only led to further problems, which are barely resolved in the present day.

Despite a history of conflict, Britain was more united than ever during the key years of 1803–5. The Irish issue was far from settled, and there was a small and ineffective revolt led by Robert Emmet in 1803, but in Britain radicals and reformers had become disillusioned with the increasing authoritarianism of the French regime and had no love for Napoleon as first consul or emperor. The working class movement was weak and repressed by the Combination Laws. The Jacobites were long gone as a political force, preferring monarchical Protestants in Britain to an upstart atheist regime in Paris.

At its highest levels, in philosophy, architecture, war and culture, British society was rational and efficient. Soldiers and warships fought in straight lines, houses in the new towns were built in terraces and squares, intellectuals looked for a complete understanding of everything, both art and science. But below that was a very different society – of cruelty, chaos and crime. This contrast was more obvious in Britain than in most of Europe, for many of the rambling medieval city centres had survived civil war and fire, but decades of prosperity had allowed many towns to expand using the latest Palladian architecture. Crime prevention was particularly weak because of the fundamental conservatism of the parliamentary system.

The British overseas empire was already claimed to be the greatest in the world, despite the loss of the American colonies twenty years earlier. It included large parts of India under the rule of the East India Company, which made great sums of money by importing silks, spices and other luxury goods. Britain also controlled many West Indian islands, where sugar was produced by slave labour at vast profit. As well as helping finance the war, the empire created jobs for the numerous younger sons of landowners and merchants, and the Scots had become particularly interested in this. When Henry Dundas was on the Board of the East India Company it was said of him, 'As long as he is in office the Scotch may beget younger sons with the most perfect impunity. He sends them by loads to the East Indies, and all over the world.'[1]

The racial composition of the British did not change greatly between 1805 and 1940. There was already a substantial non-European population in London in 1805, mostly brought in as servants to the rich. Their status was surprising to an American like Benjamin Silliman, a visiting American scientist:

> A black footman is considered as a great acquisition, and consequently, negro servants are sought for and caressed. An ill dressed or starving negro is never seen in England, and in some instances even alliances are formed between them and white girls of the lower orders of society. ... As

there are no slaves in England, perhaps the English have not learned to regard negroes as a degraded class of men, as we do in the United States, where we have never seen them in any other condition.[2]

English law was rather ambiguous about slavery, and it was certainly allowed in the West Indian colonies. In 1807, William Wilberforce would succeed in abolishing the trade from Africa but not yet in ending the institution of slavery itself.

Religion was less of a factor than in the past. Roman Catholics were no longer actively persecuted, though they were discriminated against in many ways. The mainstream Church of England was moderate in its views, while Methodists led by John Wesley brought religious fervour to the lower classes, and the evangelical movement, whose members included William Wilberforce, worked to revitalize the established church. The Church of Scotland was far more tolerant than it had been a century earlier, allowing Edinburgh its 'golden age'.

British culture was flourishing generally despite the effects of war, perhaps because the aristocratic Grand Tour of Europe was now impossible and the wealthier classes turned to support native talent. The painters Constable and Turner were both active, along with a host of lesser figures such as George Morland and Benjamin West. It was a golden age of caricature, Gillray, Rowlandson and Cruikshank all finding much material in the war situation. Sir Walter Scott was the literary 'superstar', though he was known for his poetry, including *The Lay of the Last Minstrel* and had not yet turned to novels. The poets Coleridge and Wordsworth had long lost their enthusiasm for the French Revolution, and eulogized nature instead. Jane Austen was already observing society very acutely from the English countryside, and was attempting a novel: her first would be published in 1811. Architecture found a peak in the building of elegant streets in London, the city of Bath and the new town of Edinburgh. Apart from astronomy for use in navigation, science was not of much benefit to the government in those days, but it was a golden age nevertheless. Many years later a painting was produced of 48 'Men of science living in 1807–8'. The term was defined broadly to include engineers, inventors and philosophers, and those pictured included Sir Humphrey Davy, the physicist; Sir Joseph

Banks, the naturalist; John Dalton, the chemist; Sir Marc Isambard Brunel, the father of the great Victorian engineer; Thomas Telford, the civil engineer; and James Watt of steam engine fame.[3]

The nation provided men for the armed forces that would prosecute the war with France. Merchant shipping was important here, for as well as transporting the nation's commerce it was subject to the press gang, so it trained most of the men who would crew the warships. The government enforced the Navigation Acts, by which imported goods had to be carried in British ships, or ships from the country of origin, and the crew of a British ship had to be largely natives of the country. This was essential if they were to be available for pressing into the navy when needed. In all, there were more than 18,000 ships registered in the United Kingdom in 1803, with a total tonnage of nearly two million. If fully manned, they would employ 105,000 seamen.[4]

At the top end of the mercantile marine were the ships of the East India Company, almost as big as the navy's ships of the line and commanded by officers who were almost equal in status to naval officers – some Scottish aristocratic families, such as the Elphinstones, kept alternate sons in naval and East India service, so that one would prosper in peace and the other in war. Other long-distance routes included the triangular trade to Africa and the West Indies, transporting slaves in horrific conditions during the 'middle passage'. Other ships traded direct with North America or the West Indies, returning with sugar, tobacco or cotton. The Baltic supplied naval stores such as timber and tar, and was vital for the upkeep of the navy. Closer to home, the coal trade from Newcastle and other north-eastern ports kept London supplied and was a vital 'nursery for seamen', who were not too far away when the press gangs came into action. There were many local craft serving rivers and estuaries, and the famous Thames barge was already beginning to emerge. The watermen who rowed passengers along the Thames, rather like taxis, were also expected to provide a certain number of men for the navy.

Landsmen were not subject to conscription except in a very limited sense. Small numbers could be called up into the militia, which was a part-time force in peacetime but mobilized, for home defence only, in war. Every time a new levy of militiamen had to be raised, a specific number were demanded of each county in proportion to its population. The Lord Lieutenants delegated the task to the individual parishes and their constables. Men under 5 feet 4 inches, very poor men with children, apprentices and numerous others were exempted; the rest were subjected to a ballot in which names were chosen by lot. This did not always mean that the man chosen had to go, for if he was wealthy enough he could pay a substitute. It was even possible to take out an insurance policy against being chosen, in which case a substitute would be provided.

THE BRITISH PEOPLE IN 1803

Britain's population was counted scientifically for the first time in 1801, with a national census. Among the reasons for this intrusion were two military ones: the number of men for conscription to the militia in different areas should reflect the local population; and it was necessary to know the number of seamen. England and Wales, according to the report, had just over 9 million people and Scotland had 1.6 million. The Irish were as yet uncounted but were estimated at more than 5 million. The population was increasing in practically every county of the kingdoms, but particularly in the great cities. Bath thrived on its waters and as a social venue; Bristol and Liverpool were great ports; Birmingham and Manchester were new centres of manufacturing; and the naval dockyard towns of Plymouth and Portsmouth were also growing rapidly. London was expanding as fast as anywhere, with more than a million people in the area.

London was important in the military history of the period, not just as the national capital and the headquarters of the armed forces – it was well within 70 miles of the English Channel and was a primary target for any invader, whether by sea and land, or later by air. It was the greatest port in the country, a financial centre of great wealth and dynamism, and the symbol of British prestige. Its capture or destruction, the potential invaders believed, would knock the heart out of British resistance.

37

Greater London had several distinct areas. The City of London had definite boundaries. Its wooden buildings were largely destroyed by the Great Fire in 1666 and rebuilt in stone or brick, but the medieval street pattern remained. Westminster was farther upstream and situated round the abbey. Here was the centre of government, including Westminster Hall with the Houses of Parliament and courts; Downing Street where the prime minister lived; and government buildings such as the Admiralty, Horse Guards and Treasury in Whitehall. The West End was mostly composed of large modern houses arranged in elegant terraces and squares. A grid pattern was considered ideal, but in London it was confused because it was built on a series of private estates, most of which took the names of their landowners, such as Grosvenor, Berkeley and Cavendish. The East End was developing more slowly as new docks were built, such as the London Docks, which opened in 1805, and working class housing was built around them. Southwark, south of the river, was expanding due to the opening of Westminster Bridge in 1750 and Blackfriars Bridge in 1769. For historical reasons, it contained many of the services that were essential to the running of the city but were not welcome in the West End – prisons, madhouses, breweries, coaching inns and charitable foundations.

London was not always pleasant to be in and Benjamin Silliman found that it was 'deformed with smoke and coal-dust'. It was worse after heavy rain:

> There has been a thunder storm this evening, with torrents of rain, which have disengaged such quantities of hepatic gas, from the subterranean receptacles of filth, that the air has been, for hours, extremely offensive. I am told that sudden and heavy rains usually produce this effect in London, and that sometimes the gas is so abundant as to blacken the silver utensils in the closets.[5]

Historians are divided about whether industrial changes in Britain in the late eighteenth and early nineteenth centuries amounted to a revolution or not. Certainly change was confined to specific industries, and the general effect on the economy was gradual rather than dramatic. The cotton industry went over to a factory system, made possible by inventions such as the Spinning Jenny and the power loom, which required more capital and the concentration of production in large factories, driven by water and later by steam. More closely related to defence was the iron industry, since it provided guns for the army and navy. It had recently changed from using charcoal to coke and so was re-sited from traditional areas in the Weald of Kent and Sussex to the coalfields of Wales, central and northern England and Scotland. Coal mining was also expanding rapidly, to supply the iron industry and to heat the growing cities. It used steam power for draining the mines and the new Davy safety lamp to detect underground gases. Developments in iron proved of great practical value to the armaments industry. Thomas Blomefield of the Ordnance Office had spent many years experimenting with the composition of iron used in heavy guns, and by 1800 his new pattern of cannon, with a ring above the ball on top of the breech, was almost universal in the navy and in fortresses. It offered a improved rate of fire without bursting. Other industries contributed to national defence simply by their profits, which helped to fund the war effort and made Britain the richest country in Europe, able also to subsidize allies.

As always until very recently, British society was dominated by class – the combination of birth, breeding and wealth that made it artificially difficult to move from one group to another. It was less class-bound than other European societies of the time, at least until the French Revolution, for the British upper classes have always survived by admitting selected members from below. Class was often seen as a unifying rather than a dividing factor in the 1800s, especially in the countryside, where the squire, the professions such as the vicar and the doctor, the tenant farmers and the labourers had well-established places in the community.

The true aristocracy was a small group, for only the eldest son could inherit a peerage (which brought membership of the House of Lords) or a baronetcy, while a knighthood was conferred for the holder's life only. Most of the country squires who owned the greatest part of the land had no titles; nor did the merchants who controlled much of the monetary wealth. For certain purposes there was a kind of equality within the category of 'gentleman'. In *Pride and Prejudice*, when accused of 'upstart pretensions' by plotting to marry the much richer Mr Darcy, Elizabeth Bennett replies effectively, 'He is a gentleman. I am a gentleman's daughter.'[6] Such equality also applied in foxhunting, and in the Assembly Rooms at Bath. But it did not conceal the fact that there were great variations within the class, based on education, wealth and how long it had been held. At the bottom were those who were barely clinging to their gentlemanly status, as described by Thomas Malthus:

> A man of liberal education, with an income only just sufficient to enable him to associate in the rank of gentleman, must feel absolutely certain if he is to marry, and have a family, he shall be obliged to give up all his former connections. The woman whom a man of education must naturally make the object of his choice is one brought up in the same habits and sentiments with himself, and used to the familiar intercourse from which she must be reduced by marriage. Can a man so easily consent to place the object of his affection in a situation so discordant probably to her habit and inclinations? Two or three steps of descent in society, particularly at this round of the ladder where education ends and ignorance begins, will not be considered by the generality of people as a chimerical but a real evil.[7]

A gentleman might support himself in work, especially if he was a younger son, but his choice was very limited and had to be made very early in life if he was not to lose his status.

> 'So you are to be a clergyman, Mr. Bertram. This is rather a surprise to me.'
>
> 'Why should it surprise you? You must suppose me designed for some profession, and you might perceive that I am neither a lawyer, nor a soldier, nor a sailor.'[8]

The class system did allow many people to rise, even if their style and manners were not those to be expected of a gentleman:

> The cockneys also emulate their superiors in their way, and although they cannot afford to keep coaches you will see them 'close pack'd in chaise and one', or on horseback, riding furiously into the country ... during a pleasant Sunday, the environs of London swarm with emigrants from town. Hyde Park, and the vast forests and serpentine walks of Kensington

gardens are thronged with people of all ranks – Gentry, cockneys, cits are all disgorged, and returning, in two opposite currents; and such an assemblage of burly corpulent people is probably not to be found in the world besides.[9]

The middle class was perhaps the broadest group in society, including merchants, professionals who did not quite qualify as part of the gentry, and clerks who could barely scratch a respectable living. As yet, the 'middling sort' had little identity of their own, distinguished from the gentry above them by their willingness to engage in commerce and from those below them by not working with their hands. In the professions, the medical men were rarely numbered among the gentlemen. Those at the highest level, the physicians, were generally university-trained and could make a substantial living dealing with the wealthy. Surgeons had much less status because they could not perform any kind of delicate operation in the days before anaesthetics; they usually learned the trade by apprenticeship. There was no nursing profession as such, but apothecaries sold medicines and tended to the sick poor. At the lower level of the middle classes, a junior Admiralty clerk earned £150 per year; if he rose to the eminence of Chief Clerk he would earn £800, plus an allowance of £150.[10]

Despite the growth of industry, about three quarters of the population still lived and worked in the country. Owners of the large estates tended towards reform, a process known to historians as the 'agricultural revolution'. They combined inefficient small farms into larger ones, developed new machinery and tested crop rotations. Not all areas were so advanced, and in Surrey there were still

> many of the old class of farmers; men who are shy and jealous in their communications; unwilling to adopt any new mode of husbandry; in short, with much of the ignorance and prejudice of former time, and with all its rigid and inflexible honesty – on whose bare word the utmost reliance may be placed, and who have so little of the impartial spirit of commerce, that they prefer selling their grain to an old customer at a lower price, to deserting him and accepting a higher offer from one with whom they have not been in the habit of dealing.[11]

The yeoman farmer was a figure of English mythology, a small farmer who kept his independence of spirit. Generally the class was declining, though the trend was slower in Berkshire where the houses of the prosperous yeomanry were often mistaken for those of the gentry:

> a high spirited and independent yeomanry, actively engaged in agricultural pursuit, and each forming a circle of connection around him, is the distinguishing characteristic of the county. The graduations of society have no broken links; from the highest to the lowest, there is a gradually ascending and descending scale. In such a state we may look for patriotism without interest, and a display of generous feelings without the dread of offence. It is here that the influence of love can do much; the influence of power and property, little.[12]

Most farmers were tenants of the great landowners and minor gentry, whose terms varied considerably. Some had been there for many generations. In Berkshire for example, 'Many instances occur where the same race of tenants, and the same race of proprietors have for generations managed an unbroken connection, which is equally creditable to both.' But this was not likely to continue for ever, as leases became shorter, rarely more than fourteen years and often as few as five.[13]

Those who suffered most from improvement were often the country labourers, though they too kept their independence of spirit. Berkshire

Agricultural labourers harvesting corn, from Pyne's Microcosm

labourers were paid 9 shillings (45p) to 12 shillings (60p) per week. They were 'a hardy and personable race, patient of labour, but impatient of control, when they think it improperly exerted'. But according to some, their 'love of independence' 'might be deemed dangerous words when speaking *in a general way* of the labouring classes'.[14]

One effect of the improvement of agriculture was to reduce the amount of common land, where any villager could graze his animals or collect firewood. This movement had been going on for centuries, but it was increasingly necessary for the landlords to obtain private acts of parliament to continue with it. In Berkshire it was lamented that, 'The want of a general inclosure, and the enormous expences [*sic*] attending private bills of this kind being carried into execution, not only checks on agricultural improvement, but in many cases render it impossible.'[15] Enclosure and the shortage of farm tenancies forced many off the land, into the growing factories and cities. Resentment was expressed in the popular rhyme:

> The law doth punish man or woman
>   That steals a goose from off the common
> But lets the greater villain loose
>   That steals the common from the goose.

However, the changes did lead to much greater efficiency, so that land could feed the growing cities with only a minimal use of imported food.

Artisans were skilled craftsmen, strictly regulated by local guilds who insisted on a proper apprenticeship for all their members. At worst, an apprenticeship was little more than slavery, as young people from workhouses and charitable institutions were bound to masters and mistresses for seven years to do menial work without pay. At best, a young man could gain entry to a real trade, of which there was a great variety. The first of three volumes of *The Book of Trades of Library of the Useful Arts*, published in 1804, lists 23, including wool-comber, spinner, waterman, basket-maker, hat-maker, jeweller, brick-layer, carpenter, cooper, stonemason and soap boiler. Economists like Adam Smith applauded the breaking of work down into more specialized units, but it had its drawbacks if recession or technical change hit a particular trade, for there was no regular way for an adult to learn a new trade. The most spectacular example were the hand-loom weavers, who were prosperous until the power loom came along to displace them. Men from such trades were often forced into the army or the navy, and the 124 marines of HMS *San Domingo* included twenty weavers, along with fifty labourers who had probably been forced off the land.[16]

Some artisans worked hard to establish themselves, like Francis Place with his tailoring business:

> I never lost a minute of time, was never on any occasion diverted from the steady pursuit of my business and never spent a single shilling – never once entertained any company, the only things I bought were books, and not many of them. I adhered steadily to the practice I had adopted, and read for two or three hours every night after the business of the day was closed, which never happened till half past nine o clock. I never sent to bed till twelve o'clock and frequently not until one but I indulged a little in the morning by lying in bed until seven.[17]

There were large numbers of miners. Those in the more traditional industries of tin, copper and lead were often highly skilled and quite privileged, for they had to extract valuable metals from among large quantities of soil. Those in the coal industry were less well off – theirs was hard labour to extract a bulk commodity, and those in Scotland had only been released from serfdom in 1799.

For the new factory workers, life was a drastic change from what they had known, especially if they had been displaced from the land. Instead of open fields and irregular hours, they were crammed into what William Blake called the 'dark satanic mills' around this time, to work incessantly for long hours at noisy and unforgiving machines. Children as young as five often worked long hours for minimum pay. A few factory owners such as Robert Owen at New Lanark in Scotland realized that they could do far better with well fed and contented workers, but government regulation was many years away.

There was no working class as such, for these disparate groups were not united. Trade unions were banned by the Combination Acts of 1799–1800. Artisans in established trades might still organize themselves in traditional guilds, while others could join friendly societies that might support them during illness or unemployment, or even a strike. But in general the laws against trade unionism were strictly enforced.

Francis Place noticed the difference between those who had been born to poverty, and those who had sunk into it:

> None but such can tell how disappointment preys on them, how as their number of children increases, hope leaves them, how their hearts sink as toil becomes useless, how adverse circumstances force on them those indescribable feelings of their own degradation which sinks them gradually to the extreme of wretchedness. Others there are in much larger numbers whose views are narrower, they who hoped and expected to keep on in a decent way who never expected to rise in the world and never calculated on extreme poverty. I have seen a vast many such, who when the evil day has come upon them, have kept on working steadily but hopelessly more like horses in a mill, or mere machines than human beings, their feelings blunted, poor stultified animals, working on yet unable to support their families in anything like comfort ...[18]

A fair in a market town, the centre of much social and economic activity,
from Pyne's Microcosm

Servants formed a large group in society, and their status varied greatly. Thomas Malthus thought their lives were very easy in grand houses:

> The servants who live in the families of the rich ... possess the necessaries and even the comforts of life almost, as in great plenty as their masters. Their work is easy, and their food luxurious, compared with the work and food of the class of labourers; and their sense of dependence is weakened by the conscious power of changing their masters if they feel themselves offended.[19]

That was true at one end of the social scale. At the other, there were many families not far above the poverty line themselves, who employed one or two servants. Pauper children could be apprenticed through the parish and cost practically nothing – indeed the parish might even pay a few pounds to take them on. In Jane Austen's *Mansfield Park* the Price family of Portsmouth employed two maids, one of whom was 'trollopy-looking'. Mrs Price had been brought up to higher things, and she constantly complained about the difficulty of getting good servants.

Benjamin Silliman was surprisingly optimistic when he wrote, 'the police of London must be very good, or the people uncommonly well disposed, for the place is almost as free from turmoil as a village.'[20] This was very different from the experience of the London magistrate Patrick Colquhoun, who wrote, 'all ranks must bear testimony to the dangers which both life and property are at present subjected to by the number of criminal people, who, from various causes ... are suffered with impunity to repeat acts of licentiousness and mischief, and commit depredations upon individuals and the Public.'[21]

Some people believed there was a separate criminal class. Traditionally villages and small towns had been largely self-policing communities, but the growth of cities such as London, Birmingham and Manchester had overtaken all that, and they also tended to attract those who had failed to fit into a community elsewhere. Rather than build up an efficient police force, Parliament had reacted by passing increasingly savage laws, applying the death penalty for a bizarre list of crimes – concealing the death of a bastard child, house-breaking at night, shoplifting to the value of five shillings, and many others. More than

160 offences were subject to hanging – but it failed to prevent crime. According to the legal writer Sir William Blackstone,

> The injured, through compassion, will often forbear to prosecute: Juries, through compassion, will sometimes forget their oaths, and either acquit the guilty or mitigate the nature of the offence; and Judges, through compassion will respite one half the convicts, and recommend them to the Royal Mercy.

Imprisonment in a 'house of correction' was only just becoming established as a means of punishment. The London area alone had eighteen prisons, but most were for debtors or those awaiting trial, who might linger there for many months for an acquittal and then fail to be released because they could not pay their fees. Those convicted might be whipped, or sentenced to transportation to Australia for seven or fourteen years, or for life. The harshness of naval and military discipline needs to be judged against these standards.

The social differences in London were no greater than anywhere else, but they tended to be highlighted on the city's streets:

> The number of beggars in the streets of London is very great; in some streets they occur every few steps, and among them is a very large proportion of old women, and a considerable number of young women with infants in their arms. When I have bestowed a trifle on them, I have sometimes heard Englishmen say, 'O these people are impostors, O don't mind them, they make a trade of it.'[22]

Excessive alcohol consumption was something that transcended all classes, though Silliman did not see much wrong with it:

> Immense quantities of porter and beer are consumed in London; they are very cheap and nutritious, and nothing is more common than to see Carmen and carriers in London stopping their work for a short time, and refreshing themselves with a pint of porter and a lunch of wheat bread. The porter drinkers of London reject the liquor unless it foams, or has a head, as they call it.[23]

It was just over a decade since Mary Wollstonecraft had published her pioneering and influential feminist work *A Vindication of the Rights of*

Women, but her ideas were out of fashion by this time – her scandalous sex life had been exposed, and her early support for the French Revolution helped to discredit her ideas. Though women of all classes had no political and few legal rights, some had much influence and wealth through their fathers, husbands and families. Silliman was surprised at how much liberty they enjoyed compared with their sisters in New England. 'Driving is, at present, quite fashionable among the ladies of England, and sometimes it is done when the good man sits peaceably by the lady's side – a passenger only.'[24] He met an American lady who

> remarked to me that there was much more freedom in the manners of the English ladies, particularly in their treatment of gentlemen, than with us, and that they conversed with them (in a serious style) without any consciousness of impropriety, on subjects, which it is scarcely possible to introduce in similar American circles.[25]

But these habits could be taken to extremes by the women of the lower orders:

> yesterday ... I saw a very athletic woman dragging by the collar a man much stouter than herself, and, with very appropriate eloquence, upbraiding him for attempting to go off without paying for some cherries, which it seems he had bought off this modern Amazon ... it must be acknowledged that this was an embarrassing situation, and afforded to the advocates of Miss Wolstonecraft, [sic] a triumphant example of the practical enforcement of the rights of women.[26]

This was the lively, complex, diverse and very unequal society that was to fight a war for national survival.

THE NATION IN 1940

The great wars with France finally ended with the Battle of Waterloo in 1815 and were followed by almost a century during which Britain did not fight in Europe, with the exception of the Crimean War of 1853–6, which was fought a long distance away and posed no threat of invasion. Meanwhile the country developed at an unprecedented, if uneven, rate. By 1850 a great network of railways had already reached most of the country, creating the greatest transport revolution in history.

The Victorian age lasted from 1837 when the young Queen ascended the throne, until 1901 when she died. To some it was still going on in 1940, as the shadow of Victorian puritanism and hypocrisy hung over the nation. Britain had been undoubtedly the greatest world power in those days, even if her relative position had begun to decline with the rise of Germany and the United States by the end of the century. The age had seen the beginning of police forces, universal literacy, humanitarian reform, and belief in 'progress'. It also saw the continuation of great inequalities in wealth and much hidden depravity. To others the age of Victorian optimism ended in the trenches of Flanders between 1914 and 1918. With three quarters of a million men dead and twice as many permanently injured, the horror and tragedy of these years dominated the thoughts of many long after hostilities ceased. Spiritualism boomed as the bereaved tried desperately to make contact with lost ones; pacifism was a dominant creed, and in 1933 the Oxford Union, the most famous debating society in the world, passed a motion that 'This House will not fight for King and country'. Germany had lost a war and felt the score could only be evened by winning another one. Britain had won a war (or at least been on the winning side) but had gained very little, and war was seen as a purely destructive event.

What also dominated the thoughts of most people in the 1930s was the fear of unemployment and descent into poverty. British industry was fragile after losing its technological lead in the late nineteenth century and many of its markets in 1914–18. It was on a slow climb back to prosperity when it felt the effects of the Wall Street Crash of 1929. By 1931 there were more than two and three quarter millions registered unemployed, and the figure did not go below a million until after World War II started in 1939. It remained far higher in certain industries and regions, such as mining and heavy industry in Scotland, Wales and the north of England.

Welfare benefits for the unemployed were barely adequate and were subject to the infamous 'means test' by which the applicant's resources were looked into in the most insensitive manner. In 1939 *Picture Post* featured the life of one of London's unemployed:

> He does not get up particularly early on a Friday, because until he has been to the Employment Exchange there is nothing much he can do. It is warmer in bed, and he takes up less space. When he does get up, he has breakfast, helps with the children, then goes to the local Employment Exchange.
>
> There, outside a low, grey building, groups of men, nearly all wearing cloth caps and mufflers, are waiting for the doors to open. They know one another – they meet three times a week. Some of the unlucky ones have been coming here for years.
>
> All the talk is of work – jobs heard of, jobs applied for, jobs not secured. 'Walked all the way to Houndsditch, but, when I got there the foreman said there was some mistake, there wasn't a job going at all.'[27]

It was not difficult to see Britain in 1939 as a disunited country – divided by class and level of education, by wealth and prosperity, by work and unemployment, by country and region, by town and countryside, by political views and by attitudes to war. There was a great deal of soul-searching as Victorian and Edwardian certainties were shattered and pessimism prevailed. Writers were as anxious as anyone to find the answers, usually by travelling. In 1927, H. V. Morton went *In Search of England* and found that the strength of the country was in its villages, which were under threat from suburbanization and the motor car. J. B. Priestley followed up the huge success of his travelling novel *The Good Companions* with his *English Journey* of 1934. He found that there were three Englands – the ancient one of 'cathedrals and ministers, of Parson and Squire', the Victorian one of railways, factories and slums, and the modern one:

> This is the England of arterial and by-pass roads, of filling stations and factories that look like exhibition buildings, of giant cinemas and dance-halls and cafés, bungalows with tiny garages, cocktail bars, Woolworths, motor-coaches, wireless, hiking, factory girls looking like actresses, greyhound races and dirt tracks, swimming pools, and everything given away for cigarette coupons.[28]

And in 1937, George Orwell took *The Road to Wigan Pier* and found grinding poverty and crushing unemployment in the north of England:

> There exists in England a curious cult of Northernness, a sort of Northern snobbishness. A Yorkshireman in the South will always take care to let you know that he regards you as an inferior. If you ask him why, he will explain that it is only in the North that life is 'real' life, that the industrial work done in the North is the only 'real' work, that the North is inhabited by 'real' people, the South merely by rentiers and their parasites. The Northerner had 'grit', he is grim, 'dour', plucky, warm-hearted, and democratic; the Southerner is snobbish, effeminate and lazy ... [29]

As well as the differences within England, the three other parts of the United Kingdom still regarded themselves, to a greater or lesser degree, as separate nations. Scotland suffered from the depression as badly as anywhere, with a quarter of its workers unemployed, for it had not diversified into the new industries and was still dependent on heavy industry such as steel and shipbuilding. The old division between Highlander and Lowlander had largely been forgotten, as the kilt and bagpipes were adopted as national symbols, but religion was still a divisive factor, for migration of both Catholics and Protestants from Ulster led to conflict and the setting up of powerful Orange Lodges for Protestants. The rivalry was not reflected in politics as in Northern Ireland, but it found its strongest expression in football, among the supporters of Protestant Rangers and Catholic Celtic. The cities, especially Glasgow, had grown too fast in the last century and were filled with huge slums, sometimes dominated by gang warfare. The idea of Scottish Home Rule had been abandoned by the major political parties, but there was now a small but influential National Party of Scotland campaigning for compete independence. The Scots still regarded themselves as a warrior race and contributed significantly to the new army, navy and air force that were being raised to fight for the United Kingdom.

Northern Ireland was the surviving portion of Ireland under British rule following the independence of the rest of the island in 1922, and it was the most divided portion of the Kingdom, the only one where religious loyalty was a major factor in politics. The majority Protestants were fiercely and often embarrassingly loyal to the British crown, while the oppressed Roman Catholics wanted union with the rest of Ireland. This could often lead to violence, sometimes on a local scale when Protestants raided Catholic communities, sometimes better organized, as with the Irish Republican Army's bombing campaign against Britain during most of 1939. Though the Protestants were generally enthusiastic supporters of the war, Britain never dared to apply conscription to Northern Ireland for fear of provoking Catholic resistance.

Wales maintained its separate identity, although modern transport tended to undermine it – from Cardiff it was easier to get to Birmingham than to North Wales. The Welsh identity in Britain was confirmed by leading political figures such as David Lloyd George and Aneurin Bevan in a later generation. The country, with its coal mining and heavy industry in the south, was heavily hit by unemployment, but the separatist movement had only 2,000 members in 1939.

The war had done much to dent the old British class structure and undermine the deference that had sustained it, but each class still had its own characteristics, which were defined by education, housing, leisure and sport. Dress played a lesser role – according to Orwell,

> The youth who leaves school at fourteen and gets a blind-alley job is out of work at twenty, probably for life; but for two pounds ten on the hire-purchase he can buy himself a suit which, for a little while and at a little distance, looks as though it had been tailored in Saville Row. A girl can look like a fashion plate at an even lower price.[30]

The term 'gentry' was rarely used except ironically. 'Gentlemen' was as likely to refer to a toilet as a social grouping, and the landowning upper classes tended to extend their range by including the professional and managerial upper middle classes. The old landed interests were in decline as a result of death duties imposed during the war and the death of a large number of elder sons in the conflict. Much of the great estates had been broken up and sold to tenant farmers.

The upper and upper middle classes still sent their children to so called 'public schools' where they were taught to rule. Boys at Harrow were kept apart from lesser beings with obsessive rigour, according to John Mortimer:

> Harrow-on-the-Hill is in the middle of the suburbs ... It is only a few stops from Baker Street on the Metropolitan Line and we used to sit in smoke-filled carriages to be jeered at as we went up to Lord's, dressed in top-hat, pearl-grey waistcoat, morning-coat and silver-topped stick with a dark-blue tassel. We weren't allowed to speak to the boys at the bottom of the hill, though a Prefect might occasionally give one of them sixpence to carry up his suitcase at the beginning of term. We were isolated and put in quarantine both on account of sex and class ... [31]

The classic upper-class sports were still related to the ownership of land, though the relationship was not as clear-cut as in the past. Foxhunting thrived in changed circumstances and one aficionado wrote, 'This is an age of speed and machinery ... Perhaps what appeals to the majority is to go to the meet by mechanical transport, to enjoy a hunt only comparable to a steeplechase, where the course is cut and dried and speed at its highest, and to return home the same way.'[32] This did not impress J. B. Priestley: 'The fox-hunter who begins mumbling excuses, who tells you that he hunts to rid the country-side of foxes, that hunting is valuable because it improves the breed of horses (i.e., hunters), is a contemptible fellow.'[33] Shooting was another upper-class sport where the rising middle class tried to gain entry. Traditional sportsmen deplored the influence of the *nouveau riche*, particularly in 'the pernicious habit of over-tipping'.[34]

The middle classes were the most secure group of the age, and unemployment among them rarely rose to more than five per cent, for there was a considerable growth in the financial, banking and insurance sectors, which remained very sound despite the recession. This encouraged the growth of the London suburbs. The middle classes were in constant fear of working-class activism and intrusion. The highest-paid aped the upper classes and sent their children to public schools. Others sent them to inferior versions known as 'private' schools, or to local grammar schools where children were carefully selected and the education was much cheaper. They usually studied hard for the Schools'

Certificate which was necessary for entry to a profession or university.

Cricket was a sport that went across class boundaries more than most, especially in country districts, but its own internal boundaries were particularly strong – 'gentlemen', or wealthy amateurs, were strictly segregated from 'players', or professionals. Cricket had a stronger international dimension than most sports, and the infamous 'bodyline' tests between England and Australia in 1932–3 strained relations between the two countries. Rugby football was an upper- and middle-class sport, largely developed and fostered in the public schools – though all classes played it in Wales, and Rugby League, played in the north of England, was a working-class sport. The classic middle-class game of the age was tennis, which required a certain amount of equipment but could be played by both sexes and gave unique opportunities for social contact. There were 3,220 tennis clubs in 1938, a number that had doubled since 1920. The Wimbledon championships were broadcast on the wireless from 1927, and there were British victories by Fred Perry in 1934–6.

The working classes were divided quite rigidly into two parts – those who had served an apprenticeship and become skilled workers, and those who had not. The workers looked to their trade unions to protect their living standards. There were more than a thousand separate organizations, many of them craft unions more interested in protecting the privileges of their own trades than improving the working class as a whole. The most important exception was the Transport and General Workers Union, founded by Ernest Bevin and others in 1922. The trade union movement had suffered a heavy defeat in the General Strike of 1926, and there were many who remembered Winston Churchill as the architect of that. The unemployment of the 1930s made the situation much worse, and the working-class movement responded by organizing hunger marches, which had more effect on public opinion than on government policy.

Most working-class children went to elementary schools until the age of fourteen, when they left to seek work. If they were lucky they might find apprenticeships, which they hoped would set them up in the skilled occupations, though opportunities were rare during the worst years of the Depression, so in 1939 Britain was short of skilled workers when they were sorely needed. For the working classes in most of Britain, the only important sport was football (which they never called soccer). It could be played informally in the streets where motor cars were rare. Scotland and England had separate leagues, and international matches between the countries were a focus for Scottish national pride. Otherwise the British ignored international football. Most league clubs were based in industrial towns and cities; Arsenal, the dominant team of those years, was actually founded in a factory. Huge crowds might attend, and more than 118,000 watched Rangers play Celtic in Glasgow in 1939. Millions of working-class men dreamed of an escape from poverty by betting on the results and winning the football pools. Important matches were broadcast on the wireless, especially the hugely popular English FA Cup Final, but football tended to foster local rivalries rather than national unity.

Despite the trends elsewhere, the building industry thrived during the Depression. In the mid-1930s about a third of a million new homes were built every year, largely for the new middle classes in the suburbs. A deposit of £50 or a total payment of £850 would secure a house in the London suburb of Chipstead, for example:

> These magnificent residences fitted with every up-to-date Labour-Saving device, have splendid accommodation: 2 Reception, 3 Bedrooms, Kitchen-ette (tiles) with Cabinet-dresser, 'Sentry' Boiler, Gas Copper, etc., Tiled Bathroom with marble enclosed porcelain enamelled Bath, Brick built Garage and double Coal Storage, Splendid Gardens, Gas and Electric Points, Switches, Flex and Pendants including Points for Wireless. Main drainage, Company's Water.[35]

In addition, between fifty and a hundred thousand new council houses were built each year so that some of the working classes could move out of the slums:

> One morning about September 1932 I remember the postman calling and leaving a letter which I took to my mother. On opening it she let out a wild cheer: 'Hooray! Hooray! We've got a new house.' 'With electric

lights?' I asked. 'With electric lights and a bathroom,' she replied. I didn't know that houses had bathrooms. In fact I didn't know what a bathroom was.[36]

Despite the large numbers of new 'servantless' houses, there were still half a million men and two million women in domestic service in 1931 as families tried to maintain their standards. Monica Dickens worked in service in 1937 and found much to complain of, including compulsory uniform, an invention of Victorian times that uncompromisingly marked out its wearer:

Personally, I can't see that a cap's any different from an apron – they're both badges of servitude. They only thing I have against them is that they're so madly unbecoming. Being a skivvy is drab enough, anyway, without having to make oneself look any more depressing than necessary.

Working hours were even worse:

Any maid who has only two nights a week off is bound to be green with envy at her friend the shop-girl, who goes to the Pictures and dance-halls every night and snaffles all the young men. Even on her day out her mistress may well thoughtlessly arrange a lunch-party, thinking, if she thinks about it at all: 'Oh, well, she's not supposed to get off till half-past two.' She doesn't realize that the girl is faced with the alternative of clearing up after lunch, and perhaps not getting away till three or four, or leaving everything and being confronted with a congealing, disheartening mess when she comes home tired in the evening.[37]

Britain had become a relatively law-abiding country since Sir Robert Peel founded the first modern police force in 1829. That force was now held in some affection, though popular detective fiction of the day suggested that the policemen, nearly all recruited from working-class backgrounds, were essentially stupid and unimaginative and needed the support of talented amateur sleuths such as Miss Marple and Lord Peter Wimsey. The British liked to believe that their policemen were relatively free from corruption. However, in 1931 Lord Trenchard was brought in to head the Metropolitan Police after a series of scandals. He soon found that there was indeed a good deal of low-level bribery of officers by bookmakers and publicans. He attempted reform by making the police force more like the air force he had come from, with short-service appointments and special training at Hendon for selected officers – measures that caused a great deal of resentment and did not survive his tenure.

The Economy of Britain in 1940

By the 1930s, British industry was far less dynamic than in the past and suffered from some of the disadvantages of being a pioneer – its railway system had grown haphazardly over more than a century, and there was a long-lasting legacy of bad industrial relations in her factories and complacency among the management.

Merchant shipping had emerged from World War I with great credit, and it was practically the only trade that offered a young man the chance to travel the world. But Bob Stanford Tuck (who became a fighter ace during the Battle of Britain) was not satisfied: 'At home he could talk excitedly of savage storms, of romantic islands bathed in the cool, satin light of the tropic moon, and of his wanderings in the tangled streets and alleys of foreign towns. But the more he talked, the more the novelty wore off – the more he thought about the long, uneventful periods in between.'[38] British shipping remained almost constant at around ten million tons between the wars, but it was in relative decline as the fleets of the USA, Japan, Greece and Norway expanded. It too was hard hit by the depression, and hundreds of ships were laid up to await better times. London and Liverpool had long vied as the leading port of the United Kingdom. London concentrated on imports for the prosperous south-east, while Liverpool brought in raw materials for Lancashire industry and exported the results. By value, these two had more than half the trade of the country between them. Regional ports included Greenock and Leith in Scotland, Cardiff, Bristol, Newcastle and Hull. Fishing had lost most of its export markets, but it still supported 32,000 men in 1939, largely operating out of great ports like Grimsby and Hull.

The railways were perhaps the most visible legacy of the Victorian age. There were just over 20,000 miles of track in Britain, a figure that had changed very little since 1912. The lines had mostly been built piecemeal and were ill-planned; rolling stock was small by American and European standards because the tunnels and bridges were low. In 1922 the government forced a merger of numerous lines into four regional groupings – the London, Midland and Scottish Railway; the Great Western Railway; the London and North Eastern Railway; and the Southern Railway. There was some electrification in the south, but in general the railways were powered by dirty, smoky steam. Trains, whether carrying commuters to their daily round or holidaymakers on their annual trip, were often overcrowded and uncomfortable.

The 1920s and 1930s saw a huge rise in the number of motor vehicles on Britain's roads, creating a social revolution. Motor cars had multiplied more than twenty-fold to nearly two million. There were half a million vans and lorries and almost as many motor cycles. Only tramcars were in decline, though the youthful Alan Bennett found that 'Trams were bare and bony, transport reduced to its basic elements, and they had a song to sing … ' while the buses that replaced them were 'too comfortable and cushioned to have a moral dimension'.[39] By 1939 there were 53,000 motor buses in Britain compared with 9,000 trams. J. B. Priestley travelled in a motor coach for the first time at the beginning of his *English Journey* and was 'astonished at its speed and comfort'.[40]

Road deaths peaked at over 7,000 in 1934, more than twice today's figure. There were no driving tests, and the buyer of a Morris Oxford in 1930 was advised:

> We cannot too forcibly impress upon the new purchaser of a car the vital necessity of his or her knowing the rules and the etiquette of the road before venturing forth on his or her first trip. With the roads in their present crowded state, the beginner who has not attempted to master the elementary necessities is a very real danger, not only to other people but himself or herself.[41]

There were some rather grudging improvements in road safety during the 1930s. The *Highway Code* was first produced in 1930 to give road users some guidance, driving tests came in during 1934 (but only for new drivers), and third party insurance was made compulsory. The urban speed limit of 30 miles per hour was introduced in 1935, but as *1066 And All That* put it, 'The Occasional Conformity Act was the only Act of its kind in History, until the Speed Limit was invented.'[42] A few new roads were built, such as the Liverpool-to-Manchester road, which Priestley found to be 'very broad, straight and uninteresting, the kind that chauffeurs love'.[43] There was no attempt to separate people from cars, and arterial roads like the Great West Road out of London were soon lined with new houses – Priestley saw a road that 'with its new lock-up shops, its picture theatres, its red-brick little villas, might have been anywhere'.[44] There were new by-passes and Osbert Lancaster began his cartooning career in 1939 with a mild satire on them – 'There's only one solution: we must by-pass the by-pass.' But in general the road pattern followed the old turnpikes, which in turn followed the Roman roads, or more commonly, as G. K. Chesterton put it in 1914, 'The rolling English drunkard made the rolling English road.'

Many commentators deplored the influence of the motor car. They said far less about electricity, which was to change Britain just as much, though travellers deplored the power cables and the pylons that supported them on their routes across the countryside. The national grid was set up after 1926, replacing local supplies in each town and city. The power stations were mostly fired by coal and placed near rivers so that fuel could be brought to them. Some, such as Battersea and Bankside in London, eventually became architectural icons. In 1920 there were less than a quarter of a million consumers of electricity; by 1938 there were nearly nine million, which meant that almost everyone, except the very poor or the very remote, had access to electric power.

Electricity powered most of the new factories, and it was also essential to the new servantless suburban home, allowing the use of devices such as vacuum cleaners, as well as much cleaner heating, cooking and lighting. It was also necessary to the two great communications revolutions of the age – radio (usually known as wireless) and cinema. The British Broadcasting Company was set up by the radio manufacturers in 1922 under the puritanical Scottish engineer John

Reith, and later it came under government ownership as the British Broadcasting Corporation. It was funded by an annual licence fee, and theoretically it had a monopoly of radio broadcasting in Britain – though those who wanted lighter entertainment could find it from foreign stations in Luxemburg and Hilversum. The BBC fought hard and successfully against being made a government mouthpiece, especially during the general strike of 1926. A wireless set was a substantial item of furniture, and few houses could afford more than one, so families tended to listen together. Nearly nine million homes had licences by 1939. The BBC had only a single broadcasting station until early 1940 when the Forces Programme was set up, and it provided the nation with a strong unifying force in times of crisis. Millions tuned in to listen to Edward VIII's abdication in 1936; in 1938 and 1939 various classes of reservist were called up by radio, and in 1939 it broadcast Chamberlain's mournful declaration of war on Germany.

Apart from radio, the cinema was the great mass medium of the age. Silent films had been around since the beginning of the century, but the coming of the 'talking picture' in 1927 resulted in the building of huge cinemas in every town and suburb, often using mock-Egyptian architecture inspired by the discovery of the pharaoh Tutankhamun's tomb in 1922. The cinemas became great social centres, as more than half the population went at least once a week. They displaced the old music halls and to a certain extent the pubs, but unlike radio their content was largely American.

It was an age of almost universal literacy and the habit of reading was spread by popular newspapers such as the *Daily Mirror*, by the foundation of Penguin Books in 1935, by organizations such as the Left Book Club and magazines such as *Picture Post* – all of which took a left-of-centre view. Not all writers shared this position. Evelyn Waugh was one of the most profoundly conservative, as well as the most penetrating, novelists of any period. The 1930s produced writers who would retain popularity several generations later – the crime novels of Agatha Christie and Dorothy L. Sayers, the humour of P. G. Wodehouse, the adventure stories of C. S. Forester, the children's books of Richmal Crompton, Enid Blyton and W. E. Johns, as well as the more profound works of Robert Graves and Graham Greene would provide people with amusement during the long, boring hours of war duty and sometimes give them diversion or a sense of perspective in moments of danger.

Britain was no longer an agricultural country – less than six per cent of the population worked in agriculture in 1931, and that was declining. The country produced only about 40 per cent of its own food, with 40 per cent more imported from the empire and 20 per cent from the rest of the world. There were fears for what was left of agriculture as the suburbs expanded to take over the land. A backlash in favour of the countryside included Stanley Baldwin, who was prime minister three times during the inter-war period and whose sentimental roots were in the country:

> Nothing is more characteristic of England's countryside than the village homes which, for century upon century, have sheltered her sturdy sons of toil. Who has not felt a thrill of admiration on catching sight of some old-world village round a bend of the road? The roofs, whether thatched or tiled; the walls, weather-boarded or half-timbered, or of good Cotswold stone – have been built with a material ready to the hand of the craftsman and, painted with the delicate pigments only to be found on the palette of Father Time, have grown amid their surroundings just as naturally as the oaks and elms under whose shade they stand.[45]

The industrial world, where about half of Britain's population lived and worked, was very different from Baldwin's vision. Townspeople had discovered the country and the remotest areas had been opened up by the bicycle, the motor car and the bus. The result was a great expansion in hiking, which led to conflict with the landowners. It climaxed in the Kinder Scout affair in 1932, when 500 ramblers from Manchester took part in a mass trespass. Five of them were arrested after some dubious police tactics and it was reported that 'the jubilant villagers crowded every window and door to watch the police triumph'.[46]

Although oil was now the fuel of road transport and war, it had to be imported, and the use of native coal was encouraged for other purposes. The main coalfields were still in Scotland, north-east England, South

Wales, Yorkshire, Nottingham and Derby, and Lancashire. Work underground was still hard, as Orwell discovered:

> You crawl through the last line of pit props and see opposite you a shiny black wall three or four feet high. This is the coal face. Overhead is the smooth ceiling made by the rock from which the coal has been cut; underneath is the rock again, so that the gallery you are in as only as high as the coal itself, probably not much more than a yard. The first impression of all, overmastering everything else for a while, is the frightful, deafening din from the conveyor belt which carries the coal away. You cannot see very far, because the fog of coal dust throws back the beam of your lamp, but you can see on either side of you the line of half-naked kneeling men, one to every four or five yards, driving their shovels under the falling coal and flinging it swiftly over their left shoulders. They are feeding it onto the conveyor belt, a moving rubber belt a couple of feet wide which runs a yard or two between them. Down this belt a glittering river of coal races constantly.[47]

The coal industry supplied the railways and power stations as well as providing most of the country's domestic heating, with about a quarter of its production going for export. Its labour force –more than three quarters of a million men in 1937, but hardly any women – mostly lived in isolated villages and were fiercely proud of their work and their culture. But they were discontented with the largely aristocratic owners, and labour relations were worse than in any other industry. It was particularly vulnerable to unemployment, and more than a third of miners were out of work in 1933.

Shipbuilding was another proud trade. It had coped with huge changes during the nineteenth century, as steam replaced sail, and iron and then steel replaced wood. It had largely been relocated from the south of England to the north-east, Merseyside and the Clyde. The pace of technological change slowed down in the twentieth century, though diesel was becoming common for small ships, while at the other end of the scale Atlantic liners were becoming ever larger. The industry had great strategic value, but it suffered even more from unemployment, with a catastrophic 60 per cent out of work in the worst year of 1932. Many yards were closed in the early 1930s, and famous names such as

Beardmore of Dalmuir and Palmer of Jarrow disappeared – the latter town was devastated. 'Jarrow in that year, 1932–33, was utterly stagnant. There was no work. No-one had a job, except a few railwaymen, officials, the workers in the co-operative stores, and a few workmen who went out of the town to their jobs each day. The unemployment rate was over 80 per cent.'[48] In Clydebank work was stopped on the great new Cunard liner, No. 534. When it resumed in 1934, the town was decorated with flags, and pipers led the workers on their first day back at work. The ship was launched as *Queen Mary* later in the year.

The textile industry employed women far more than any other – nearly half a million men and three quarters of a million women in 1939. Wool was still important and employed more than 200,000 people, spread around the country, while such industries as silk, lace and canvas were rather smaller. Cotton manufacturing was by now largely confined to Lancashire. It too had suffered badly during the war, as it relied totally on imported materials, and now it faced fierce competition from Japan.

Engineering was still an important British industry. There were great steelworks near the coalfields, while factories produced machinery and locomotives for home use and export.

The motor industry was a great growth area and one with strategic consequences because it could be converted to aircraft or military vehicle production. It supplied almost all of the home market, and the tax system encouraged slow, underpowered vehicles, though Rolls Royce and Daimler had strong places at the top end of the market. Car production was usually sited near the main centres of population, with large factories in the Midlands, Morris at Oxford, and a new Ford works that was set up at Dagenham down the Thames from London. The industry used mass production, so the proportion of skilled workers was smaller than in traditional engineering industries. The chemical industry, which among other things produced dyes for textiles and explosives for the armed forces, was dominated by the huge Imperial Chemical Industries, formed by a merger of four firms in 1926.

London regarded itself as the greatest city in the world in 1939. It did not have the beauty of Paris or the history of Rome, but it was the largest, a conurbation of eight million people. It was the centre of a huge empire, and decisions made in London were felt all over Africa, India and the Middle East. As well as the political capital, home of both the monarchy and parliament, it was the financial centre, the greatest port and contained the finest museums, art galleries, theatres and libraries. It was the centre of communications and had a good deal of industry. There was no agreement about the exact boundaries of London. Unlike Paris, it did not expand across a series of city walls, and unlike modern London, its areas were not defined by orbital roads. There was the ancient City of London, the 'square mile', which had few inhabitants and was a centre of financial business. Then there was the County of London with nearly four-and-a-half million people, all within ten miles of the centre. And, probably most relevant, there was the Metropolitan Police area, which extended well into Middlesex, Kent, Sussex, Essex and Hertfordshire. This was the area into which the suburbs had expanded in the last two decades.

London as a whole had a large proportion of workers in small companies, especially in the clothing trades. Larger industries were often concentrated on the banks of the Thames, including gas works and electricity power stations, sugar factories and grain mills. The biggest single group of employees, apart from domestic servants, was the transport workers, for London was the centre of the national distribution system as well as needing extensive transport of its own to cater for its vast suburbs. London Transport was formed in 1933 by merging several bus and rail companies. The famous London tube map was designed by Harry Beck, while new lines, no longer underground as they were in central London, extended out to 'Metroland', the new suburbs where new stations were built in modern style.

The British went reluctantly to war in 1939, less prepared in many ways than in the past. The invasion crisis of 1803–5 was just the latest in a long series, but there had been no real threat of invasion during 1914–18 (despite many paranoid fears), and it did not seem very likely even at the outbreak of war in 1939. In other ways the nation was far more prepared. The last war had sent a whole generation into the conflict, so there were millions of men with front-line experience. This time no-one had any doubt that the war would affect everyone's lives, so there was no shock when children were evacuated from cities, conscription was applied generally, and a host of wartime regulations was introduced. There was no Jane Austen to treat the conflict as a distant struggle; in 1939 people closed their blackout curtains, built their air-raid shelters, worked long hours in their jobs, waved goodbye to family and friends in the armed forces, tried to make the best of their rationed food and clothes and wrote letters to their homesick children in the country.

London had not been vulnerable to invading armies as Paris, Madrid and Berlin had been in recent years. But it felt very vulnerable to the new threat of bombing raids. H. V. Morton noticed the preparations as he drove through the south-eastern suburbs in May 1939:

> I think it was at the Elephant and Castle that I was held up for a long time by a line of lorries loaded with gas-cylinders; as I passed through Lewisham the sun was pitilessly illuminating those tall houses of Georgian brick and Regency stucco which have come down in the world to a shabby, divided life of flats and tenements, and I noticed it the front gardens here and there, if I dare call those sooty strips by such a name, uneasy mounds and tumuli roofed with galvanized tin. In those soggy depths the householders proposed to take refuge if war came. The old, black houses gazed down on those dug-outs with an expression of utter amazement. And I too was amazed. I never thought the Ypres Salient could be reborn in a London garden.[49]

It was the civilian population of the nation that provided the soldiers, sailors and airmen to fight the war, largely through compulsion this time. Early in the century, conscription had been the subject of fierce debate, and Britain, uniquely among European powers, relied on a voluntary army until halfway through World War I. By the beginning of the second war it was accepted that conscription was the only fair way to raise mass armed forces, and it was just as necessary to meet the needs of industry. Conscription was first applied in peacetime in June 1939, when men were called up for service in a new militia, for six months training. This was quickly overtaken at the start of the war when a National Service (Armed Forces) Act was passed, making all men between the ages of 18 and 41 liable. After that, men were called out to register by age group as required. The process started in October 1939 with men aged 20 and 21, and after that the younger men were called up when they reached the age of 20, plus older men when the forces were ready to receive them. Thus on 9 December men born between October and December 1919 were called, as well as the older ones born in 1916 and 1917. The age gap within each successive group naturally tended to widen, so on 16 November 1940, men born in 1905 registered alongside those who had been born between July and November 1920. 1940 was the most important year for conscription, for more than a million men were called up, along with half a million more who volunteered before they became liable.

Each man was called to an interview in which he could state his preferences for the navy or the air force, but the army was hungriest for men in 1940 and took a total of more than 1.1 million, while the air force took less than 300,000, and the navy, still awaiting new ships under construction, needed only 124,000. Britain had quite liberal laws on conscientious objection. A man could decline to serve in the armed forces for political, religious or pacifist reasons. He appeared before a tribunal, which inspected the sincerity and validity of his beliefs. Occasionally it might register him unconditionally as a conscientious objector, but it was more likely to register him conditionally and put him into non-combatant duties, or occasionally to dismiss his case. It is significant how quickly the numbers of conscientious objectors fell with each registration during the crisis of 1940, from more than 5,800 in March to less than 2,000 in July and August. There were some who had not believed that the Chamberlain government was serious about fighting the Nazis, and in April George Orwell wrote: 'Except for small sections such as Pacifists etc. people want to get it settled & I fancy they'd be willing to go on fighting for 10 years if they thought the sacrifices were falling equally on everybody, which alas isn't likely with the present government in office.'[50] But the Conservative government was replaced by an all-party coalition just as the German attack on Western Europe began and J. P. W. Mallalieu had a change of heart 'when Churchill formed a National Government with the full support of the Labour Party and when Germany smashed through Belgium, Holland and France and what remained of the British army escaped through Dunkirk; my own previous attitude to the war seemed irrelevant and possibly wrong-headed. I had registered as a Conscientious Objector, on political, not pacifist grounds; and I now withdrew this registration and awaited call-up.'[51]

This was almost the last stage in forging national unity to face the crisis. Fascists were isolated or had renounced their faith, Conservatives, Labour and Liberals were in government, and only the small Communist party remained outside, at least until Hitler invaded Russia a year later. Already there were more than two million men and 56,000 women in the armed forces, with many more to come. This was the moment when Churchill made some of his most famous speeches, using the medium of radio to unite town and country, labour and capital, servants and masters, north and south, England, Scotland, Northern Ireland and Wales, as never before.

3

THE CIVILIANS

CIVILIANS AGAINST NAPOLEON

Civilians were not expected to be in the front line in most wars, but they paid taxes and made savings that would provide finance for the war. A proportion of them voted for or against the politicians who declared and conducted the war. They worked on the land and in manufacturing to produce food and munitions. They said goodbye to friends and relatives, they bore mental and material hardships for the sake of the war effort, and in the longer term they produced and reared the children who would fight future wars. In the meantime they were the loved ones the forces were fighting for, and gave them something to make their efforts worthwhile.

But not all civilians were materially useful. The young were just mouths to feed until they were ready to make a contribution. The old and the infirm were simply liabilities. Criminals were a problem in any society, and crime rates tended to rise slightly in 1940, but a full-scale invasion might bring on a breakdown of law and order that would distract and undermine the fighting forces. Even the most valuable civilian, such as an industrial worker, could be a liability in certain circumstances, if he panicked and became a refugee, for example, while groups of civilians might be used as cover for spies or traitors.

Any land war, except perhaps the one that was to take place in the North African desert from 1940 onwards, is fought over territory inhabited by civilians, who would feel the destructive effects of both enemy and friendly action. In a sea war, the enemy would attack merchant shipping and attempt to starve the population or destroy their trade. A war in the air might involve bombing them deliberately, or at the very least they would suffer from near-misses and all the restrictions that a bombing campaign brings. The British were used to fighting their wars at a distance, in Europe or the empire. An invasion, or the threat of invasion, would subject her people to land and sea war plus, in 1940, an air war as well. In 1803, the government made quite serious demands on all its citizens, though most of them had little material stake in the country – only a small minority had the vote and wealth was unevenly spread.

There is no sign that novelists took up the anti-invasion cause with any great enthusiasm in 1805, but other writers and artists did. New plays did not generally deal with the war, but an old Shakespearean favourite like *Henry V* had the subtitle 'or the conquest of France' when shown at the Theatre Royal, London, in September 1803, and the interval had a presentation called 'All volunteers!' that included a song called 'The country squire a volunteer'. At a more populist level, the Theatre Royal put on one of many plays mocking the 'Corsican tyrant':

...AN OLD PANTOMIME FARCE, CALLED
HARLEQUIN'S INVASION
OR THE
DISAPPOINTED BANDITTI
With New Machinery, Music Dresses and Decorations.
Harlequin Butcher by Mr Bonaparte, from Corsica,
(Who performed that Character in Egypt, Italy,
Switzerland, Holland &C.)[1]

When the King and some of the royal princesses went to see *School for Scandal* at Drury Lane in June 1805, there was,

> a poetical prologue to the interlude, all the lines of which ended in ation, and Bonaparte, under the nick-name of Bony, by which appellation he is contemptuously and jocosely called in England, was severely satirized, as well as his long threatened invasion. The king seemed more delighted with this than with any-thing; he laughed, almost continually, and the queen even exceeded him.

The entertainment ended with *Rule Britannia*, which was 'sung by the whole house, and the princesses joined in this chorus also'.[2]

In poetry, William Wordsworth had long forgotten his early support for the French Revolution and addressed those who would face the invasion:

Confirmed the charters that were yours before; –
  No parleying now! In Britain is one breath;
We are all with you now from shore to shore:
  Ye men of Kent, 'tis victory or death![3]

But the most savage intellectual weapon against Napoleon was the caricature, which was enjoying a golden age. Perhaps the greatest single feature in British morale was the fear of Napoleon, alternately a figure of fun and of fear. Artists like Gillray, Cruikshank, and Rowlandson were highly active in the cause. Some cartoons emphasized political unity and showed the opposition leaders Fox and Sheridan falling in as volunteers under Pitt as an officer. Others showed a diminutive Bonaparte, perhaps facing George III as the King of Brobdingnag in *Gulliver's Travels*. Another favourite theme was how different trades would deal with him when he landed. In a strip of August 1803, an apothecary says, 'I'll pound him', a publican proclaims, 'I'll cool his courage in a pot of brown stout', and an epicure concludes with, 'I'll eat him'. Cartoonists did not lack confidence in their nation's armed forces and delighted in showing the defeated Bonaparte enduring every possible humiliation – he was knocked out by a sailor in the English Channel, captured and put in a parrot cage, forced to ride in a triumphal procession facing backwards on a horse, hanged from a gallows or his head impaled on a pitchfork, or even more bloodily on a spike with the heads of his minions decorating the lower levels. All classes united against Napoleon under this cultural bombardment. Unlike World War II, there was no organization like Mass Observation to record the feelings of the people, but the poet Hannah More attempted to reproduce those of a ploughman:

Tho' my house is but small,
  Yet to have none at all, –
Would, sure, be a greater distress, Sir;
  Shall my garden so sweet,
And my orchard so neat,
  Be the prize of a foreign oppressor? ...
Then I'll beat my ploughshare
  To a sword or a spear,
And rush on these desperate men, Sir;

Like a lion I'll fight,
That my spear, now so bright,
 May soon turn to a ploughshare again, Sir.[4]

European society was generally free of peacetime travel restrictions during the eighteenth century, and it was expense, slowness of movement, danger and discomfort that prevented large-migrations rather than any legislation. Internally there was freedom of movement, except that vagabonds who were unable to support themselves were liable to be sent back to their home parishes. Passports were not needed for normal foreign travel, only for special purposes such as visiting war zones. Britain had welcomed many French émigrés after the Revolution and often put them in positions of trust. It had a long tradition of absorbing waves of French refugees, notably the Protestant Huguenots who arrived in the 1680s and were now established in London and elsewhere. The new refugees from the French Revolution were useful in terms of propaganda, and also for the information they might give, including that by General Dumouriez; he had commanded French revolutionary forces at the decisive battles of Valmy and Jemappes in 1792 but defected to the Allies soon afterwards and knew a great deal about past invasion plans.

Control of aliens within Britain only began with the Aliens Act of 1793, which was a reaction to the influx of tens of thousands from France. Its aims were described by its sponsor Henry Dundas:

> It was intended in the first instance, to make all foreigners, arriving in the kingdom, give an account of themselves; to make them give up such arms as they might have in their possession; he did not mean such arms as were natural for gentlemen to wear, but such as might naturally excite suspicion against the owners. It was also intended that, in their several removals through the country, they should use passports, by which the actual residence or occasional movements, might be notorious. For the same reason it was also intended to distribute those who received support into certain districts, where also they would be more liable to the cognisance of the civil power. Finally, it was proposed to pay particular attention to those foreigners who had come within the present year, or who may hereafter come without obvious reasons, and thus be rendered more liable to suspicion.[5]

71

It was seen by some as an ending of traditional liberties going back to the Magna Carta and was not unopposed. During the debate in the House of Lords, the Marquis of Landsdowne stated that, 'He considered the Bill in no other light than the partial suspension of the Habeas Corpus Act.'[6]

Arguably, the act was less necessary by 1803. Many of the French refugees had taken advantage of an amnesty offered by Napoleon and had returned home at the Peace of Amiens, and there was no great fresh influx in the new war. Nevertheless, it remained in force and applied to citizens of neutral as well as enemy countries. On registering in 1805, the American Benjamin Silliman was told that, 'I might think myself very fortunate in obtaining so soon my written permission to reside. I am restricted to London and the country within thirteen miles of it, for three months, with directions to communicate every change of lodgings ... Such are the mildest restrictions imposed on every foreigner ...'[7]

The first act that demanded the service of the general population, (apart from recruitment to the Militia) was that 'to provide for the Defence and Security of the Realm during the present War', which was passed into law on 11 June 1803.[8] The Lord Lieutenants were to provide returns of men between fifteen and 60 years of age, showing which were fit to serve in the volunteers and which were willing to be trained. They were also to list all wagons, boats and horses the owners would furnish for the public service. At the same time, they had authority to remove them if they were in danger of falling into enemy hands. Each Lord Lieutenant had the authority to 'mark out any Piece of Ground wanted for the publick service', though only with the consent of the owner 'unless the Necessity be first certified, or in case of actual Invasion'.

It had long been policy to deny all resources to the enemy in the event of an invasion, even at the cost of considerable hardship to individuals. On 1 July 1803 the War Office sent instructions to the Lord Lieutenants to 'drive the country', with particular emphasis on removing horses and cattle. In Pevensey Rape, the middle third of East Sussex, there were more than 5,000 oxen and 200 other cattle, eleven goats and 12,000 pigs, but it was mainly a sheep-farming area, with more than 95,000 of the animals. There were 4,430 horses, 1,572 wagons and 2,505 carts as well as 38 barges on the River Ouse. Also of strategic value to one side or the other were the 29 water-mills and 20 windmills, capable of producing a total of 201 sacks of flour a day.[9]

The Lord Lieutenants were to divide the county into districts then decide the routes by which the stock was to be withdrawn, using secondary paths as far as possible so that they would not get in the way of British troops.[10] Each district was to appoint men to carry them out. In Folkestone in Kent, eight were appointed 'for the Removal of Horses and Waggons conveying such persons as are unable to move themselves'. Sixteen more were to remove cattle, and 19 more sheep, while thirteen more were 'to take Charge of the Dead Stock, and to be stationary in their respective Districts'. Proprietors were recommended to mark their cattle with their initials, and a special parish symbol was advisable, as flocks might be mixed in the receiving areas.[11]

Reducing the enemy's mobility was a primary aim and later the War Office asserted,

> One of the most material objects to be attended to is the removal of the Horses & Draft Cattle, as well as Wheel Carriages or the rendering of them totally useless to the Enemy in the case of his effecting a Landing. All Horses or Draft Cattle that are not wanted for the Service of the Army, for the more speedy conveyance of Troops, and for forwarding the Military and Commissariat supplies of all Kinds, as well as the Transport of the Infirm Women and children, & that are in danger of falling into the hands of the Enemy, should be shot or hamstrung, and the Axletrees or Wheels of all Carriages, in the same predicament, should be broken to pieces or damaged as much as possible.[12]

Proprietors whose animals or goods were destroyed or mutilated in this way were promised indemnification, though not those who allowed them to fall intact into enemy hands through 'want of proper exertion'.

Not everyone was happy with this policy. Dumouriez advised:

> There must be no thought of denuding any counties threatened with invasion – that is removing the inhabitants, cattle &c. This fearful and ruinous measure could never be carried out even if it was to pass into law. The French themselves have never had recourse to these barbarous means, whether at home or in a hostile country.[13]

The Duke of Richmond, a field marshal and Lord Lieutenant of Sussex, thought that the scheme was impracticable on many levels and was a 'cruel idea'. It would require very detailed planning: that draught animals would have to be retained if women and children were to be removed, that stock would have to be left behind to feed any inhabitants still there; and that the roads would become clogged up:

> The removal of infirm women and children in carriages, such as wagons and carts, must be a slow operation from its nature, the numbers that must go from any considerable extent of the country, the cross roads they must take, and the unavoidable delays they must meet with, which may occasion both the miserable inhabitants and the draft cattle to fall into the hands of an alert enemy, who may thereby obtain in a considerable degree that most essential object for him, cattle to draw his artillery and ammunition ...[14]

The scheme was quietly dropped after that.

Lord Lieutenants were instructed to form corps of pioneers, civilians whose duties were 'in opening Communications for the March of our own Army, in closing such Roads as may be of use to an Enemy, or by assembling to fortify such Posts and Camps, as may be calculated to give Security to the Country in the Rear'.[15] In Folkestone, 39 men were found, enough to establish them in a company. Each was to bring his tools, including felling axes, pickaxes, spades, bill hooks and saws.[16]

Another act that reached well into the resources of the general population was the Levy en Masse Act of July 1803, which in theory mobilized the whole male population to fight an invader. Lord Lieutenants were to make lists of the men, dividing them into four categories according to age, marital status and number of children. Those in the first three classes, that is men under 30 without children and others under the age of 50, could be called out for compulsory military training for a minimum of two hours every Sunday. But the act also allowed exemption for areas that produced a sufficient quota of volunteers. In certain areas, such as Cambridge and Buckinghamshire, potential recruits were suspicious of clauses that seemed to allow them to be drafted into the regular army, and failed to come forward; but in most areas the act was successful, and it was not necessary to call men out for compulsory training.[17]

Lord Lieutenants and their deputies were ordered to survey the arms that the men of their country might provide. Men were asked whether they would arrive mounted or on foot, and whether they would provide firelocks or pitchforks. If carrying the former, they were asked to bring 'a Bullet Mould for the Calibre of their Gun of Pistol, a small Bag for Bullets and a Powder Horn lest the Bore of their [weapon] being smaller than those of the Army should prevent their using the Ammunition made for the King's Troops, in which case a delivery of Lead and Powder will be made to them'. It is not clear how they were expected to find time to produce their own ammunition in the heat of battle. In any case, the take-up seems to have been small, as most suitable men joined the volunteers in any case. In Folkestone, only four were 'willing to serve with Arms ... in Troops or Companies under such persons as are chosen from amongst themselves and approved of by the Civil authority of the County'.[18]

Beyond the volunteers, the War Office envisaged a different kind of warfare, carried out by small groups of men who knew the country and one another: 'no Company should be formed of a greater Number of People than what are already known to each other, to act under Leaders known to each Individual, and whose Intelligence and Prudence all have equal Confidence.'

The War Office reasoned that the invasion could not be reinforced by sea, and therefore, 'whilst our own Army becomes every Day more powerful, several Causes must operate towards the Diminution of his [the enemy's] original Numbers. His Losses from partial Engagements, constant Fatigue, and precarious Sustenance, are in themselves sufficient to decide his fate, independent of any decisive Action being fought, which may annihilate his Army at one Blow.' As to the form of the attack on the enemy,

From the first Moment of a Landing being made, the great Object of the Irregular Troops must be to Harass, Alarm and Fatigue an Enemy.

Nothing can more effectually contribute to this Object than the Operations of small Bodies of Men well acquainted with the Country, who will approach and fire upon the Advanced Posts of his Army, without ever engaging in serious Action, or hazarding themselves, in any situation where their natural Intelligence and Watchfulness does not ensure the Danger of being cut off. So long as they are watchful to this Point, it must be evident, that with the Country open in their Rear, and with the Advantage of knowing all the Avenues and Roads, having an Enemy who is ignorant of them; and who can likewise have but a small proportion if any Cavalry; that nothing can expose them to any other Danger than what their own Energy and Courage had determine them to face.[19]

This was a remarkable description of guerrilla warfare as it would soon be seen in Spain against the French. But it was rather naïve of the rulers of 1803 to miss the point that such a war demanded full political rights for those who took part in it, and it would almost certainly have led to radicalization of the population afterwards. But the proclamation made no appeals even to vague concepts of equality or liberty – only to 'the bold unconquerable spirit' that was 'the Birth-right of every Briton'.

The ruling classes of 1803 were assuming a high level of morale and huge degree of commitment to the war among those who had little formal stake in the country. They were, of course, quite right in believing that shopkeepers, clerks, artisans, servants, small farmers, labourers and many others were patriotic and would unite against what they had been told was the certainty of robbery and slavery; but these people would have demanded a greater share in society after they had won, and the domestic crisis that followed the war would have come sooner, been more intense and perhaps advanced the real liberty of the Briton by many decades.

CIVILIANS AGAINST HITLER

Unlike his ancestor in 1805, the citizen of 1940 could not help being aware of the war every day and probably every waking hour. As he awoke in the morning, he would be thankful if his sleep had not been interrupted by air-raid sirens; indeed, on 23 August, George Orwell complained: 'The fact that at present the alarm sounds all over a wide area when the German planes are only operating in one part of it, means not only that people are unnecessarily woken up or taken away from work, but that an impression is spread that an air-raid alarm will *always* be false, which is obviously dangerous.'[20] Even the alarm clock reflected the realities of war. British Summer Time, introduced in World War I, was now extended throughout the year to make the best use of daylight during the blackout, so he got up an hour later than Greenwich Mean Time would have allowed – unless he was one of the farmers in remote districts, who preferred to work in 'God's time'.

He or his wife might pull back the heavy black-out curtains, which prevented any chinks of light being seen by enemy bombers, and peer through windows criss-crossed with sticky tape to prevent glass splinters. As he dressed, the citizen was not as short of clothes as he would be a year or so later, for clothes rationing was not introduced until June 1941. But as soon as he got to the kitchen he would feel the effects of food rationing, which had begun in January 1940. It was not common for men to cook in those days, but his wife might have bought one of the numerous wartime cookbooks being published. At least a dozen were in the bookshops by 1940, heralding a flood that was to come in later years. These included *A Kitchen Goes to War*, with 150 recipes contributed by famous people such as Agatha Christie ('Mystery Potatoes'), John Gielgud, Mrs Neville Chamberlain, Sir Kenneth Clark and many others whose names are less recognizable today. Other books included *The Penny Guide to the Most Profitable Cooking of Vegetables Grown in Allotment Gardens, Some Recipes for Wartime Dishes* by the Glasgow and West of Scotland College of Domestic Science and *They Can't Ration These*, whose title seemed to reflect a populist mistrust of authority. Fortunately eggs, the British breakfast favourite, were still available at a price and he did not have to resort to the powdered variety.

The house of a city dweller might seem strangely quiet if the younger children had been evacuated to the country. A million-and-a-half mothers and young children had left for the country in the first days of the war, but nearly two-thirds returned home when large-scale bombing did not materialize. There was a smaller wave of evacuation in the summer of 1940, as people moved away from the areas threatened by invasion, so in August 1940 439,000 unaccompanied children, 64,000 mothers and children, 29,000 teachers and helpers and 14,000 other adults were still away from home. If the citizen lived in the country the opposite might be the case, and his house could be filled with the noise of unruly boys and girls. In either case there was a distinct absence of young men, as so many had been called up into the forces.

He might read his newspaper over breakfast. It was far smaller than it had been before the war, with only six pages. If he was from the upper middle class or had aspirations he might read *The Times*, which printed no news on the front page, only discreet personal advertisements. In other papers, the headlines were dominated by hot war news, and most of that was bad during the summer of 1940. The favourite paper of the middle and lower middle classes was Lord Beaverbrook's *Daily Express*. It was relentlessly optimistic even in the darkest days. On 13 August, as the air battle in advance of an invasion intensified, it carried the main headline, 'Biggest Air raids of All', followed by 'R.A.F. shoots down 39 more Nazis and loses only nine fighters'. There was a story that the Albanian allies had killed 400 Italians, and of a 'terrifying new weapon' said to be the answer to the dive-bomber. And at the bottom of the page there was a report on a raid on Germany under the headline, 'And WE did this to THEM'. Working class families read the *Daily Mirror*, the first newspaper that was aimed specifically at them apart from the rather didactic *Daily Herald*. The *Mirror* was a particular bugbear of Churchill's, but the paper was stalwart in support of the war, though not the way it was conducted. According to a report to the War Cabinet,

> On September 17th, 18th and 19th the leaders were devoted to the lack of forethought and preparation in connection with the shelter policy. 'There is still time, but not too much, to get on with further evacuation schemes and the provision of deep shelters, hitherto rejected with unparalleled obstinacy by Sir John Anderson.'

Herbert Morrison, the Labour Home Secretary, saw the essence of the problem:

there is much in these papers which is calculated to promote a war spirit. They seem to be clearly anxious for the defeat of Hitlerism. In the Daily Mirror of today occurs the sentence: 'Bad as our "pluto-democratic" world may be, it is at least better than the slavery that would suppress all independent thought in the devilish way of life commended by the Nazi fanatics.'[21]

If Hitler himself was comic to the British, his actions and his supporters were not. The British were well aware of Nazi persecution and torture, for example from an article in *Picture Post* in November 1938 called 'Back to the Middle Ages', which highlighted early Nazi atrocities against the Jews. No one had any doubt that the Germans would be just as ruthless in any conquest of Britain. Inside the typical newspaper, feature articles often told the citizen how to conduct his duties in the Home Guard or fortify his home against raids. Even the cartoons did not avoid war topics, and the *Daily Mirror*'s famous *Jane*, labelled as a 'bright young thing' in peacetime, was now deploying her charms for the secret service.

It was unlikely that the citizen would drive to work – few people had owned cars before the war, and the number was declining, for petrol rationing made it very difficult to use one except for essential purposes. Many factory workers lived close enough to walk, others crammed into overcrowded buses or got on to much-delayed trains. The citizen might well be thankful to have a job, for the one positive effect of the war was to create work. Once he got there he would feel the effects of the war yet again. Unless it was a factory producing war supplies or employing people in reserved occupations, he would notice that the workforce was older than it had been in peacetime. There was plenty of work to do, and in the summer of 1940, before cynicism set in, he would probably throw himself into it. He might eat his lunch (or dinner as the working class called it) in a works canteen. And it is quite likely that he would be asked to do several hours of overtime in the evening.

Schemes to give women a greater part in the war effort had not yet got under way, and it was not common for married women to go out to work. The female workforce expanded by less than ten percent between June 1939 and June 1940 – after all there were still 434,000 unemployed men as the army was evacuated from Dunkirk. Of five million women in work, most were single and employed in the traditional fields of textiles, domestic services, teaching, nursing and typing.

Instead, the housewife worked hard just to find the food she needed for her family. She had to bring her ration book so that coupons could be torn off by the shopkeeper. She had to calculate carefully to make the best of her allowance of four ounces of bacon, ham and butter and 1s 10p [9 pence] worth of meat per adult per week. Even tea was rationed from July 1940. There were no supermarkets, and she would have to visit butchers, bakers, grocers and greengrocers in succession. Often there was a queue in each, and no guarantee that the goods would still be available when she reached the end of it.

If she had time and energy left, she might take part in voluntary work. Women's Voluntary Service had been founded in 1938 specifically to help women take part in civil defence and support their families in difficult times. It had hundreds of thousands of members by mid-1940, far more than the Women's Institute, which had pacifist origins and was reluctant to get involved in war work. The WVS helped with evacuated children, darned socks and knitted goods for servicemen, and carried on all kinds of social work. It had a practical green uniform, but hardly any of its members were full-time, and they continued to live at home.

Other women's services offered varying chances to escape from the routine of peacetime life. It was possible to volunteer as an 'immobile' Wren, wearing a version of naval uniform but living at home and not liable to be transferred away. The Women's Royal Naval Service, or Wrens, was probably the most popular of the women's services, closely followed by the Women's Auxiliary Air Force, or WAAFs, who made a name by operating the control rooms. The army's service, the Auxiliary Territorial Service, or ATS, was the least popular. It had a weak and meaningless title, an unattractive uniform and a reputation for immorality. None of the women's services were subjected to the full rigour of military discipline at this stage. This only came to the WAAF and the ATS in 1941, and not to the Wrens for many years later. In the services, women mostly still served in traditional domestic and administrative roles. No servicewomen were sent abroad at this stage, and they had no combatant role. Women could also serve in uniform in the Land Army, working in the fields to increase the food crop, or as members of the Auxiliary Fire Service.

After work many men had commitments with the Home Guard or civil defence. Air Raid Precautions, or ARP, had been founded in 1935 after the government began to fear the dangers of enemy action. As well as around 125,000 full-time, paid members, ARP employed nearly 720,000 part-time men and 137,000 women in June. Some worked at local headquarters or in rescue teams, and large numbers were employed in the role of local warden, a 'person of courage and personality with a sound knowledge of the locality, to advise and help their neighbours, and generally to serve as a link between the public and the authorities'.[22] But that summer few bombs fell on civilian targets, and the warden was left with the thankless job of enforcing the blackout. Equally unpopular was the Auxiliary Fire Service, which was to supplement the work of the regular services. Its full-time members were accused of avoiding military service for well-paid jobs near home.

Gardening was more than a hobby in 1940 – it was a patriotic duty. Encouraged by the government's 'Dig for Victory' campaign, flower beds and lawns were turned into vegetable patches so that the meagre ration of food could be supplemented. More than 800,000 people had allotments in 1939, and that number rose during the war. But many people were too exhausted after a long day at work to do more than eat a meal and listen to the radio. Dinner, or tea as it was known to the working classes, was usually of plain food to the British taste of the age, made even plainer by war restrictions, but some of the recipe books offered ideas. If the cook followed the frugal ideas of the Glasgow and West of Scotland College of Domestic Science, the meal might begin with giblet soup, followed by kedgeree, steamed ox, kidney and macaroni or butter-bean roast. Suet pudding could be on offer, possibly made without eggs if they were expensive, with syrup instead of sugar, and even with margarine or nut butter instead of suet.[23]

The main BBC radio station was now known as the Home Service, and it was supplemented by the Forces Programme, which started early in 1940, initially for troops at home and in the BEF. It proved highly popular with civilians too. The BBC also had to provide services in foreign languages, including French, Norwegian and German, and domestic ones in Welsh and Gaelic, so its time was limited. There were serious reports, forces programmes such as *Naval Log* and *Ack-Ack*, *Beer-Beer* for anti-aircraft gunners. There were plenty of light entertainment programmes, including the favourite *ITMA*, or *It's That Man Again* (a reference to Hitler), which began in 1939. It provided a diet of catchphrases such as 'Can I do you now sir?' and 'I don't mind if I do'. It was listened to by nearly a third of the adult population every Thursday night.

Churchill's broadcasts were rare and irregular events and there were only three during the period when invasion threatened seriously – on 19 May, for which only the notes survive, on 14 July and on 11 September. George Orwell's cleaner, Mrs Anderson, was 'impressed by Churchill's speeches, though not understanding them word for word'. Orwell believed that 'uneducated people are often moved by a speech in solemn language which they don't understand but feel to be impressive'.[24]

Churchill's parliamentary speeches contained his most ringing phrases but were not broadcast. There were other official talks, on food economy, evacuation and may other subjects, and the government found the wireless was an excellent way of publicizing new policies on rationing or call-up. The most popular talk programme of 1940 was J. B. Priestley's *Postscripts*, whose run between June and October coincided almost exactly with the invasion crisis. Priestley was already a very successful novelist and playwright. He caught the spirit of the age with his stolid north-country voice and his plain tales. He often started with an image that people could relate to, of familiar pleasure steamers lost off Dunkirk, or farmers guarding their fields against paratroopers. He went on to link it to the world situation, with literary references to Shakespeare and Dickens. But he was too left-wing for some, and his broadcasts caused hysteria in the right-wing press.

Everyone had heard of Lord Haw Haw's propaganda broadcasts from Germany, and rumours circulated that he had predicted individual events or had strange and detailed intelligence of life in Britain – though hardly any of it was true. Research in the winter of 1939/40 showed that about a quarter of the population listed regularly, and two-thirds occasionally. Most claimed that they only listened because 'his version of the news is so fantastic that it's funny', but there is evidence that it had some effect on people's beliefs.[25]

Many men, especially those living in overcrowded houses or flats near the city centres, would go out to the pub in the evening. Shortages of drink were not yet drastic, and a pub might be filled by servicemen from a nearby base or anti-aircraft battery. Pianos were common, and music was encouraged in England, where *We'll Meet Again, There'll Always be an England* and *Roll out the Barrel* were popular hits.

The cinema flourished during the war. Newsreels would almost certainly show film of events such as the retreat from Dunkirk, the preparations of the Home Guard or the growing battle in the air, but that was only the prelude to a long programme. There were a few British war films in 1940, such as *Convoy* with a rather old-fashioned view of naval combat. But most people had come to the cinema to get away from all that for few hours. The programme probably began with advertisements then cartoons (though it was not necessary to enter at the beginning of a continuous programme, hence the phrase 'this is where we came in'). Apart from the familiar Disney characters, 1940 audiences could see *A Wild Hare*, which introduced Bugs Bunny and his catch phrase 'What's up, doc?' and *Puss Gets the Boot*, whose cat and mouse characters were not yet named Tom and Jerry and had not reached their later level of surreal violence. There was usually a short B-feature, often a British 'quota quickie' made cheaply to meet government regulations. The main feature was usually American, and the hits of 1940 included *The Westerner*, with Gary Cooper, and *Broadway Melody of 1940*. British characters and settings were used for *Pride and Prejudice* and Alfred Hitchcock's *Rebecca*, both starring Laurence Olivier as the haughty owner of a stately home. The feature-length Disney cartoons of the year were the classics *Pinocchio* and *Fantasia*. Costume fantasies included *The Thief of Bagdad, The Mask of Zorro* and *The Sea Hawk*. It was not all escapism – *The Grapes of Wrath* was a powerful drama about the horrors facing migrants from the Oklahoma dustbowl during the Great Depression. The world situation was reflected in Charlie Chaplin's farcical satire on Fascism, *The Great Dictator*, in which the character of Adenoid Hynkel was not hard to identify. In *The Long Voyage Home*, John Wayne, not yet established as the all-American hero, was cast as a weak-willed Swedish seaman facing dangers from U-boats among other things.

Audiences emerged from the cinema trying to adjust to real life outside, to find themselves in the blackout, for even in the high summer of 1940 it was probably dark by the time the programme finished. With or without air raid warnings, returning home was dangerous in itself. Signposts had been removed because they might help paratroopers, and station names were painted over. Road vehicles were only allowed with masked headlights. Buses and trains were probably just as crowded as they had been in the morning. The shortage of torch batteries had largely been resolved by the summer of 1940, but minor injuries were quite common in the dark. Once he was safely home, the citizen might well have a cup of tea, if his rationed supply was sufficient, then retire thankfully and hopefully to bed.

GOVERNMENT CONTROL, 1940

The British public was under terrifying pressure during the invasion crisis, but it could not respond to it directly. Working people could get on with their jobs, housewives could do their best to save food, Home Guards and ARP members could continue their patrols and precautions – but the great majority, including most of the army, could only watch and wait for the cataclysm that might come any day. In these circumstances civilian morale was of the greatest importance. And, according to orthodox opinion, there were two great and closely related dangers within: the fifth column and the Quislings.

Both concepts were new. The first one dated from the Spanish Civil War. In 1936, as his rebel armies approached Madrid, General Franco remarked that he had four columns outside the city, and the 'fifth column' inside would also support him. This was a natural belief in the ideological conflict of a civil war. But it did Franco little good: it took him three more years of savage fighting to capture Madrid. Britain's war with Germany was far less ideological, and almost all sectors in the community had good reason to support it. Conservatives saw Germany as the national enemy. Liberals were not likely to support the savage methods of the Nazis. Socialists had good reason to hate the party that had imprisoned and killed their comrades in Germany and was determined to suppress their beliefs. Apart from a few tiny fringe groups, dissent was only to be found on the extremes. The Communist Party supported the Moscow line during the Nazi-Soviet Pact, and Churchill felt it necessary to suppress their newspaper, the *Daily Worker*, though it is clear that the party lost ground because of its policies. On the other side of the spectrum, fascist leaders such as Sir Oswald Mosley were locked up, though no evidence was ever offered that they were collaborating with the enemy. Despite extensive scares and the frantic activities of the Home Guard, even the rather panicky General Ironside began to have doubts about their importance and wrote at the beginning of July, 'It is extraordinary how we get circumstantial reports of 5th Column and yet we have never been able to get anything worth having. One is persuaded that it hardly exists.'[26] Britain never had a large Fascist party in the 1930s. The lower middle class, the likely core of such a movement, had less reason to fear Bolshevism than the Germans and Italians. Inflation, which had ruined the small savers in Germany, hardly existed in Britain. There was no great national humiliation such as that which the Germans had suffered. Britain's empire was bigger than ever and provided an outlet for her active young men. And the middle classes had often prospered in the 1930s, against the national trends.

It was the presence of many refugees and foreigners that confused the issue. The British government had not been over-generous in accepting refugees from the Nazis before the war, but there were 73,000 Germans and Austrians in the country, the great majority fleeing from persecution. At first the government was determined not to repeat the experience of the previous war, when 30,000 had been interned. This time the enemy aliens were divided into three groups: Category 'A' consisted of dedicated Nazis who were to be interned; Category 'C' were those who had arrived in the country fleeing from the Nazis and could be trusted; and in between was Category 'B', those long settled in the country and involved in British life, who were to remain free subject to guarantees and restrictions. Tribunals were set up to assess them, and by the end of November they had interned around one per cent of those who had come before them.

Unfortunately this was overtaken by the events of the end of May, when the fifth column seemed to be allowing the Germans to sweep all before them in France. The issue was confused by a treasonous affair involving an anti-Jewish activist, an official of the American embassy and a right-wing Conservative MP. Churchill now supported mass internment, and when Italy entered the war he ordered, 'Collar the lot', the mass arrest of Italian nationals. Personally he was far more loyal to his country than to any political belief – he had changed parties twice during his career. Perhaps he had difficulty understanding that the horrors of Nazi Germany would over-ride any national loyalty among the aliens. By orders of 23 May, aliens in Category 'C' were also to be interned. It was a crushing blow to the refugees, who were often keen to help the war effort, and was unplanned and badly handled. Families were split up, some went to requisitioned hotels behind barbed wire on the Isle of Man, others were sent overseas to Canada or Australia and in some cases their ships were sunk by U-boats.[27] In the autumn selected internees were released, but many were held until 1941.

The other phrase on everyone's lips in 1940 was 'Quisling', after the fascist leader who had apparently betrayed Norway in 1940. Again the mythology had far overtaken reality. It is true that Vidkun Quisling had visited Hitler after the war started and perhaps helped sow the seeds of an invasion plan in his mind, but the Norwegian's ideas for a coup were rejected, and the actual attack needed no help from inside elements. Quisling confused the issue in a radio broadcast on the morning of the invasion, but that was not authorized by the Germans. Once they had landed, they allowed Quisling no power in running the country. In Britain, the word 'Quisling' was bandied around to describe any individual who was not enthusiastic enough about the war effort. But there was no body of traitors prepared to sacrifice their country to the Nazis, and no significant individuals in contact with the Germans.

The Home Defence Executive was set up in May 1940. Its title was something of a misnomer: it had no executive authority. Its role was to coordinate the work of the services at home and the civilian ministries in anti-invasion preparations. The committee, which met daily, consisted of representatives from the home commands and the Home Office, and the ministries of Home Security and War Transport. At its 60th meeting, on 8 August 1940, it considered the allocation of mechanical diggers for defence works, some of which were seen lying idle; the danger of gas attacks from the sea; the perennial subject of the immobilization of civilian vehicles; the information that the army did not use the BBC to issue operational orders to its troops; the allocation of steel helmets to the Home Guard; the immobilization of factories; the question of whether visitors should be allowed to the seaside resort of Bournemouth; the possibility of evacuating miners from the collieries of Kent; and the risk that advertisements for local beers might give away locations to the enemy.[28] The committee had a small staff of civil servants headed by Sir Findlater Stewart. They were Whitehall insiders who knew who to contact in an individual ministry to get things done; most of the problems could be sorted out by a telephone call without reference to ministers.

One of the questions to be faced at the highest level was how far the civilian population, excluding those in the Home Guard, should be encouraged to resist an invader. At one extreme, a leaflet 'Wake up and Face it!' used the slogan, 'Everyman and every woman a soldier':

> What happens today, ask yourself, if a German tank comes down the High Street of your own town. Nothing. It can go by as it chooses, and you must stand and gape at it. But if everyone has a handgrenade, the tank must move through a barrage of explosive. Ninety-nine times it might escape, but if EVERYONE had a handgrenade, the hundredth time comes very soon. From being the lord of destruction trampling all before it, the tank become the death trap of its crews.

Apart from the obvious political risks of arming the people, there were the more practical points – the shortage of arms and the danger of enemy reprisals. As Mr Rootham of the Home Defence Executive put it, the over-riding thing is for us to have to meet the enemy a disciplined force equal or superior in fire power to his disciplined force and that in these circumstances the claims of the army must come first. To spread the supply of arms thinly over the whole population would only invite acts of frightfulness by the enemy on those sections of it least able to defend themselves.[29]

This left the possibility of passive resistance. General Elles of the Ministry of Home Security suggested, 'until there are arms for the whole population, passive resistance was the most that civilians could be allowed to attempt; improvised arms would not be effective and would only provoke harsh treatment.' Passive resistance as developed by Gandhi in India was to have considerable effect on British forces there, but German troops were far more ruthless and had no respect for law. The issue was never clearly resolved, but commanders-in-chief of the army districts were given authority to 'issue orders to individuals for the purpose of organising civil resistance'.

Apart from mothers and children evacuated from industrial towns, there was now the question of emptying the coastal areas where the enemy was likely to invade. This was a different issue in principle – the first evacuation had been for humanitarian reasons, while this was for military purposes. Experience in France had shown how much civilian refugees could clog up the roads, and this was confirmed by General Sir Douglas Brownrigg:

> I had particular experience of this problem around Boulogne and Calais. Crowds of cars, horse-drawn vehicles, cyclists, pedestrians and disorganised soldiers of France, Belgium and Holland, made movement in the coastal roads and roads leading to the coast almost impossible ...
>
> I do not suggest that British crowds will necessarily behave in the same way – but 'evacuation' by road is infectious. A few people start to leave an area and others follow. This is soon taken up by others further away from the anticipated danger who have become infected with panic by seeing crowds pass through their own towns and villages. So the crowds go on the roads without any definite idea where they intend to go.[30]

One way of avoiding this was to evacuate 'useless mouths' from the coastal areas in the east and south. Plans were drawn up for the evacuation of nineteen towns, from Great Yarmouth in the north of East Anglia, to Hythe on the coast of Kent. They varied in size from Southend in the Thames estuary, with 120,000 people, to the village of Minster with 2,200. Some, such as Great Yarmouth, had substantial port facilities and industry, and many workers would need to stay; others such as Margate had none, and 'the right course would probably to allow all the inhabitants to go with the exception of certain Government employees (such as G.P.O. telephone and engineering staff), the local authority and its servants, police, fire brigade, civil service, public utility undertakings and so forth.' Evacuation would be compulsory, both as to who should go and who should not. It was to be kept confidential for the moment, but if implemented it would need 12–24 hours' notice to start it, then up to 48 hours to complete. On 20 June the police in the nineteen towns were ordered to put up posters to tell the population to be at twelve hours' notice. But officials were already beginning to have doubts about the scale of the scheme – up to 90 per cent of the population might have to be evacuated from certain towns, and intelligence was beginning to suggest that the south coast was just as likely a target for invasion. Towns like Brighton had far greater populations than the east-coast resorts. On 27 June, the War Cabinet decided,

> That the scheme for the compulsory evacuation of all but essential people from the nineteen East Coast towns between Sheringham and Folkestone should not be put into operation for the present. A scheme on the scale now proposed should not be carried out except as a military necessity, in the face of an invasion or an imminent invasion.[31]

There was an essential snag, as the Chiefs of Staff pointed out: 'We cannot be certain that we shall receive any more definite information than is in our possession at present as to the day and hour that operations will commence ... We are unable to give an assurance that we shall receive three days notice of attack.' Ironside wanted to evacuate right away, but he was overruled. In fact there had already been a good deal of voluntary evacuation, partly inspired by the plans for compulsion: 43,000 out of the 120,000 inhabitants of Southend had left by 3 July, half the 22,000 citizens of Deal and two thirds of the 2,500 people who had lived in Aldeburgh before the war.[32]

It was much simpler to restrict visits to the coastal areas under threat. This would reduce the income of the hotel owners, but already the beaches were mined and covered with barbed wire and anti-tank obstacles, and many of their premises had been taken over for military purposes. Nevertheless, a deputation from Bournemouth approached the Home Defence Executive in August asking, 'whether it would be possible to relax the orders prohibiting visitors to Bournemouth and other places in defence areas in the autumn and winter'.[33] The Chiefs of Staff vetoed this, as it would leave visitors 'free to study details of the beach and other defences and to wander round aerodromes and similar establishments'. There might be casualties from mines, and, 'If the restriction on visitors were to be removed, sudden invasion might find road and rail communications congested with holiday-makers.'[34]

Throughout the country the government urged a policy of 'stay put' for all civilians who might find themselves close to an invading force. A leaflet of that June, 'If the Invader Comes, What to do – and How to Do It', outlined the policy. In the first place, 'If the Germans come, by parachute, aeroplane or ship, you must remain where you are. The order is "stay put".' Secondly, one should not believe or spread rumours, which might well be created by the enemy. Thirdly, keep watch for anything suspicious. Fourthly,

> Do not give the German anything. Do not tell him anything. Hide your food and your bicycles. Hide your maps. See that the enemy gets no petrol. If you have a car or motor bicycle, put it out of action when not in use. It is not enough to remove the ignition key; you must make it useless to anyone except yourself.

Fifthly, the citizen should be ready to help the military in any way possible but should not block the roads. And if he was in charge of, or worked in, a factory he should be ready to defend it against a sudden attack. In conclusion he was instructed, 'Think before you act. But think always of your country before you think of yourself.'

A leaflet issued early in August told the people:

> If this island is invaded by sea or air everyone who is not under orders must stay where he or she is. This is not simply advice: it is an order from the Government … If you do not stay put you will stand a very good chance of being killed. The enemy may machine-gun you from the air in order to increase panic, or you may run into enemy forces which have landed behind you …

A citizen should help by setting a good example to others:

> If fighting by organised forces is going on in your district and you have no special duties elsewhere, go into your shelter and stay there until the battle is past. Do not attempt to join in the fight. Behave as if an air raid was going on. The enemy will seldom turn aside to attack separate houses.
>
> But if small parties are going about threatening persons and property in your area not under enemy control and come your way, you have the right of every man and woman to do what you can to protect yourself, your family and your home.

There were many who felt almost elated at the situation, including Harold Nicholson, who was a junior minister at the time. 'I am quite lucidly aware that in three weeks from now Sissinghurst may be a waste and Vita and I both dead. Yet these probabilities do not fill me with despair. I seem to be impervious both to pleasure and pain. For the moment we are all anaesthetised.'[35]

One thorny issue was the police force, whose numbers included 64,000 regulars, 31,000 full-time special constables and reservists, and 159,000 part-timers, but only a thousand or so women. Recruitment to the reserve was rushed as the war began, and the future serial killer John Christie was taken on even though he already had a criminal record. George Orwell thought that 'The police are the very people who would go over to Hitler once they were certain that he had won.'[36] This opinion was not borne out by the activities of the force in the village of Storrington, ten miles inland from the south coast. The village headmaster was a sergeant in the Special Constabulary, and he and a constable went out armed with truncheons to look for suspected paratroopers. 'The Good Lord only knows what we would have done had we met any invaders – I'm sure I don't!'[37]

The police were not part of the armed forces of the crown. About ten per cent of them were armed in wartime, but they maintained their traditional reluctance to carry weapons. They had a role in maintaining order during air raids and their aftermath, but the question arose as to what would happen to policemen who found themselves in enemy-occupied areas. Two cases were considered. If the enemy landed in force and looked likely to occupy the area, the main body should control movements and then withdraw with the troops. A smaller number, mostly beyond military age or with families that had not been evacuated, would stay behind, 'to ensure that all necessary measures have been carried out to guard against agents making contact with the enemy'. They should assist the army rearguard and, if possible, withdraw with them.

If only small parties had landed with the aims 'to attack civilians, destroy property and cause confusion or devastation', then the police, along with other civilians, would not be debarred by international law 'from resisting, and if possible, destroying the enemy, in order to prevent him carrying out these objects'. Likewise, the fire service was to remember that it was not a military force and that 'the first consideration is the readiness of its members for the purpose of fire-fighting ...' and should only attempt to resist small and isolated parties of the enemy.[38]

The great test for civilians, however, would come when the bombing of cities began in September 1940. The RAF, who had been sneered at and assaulted after Dunkirk, were now the heroes, and so were the ARP and Auxiliary Fire Service, whose inactivity was much mocked during the summer of 1940 but who were now at the centre of the action.

4

THE LEADERS

POLITICAL LEADERSHIP IN 1805

One of the many things in common between Britain in 1803–5 and 1940 was that the country went to war with weak prime ministers – Henry Addington and Neville Chamberlain – but soon came under the leadership of great men – William Pitt, Horatio Nelson and Winston Churchill. Faced with enemies where power was absolute and the leader was everything, these men had to develop their own styles within the political and military hierarchies of their times.

In France, power was increasingly concentrated in the hands of Napoleon, but in Britain it remained decentralized and complex. Responsibility for the defence of the country rested with the King; with the Prime Minister and about half a dozen government departments; with various local authorities and other institutions; with parliament; with the officers of five separate armed forces; and ultimately with the people themselves, organized as a levée en masse. The organization of defence presented many contradictions, with areas of overlapping responsibility and confused boundaries. Many elements, such as recruitment to the militia and navy, were feudal in origin. Some government bodies had been deliberately created in rivalry to one another, as part of a system of checks and balances, and many institutions were jealous of their power.

King George III was head of the state, of the armed forces, and of the executive arm of government. In theory he had a veto on acts passed by parliament, and the King's influence over legislation could be quite strong – he had prevented the passing of a Catholic Emancipation Bill at the turn of the century. In practice the King was old and tired, and subject to bouts of an illness that at the time was taken for insanity. The real executive authority lay with the prime minister, but he depended on the support of both king and parliament to stay in office. Even a strong minister like Pitt had to accept that he would not always get his own way – during the 1780s he had to drop proposals on parliamentary reform and the slave trade because of opposition from one side or the other.

Parliament consisted of two houses, the Lords and Commons. It debated and voted on all new laws, and it was kept busy during the threat of invasion: numerous acts were passed on recruitment to the militia and the role of the civilian population in the event of a landing. Parliament also passed the laws on which all military and naval discipline was based. The Articles of War that governed the navy were permanent, but the Mutiny Act, which provided a framework for army discipline, had to be renewed annually, a measure of Parliament's distrust of standing armies. The House of Commons claimed the sole right to raise taxes and to allocate them to different departments. The army and navy estimates were passed through the house each year, and gave some control over the numbers of seamen and soldiers in service. The House of Lords was hereditary, while the Commons was elected on a narrow franchise, which varied from place to place but in general represented men of wealth and property. Corruption and manipulation caused electoral power to be concentrated in few hands, and the 'common people' were very little represented. There were two political parties: the Whigs, who were broadly in favour of parliamentary government against the King, and the Tories, who were the forerunners of the Conservatives. But the party system was not very strong. Members were far more involved with family or local interests, and large landowners might control several seats and form groups of their own. General elections rarely led to a change in government, just to a realignment within the existing system. Parliament was generally a very conservative body, which supported the constitutional balance between king and parliament as set up in 1689. It had no mission to reform society, and changes were only brought in after great political effort. It became even more conservative after the excesses of the French Revolution appeared to show the dangers of change. At the height of war in 1803–5 there was no political unity, and sectional interests were as strong as ever. William Pitt's long-standing feud with Charles James Fox continued, and there was no coalition government during the rest of Pitt's lifetime, as there would be in 1940, to meet the threat from abroad.

Though not recognized by any legislation, the prime minister had been the real head of government for the last 80 years or so. At the beginning of the war in 1803, the post was held by Henry Addington, born in 1757 and formerly Speaker of the House of Commons. He had long been a friend of his great predecessor, William Pitt. In 1801 Pitt resigned over Catholic emancipation, and Addington took power as a compromise candidate and supporter of peace. He had always been overshadowed by Pitt, as expressed in a popular rhyme, 'Pitt is to Addington as London is to Paddington.' He was the son of a doctor and Britain's first middle-class prime minister, the first who was not from the landowning classes. As was said at the time, he was not an aristocrat, he was not an orator and he was not William Pitt. In May 1804, the Addington government fell, and Pitt became prime minister again.

Unlike other great leaders of these two periods – Horatio Nelson and Winston Churchill – William Pitt is barely remembered by the British public, and then mainly for the fact that he first became prime minister at the age of 24. He impressed Benjamin Silliman when he visited the House of Commons in 1805:

> In his person he is tall and spare; he has small limbs with large knees and feet; his features are sharp; his nose large, pointed and turning up; his complexion sanguine; his voice deep-toned and commanding, yet sweet and perfectly well modulated, and his whole presence, notwithstanding the want of symmetry in his limbs, is, when he rises to speak, full of superiority and conscious dignity.[1]

William Pitt the Younger was the second son of William Pitt, Earl of Chatham, who had steered the country through its greatest victory in modern times, in the Seven Years War of 1756–63 against France and Spain. He entered Parliament in 1781 at the age of 21, but had little time to begin his intended career in law before he was appointed Chancellor of the Exchequer a year later. The greatest surprise of all was when he became prime minister at the end of 1783, with the collapse of the Fox-North coalition. The country was in a sorry state after defeat in the American War, and there was a huge National Debt. Pitt had no majority in Parliament but gradually built one up through his oratory and strength of character. Over ten years of peace he restored the finances (though not his own, which were always in a mess). He kept the country out of war several times without surrendering any important points. Like many people he supported the principles of the French Revolution when it first broke out in 1789 but became horrified is it turned increasingly to extreme measures. Early in 1793 he announced Britain's declaration of war against France, hoping that it would be a short affair.

Despite his outstanding political skills, Pitt was never a great war minister. His efforts were largely wasted on supporting ineffective allies, or on colonial expeditions that did little towards defeating the French. He had no great strategic vision, though more than some of his contemporaries such as Addington. Like Winston Churchill, he was often accused of interfering too much with the generals, but he had less excuse than Churchill, for he was an outsider in military affairs (until when out of office he became colonel of the Cinque Ports Volunteers). During this time, according to his friend Lady Hester Stanhope he 'absolutely goes through the fatigue of *a drill sergeant*', riding hard from one parade to another and buying a collection of books on tactics.[2]

Pitt was an austere and private man who never married and apparently only had one intimate but short-lived relationship with a woman; his early entry to high political office meant that he never experienced a normal youth and early manhood. He was very convivial with a few close friends, but the rest of the world respected rather than loved him. His intelligence was extraordinary, allowing him to grasp the essence of any problem, and his oratory was among the greatest ever heard in the House of Commons, though most of it was exercised in an age when parliamentary speeches were reported inadequately, and he did not produce anything like Churchill's array of ringing phrases. But Pitt lived in an age when a great speech really could sway the House and decide the fate of a government. Despite his many ups and downs

Above: John Bull knocks 'Bonaparte' into the English Channel, to the delight of the British sailors to the left, and the dismay of the French soldiers on the right. (The Trustees of the British Museum)

Right: King George III looks at the tiny Bonaparte in James Gillray's highly popular caricature. (Courtesy of the Warden and Scholars of New College, Oxford/The Bridgeman Art Library)

THE CORSICAN LOCUST.

Above: West's cartoon of 1803 shows an Englishman eating roast beef, an Irishman eating potatoes and a Scotsman in a kilt, demonstrating national unity against 'The Corsican Locust.' (The Trustees of the British Museum)

Opposite page, top: Royal Crescent at Bath, perhaps the pinnacle of British architecture and social life of the Georgian period. (Victoria Art Gallery, Bath and North East Somerset Council/The Bridgeman Art Library)

Left: A view of London in 1803 by William Daniel, showing the new docks at Wapping with many ships in the river awaiting unloading. (Guildhall Library, City of London/The Bridgeman Art Library)

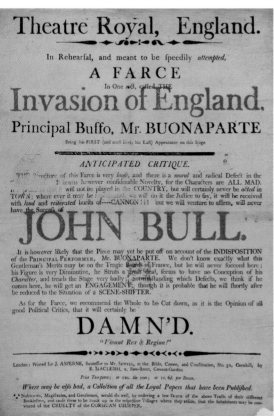

Above: The blockade of Boulogne. French invasion craft are in line close to the shore. Farther out to sea, a Dutch merchant ship is about to be intercepted. A line of British sloops and brigs is backed up by frigates and ships of the line at the bottom of the picture. (National Maritime Museum)

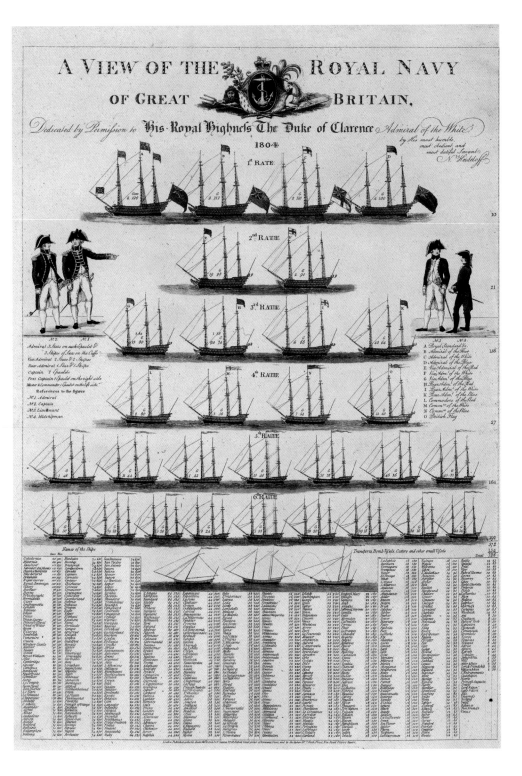

Left: The militia on the march to Portsmouth in record time, 1803. (The Trustees of the British Museum)

Above: A view of the Royal Navy of Great Britain, 1804. (National Maritime Museum)

BRITANNIA between DEATH and the DOCTOR'S. ___ " Death may decide, when Doctor's disagree "

Above: In this 1804 Gillray cartoon a skeletal Napoleon threatens Britannia as Pitt kicks Addington out of the door, while simultaneously trampling on Fox. (Library of Congress)

Left: Thomas Rowlandson's view of the 'Light Infantry Volunteers' in 1804 is less than flattering. (Chris Beetles, London/The Bridgeman Art Library)

and a rather unhappy private life, he had a great self-confidence, which reassured his followers and daunted his opponents.

The cabinet was the body where the most important executive decisions were taken and it met regularly at 10 Downing Street. Apart from the army and navy ministers, the members were the Secretaries of State for Home and Foreign Affairs, the Lord Chancellor, who was chief legal officer, and the holders of three formal posts: the Chancellor of the Duchy of Lancaster, the Lord Privy Seal, and the Lord President of the Council. The Chancellor of the Exchequer was in charge of finance, but both Addington and Pitt combined the post with that of prime minister. Most cabinet ministers were from the House of Lords, but the prime minister was usually from the House of Commons. The cabinet decided the strategy for the armed forces and planned the numbers of ships for particular fleets, and regiments for the different commands. In addition, the Home Secretary was the head of the militia in peacetime, and responsible for raising and organizing it.

Compared with the army, the organization of the navy was relatively simple. At its head was the Board of Admiralty, presided over by the First Lord of the Admiralty, who could be a civilian politician or a politically active admiral. In the Addington government, the First Lord was Sir John Jervis, Earl of St Vincent, a vastly experienced admiral who had defeated the Spanish fleet off the cape from which he took his title. He was a fierce disciplinarian, but his 'quarterdeck manner' was unsuccessful in politics. Believing that the peace of Amiens was permanent, he devoted his efforts to reform in the dockyards, and as a result British naval forces were in disarray when war broke out in 1803. St Vincent did his best to remedy this by a ruthless mobilization, making full use of impressment.

When the Addington government fell in 1804, the new First Lord was Henry Dundas, Viscount Melville. He was noted for his ability to get the best out of a rather corrupt political system and for his political dominance of his native Scotland. He had many administrative talents, some knowledge of naval affairs and a good strategic brain – in 1798 he was one of the first to suspect that Napoleon's fleet was heading for Egypt. Dundas was far more than a departmental minister – he ran intelligence services, controlled a great deal of patronage and was the Prime Minister's right-hand man. But Melville fell from office in 1805, the last British politician to be impeached, albeit unsuccessfully. It was a disaster for the Pitt administration, most of whose members were lightweights, and the Prime Minister was in tears as the vote was announced – he considered it was as bad as losing a battle. However, Melville was succeeded by Sir Charles Middleton, who was hastily created Lord Barham. He too was an admiral, though his experience, rather than at sea, was mainly in the offices of the Navy and Admiralty Boards, where he had carried out many important reforms. He soon showed himself a great master of naval strategy, and he was to direct the Trafalgar campaign.

The junior Lords of the Admiralty were either admirals or civilian politicians. The term First Sea Lord was just coming into use to denote the senior naval figure apart from the First Lord, but the junior political members of the Admiralty Board had tended to regard their posts either as sinecures or as training for higher office. The Board met almost daily and was responsible for the appointment and commissions of naval officers. It supervised the work of the lower boards, and in theory had direct control of recruiting through the impress service. It allocated ships to specific tasks; the broader strategic questions were decided in cabinet. The Admiralty was based at its office in Whitehall, protected against rioting seamen by a screen that was its most distinguished architectural feature. The boardroom was equipped with globes and charts, reflecting the world-wide scope of its work. A wind indicator told their lordships of its current direction, and a telegraph on the roof allowed a message to be sent to most of the major home naval bases within minutes.

The Admiralty had various auxiliary boards, mostly based in Somerset House in the Strand. The Navy Board was in charge of the Royal Dockyards, the building of ships and supply of naval stores, and the appointment of certain warrant officers to ships. The Victualling Board purchased food supplies, and issued them to ships. The Sick and Hurt Board was largely composed of medical men, and was responsible for naval hospitals and the appointment of ship's surgeons. The Transport Board hired merchant ships for the movement of troops and military supplies. The only body concerned with naval affairs that was not under the control of the Admiralty was the Ordnance Board. In addition to its numerous military functions, it supplied guns, ammunition and gunners stores to the navy.

The army had been deeply mistrusted for a century and a half, ever since the days of military rule by the New Model Army under Oliver Cromwell. The ruling classes feared a military government, which might usurp their traditional rights, while the common people saw soldiers as a force for repression, or as drunken hooligans. The administration of the army was deliberately kept complicated, as part of a system of checks and balances. There were four main officials who had responsibility for the army.

The Secretary of State for War and the Colonies was a member of the cabinet, with a role in planning strategy. He was largely responsible for the overseas operations of the army, appointing commanders-in-chief on foreign stations, and coordinating the efforts of the other departments. In 1803 the post was held by Lord Hobart; when the Addington government fell he was replaced by Lord Camden. In July 1805 the latter was replaced by Lord Castlereagh, who was eventually to become a great war minister, but had little opportunity to make his mark during the period of the invasion scare.

The Secretary at War had a confusingly similar title but much less status and power. He was not normally in the cabinet but was in charge of much of the administrative work of the army, operating from the War Office in Horse Guards Parade, Whitehall. He served as a check on military extravagance, or any attempt at military intervention in politics; every movement of troops within the country had to be approved by his office, down to the details of the route by which the men would march and where they would stop for the night.

The Master General of the Ordnance was a figure of considerable status. During the invasion crisis the post was held by the Earl of Chatham, elder brother of William Pitt. His administration was not very efficient, and he was accused of laziness and neglect. His department was responsible for all the technical side of army affairs – engineers, fortification, artillery, property and barracks. It acted as a ministry of supply, producing or buying munitions for the army and navy. The Master General acted as chief military adviser to the government and sometimes took command of expeditions in the field.

The fourth official at the head of the army was the commander in chief, responsible for the defence of the United Kingdom. This post had been in existence for more than a century but had only been put on a permanent basis in 1793. From 1795 it was held by the King's second and favourite son, Frederick, Duke of York. His rise, as was to be expected of a royal prince, had been meteoric: a major general at 19 and a field marshal by 31. His conduct of a campaign in Flanders in 1793 had led to accusations that he and his officers lived well while the troops starved. His private life was no better: he was heavily in debt to tradesmen and gamblers. His marriage of 1791 had soon collapsed, and recently he had become involved with Mary Anne Clark, who openly sold promotions to officers. Despite all that, he was a competent administrator and carried out much-needed reforms. He supervised the cavalry and infantry, having authority over training, promotion of officers, recruitment, and administration. But, since the Flanders campaign, there were serious doubts about his fitness as a field commander.

Defence of the country relied on local government for several purposes, including raising men for the militia and controlling the civil population in the face of enemy attack. The system was antiquated, complicated, and generally undemocratic. The most important unit of administration, especially for military purposes, was the county. There were 52 of them in England and Wales, varying in size from 2,600 square miles (Devon) to 150 square miles (Rutland). Scotland had a further 33 counties, and Ireland 31. The county was run by a committee of Justices of the Peace, who were generally local landowners appointed by the Crown. Far above them in social status was the Lord Lieutenant, also appointed by the Crown for life, or at least until he was removed by some major political change.[3] He was invariably a great landowner and usually a member of the aristocracy. The Lord Lieutenant was first and foremost the commander of the military forces of the county, especially the militia. He was in charge of the raising, supply and organization of all such forces, including those areas that did not come under the jurisdiction of the county for other purposes – from 'all cities, boroughs, liberties, places incorporated or privileged, and other places whatsoever within the said county and limits and precincts of the same'.[4] He might take operational control of the local forces in an emergency, but normally command of the militia and volunteers was exercised by the generals commanding the military districts, and in wartime most militia regiments were serving away from their home counties. In the event of invasion the Lord Lieutenant, like other county officials, would organize the citizens in a levée en masse, and supervise the destruction or evacuation of stores.

Each county was divided into parts, known variously as hundreds, lathes, wards, wapentakes and rapes, which had little modern relevance except as a convenient way of subdividing the county for raising the militia. A smaller but more relevant unit was the parish, headed by the churchwarden, constable, surveyor of highways and overseer of the poor, all appointed by rote and generally unwilling to serve. It was also the main subdivision for raising the militia in the countryside: each was asked for a certain number of men according to population. If the enemy landed, parish officials would be appointed 'for the removal of wagons, cattle, horses, and live stock', and they drew up 'parochial returns ... showing the number of persons between the ages of 15 and 60 willing to serve with arms who will assemble in troops or companies under such persons as are chosen from amongst themselves and approved of by the civil authority of the county'.[5]

Long-established towns had their own governments, though again the system was antiquated. Growing industrial cities such as Birmingham were still part of the county, while decayed towns, like Old Sarum in Wiltshire, enjoyed borough status. The constitution of boroughs varied: some were run by 'closed corporations', which filled vacancies by a vote amongst themselves, while others were relatively democratic. For defence purposes, the town council and magistrates had many of the functions of parish officers in the countryside; they organized the ballots for the militia, ran the volunteers and prepared for the defence or evacuation of the area on the approach of the enemy.

This was the venerable and complicated system that was going to take on the ruthlessly efficient Grande Armée of Napoleon Bonaparte, perhaps fighting him in their own streets and fields. Would the defence have fallen into hopeless confusion, or would the urgency of the situation have compelled some kind of agreement?

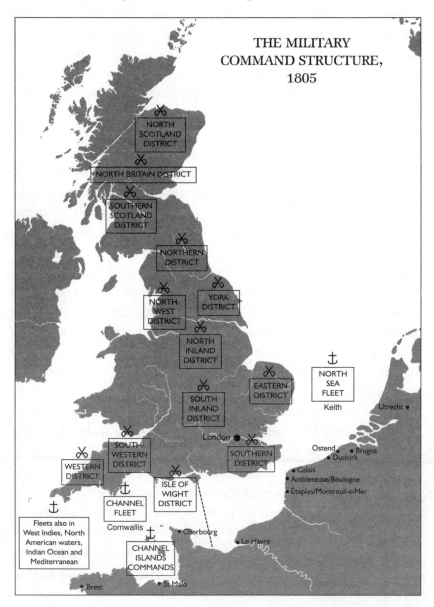

THE MILITARY COMMAND STRUCTURE, 1805

MILITARY LEADERSHIP IN 1805

For the naval defence of Great Britain, there was no single authority below the Admiralty Board in London. The commanders-in-chief of the various fleets and stations enjoyed considerable powers within their own areas and could even operate outside those areas if the situation demanded it – Nelson took the Mediterranean Fleet across the Atlantic in 1805. But there was no unified command for the defence of the United Kingdom as there was with the army.

For the purposes of home defence, the most important naval command was that of the North Sea Fleet. Like most British fleets, it had a title that was rather misleading – its boundaries extended well into the English Channel, to Selsea Bill, just outside the Solent, where the Portsmouth Command began. The North Sea Fleet was also responsible for the defence of the whole east coast of Britain, as far north as the Shetlands. It provided the ships that blockaded the French invasion ports, at Boulogne, Flushing and many smaller harbours, and it patrolled the coast on the British side and escorted convoys within the area.

The command was held by one of the navy's most efficient admirals, George Elphinstone, Viscount Keith. He never led a fleet in a major battle but had a very solid record of fleet administration, culminating with the command of the Mediterranean Fleet at the end of the last war. He had helped put down the mutiny at the Nore in 1797 and organized a successful invasion of Egypt in 1800. He was 59 in 1803 and had his headquarters ashore at Margate in east Kent.

The North Sea Fleet was divided into six subordinate commands, each serving different purposes. There was a squadron at the Downs, providing an important cover against invasion. Another force, mainly of frigates and smaller ships, operated between Dungeness and the French Channel ports, forming the front line of British defence. A largely static force was based in the Thames estuary, with headquarters at the Nore, a sandbank at the mouth of the estuary, which provided an anchorage for ships coming down from Chatham or Deptford and Woolwich. A squadron operated against the Dutch bases in the Texel and Scheldt, and another was based at Yarmouth. The Leith squadron was relatively weak but formed the main naval defence of Scotland and escorted convoys in that area. Lord Barham disapproved of having 'so extensive and complicated command under one flag', but the system was not changed until some years later.[6]

The command of the Channel Fleet was almost as important as that of the North Sea. Again the name was misleading. It blockaded all the ports of Western France, and later Spain as far as Cadiz. Its biggest responsibility, perhaps the greatest of any in the British armed forces, was to keep the French main fleet bottled up in Brest. After that, any ships that could be spared were used to blockade the other enemy ports, especially Rochefort and Ferrol. It was responsible for the immediate defence of the Channel west of the Isle of Wight. However, the areas round Plymouth and Portsmouth dockyards were defended by the port admirals at the respective harbours. The commander of the Channel Fleet was Sir William Cornwallis, who had been in the service for more than 40 years. His most distinguished actions included 'Cornwallis's retreat', when he skilfully led his squadron to safety from a much-superior French force. He was a very active admiral, and his service nickname 'Billy Blue' referred to the fact that when in port he continually kept the 'Blue Peter' flying, to show that his ship was about to sail.

There were several minor commands. The Channel Islands squadron was to defend those islands against French invasion and to blockade some of the ports of Brittany and Normandy. The Irish squadron was based at Cork for the defence of that country. There were also fleets in the West Indies, North America and the Indian Ocean, which had less immediate effect on home defence, as there were no large enemy naval forces in these areas. The main overseas naval force was the Mediterranean Fleet, commanded by Lord Nelson. It too had some part to play in the prevention of invasion, for its primary role was to blockade the French Mediterranean Fleet at Toulon; indeed, a very important element in the French plan was for that force to break out and take control of the English Channel.

Nelson was a complement to Pitt as a great leader – a warrior rather than a politician, an emotional man who was popular with the common people, and one whose love life was 'a little too involved'. The son of a country parson, he was born the year before William Pitt, and he too had a rapid rise within his profession – when rebuked for his high-handedness by a West Indian governor in 1785, Nelson replied that he was the same age as the prime minister and 'thought himself as capable of commanding one of H. M. ships as he was of governing the state'. Nelson's career was greatly helped by his uncle Maurice Suckling, the Controller of the Navy, who found him suitable appointments in war and peace. He was a full captain by the age of 20, and by-passed the bitter rivalries among lieutenants vying for promotion. During the American War he served in various small ships on convoy escort and amphibious operations. Until he was appointed to the 64-gun ship of the line *Agamemnon* in 1793, he had always had independent commands and had no experience of working with a fleet under the eye of an admiral. Like Pitt, he came to responsibility early in life, with a fresh eye and an open mind. He had his first taste of fleet action under the mediocre Admiral Hotham in 1795. When his admiral failed to pursue the defeated French fleet, Nelson stormed on board the flagship only to be told, 'We must be contented. We have done very well.' Nelson wrote to his wife, 'Had we taken ten sail, and allowed the 11th to escape when it had been possible to have got at her, I could never have called it well done.' This was the credo for the rest of his life.

Nelson found a more active role under Sir John Jervis. In 1797 he anticipated Jervis's orders and made headlong for the Spanish fleet off Cape St Vincent – the result was a decisive victory, much needed at a time when the war was going badly elsewhere. As often happened, triumph was followed by disaster. He landed with a force in Tenerife but was wounded, and his right arm was amputated. He recovered in time to take charge of a force of ships of the line that defeated Bonaparte's fleet in the Battle of the Nile, perhaps the most decisive naval victory of the war and one that changed the whole balance of power. Again his career took an unfortunate turn: he became involved with the reactionary government of Naples, and he was responsible for several very poor decisions. He also became close to the British Ambassador Sir William Hamilton and even closer to his lower-class, beautiful and emotional wife, Emma (an affair that pushed aside Frances, Nelson's worthy and loyal wife). The three returned home under a cloud, but as soon as they landed on British soil Nelson knew how popular he was, as the people of every town between Great Yarmouth and London turned out to greet him.

Nelson was second-in-command of a fleet under Sir Hyde Parker when in 1801 he engaged the anchored Danish fleet off Copenhagen. Parker tried to recall him, but Nelson famously put his telescope to his blind eye (the sight of which he had lost during a siege in Corsica) and ignored the signal. It was the tightest of Nelson's battles, but it resulted in another victory. After this, he took command of the forces in the English Channel facing the latest French invasion threat. Again there was disaster with a failed attack on Boulogne, but Nelson was now strong enough to escape any blame. During the Peace of Amiens he settled down to a menage à trois with Sir William and Lady Hamilton, until the former died in 1805. When war broke out again in 1803, he was recalled to lead the Mediterranean Fleet, now a viscount and a vice admiral.

Nelson knew that his own sailors were skilled and battle-hardened, while the French had been disrupted by revolution, and he never gave them the chance to recover. He was often unsuccessful on land, as at Corsica, Tenerife and Boulogne, but at sea he was a highly skilled tactician who could spot the enemy weakness with an unerring eye. He was fearless for his own safety and was wounded many times in the King's service. Although undistinguished in appearance, he had a charismatic style and an ability to engage the affections of everyone under him, as well as the general public. According to Benjamin Silliman,

> His features are sharp and his skin is now very much burnt, from his having been long at sea; he has the balancing gait of a sailor; his person is spare and of about the middle height, or rather more, and mutilated by the loss of an arm and an eye, besides many other injuries of less magnitude.[7]

His popularity was evident when Silliman happened to see him embark for his final voyage at Portsmouth:

Lord Nelson, who had been doing business on shore, preparatory to his contemplated expedition, endeavoured to elude the populace, who were assembled, in great numbers, in the street through which he was expected to pass. He went out through a back door and through by-lane, attended only by Admiral Coffin and a few private gentlemen. But, but the time he had arrived on the beach, some hundreds of people had collected in his train, pressing all round, and pushing to get a little before him to obtain a sight of his face. I stood on one of the batteries near where he had passed, and had a full view of his person. He was elegantly dressed, and his blue coat was splendidly illuminated with stars and ribbons. As the barge in which he embarked, pushed away for the shore, the people gave him three cheers, which his lordship returned by waving his hat.[8]

Nelson had the job of defending his country in distant seas, while most of the military leaders had to operate much nearer home. The army had a unified command in the person of the Duke of York. However the burden of local defence, and of military action in the event of invasion, would naturally fall on the generals commanding the military districts.

In 1803 the country was divided into seventeen districts, each commanded by a general or lieutenant-general. The vital Southern District comprised Kent and Sussex, and was headed by Sir David Dundas, a very experienced officer. Born in Edinburgh around 1735, he was a cousin of the ubiquitous Henry Dundas. He trained as a military engineer and commanded infantry and cavalry regiments as well as serving as a staff officer. In peacetime he had observed the French, Austrian and Prussian armies. He fought in three wars, in Europe and the Caribbean. He had compiled the army's drill regulations ten years earlier, and surveyed the coast during the last threat of invasion. By this time, at 68 years of age, he was past his best and was not popular – his officers called him 'old pivot' because of his emphasis on drill, and to one he was 'a tall, spare man, crabbed and austere, dry in his looks and demeanour'.[9] In August 1803 he had 24,000 troops under his command, more than a quarter of the whole home-defence force. He had three lieutenant generals, in charge of West Kent, East Kent and Sussex respectively. Under them were seventeen brigadiers or major generals as brigade commanders, among them Major General Sir John Moore, one of the most brilliant soldiers of the day. Based at the

Shorncliffe camp overlooking the Strait of Dover near Folkestone, he was using innovative methods to train a highly-effective force of light infantrymen.

The Eastern District included Essex, Suffolk and Norfolk, and was commanded by Sir James Craig, born in Gibraltar to a Scottish family, who had started his career forty years earlier and had gained distinction by commanding the land forces that took the Cape of Good Hope in 1795. He had 17,500 men under his command in August 1803.

Other areas that might face invasion were the South-Western District (Hampshire, Dorset, Somerset and Wiltshire, with less than 4,000 men), the Western District (Cornwall and Devon, with over 7,000), and the Isle of Wight, with just under 2,000 men. London had more than 4,000 men for the immediate defence of the capital, and the 'home' district, in the area around London, had nearly 4,000 more. The Channel Islands had two separate military commands, with nearly 3,000 men on Jersey and more than 2,000 on Guernsey and Alderney. Less important areas were the Northern District, with 1,300 men; York, with just over 2,000; Severn, with 462; and the North-West, with only 413, all cavalry. The North and South Inland Districts could muster 500 men between them, and 'North Britain', or Scotland, had about 9,000 men.

In general, the naval commanders were experienced and well chosen, while those of the army were often too old for their tasks. The civilian politicians were not all suited for the roles they might have to play, and the numerous local officials would probably have found themselves overtaken by events very soon after any attack by enemy troops. Yet the system held together somehow, and certainly an invader would have encountered fierce resistance, by land as well as by sea.

POLITICS IN 1940

On the surface, the British system of government did not change much between 1805 and 1940. The country was still ruled by a King George, the sixth rather than the third. Parliament still consisted of the hereditary House of Lords and the elected House of Commons, the judges wore eighteenth century wigs, the navy was run by the Admiralty and the army by the War Office, with little cooperation between the services. But that impression only demonstrates the British genius for adopting radical change while keeping the old form. The King's personal power, already restricted by 1803, was even more limited by 1940. The House of Lords had been cut down to size by the rise of popular democracy and the Parliament Act of 1911. The Commons was now elected on a much wider franchise – all adults over the age of 21 (male and female) who were not convicts, lunatics or members of the Lords.

The government was still headed by the Prime Minister and his Cabinet. Neville Chamberlain, Prime Minister from 1937 to 1940, had a good deal in common with his predecessor Henry Addington – he was a middle-class, peace-loving man with a strong interest in government finance but no great breadth of vision. Like Pitt and Churchill, he was the son of a well-known politician: Joseph Chamberlain had split the Liberal Party in the 1880s over Irish Home Rule. Neville was born in Birmingham in 1869 and became Lord Mayor of the city before entering parliament. During the Conservative hegemony of the 1920s and 1930s he was Chancellor of the Exchequer for seven years before becoming Prime Minister.

He was wildly popular when he brought back 'peace in our time' from his Munich meeting with Hitler in 1938, but that bubble soon burst when Hitler ignored the agreement: instead, Chamberlain's lugubrious face and his umbrella became the subject of the cartoonists' mirth. His mournful voice was unforgettable as it announced the British declaration of war with Germany on the wireless in September 1939. Like Addington, he had no idea other than to conduct a defensive war and wait for something to happen. His stock fell still further when Germany invaded Norway in 1940. Now that the war had turned serious, a coalition government was clearly necessary, but the Labour Party refused to serve under him. He was replaced on 10 May 1940, just as the crisis escalated still further with the German invasion of the Netherlands, Belgium and France.

The two main parties were now the Conservatives (still known informally as the Tories) and Labour, with the Liberals, successors to the

Whigs, running a rather poor third. With the fall of Chamberlain in May 1940, all of these joined a coalition, leaving only tiny groups like the pacifist Independent Labour Party outside it. Political unity was much stronger than in 1805. 'Total war' demanded a compact war cabinet of five to seven members, who met almost daily. Some of its members had grand-sounding titles that carried few departmental duties and allowed the holder to think about the war effort as a whole. Until his fatal illness in October, they included the former Prime Minister, Neville Chamberlain, and Clement Attlee of the Labour Party as Lord Privy Seal and Deputy Prime Minister. His colleague Arthur Greenwood was the Minister without Portfolio. Until December the Secretary of State for Foreign Affairs was Lord Halifax, who had considered a deal with Hitler in 1940; he was replaced by Churchill's friend Anthony Eden. The Chancellor of the Exchequer was Sir Kingsley Wood a former civil servant; Lord Beaverbrook, the newspaper magnate, was Minister for Aircraft Production; and Ernest Bevin, another Labour member, was brought in as Minister of Labour and National Service, in charge of mobilizing the population for war.

Before he took office as Prime Minister on 10 May 1940, Winston Churchill seemed an unlikely focus for national unity. He was a political maverick who had changed party twice during his career. In an age of 'people's war' he lived an opulent lifestyle, he had never been on a bus, and he did not know how to run a bath. In a long political career, he had given every sector of opinion some cause to dislike him. He was a fervent anti-communist, who had motivated the British expedition against the Bolshevik government in Russia in 1919. He was almost equally anti-socialist and during the 1926 General Strike he had led the government against the trade unionists with his usual panache. He had deserted the Liberal Party in 1923—as its fortunes seemed to be fading. As to his own Conservative Party, he had spent most of the last decade in open opposition to its policies, first on self-government for India, and then on their attitudes to Nazi Germany. But none could doubt his opposition to fascism. Churchill offered strength and experience as a military leader, but there were many who remembered the Dardanelles expedition of a quarter of a century ago, when he took the blame for a disastrous failure. There were always those who suspected his judgement, and his close associates knew that his wilder schemes had to be kept in check.

Churchill was the most aristocratic of the great British war leaders of the nineteenth and twentieth centuries. Born in Blenheim Palace in 1874, he was a descendant of the Duke of Marlborough, who had won many victories against Louis XIV of France. His father was a distinguished politician who lost office and died of syphilis. His mother was an American heiress. Winston became an army officer and then a war correspondent and saw wars in India, Egypt, Cuba, and South Africa. He entered parliament in 1900, and soon left the Conservatives to become a leading light of the reforming Liberal government of 1906 to 1916. He served as Colonial Secretary and Home Secretary, throwing himself into each role with great energy. He found his forte as First Lord of the Admiralty from 1911, and he played a vital role in getting Britain ready for war in 1914. He fell from office in 1915 over the failed expedition to the Dardanelles and served as a battalion commander on the Western Front, before returning to office as Minster of Munitions. In peacetime he served as Chancellor of the Exchequer, where some of his decisions, such as the Ten-Year Rule, were used by his successors to postpone rearmament. He was out of office during the 1930s, and his lack of judgement and moderation over India, as well as his reputation as a warmonger, did not help his campaign to stand up to the Nazis. He came back as First Lord of the Admiralty on the first day of the war in 1939 and was almost the only minister of Chamberlain's government who seemed to pursue the war with any vigour.

As Prime Minster there was no doubt about Churchill's dominance, even if he did not always get his own way. He also took on the title of Minister of Defence, which had no constitutional status and no actual ministry under it, but it gave Churchill authority over the armed services, and he had no compunction in interfering directly in the detail of the war effort. The service ministers – the First Lord of the Admiralty, the Secretary of State for War and the Secretary of State for Air – were outside the War Cabinet and, apart from Anthony Eden, they were relatively minor political figures. Churchill tended to confine them to administrative duties and deal directly with the Chiefs of Staff on matters of strategy.

If Nelson's working life was entirely confined to the Royal Navy, Churchill had a much wider perspective. One of his greatest assets was his intimate knowledge of all three services. There were plenty of retired admirals, generals and air marshals who knew their own service in great detail, but very few could rise above their own service interests. During his service as an army officer, as First Lord of the Admiralty and as Air and War Ministers he had always adopted a hands-on approach and knew all the services from the inside. No one else could have had such detailed knowledge of all the services without prejudice in favour of one or the other. Furthermore, he had no doubt about his military competence. As General Brooke wrote, 'Winston never had the slightest doubt that he had inherited all the military genius from his great ancestor Marlborough.'[10] But his dominance was not always to the good, and his subordinates knew he interfered in military affairs too much. Nevertheless, it gave him an ability to assess the different claims of the services and to inspire them to cooperate as they had never done before.

In private, Churchill tended to be sceptical about the possibilities of invasion. Even in public, he told the House of Commons in June 1940, 'it seems to me that as far as seaborne invasion on a great scale is concerned, we are far more capable of meeting it to-day than we were at many points in the last war and during the early months of this war ...' Early in July he told his staff that he hoped 'to drown the bulk of them in the salt sea'. But Churchill recognized the morale value of the threat, and on 12 July he told some of his staff, 'the great invasion scare ... is serving a most useful purpose: it is well on the way to providing us with the finest offensive army we have ever possessed and it is keeping every man and woman turned to a high pitch or readiness. He does not wish the scare to abate therefore, and though personally he doubts whether invasion is a serious menace he intends to give that impression, and to talk about long and dangerous vigils, etc., when he broadcasts on Sunday.' He may have had doubts, but by 12 August he was able to tell his ministers that he was feeling 'more confident than two month ago. Our defences on this island have been immensely improved.' His mood varied from time to time, and during a critical point in September his private secretary reported, 'The PM seems more apprehensive than I had realized about the possibility of invasion in the immediate future and he keeps on ringing up the Admiralty to ask about weather in the Channel.'[11]

Churchill also had very obvious talents, which proved invaluable during the feverish summer of 1940. He had enormous self-confidence, for he had been born into the ruling classes at the zenith of the British Empire; he had overcome youthful difficulties and disappointments, and he had been proved right about the need to meet the Nazi threat (though not about his other campaign of the 1930s, on India). During the critical month of May 1940, it was his resolution that made the difference between a deal with Hitler and fighting on. He had an enormous capacity for work and knew every detail of the war effort while leaving domestic affairs largely to Sir John Anderson, a former civil servant, and the Labour members of the coalition. And, of course, Churchill's oratory turned out to be a weapon of war in itself – according to the American journalist Ed Murrow, he 'mobilized the English language and sent it into battle'.[12] His speeches were always carefully prepared and were rather ponderous in their structure, but they provided as great an oratory as Pitt or anyone else had ever done. He had the advantage that those in the House of Commons were fully reported in the press, while he could also appeal direct to a wider audience by radio broadcast. And he had a far greater capacity for the ringing phrase than Pitt.

Unlike the other great British war leaders, Churchill had a successful if stormy marriage, and his wife Clementine was a frank and intelligent critic and a great support to him. Late in June as he faced the enormous strain of taking office in the middle of the greatest crisis in his country's history, Clementine was shocked about his attitude to his subordinates. She wrote to him,

> I hope you will forgive me if I tell you something that I feel you ought to know.
>
> One of the men in your entourage (a devoted friend) has been to me & told me that there is a danger of your being generally disliked by your colleagues & subordinates because of your rough sarcastic & overbearing

manner ... If an idea is suggested (say at a conference) you are supposed to be so contemptuous that presently no ideas, good or bad, will be forthcoming. I was astonished & upset because in all these years I have been accustomed to all those who have worked with & under you loving you – I said this and was told 'No doubt it's the strain' ... with this terrific power you must combine urbanity, kindness and if possible Olympian calm ... I cannot bear that those who serve the Country & yourself should not love you as well as admire and respect you.[13]

She tore it up then pasted it together again and handed it to him. It seemed to work, and there were no further complaints, but Churchill was never an easy man to work with.

Unlike Nelson and Pitt, Churchill used a very large staff – he travelled with 'a retinue that Cardinal Wolsey might have envied', as one of them put it. He had his political favourites, such as Anthony Eden and Lord Beaverbrook, whom many regarded as an evil influence. He had close associates of a slightly lower rank such as his Minister of Information, Brendan Bracken, and his scientific adviser, 'Prof' Lindeman. In his capacity as Minister of Defence he employed three of the cleverest soldiers of the day, General 'Pug' Ismay, Brigadier Leslie Hollis and Colonel Ian Jacob. For his office as Prime Minister he was assisted by three or four very able private secretaries, all graduates of the best universities. According to one of them, 'there was never a day or night when at least one Private Secretary was not with Winston Churchill – that is to say capable of being physically present at his desk or at his bedside within a couple of minutes, or on the same train, ship, aircraft or car and able to comply with any request, reasonable or not, on the telephone or in person.' His naval aide de camp, Commander Thompson, accompanied him on every trip, as did his bodyguard, Inspector Walter Thompson of Scotland Yard. Below that Churchill deployed teams of typists to take down his thoughts, and his personal needs were served by his valet, Frank Sawyer, who was 'a little, baldish Cumbrian with a round, florid face, piercing blue eyes, and a pronounced lisp ... Something of a wag, he had a way with Mr. Churchill that no-one else dared to emulate.' John Colville, one of the secretaries, thought, 'He was a considerable character, and would have made a fortune on the stage.'

Having gone through the Victorian period of reform when almost anything seemed possible, with tightly organized party discipline, with practically the whole nation solidly behind the war effort and with far less taboos than in the past, Parliament was powerful enough to give the government practically anything it wanted. It could raise taxes to a far higher level than ever before, impose conscription, direct labour into specific industries and factories, imprison aliens and suspected persons, ration food and clothing and impose all kinds of restrictions on the population. Churchill enjoyed a real power over the country that Pitt could only have dreamed of.

The civil service was a much also larger and better established body than William Pitt had known, appointed by competitive examination rather than patronage. It had many critics, who claimed that it was over-cautious, that senior civil servants knew little of the outside world, that it relied on committees which reduced individual initiative and responsibility, and that its career structure and guaranteed pensions made its members complacent. But it was capable of organizing everything that was needed for a major modern war – conscription, food supply, orders for the armed services, maintaining law and order in the face of air raids, and many other duties.

Local government had been totally restructured in the nineteenth and early twentieth centuries, and on the surface it was far more rational and efficient than in 1805, though its structure could baffle an old soldier like Brigadier Green of the Sussex Home Guard:

> The essential feature of the 'chain of command' in the Army is the invariable principle that the Commander really does command all formations under him ... In local government his principle does not apply. You would suppose in a system consisting of Ministry, County Councils, Borough and other Councils and Parishes, there would be the same sort of chain of command, but this is not so. The lay-out looks like a military lay-out, but the machine functions differently.[14]

The old counties were retained, but now they were governed by elected councils rather than appointed justices of the peace. Large towns and cities were detached from them and given independent status as county boroughs, while small boroughs were independent for certain functions. London was a case in itself, with 28 boroughs under the London County Council, which had been set up in 1889 but had not been extended to cope with recent suburban growth. Local government at various levels was responsible for matters such as roads, police, education and public health, all supervised to a greater or lesser extent by ministries in London, Edinburgh or Belfast. It tended to work through committees, even more than the civil service. In wartime many new functions were added, including civil defence and air-raid precautions and evacuations of the population. Local government was still held in some respect, for councillors and mayors were figures of some authority, though perhaps not as much as they had had in Victorian times. As a reminder of older times, the Lord Lieutenants of the counties were still in service, with authority over the reserve military forces until they were mobilized and went to war.

MILITARY LEADERSHIP IN 1940

Apart from Churchill himself, who could never be disregarded as a military authority, the main group for the coordination of the three armed services was the Chiefs of Staff Committee, or COS, which consisted of the three service chiefs – the First Sea Lord, the Chief of the Imperial General Staff and the Chief of the Air Staff. Churchill was determined that the services should work together better than during the previous war, and the chiefs met daily for two or three hours to discuss planning and strategy.

The navy was still headed by the Board of Admiralty in its office in Whitehall, though naval bureaucracy had expanded vastly, and it now occupied several large extensions and many offices in the London area. The First Sea Lord was Admiral of the Fleet Sir Dudley Pound, who ran the navy as if he were the executive officer of a battleship. His main combat experience was as a captain at Jutland in 1916, but he had spent much of World War I in staff posts, which gave him early experience of dealing with Churchill. After the war he alternated between staff and operational posts, but it was only the death or illness of several more likely candidates that brought him to the post in June 1939. He was a dedicated and mild-mannered man, who tended to deflect Churchill's wilder ideas by diplomacy and careful staff work rather than confrontation. His health was beginning to decline at the age of 63, and he showed symptoms of narcolepsy. According to John Colville, 'He wore a lugubrious air and his mere entry into the room made the occupants feel grave.'[15] His deputy was Sir Tom Phillips, a traditional battleship admiral who would later pay for his faith with his life when he sailed without air escort and went down to Japanese bombers in *Prince of Wales*.

Unlike the other service ministries, the Admiralty was an operational as well as an administrative headquarters, and it is not clear where the boundaries of its authority would have lain in the event of invasion – it would certainly have been entitled to take over control of home defence. However, the command structure under it lacked cohesion. The naval forces at home were divided into various commands. Charles Carrington claimed with some exaggeration that the navy had 'a string of vice admirals down to the Flag Officer-in-C Falmouth, all of them having ranked as Commanders-in-Chief since Samuel Pepys established them under Charles II'.[16] In fact Falmouth was only a sub-command, and in 1940 home waters were divided into six major commands. Of these, Western Approaches, from the south-west of England to the Hebrides, was unlikely to face an invasion and was mostly concerned with the developing submarine campaign in the Atlantic. Orkney and Shetlands was responsible for the base at Scapa Flow and for sealing off the northern end of the North Sea to German shipping. Rosyth Command had a large stretch of the east coast of Scotland and England north of Flamborough Head; an invasion there could not be ruled out, but it was far more likely in the three commands to the south.

The Nore Command could indeed could trace its history back to Pepys and beyond. It covered a coastline of more than 200 miles as the crow flies, from Flamborough Head to the north-east corner of Kent, and was divided into three sub-commands, Humber, Yarmouth and Harwich, which included the Thames Estuary. Its commander-in-chief was Admiral Sir Reginald Plunkett-Ernle-Erle-Drax, better known as Admiral Drax. Born into an aristocratic family in 1880, he was a radical figure in the naval circles of his youth. He served on the staff of Admiral Beatty during most of the great battles of World War I. Successful as a

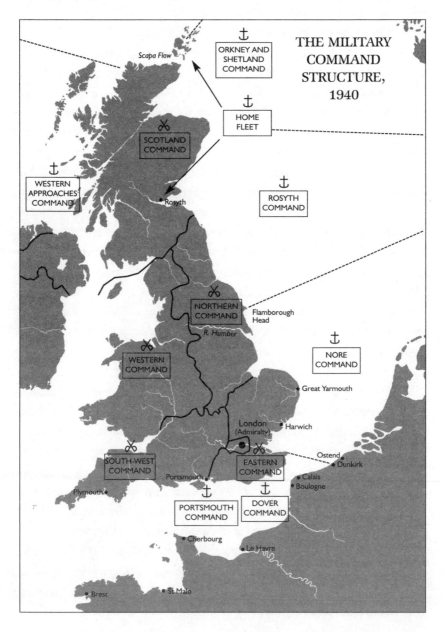

staff officer and captain of a cruiser, he was unsuccessful on a military mission to Russia in 1939. He was deeply involved in the evacuation from Dunkirk and threw himself into the organization of defensive measures on what seemed the most likely stretch of coast for an invasion. As well as that, he had to protect the vital convoys along the east coast into London.

Dover Command was a much newer and smaller one, guarding the south-east corner of England. It was headed by Bertram Ramsay, one of the most outstanding officers in the navy. He was born into a military family in 1883 and specialized in signals rather than gunnery, which was considered the path to high rank, for he was more interested in the tactical problems of moving fleets than with the technicalities of armament. Unlike his fellow commanders-in-chief, he spent most of World War I in small ships. He was given the plum post of chief of staff to Sir Roger Backhouse of the Home Fleet, but soon resigned because Backhouse was a traditional admiral who did not need a staff. Ramsay was a strict disciplinarian but open to new ideas. He was one of the key figures in the Dunkirk evacuation, and his talent for improvisation did much to save the day. As well as protecting a key area against invasion, he had to try to get convoys through 'Hell-fire corner' in the English Channel and to prevent the Germans using the waterway for their own purposes.

Portsmouth Command was another traditional one. The C-in-C, Sir William James, was a courtly and multi-faceted man – in his youth a painting of him by Millais was used in a Pears' Soap advertisement that was as famous as any television commercial of modern times, and to his embarrassment he was still known as 'Bubbles'. He was another intellectual sailor, who published books on ship organization and naval history. Major Carrington of Bomber Command visited him in his office in Nelson's cabin in HMS *Victory* to find, 'His golden locks time hath silver turned and that baby's-bottom complexion had matured into a rich port-wine purple', but he was still recognizable as the boy in the Millais picture. He was still energetic at the age of 59 and spent much time visiting the outstations of his command, as well as sending ideas for its defence into the Admiralty.

The Home Fleet was the navy's main striking force in these waters, by far the strongest unit in terms of gun power apart from the Mediterranean Fleet. It was based much farther north at Rosyth and Scapa Flow, where defences had been hurriedly set up after the loss of the battleship *Royal Oak* in October 1939. Its commander-in-chief was Admiral Sir Charles Forbes, a typical 'big-ship' admiral. He had been unfortunate in failing to intercept the German invasion fleet on its way to Norway, thereby gaining the nickname of 'Wrong-Way Forbes', but he was one of the few senior officers, like Dowding of Fighter Command, who had the stature and confidence to say 'no' to Churchill.

The army had a much simpler organization at the top than in 1805 and was directed by the Army Council, which roughly paralleled the Admiralty. As well as the Chief of the Imperial General Staff, its military members included the Adjutant General, the Quartermaster General, the Vice Chief of the Imperial General Staff and the Deputy Chief. From the beginning of the war, the Chief of the Imperial General Staff was General Sir Edmund Ironside, a gargantuan 60-year-old Scot and one of the army's most thoughtful and far-sighted officers. His adventures in South Africa led him to believe that he was the model for Richard Hannay, John Buchan's hero who was the James Bond of the day. His appointment to the CIGS post was despite a lack of experience of the politically charged offices of Whitehall. He did not do well dealing with the attacks on Norway and France, and by 25 May he saw that the post of Commander-in-Chief, Home Forces, was likely to be the centre of the army's next battle. He wrote in his diary:

> I am now concentrating on Home Defence. The Cabinet are still wondering what to do about appointing a Commander-in-Chief ... They want a change to some man well known in England. They are considering my appointment. I have said I am prepared to do anything they want.[17]

Ironside put this to Churchill and two days later he was appointed to the crucial post as the evacuation from Dunkirk got under way. It was 'an honour to me and a new and most important job, one more to my liking than C.I.G.S. in every way'.[18]

His successor as Chief of the Imperial General Staff was Sir John Dill, who projected the image of a perfect English gentlemen, though he had been brought up in Northern Ireland. He was 'lamb-like, a mild-looking scholarly old fellow with a pink flabby face. Slow moving, looks every year of his age (59).'[19] He had been a very efficient staff officer and a lecturer of genius in the staff college, though he had seen very little regimental service. He had very great energy in the early 1930s, but his health was in slow decline, perhaps because of the onset of aplastic anaemia. He often failed to convince the Prime Minister by written arguments, and his verbal comments were mishandled – he admitted that he often thought of the perfect reply when it was too late. Churchill came to call him 'Dilly-Dally'; Dill for his part was reported to be 'very fed up with Churchill' by the end of November.[20]

General Sir Alan Brooke had done much to organize the defence of the British army during its retreat to Dunkirk. He had escaped from France not once, but twice, and as soon as he got back he was put in command of the Southern District, responsible for the defence of England from Portsmouth to Land's End. Churchill was impressed with him during a visit to Southern Command in mid-July: 'His record stood high. Not only had he fought the decisive flank-battle near Ypres during the retirement to Dunkirk, but he had acquitted himself with singular firmness and dexterity, in circumstance of unimaginable difficulty and confusion, when in command of the new forces we had sent to France during the first three weeks of June.'[21] This inspired Brooke's appointment as C-in-C Home Forces two days later. He was called to Whitehall to see Dill. 'I find it hard to realize fully the responsibility that I am assuming. I only pray to God that I may be capable of carrying out the job.'[22] Ironside took his dismissal very well: 'the Cabinet wished to have someone with late experience of the war. I told Eden that he needn't worry and that I was quite prepared to be released … I can't complain.'[23] But he did not make it easy for Brooke, who arrived to find, 'Not a word concerning the defences or his policy of defence, etc., absolutely nothing!'[24]

Brooke was a general of great efficiency – 'without question the dominating personality, very shrewd, decisive, expresses himself well in

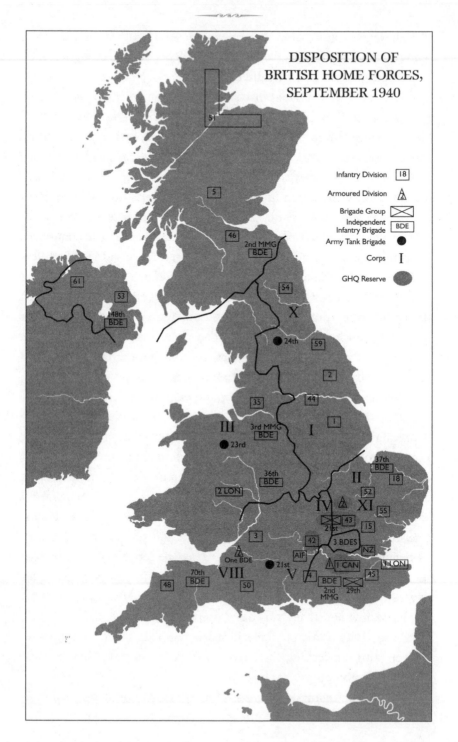

DISPOSITION OF
BRITISH HOME FORCES,
SEPTEMBER 1940

Infantry Division   18

Armoured Division   △

Brigade Group ⊠

Independent
Infantry Brigade   BDE

Army Tank Brigade   ●

Corps   I

GHQ Reserve

a high strong voice. Looks better sitting down; he sags a little, looks too heavy. Long head, iron-grey hair, wears horn-rims and looks not so much like an eagle as a wise old eagle-owl.'[25] But his diaries reveal a far more sensitive man, full of self-doubt and finding relief in the love of his family, and in bird-watching.

The army at home was divided into eight major commands, each under a senior general. London and Aldershot districts had few troops and were more concerned with administration and training. There was a small force in Northern Ireland, which might become important if the Germans moved against Eire to the south. Scottish Command was not likely to face an invasion but had several naval bases to protect. Western Command covered north-west England and Wales and was even less likely to have to deal with an immediate threat. The Northern Command faced the Germans across the width of the North Sea and was kept strong, with six divisions. Southern Command covered the south-west peninsula of England and was opposite the enemy 60 miles away in Cherbourg, but it was not considered a major risk area, and so only had three infantry divisions and one armoured.

The most vital sector, whether the invasion was to come from the English Channel or the North Sea, was Eastern Command stretching from the Wash to Portsmouth. Throughout the crisis it was under the rather undistinguished command of General Sir Guy Williams, and none of his corps commanders, Lieutenant Generals Massy, Thorne and Osborne, made much impression either. Massy was only noticed by Churchill when he visited his corps headquarters in June and made the mistake of introducing the Prime Minister to his staff rather than showing him the troops in action. Thorne was invited to lunch at Chequers and was impressed with Churchill, whom he thought was 'more vital to this country than Hitler was to Germany', but there is no sign that the Prime Minister reciprocated this regard.[26]

The division was the internationally recognized measure of military power, though there was no general agreement about its actual strength – it might be any number of men from about 10,000 to 20,000, it might be infantry, it might be armoured – but when Britain planned for a force of 32 divisions in March 1939 the world military community knew what that meant. Stalin once famously asked, 'How many divisions has the Pope?' while Churchill said of the arrogance of the exiled French General de Gaulle that he might be 'Stalin with 200 divisions behind him' rather than a refugee whose country had collapsed. According to Brian Horrocks, 'A division is probably the best command in the British Army because it is a tactical unit complete with its own gunners, sappers, supply and medical services ...'[27]

An infantry division consisted of three infantry brigades, each of three battalions. Compared with a division above it or a battalion below it, the brigade was a unit that attracted less loyalty – its commander, the brigadier, was not even a 'proper' general. The division also had a battalion of light tanks, three field regiments of Royal Artillery and an anti-tank regiment, three field companies of Royal Engineers, transport and supply units of the Royal Army Service Corps, three field ambulance units, divisional signals, a provost company of the military police and a postal unit. In theory it consisted of 13,863 men. It was commanded by a major general, and the most dynamic one in Home Forces in 1940 was Bernard Montgomery, who was not universally popular but made a good impression on Churchill in July.

There were only two armoured divisions in service during the summer of 1940. The 1st had returned from France and had to be re-equipped. The 2nd had remained in the United Kingdom but was still under strength. Later the 6th was formed in September, the 8th in November and the 9th in December. An armoured division had a theoretical strength of 10,750 men in April 1940, with 340 tanks organized in two brigades of three armoured regiments each. It had an artillery regiment, an anti-tank and light anti-aircraft artillery regiment and two motorized infantry battalions, as well as Royal Engineers units. In a reorganization in October, the motorized infantry were integrated with the armoured brigades so that they could fight more closely with the tanks.

Divisions in Home Forces were mostly allotted to the area commands and grouped in corps when there were enough of them. In August, after Brooke had completed his moves in accordance with his new strategy, Eastern Command had three corps consisting of six divisions as well as an armoured brigade, an independent brigade and a motor infantry brigade. Northern Command had two corps with six divisions and a motor brigade, and the other districts had a single corps each, or no corps structure like Scottish Command.

The RAF was ruled by the Air Council, which was roughly similar in function to the Board of Admiralty and the Army Council. It has been observed that young army and navy officers join because they want to take command, but air force officers simply want to fly. Certainly most of the men in the higher commands of the Royal Air Force in 1940 were exceptions to that rule, men to whom the actual piloting of aircraft had played a secondary role in their careers.

The Chief of the Air Staff in the summer of 1940 was Sir Cyril Newall, whose appointment was a surprise in 1937, as there were several better-qualified, though less pliable, candidates. Like most of his generation he had started off in the army and he learned to fly in 1911. As a squadron commander in 1915 he preferred ground administration to leadership in the air. He aided the development of the Hurricane and Spitfire, but he knew very little about modern bomber or fighter tactics, and he lacked any charisma – he preferred to stay in his office in the Air Ministry, retreating to an underground shelter at night. In October 1940 he was replaced by Sir Charles 'Peter' Portal, the former head of Bomber Command.

Unlike the other services, the RAF had functional rather than geographical commands, set up in 1936 when the old Air Defence of Great Britain was divided into Bomber, Fighter and Coastal Commands. Coastal Command was the weakest, but it was fortunate in its commander-in-chief, Sir Frederick Bowhill, who had started as a merchant navy cadet. He had joined the Naval Air Service in 1913 and at the outbreak of World War I took command of HMS *Empress*, a pioneering seaplane carrier. Later he led Royal Naval Air Service units in Mesopotamia and Zanzibar. During the peace he spent some time as chief staff officer in Coastal Area, the forerunner of Coastal Command, Air Officer Commanding Fighting Area and at the Air Ministry as Air Member for Personnel. Appointed to Coastal Command in 1937, he led the force energetically.

Bomber Command was headed by Portal from April 1940. He was the most intellectual of the air marshals, having studied law before going to the Western Front as a corporal dispatch rider in 1914. He trained as an air observer, then as a pilot and was a major in command of a squadron by 1917, at the age of 24. He was to fly more than 900 operational missions. He served as a flying instructor and staff officer in peacetime, then took command of RAF forces in Aden before joining the Air Council as Air Member for Personnel to oversee the great expansion programme. He took over Bomber Command a week before the 'phoney war' ended with the invasion of Norway and began to set realistic targets for the bombing offensive against Germany, as well as working towards better navigation and the use of radio aids. His efficiency impressed Churchill, who promoted him to replace the inadequate Newall. Portal was an austere man, though unlike William Pitt he had a happy marriage. Like his predecessor as CAS, he had no urge to visit air stations, but his administrative competence and force of personality made him highly efficient. According to Churchill's secretary, John Colville, he was 'Quiet, unforthcoming and not easy to converse with, he was shrewd in his judgement and seldom averse to risk and adventure.'[28] However, as a true creation of the air force of his day, he favoured the bombing offensive above all, while the defence against invasion was seen as a distraction.

Fighter Command was led by Sir Hugh Dowding, whose rather severe appearance and nickname of 'Stuffy' showed how unlikely he was as a popular hero. Failing to follow his father into the academic world he had become a professional artilleryman before volunteering for the Royal Flying Corps in 1914. He found it difficult to learn to fly at the age of 32, but eventually he took charge of a squadron in France, where he was said to be aloof and reserved. At the end of the war he clashed with Trenchard, the head of the new RAF, but came back into favour in the 1920s. He was Air Member for Research and Development in the early 1930s until he founded Fighter Command in 1936. As well as developing the new fighters, he promoted radar stations and the Observer Corps, the building of concrete runways, the use of barrage balloons and the setting up of a highly effective control system. He was passed over for Chief of the Air Staff in 1937 and was due to retire in 1939, but his tenure was extended. As the threat of a German attack on

Britain drew nearer, he remained determined to keep his force intact during the coming struggle and in 1940 refused to send any more fighters to be lost in France.

Dowding's subordinates were also to play key roles in the battle that followed. Sir Keith Park was a New Zealander who came to flying rather slowly – he had already served in the bloody campaigns at Gallipoli and the Somme before he learned to fly in 1917, but he found time to win four medals before the war ended. He was involved in the development of fighter aircraft and tactics between the wars, and he received an honorary MA as commander of Oxford University Air Squadron. Dowding's deputy in Fighter Command, he was promoted to command 11 Group, whose fighters were in the front line after the Germans occupied France.

Park's colleague and rival was Sir Trafford Leigh-Mallory, commander of No. 12 Group, to the north. He was appointed to 12 Group in December 1937, though he had no experience of fighter operations. Dowding and Park complained of his conduct of exercises and remarked that he had 'a misconception of the basic idea of fighter defence'. Tension between these three, creative or otherwise, remained in the summer of 1940.

There were serious faults in the British command structure in 1940. Churchill was aggressive, confident and determined but did not know his own limitations or those of the forces under his control. The other political leaders, with the possible exception of Eden, were little involved in the war effort and left everything to the military. At the top military level, none of the chiefs of staff was entirely adequate, at least until Portal was appointed in October. The real fire in the resistance would come from lower down, particularly from Ramsay for the navy, from Brooke, and Montgomery from the army and from Bowhill, Dowding, Park and possibly Leigh-Mallory from the air force. With a rather erratic and weak command structure above them, they would have had to find ways to cooperate in the supreme test of invasion.

5

INTELLIGENCE

INTELLIGENCE IN 1803–5

Intelligence, in the sense of gathering and assessing information, was not new to the British government in 1803; it had been operating services for several centuries. The term was more ambiguous then than it is now, for it might include what we would simply call news – indeed, newspapers and magazines often carried headings such as 'Interesting intelligence from abroad'. Secret service funds were available to the government, but that just meant they were not subject to normal parliamentary accounting, and they could be used for bribery and propaganda as well as finding out the enemy's secrets. Intelligence was not regarded as a profession in 1803, and hardly anyone could be described as a full-time agent, but governments and military leaders did everything in their power to get information about enemy forces and movements. The methods of both intelligence and counter-intelligence might seem amateur and dilettante in comparison with later ages (not to mention the superhuman efforts of fictional spies), but the British government did succeed in finding out a great deal about the enemy, by various means.

Naturally the government collected as much information as possible before war broke out. On 10 May 1803, during the last few days of peace, a loquacious French commissary in the Dutch port of Hellevoetsluis about to embark for Louisiana gave information that was repeated to one Charles Sevright:

The number of French troops already in the Batavian Republic amounts to 25,000 ... These troops are to be followed by several additional corps; it being the intention of the French government, in the event of war, to keep in this country an army of 50,000 men, as well for the sake of the military objects as may be in view, as on account of some apprehension of insurrection against the French authority ...

In the mean time every effort is to be tried to invade England. This undertaking is allowed to be connected with peculiar difficulties, but it is nevertheless considered as practicable with success. Several expeditions are to be prepared in the different ports, and the different places on the coast, of this country, for that purpose ...

The immediate object of the operations thus commenced will be to gain some tenable point or post, where the troops can maintain themselves, till the arrival of reinforcements, which both in men and stores, every opportunity is to be seized of sending, or till they are joined by their adherents among the inhabitants. Of these many desirous of change and preferring republican liberty, are expected to promote their views in different parts of Great Britain ... the schuyts are not to steer for any harbour, but are to run at once upon the coast; the troops are to jump on shore with the utmost expedition.[1]

This was not the only report to suggest that the invasion relied on gaining support once it had landed. A traveller who left Calais in August 1803 wrote that, 'Informant thinks some treachery ... is going on in our fleet in the Downs ...' and described some rather fantastic plans to capture admirals in advance of the invasion. [2]

Reports also suggested that the metropolitan French, in contrast to their reluctant allies and the provincials of Brittany and Normandy, were enthusiastic about invasion. A report from Paris said, '*The general hatred against all the English is beyond description*.'[3]

Many correspondents sent on letters from friends and business associates in French-held territory but disclaimed responsibility for their accuracy. Charles Deane of London received a letter from Paris, and his father sent it on to the authorities, noting, 'He does not pretend to attach any importance in the extract.'[4]

There were no professional spies in 1803, but there were several men who made a habit of collecting information in one way or another. One of these was Nelson's chaplain, Alexander John Scott, who among other talents had a remarkable flair for languages. He operated with Nelson's fleet in the Mediterranean, developing networks on Sardinia and Sicily and expanding his remarkable book collection during his trips ashore.

Philippe d'Auvergne was another remarkable character. Born on Jersey in 1754, he was naturally fluent in French as well as loyal to the British crown. He became a naval officer, serving alongside Nelson on an Arctic voyage. As a prisoner of war in France he made the acquaintance of a namesake, Charles de la Tour d'Auvergne, Duc de Bouillon and ruler of a tiny principality on the borders of France and modern Belgium. He convinced the Duke that he was descended from the same stock, and with his immense charm he persuaded him to adopt him as his heir. As a result, from 1802 he was usually known as the Prince de Bouillon, although the actual territory was under French occupation, and in any case d'Auvergne's legal right to it was never established. But the title alone gave him some standing among French émigrés, many of whom had equally empty titles.

In the 1790s d'Auvergne was posted to his native island and supported the Chouan rebels in nearby Brittany, while building up a network of contacts in Normandy, where the Vendée revolt had been crushed by 1796. In 1803 he restarted his intelligence activities from Jersey. Boats from the island could cross to Brittany or Normandy in a few hours and land secretly among the numerous harbours and coves. There were no revolts this time, but plenty of royalist sympathizers to provide information – the French police files recorded 108 people 'devoted to the Prince of Bouillon', 132 more suspected of being in touch with him, and 160 boatmen 'presumed to be in English pay'. [5] He had a substantial fund to support his activities, even in peacetime. In January 1802 he paid out £2,088 to agents Bertin and Thysauron 'for their journey to the interior of Bretagne, on account of secret service'; in December that year he paid out £2,049 to 25 different informants.[6]

The Prince had informants as far away as Paris. One report described 500 boats being constructed on the Seine, each about 36 feet long and drawing three feet of water or less. Each was to take a crew of up of 150 soldiers and a dozen paddlers. They were for a 'general dash under the guns of the several batteries of the intended places of invasion'.[7]

At the northern end of Napoleon's empire, the British used the services of John Sontag, recently promoted to colonel in the British army. He was based in neutral Altona, near Hamburg in the domains of the King of Prussia, under the cover of the post of 'inspector general, foreign allowanced officers' from May 1804. He was able to build up a detailed picture of what was happening in the Dutch ports from travellers to and from the country. Much of his intelligence was political, but he also produced detailed reports on the movements of ships, large men of war as well as invasion craft. In December 1803, for example, he listed five Dutch ships of the line that were fit for service, along with seven frigate and smaller vessels. He described a number of gunboats carrying 'two 18 pounders in the Bows one 26 Pounder in their stern and two 3 pounders on each side'. The crews were mostly landsmen recruited in Germany, and the general opinion was that 'the greatest exertions will be made from Walcheren, where all the flat bottom boats have been sent to'. He also reported,

> The exertions for the intended invasion in Holland are continued with vigour; all the gun boats, flat-bottomed boats and small crafts are sent from Holland thro the rivers to Flushing; 46 gun boats were sent there from Amsterdam, and all the small vessels from Rotterdam; it seems that the dread of the frost taking place has been one of the causes to accelerate the departure of the boats for Flushing.[8]

In January his information was mainly military, and he listed fourteen battalions of the Dutch infantry and four squadrons of cavalry as having been moved to various ports, where they could be embarked at four days' notice. His contacts also extended into France, and he reported, 'The greatest exertions are still continued. Troops making for the coast from all parts of the interior. The French regiments not intended for the expedition are to send a certain number of chosen men to form a *corps d'elite*, which is to be assembled at Arras, and is supposed will attend Buonaparte.'[9] But Sontag began to feel unsafe in his role as the French put increasing pressure on the government of Hamburg. 'My situation here is far from being pleasant. I know from very good authority that I have been the subject of a conversation made by Mr Reynhard the French minister,' he wrote in November 1804.[10]

These two agents were very useful in their ways, but they were at different ends of Napoleon's empire, leaving a gap in the middle around

Boulogne, where the main danger was likely to come from. Travellers returning from France and the Netherlands were another important source in the early stages at least. The trade between the two countries was formally banned, but neither the British nor the Dutch authorities made much effort to stop it. Benjamin Silliman travelled from the Thames in September 1805:

> The traffic is carried on in this way. The Dutch boats, commanded, manned and owned by Dutchmen, clear off from Holland as Prussian, and sail under Prussian colours; they state their destination as being for Embden, a neutral town, north of Holland; their papers state that the ship is bound to Embden; the passports of the travellers are all for the same place and the captain kisses the Bible, and deliberately swears that this is his destination.
>
> With this solemn parade, known to both sides to be a mere fiction, the boat proceeds directly to the Thames, and when she returns, the same farce is repeated …[11]

With their trade ruined and their nation subjugated and forced to send men to fight for the French, it is not surprising that the Dutch were resentful. According to Silliman, 'a young man of excellent understanding … declared his hatred of the Gallic dominion and lamented the misfortunes of his country, but seemed to despair of her deliverance.'[12] Intelligence reports tended to reflect apathy, and according to Colonel Sontag in May 1804, 'In Holland the inhabitants in general are thro fear grown perfectly indifferent about Political News, everybody seems to think about themselves and their property only …'

Both sides employed smugglers, with the same people often working for both, but their reports rarely appear in the intelligence files. They tended to land at isolated coves rather than the main harbours, so they could not report on the movements of large bodies of vessels. Their word was not to be trusted, but they could be useful in bringing back newspapers and other documents. D'Auvergne also supplied a variety of these from Normandy and Brittany, taking care that his agents bought them in different places to avoid suspicion. The news in them took a long time to reach London, whereas smugglers could bring them back literally overnight. Thus, for example, on 1 July 1803 it was gleaned from a 'Paris paper' that,

> The [Dutch] ship of the line *John deWitt* is not entirely armed. It has taken up its station near the Texel. The council of the Marine has given authority to put three ships of the line into service. There is great activity in the shipbuilding slips to fit out 16 or 20 other warships destined to defend our coasts.[13]

A contract of November 1803 between the Commissioners of the Batavian Marine and the masters who would engage to charter their vessels supplied details of the types to be used in the invasion fleet:

> 1st Class – fast sailing ships, as frigate built brigs, to carry horses and men, or to be lightly armed.
> 2nd Class – large flat-bottomed two deckers etc for ditto and for hospital ships.
> 3rd Class – one mast flat bottomed ships etc for ammunition and other objects.
> Ships to be fitted up for the reception of troops etc by the freighters.
> Ships to be ready by November, when the freight commence.
> Time to go to the Texel for 1st and 2nd Class 12, and for 3rd Class 8 days.
> Ships are chartered for 4 months.[14]

The movements of a sailing vessel are naturally easy to observe, and its tall masts are visible from a long way away. The blockading ship has masts of her own, so the captain can climb up 110 feet up to the main cross-trees of a frigate to take a look for himself through a telescope. Thus on 10 December 1803, Captain Owen of the famous frigate *Immortalité* personally counted in Boulogne harbour mouth '17 brigs and schooners alongside the quay – 3 small brigs further up the Harbour – the space between occupied by luggers'. Even the signal station across the channel could make reports of movements when the visibility was good, and in January it was reported, 'Observe 55 vessels from Dunkirk and Calais proceeding towards Boulogne – 6 ships, 3 brigs, the rest luggers.' It was slightly more difficult to find out what was going on inside the harbour, but fisherman and neutral sailors proved helpful. By 17 March Lord Keith was 'of opinion that the account of the number of vessels at Boulogne is not at all exaggerated at 1200'. By the summer of 1804 there was no doubt about the build-up inside the harbour.

The deeper harbour at Dunkirk was more difficult to observe, and there was a slow start there. Moreover, the French revolutionaries with little regard for religious sensibilities, were reported to have found a unique way to conceal their shipbuilding efforts: 'The Great Church is appropriated for the Frame Building of the boats and the Street leading therefrom is completely filled with them. Nothing can exceed the active exertions of the workmen.'[15]

The captains of the ships off the coast interrogated passengers and crew in the ships they stopped and often found them quite forthcoming. One man who left Flushing in mid-January 1804 told Sir Sidney Smith,

> there were at that place the following vessels. 110 Schuyts are now carrying each one long gun and adapted for transporting from 60 to 80 soldiers; 17 schooners carrying each six 6-pounders in the waste [sic], 2 long 24 pounders forward and one abaft also a Dogger brig of 10 guns one French frigate of 44 guns (La Furie) ... Her men said to be distributed in the above mentioned vessels.

Helpfully the informant provided a drawing of the bow of one of the vessels. [16]

Fisherman could also be useful, and Captain Brenton of HMS *Harpy* wrote in December,

> The fishermen say that in the late gales upwards of 40 gunboats have got out of St Malo and Cherbourg, and that they have gone to Boulogne. They say that at Havre there are 62 gun boats besides others building, and 14 at Honfleur, capable of carrying 100 men each.[17]

The Regulating Captain at Dover took time off from running the press gang to report a conversation with a Dane, that 'at Ferrol [in Spain] are 3 two decked Dutch ships of war and 2 frigates'.[18] Along the coast at Ramsgate, Mr David Banks wrote to the authorities:

A man who lives at Flushing and left it last Tuesday says that there are at present only 42 guns boats, schuyt rigged with one mast and the gun brig that was taken out of Dungeness Road, but they cannot get any men to man them. There are 10 schooners with 4 to 6 guns each. The new frigate is launched, and the French frigate that was in the road is now at the Rammekins.[19]

Off the Dutch coast in December 1803, Captain Hope of the *Defence* provided a detailed report:

Spoke several vessels just out from the Texel, and all of them agreed in their reports of a number of transports fitting at Amsterdam; the general part of which was hauled out into the stream with their sails bent, but detained by want of seamen. They are all under Dutch colours, and it was reported they were to drop down immediately to the Helder to embark troops.[20]

Back in London, the Admiralty clerks filed the various letters, reports and summaries the information on each port throughout the French empire in a book entitled 'Intelligence'.[21] From this it is possible to follow the build up of forces in each of the invasion ports, though the information was often scanty and contradictory. At Boulogne, most of it was visible from the fleet off the coast.

During the two and a half years in which they were threatened with invasion, the British built up a very detailed picture of their enemy and his means of attack. They knew that the French in general were keen to invade, but the Bretons and Normans were far less so, and the Dutch were very reluctant indeed. They knew a good deal about the movements of the great French Army, and had much detail of the numbers and qualities of the boats which were likely to invade. They had observed the movement of his forces towards Boulogne, and knew that it was the main port for launching an invasion, but they did not rule out others – Lord Keith, for one, thought that Le Havre offered distinct possibilities to the enemy. They knew far less about the enemy's tactics, when he was likely to launch his attack, and even less about where he might land.

INTELLIGENCE IN 1940

Intelligence was far more of a profession by 1940, and the armed services had their own agencies, while information was also supplied by the Foreign Office and other government departments. Spy fiction was already well established before the war, including the works of John Buchan and the early Somerset Maugham. It boomed during the 1950s and 1960s, especially with the works of Ian Fleming, who had been in Admiralty intelligence, but in fact it was based on a myth. When Churchill published his six volumes on *The Second World War* between 1948 and 1954, he was not allowed to reveal the true nature of his intelligence and wrote for example, that fore-knowledge of the invasion of the Soviet Union came from 'one of our most trusted sources', which might be taken to mean a high-placed spy but was actually acquired by a very different means.[22] In fact the secret agent played a relatively minor role in what the British knew about the German invasion plans. Britain had no well-placed spy in the German hierarchy, though there were many in occupied Europe who were only too willing to help the Allied war effort. Resistance operatives could be supplied with radio sets and report shipping movements, for example; but this network was in a fairly primitive state in 1940. Technology did not necessarily work in the spy's favour, for modern communications gave the Germans many methods of detecting and trapping him, and Nazi ruthlessness was deployed to the full. It is difficult to imagine any German official reporting that he knew of more than 300 people suspected of being in the pay of a foreign agent, as the French police did about the Prince de Bouillon's contacts; he would simply have passed the names on to the Gestapo to deal with.

A direct and close blockade of the invasion ports was not possible in the days of submarines, mines, long-range coastal artillery and dive-bombers. In any case it would not have yielded the intelligence results of 1803–5, as vessels no longer had to step their masts or cross their yards before putting to sea, and a Dutch barge fully loaded had a very low profile. Fortunately there were other ways of keeping an eye on the ports.

Aerial photo reconnaissance, like radar, was developed just enough to be useful in the crisis of 1940. It had been used in the previous war with the limited aims of plotting enemy trench systems and helping artillery spotting. Between the wars most of the development had been done by private companies such as The Aircraft Operating Co. Ltd., which carried out aerial surveys in Britain and the Empire, and F. S. Cotton, a freelance photographer, had carried out clandestine aerial reconnaissance over Germany before the war. A photographic interpretation cell was set up at the Air Ministry in March 1938. Blenheim bombers soon proved too slow, but Cotton, a former World War I pilot who was now commissioned as a wing commander, set up a unit at Heston near London. A machine known as Wild Rectifier was acquired in Switzerland to produce mosaics from angled shots, and a series of huts and bomb-proof shelters were taken over in Wembley for an interpretation unit. But it was not impervious to enemy action: on 2 October a leading aircraftsman was killed by a bomb. Early in 1941 the unit moved to Medmenham on the banks of the Thames west of London.

Speed and height were the best ways of avoiding enemy action, and it soon became clear that the Spitfire, stripped of its guns and polished all over, was the best aircraft available. By the beginning of 1940 the reconnaissance version was making speeds of 375mph, compared with 355mph in its configuration as a fighter, and flying at 30,000 feet or more. Cotton wanted at least 400mph and asked for aircraft to be constructed with flush riveting and butt joints, their gun holes welded over, an improved windscreen (as a flat surface was only needed for gunnery purposes) and a more powerful model of the Merlin engine. He did not want to use fighter pilots – 'it is much easier to teach a man to fly a Spitfire than to teach a Spitfire pilot with the wrong temperament to do the work we are doing.'[23]

The Spitfire was reasonably safe over enemy territory at this height and speed but more vulnerable on the way up. As a result, Pilot Officer W. B. Parker was shot down by two Messerschmitt 109s over Kent at 29,000 feet while setting out on a mission. He baled out, but his flying suit caught fire, he was temporarily blinded and broke his arm when he made a landing, but he eventually returned to operations.[24]

There were several flights every day during the summer and autumn of 1940, over all the invasion ports from Norway to the Bay of Biscay and sometimes heading a long way inland. A typical flight was that which took place on 17 September, the pilot flying at a height of 32,000 feet over Cap Gris Nez opposite Dover, then south to Boulogne, Étaples and Nuncq-Hautecôte, followed by Dunkirk, Gravelines and Calais to the north. Back at Wembley, the interpretation officers studied detailed changes in gun position at Cap Gris Nez. They noted that nothing seemed to have changed on the aerodrome at St Inglevert, but a new telephone line made them suspicious that some aircraft were hidden at a nearby landing ground, and an anti-aircraft battery had suddenly appeared to the north. There was no definite change in the gun batteries at Wimereaux, but eighteen E-boats were to be seen in Boulogne harbour. At Etaples they noted the detail that the guns were moved 20 degrees and back again between sorties, while at St Pol sur Termoise a new aerodrome was 'far from incomplete' but not yet in service. There was no change in the shipping and barges at Dunkirk and Gravelines, but six small craft, 'not of Naval appearance' had arrived at Calais. At the town's central station the rolling stock had been moved and 'Three trains of trucks which appear white in the photograph have arrived.'[25]

The first photo interpretation manual was issued in March 1940, at a time when its main function was to support the BEF and aid Bomber Command. Nevertheless it was quite prescient in considering the possibility of a German invasion of Holland and Belgium and in reporting the activities on the German canals and their barges. It commented that most people had a dual vision of interpretation work. 'It is contested [contended?] that on one hand that anyone can, without training, read and obtain information from air photographs, and on the other that interpretation is a slightly mystic art which can only be practiced by the select few.' It advised interpretation officers to make full use of shadows, which could give a good idea of the orientation of the photograph if the time was known. Furthermore, they could give an idea of the height of an object: 'This will prevent such errors as interpreting an embankment as a cutting, or a slag heap as an excavation.'[26]

The second volume was issued soon afterwards, in a time of great flux. It had a detailed section on the Siegfried Line, the German land defence, which was not likely to trouble the British army for some time to come. It also had aerial photographs of Boulogne, which had recently fallen to the enemy. The section on canal barges was supplemented with basic descriptions of the most common types, and officers were informed that, 'The volume of traffic on canals is best judged by the numbers waiting to proceed through locks which are always bottle-necks …'[27] Detail was everything in the interpretation of photographs, and it was essential to visit the site many times, as changes were the only way to spot activity.

The most dramatic and secret means of finding out about the enemy was by intercepting and decoding his radio messages – the first part was simple, the second needed a huge amount of skill and ingenuity. The navy had a good deal of experience of this from the previous war. A skilled team of code-breakers had been built up in Room 40 at the Admiralty, and many of them, such as the Director Alistair Dennington, Nigel de Grey and Dillwyn, or 'Dilly', Knox, would serve in senior positions in the next war. During the peace, a small organization was kept up in the form of the joint-service Government Code and Cipher School, whose title understated its role.

The German Enigma machine was first developed for commercial purposes in 1923, and made far more sophisticated when it was taken up by the military. The Poles, who had as much to fear as anyone from German expansion, acquired models and studied them in some detail. The Enigma machine looked like a portable typewriter in a box and had a keyboard. Its coding was done by a series of rotors, each bearing the letters of the alphabet, with rings attached to each. Using all of these, many millions of combinations could be used, and the letters did not repeat themselves in the finished message, so it was not possible to decode it by counting common letters such as 'e's. The system was changed every day by using a different position on the rotors and rings. The Poles discovered that the Germans were using a simple ABCDEF keyboard and that they usually repeated the three letters used in the preamble, which made decoding much easier. The Polish team escaped when their country was overrun and provided machines as well as information to the Western Allies.

As with many government departments, the GC&CS was evacuated from London on the outbreak of war. Admiral Sir Hugh Sinclair, the head of the service, privately bought Bletchley Park, 50 miles north-west of London. A large Victorian house that had been built by Sir Herbert Leon, with 55 acres of land attached, it was ideally situated, with good rail links to London as well as the university towns of Oxford and Cambridge, where many of the code-breakers would be recruited. Soon extra accommodation was added in the form of huts in the grounds, but most of the staff were billeted out in nearby hotels and houses.

Bletchley Park had no radio facilities of its own, as that would draw the enemy's attention. The enemy messages were actually intercepted in stations at Chatham, Flowerdown near Winchester, Scarborough and Cheadle. More were set up, and there were 132 receivers in use by September 1940. Coded messages were noted down and sent to Bletchley by teleprinter if they seemed urgent, or by motorcycle dispatch rider.

The centre recruited its staff from several sources. Mathematicians included Alan Turing of King's College, Cambridge, as well as academics, chess players, museum curators, lawyers and many others. Some were in uniform and some were civilians employed by the civil service. Between them they brought a great deal of variety and creativity to the problems. There were translators in German, Italian and Japanese. There were separate groups working on the German army, navy and air force codes. There were intelligence experts to assess and collate the value of the information received. For more routine duties, teams of servicewomen were drafted in, but service personnel generally wore civilian clothes to maintain secrecy and to foster a creative atmosphere, while academics continued with their informal and often eccentric styles of dress and behaviour. By December 1940, Bletchley Park had a total staff of 550, plus a hundred more in outstations.

Just before the invasion of the Low Countries and France, the Germans changed the system and decoding became much more difficult. The intellectuals at Bletchley enjoyed the challenge of finding a solution, which depended on the carelessness of the operators.

> Those first few days after the change on May 10, 1940, were quite fantastic. Many people contributed bright ideas ... We were like a pack of hounds trying to pick up the scent. Till now the observed habits of individual Enigma operators had been regarded as interesting oddities rather than as a means of breaking the Enigma keys. Suddenly they were all we had, and we had to find ways to take advantage of them.[28]

John Herivel was the first to spot a solution:

> I thought of this imaginary German fellow with his wheels and his book of keys. He would open the book and find what wheels and settings he was supposed to use that day. He would set the rings on the wheels, put them in the machine and the next thing he would have to do would be to choose a three-letter indicator for his first message of the day.
>
> So I began to think, how he would choose that indicator. He might just take it out of a book, or he might pluck it out of the air like ABC or whatever. Then I had the thought, suppose he was a lazy fellow, or in a tearing hurry, or had the wind up, or something or other and he were to leave the wheels untouched in the machine and bang the top down and look at the windows, see what letters were showing and just use them.
>
> Then another thought struck me. What about the rings? Would he set them for each of the three given wheels before he put them into the machine or would he set them afterwards? Then I had a flash of illumination. If he set them afterwards and, at the same time, simply chose the letters in the windows as the indicator for his first message, then the indicator would tend to be close to the ring setting of the day.

This was the 'Herivel tip' which would provide one method of decoding during 1940. The other was by means of the 'Cillies', a name which was possibly based on the mythical girlfriend of one of the operators. Each one had to use two three-letter codes, and he might use a proper name, including 'HIT' followed by 'LER', or he might use three letters from a diagonal on the keyboard. One operator tested his machine by typing the letter 'L' many times. Since the Enigma machine would come up with any letter except the one typed in, it was possible to find the settings from that.

There was a good deal of skill and excitement in working out the settings for an individual day.

> Having spotted the dispersed cluster, I made up the usual menus for the DR and spent most of the watch with Pat Hempsted testing the results on the machine ... as the night wore on, she got more and more fed up with the whole proceeding. Then, probably around seven A.M., I saw signs that I was at last working on the correct wheel order and ring setting. After a few more test operations Pat saw the signs too and exclaimed incredulously, 'It's coming out.' Tired but happy, we had almost completed the break by the end of the shift.[29]

This meant that the rest of the signals in that particular system, code red, for that day could be deciphered. The next task was to distribute the signals, so that they could be acted on by the best authorities without compromising the secrecy of the operation. Those of immediate tactical significance were relayed to the appropriate headquarters by telephone, those of less urgency by teleprinter. Routine messages were bundled up and sent by dispatch rider, while those of no significance were filed. On 27 September 1940, Churchill requested to see all decrypts, but that would have been impossible, and he was sent a box every day containing about twenty of the most important.

By September, Alan Turing had developed a machine called the Bombe, which could work out the settings mechanically and electrically, making the Herivel tip and Cillies redundant. The naval code would have proved the most useful in revealing the plans of U-boats at sea, but it used four rotors out of a possible eight, while the army and Luftwaffe ones used three out of five, so it was much more difficult and remained unbroken at this stage. The one that was broken first was the Luftwaffe code red, used for signals between headquarters. Over the months from June 1940 onwards it provided a sketchy but very useful indication of the German invasion plans.

'Ultra', the codename for the decoding of Enigma, was not the only type of signals intelligence. Another form of intelligence was direction-finding, using cross-beams to plot where a signal originated from. Another was Traffic Analysis, or TA, which was done by measuring and comparing the output of radio signals, either generally or from particular stations. It was becoming clear, for example, that there would be a lull as radio silence was imposed before a major attack, followed by a surge as it got under way, and that might give an indication that an invasion was imminent. On a lower level, TA could reveal the movement of particular units, perhaps getting into place for an attack. It was also used to estimate the number of German aircraft in service by picking out and counting their identification signals on landing – it was calculated that there were 1,153 bombers in September 1940.[30]

INTERPRETING THE INTELLIGENCE, 1940

The separate intelligence services, including the army, navy, air force and Foreign Office, had a tradition of rivalry and reluctance to share their sources or information. This came to a head with the invasion of Norway when there were reports from the British Embassy in Stockholm, from a secret Foreign Office source inside Germany, from the American Ambassador in Copenhagen and from photo reconnaissance – all pointing in the same direction.[31] The failure to put these together, plus a naval belief that an invasion on this scale was impossible without control of the sea, led directly to defeat. After that the position improved drastically. At the centre was the Joint Intelligence Committee, first set up in 1936, with representatives from all the service intelligence services – the Military Intelligence organizations for the army, the Naval Intelligence Department for the navy and Air Intelligence for the air force. In May 1940 the Ministry of Economic Warfare and the Special Intelligence Service joined the committee, and a special sub-committee, the Combined Intelligence Committee, was set up specifically to deal with the threat of invasion. Their task was to find out how, where and when the enemy was likely to attempt a landing.

The timing of a landing could probably be assessed by the weather, the state of the tides and the degree of German air superiority. Signal intelligence and photographic reconnaissance gave indications of the movement of troops and invasion craft, and the kind of training they were doing. In June the army tried to collate all information on possible dates, and found a considerable variety. The German minister in Lisbon was reported as saying that 'Machinery for attack' had been fixed for 1 July; MI 14 predicted the 3rd. Neutral naval attachés in Berlin reported that several transports were to leave Frederickshaven for France on 7 July, to visit the French ports. And three escaping Dutch officers reported gossip in their homeland that it would take place on or after 11 July – 'the German slogan is "London on the 15th July".' The Admiralty assessed the effects of tides. For at the time it was assumed by both sides that a high tide around dawn was needed for landing; at Harwich on the east coast, it would be possible on two days either side of 6 July or 8 August; at Dover it would be around 11 July or 10 August; at Plymouth it would be either side of 2 July or 1 August. A possible date for much of the east coast was 15 July, and this seemed to fit the military plans, the need to finish the matter quickly, and the possibility that it could take place soon after Hitler's review of the armed forces.[32] But the Germans were not ready, and nothing happened.

Tension increased again in September as the air battle came to a climax. Aerial reconnaissance spotted a 'procession' of at least 50 boats, each about 100 feet long, heading round Cap Gris Nez towards Boulogne on 4 September. That afternoon they were seen moored in the Bassin Loubet, and on the 5th there was speculation about what they were. 'Large scale photographs suggests these craft combine the features of small self propelled barges with some of the characteristics of "E" boats.' The number of barges in Waalhaven, Rotterdam, was seen to increase from 40 to 150 by 26 August, while on 4 September it was noted that the number in the Ghent–Terneuzen canal in Belgium was tending to decrease. Meanwhile five motor boats were entering Ostend, of a type that had not been seen there before. The same day an increase was observed in the barges in Amsterdam, and a dozen small boats arrived in Veere on the southern Dutch island of Walcheren, and a hundred more at Flushing nearby. Farther east at Le Havre, bathing huts were removed from the beach, and fifty vehicles and their stores took their place. Nearly 50 barges were seen moving south on the Dortmund–Ems canal, away from the sea, but in the Hollandsch-diep, south of Rotterdam, they were nearly all heading westwards towards it. The army's appreciation of German intentions stated:

> During the first half of September the general movement of German craft has been from the German northern ports and those of the Netherlands and Belgium to the south west. By the 15th September approximately 1,625 barges had been assembled in ports from Antwerp to Boulogne. Further to the south west merchant vessels, mostly, apparently, from Hamburg, Bremen, Wilhelmshaven and Emden, have been moved to ports between Boulogne and Cherbourg whilst merchant shipping in Belgian ports has been increased. Between inclusive Antwerp and Cherbourg [sic] it has been estimated that there is about 213,000 tons of merchant shipping.[33]

All this contributed to a feeling that the invasion was not far away, and Britain went on the alert.

Meanwhile the Admiralty assumption about the amount of shipping needed for an invasion was challenged by some intelligence officers. On 26 July they had estimated that 180,000 tons of shipping would be needed to sustain 150,000 troops for a month; but, it was claimed, that was based on the idea of a British Expeditionary Force moving to France for a long war, not a German blitzkreig. More important would be the provision of berths where the ships could unload, though a good deal could be brought in by barge and unloaded on the beaches. If each barge contained troops and equipment to form a tactical sub-unit, it could still fight on shore no matter how many of its companions got lost or were sunk. There was also the possibility of the enemy using 'Trojan horses', merchant ships disguised as friendly vessels and allowed into port. In all, it was felt, the Germans could launch an invasion with 60,000 tons of shipping.[34]

It was 10 October before the intelligence services became aware that the invasion of Britain had been allocated the codename 'Seelöwe' or 'Sea Lion' – not a very good cover name, as it pointed too obviously to the British lion and its seapower. With hindsight, the intelligence services noticed that it had probably been in use for some time, for it had been used in a message of 25 September, and there was a previous reference to operation 'S' on 29 August, which probably meant Seelöwe.[35]

The most open question was where the enemy would land, for the defence of a particular stretch of coast had to be planned well in advance. In the early stages the authorities were convinced that the east coast was the main target area. The bulk of the German navy (such as it was) was in the North Sea or the Baltic. Possible invasion barges were concentrated in the Netherlands, and it was believed, probably wrongly, that it would be too risky to take them through the Strait of Dover. There were reports from many sources, most of which added to the confusion. One suggested troop-carrying planes from Stavanger in Norway, while a neutral traveller had heard that they might use electrically propelled one-man canoes to get across the Channel.[36] Churchill subscribed to the east coast theory, and on 9 July he told the War Cabinet that he 'did not think, however, that in the immediate future, at any rate, there was much possibility of an attack being launched from the French coast'.[37] On 5 August he proposed the defence of the different areas on a scale of three units guarding the east coast north of the Wash, and five to the south of that. (The whole of the south coast, from Dover to Land's End, had only 1½ units.) Within five days General Brooke had piped up to say, 'Yet the threat of invasion seems just as great on the south coast towns as on the east coast.' Churchill queried this: it ran counter to Admiralty assurances that there were no concentrations of enemy warships to the south except a score of motor launches.

By the 15th the General Staff of the army had produced an appreciation 'to decide whether a German invasion of GREAT BRITAIN is more likely to take place on the East or the South Coast'. It considered the possibility of launching it from Norway or Denmark, where there were plenty of ships and about thirteen army divisions, of which six might be spared. The bulk of the German navy was in the Baltic, which was a closed book to British intelligence, and it was difficult to know what they were plotting there. But an invasion would involve a long sea voyage, during which troops in small craft would be debilitated by seasickness, while there would be plenty of opportunity for the British Home Fleet, based at Scapa Flow, to interfere. Most significant of all, there was little prospect of air cover, so an invasion from Norway, or one anywhere on the British coast north of the Wash, would almost certainly be a diversion. An invasion from Holland and Belgium to East Anglia or the Thames Estuary was more likely, but it would have to cross the mine barrage parallel to the coast, which was possible for barges but not for ships of more than fifteen feet in draught. It was reckoned that 20 to 30 per cent of these would be sunk unless they were preceded by minesweepers. The east coast was the most strongly held by the army, which the enemy probably knew, and they had a history of avoiding frontal attack.

The south coast, on the other hand, offered relatively short sea crossings. It would turn the flank of the British defences, which the Germans were always keen to do. An attack there would do more to disrupt British lines of communication and it would soon cut off London. There was much intelligence about German build-up in the launch area, though they had not yet moved transport aircraft and ships in. Enemy air reconnaissance seemed to suggest that they were more interested in that area. The report concluded:

> The naval and military difficulties and disadvantages of launching a sea-borne expedition against the east coast in the face of strong air defences are probably sufficient to discourage the Germans from attempting initially more than diversions here, from NORWAY to the BALTIC. It must be emphasised that if an invasion is attempted it will be pushed on regardless of losses until they become overwhelming. The main thrust will be directed from the area where the maximum co-operation between the three services is possible and against a wide front. The south coast, therefore, offers many advantages which, combined with the increasing activity opposite this coast, suggest that this may well be where the Germans will attack.[38]

This view was probably reinforced on the 15th when the Luftwaffe raided the north of England from Norway and was heavily defeated.

If an invasion fleet should indeed be launched and not detected by any of the intelligence means available, there was a final warning system in the newly invented radar, or RDF as it was known at the time. It had

147

been developed by Sir Robert Watson-Watt in 1936. Priority was naturally given to anti-aircraft radar, and by 1940 a chain of stations had been built round the east and south coasts of Britain. The ordinary stations, the 'Chain Home', or CH, were designed for relatively long-distance detection. Alongside them were the 'Chain Home Low', or CHL, stations to detect low-flying aircraft, and it was soon realized that they could also find small ships. There were ten stations in operation on 4 July, and 14 more were under construction. On 18 June, Fighter Command Headquarters told its operators:

> In the event of the enemy attempting to invade this country, it is considered that some of the enemy troops would be conveyed in large numbers of small ships, which would be beached at suitable parts of the coast. Larger ships might also be used to a port after it had been occupied. It is probable that the approach of these ships would be observed by C.H.L stations.

Observers were ordered to report any concentration of five or more ships to higher authority and to keep watching it, while the naval liaison officer would check if there were any British squadrons or convoys in the area.[39] A sub-lieutenant was appointed to each station to filter out the naval information. 'The main requirement of the officers is commonsense, ability to plot on a chart and read from a map and ... the ability amiably to co-operate ...'[40] Direct telephone lines were set up with naval headquarters, which proved reasonably successful. From Dover it was reported at the end of October, 'It has been found that on request and having provided an indication of their whereabouts, the position and frequently the number of our own patrolling craft or convoys can readily be obtained from C.H.L Stations.' On the other hand, CHL stations did not always take the initiative in making new reports, and the Flag Officer in Charge, Tyne Area, reported in January 1941 that only about one in ten of the numerous shipping movements in his area were actually reported to his headquarters. He recommended more naval staff in the stations. Meanwhile they tended to grow in confidence and skill. A report from Whitstable at the end of November stated,

The crew is keen and the Officer-in-Charge is anxious to improve his operators experience in surface craft detection. Operators vary considerably in skill, but one or two seem fairly confident in differentiating between moving vessels, stationary surface objects, e.g. buoys, and cloud effect. The whole crew is improving with this now considerable practice.[41]

The army was allocated fifteen sets for watching beaches. By October the navy was asking for eleven more to watch the main ports, though mainly to monitor convoys, to protect against torpedo-boat attack and to activate controlled minefields (which were only live when there was a danger from the enemy or no friendly shipping in the area) rather than invasion.[42] In any case, fog or darkness was no longer a protection to an invading force.

Churchill was generally sceptical about the prospects of invasion. As early as 16 June he wrote, 'We are asked to consider many plans of possible invasion by Germany. Some of these seem to be very absurd.'[43] On 10 July he told his generals, 'it would be a most hazardous and even suicidal operation to commit a large army to the accidents of the sea in the teeth of our very numerous armed patrolling forces ... They could immediately break up the landing-craft, interrupt the landing, and fire upon the landed troops ...'[44] By 21 August he was telling General Ismay on his staff, 'The prospects of invasion are rapidly receding.'[45] By 11 September, as a telegram from the ambassador in Spain reported that the real enemy objective was Egypt, he told the War Cabinet, 'it was by no means impossible that the Germans would in the end decide not to launch an attack on this country because they were unable to obtain the domination of our fighter force.'[46] Later that day he told the House of Commons, 'for him to try to invade this country without having secured mastery of the air would be a very hazardous undertaking.' But his secretary, John Colville, found him 'more apprehensive than I had realized by the 21st, and he kept ringing up the Admiralty to ask about the weather in the Channel'.[47]

General Sir Alan Brooke, in charge of army forces in the United Kingdom, was far more nervous, and his diaries show constant relief when nothing happens. On 15 September: 'Still no move on the part of the Germans! Everything remains keyed up for an early invasion ...' And the next day: 'Still no invasion. Rumour has it that tonight is to be the night.'[48]

6

WHERE AND HOW?

THE SEA AND THE LAND

The factor that had changed least between 1805 and 1940 was the British coast. It was still exactly the same distance from the continent of Europe and faced by enemy bases in the Netherlands and northern France. No large areas of land were reclaimed in Britain during the period (though many marshes were drained), while only small areas were lost to the sea. It is interesting that over the centuries the French should use the same terms to describe the English Channel as Britain faced invasion. Napoleon said: 'It is a mere ditch, and will be crossed as soon as someone has the courage to attempt it.' And as France was about to surrender in 1940, General Weygand remarked to Churchill, 'You have a very good anti-tank trap in the Channel.'[1] The main change was in the development of the coastline for leisure and housing, which was much less advanced in 1803.

The coast of Britain is about 6,000 miles long, but not all of that was suitable for invasion. Much of it is faced with cliffs or rocks, and large areas of the country were too far away from enemy bases to need strong defences. Nevertheless in 1803, as in 1940, the country was faced with a resourceful enemy who was full of surprises. Every option that might conceivably be open to him had to be considered. In addition, the defence of Ireland posed different problems.

It is unfair to claim as one historian does, that, 'It is hard to realise how inadequate was the information on which the defence of England had been planned between 1795 and at least 1805.'[2] In fact there had been many surveys of the coast over the preceding 40 years, either for producing maps or, more commonly, for assessing the defensive potential of the different stretches of shore. One of the first had been produced by William Roy, a great pioneer of British map-making, in 1765.[3] In 1783–4 he and others began a great triangulation of the land between London and Paris, work that was to provide the basic framework for later studies. William Mudge of the 'Drawing Room' in the Tower of London carried out a very detailed survey of Kent, accurate down to the field boundaries. This was published in 1801 and was the real foundation of the Ordnance Survey. Further maps were added on a county basis over the next few years, replacing the rather inaccurate county maps that had been produced by private enterprise. The Ordnance Survey map of Essex was published in 1805, and the south coast had been completed by the end of the wars with Napoleon.

By the 1930s the Ordnance Survey had gone through several editions and become a national institution, its military role almost forgotten by the public. It was finding it difficult to keep up with such changes as the new suburbs that dominated the London area, and soldiers of 1940 were warned, 'Even maps of Great Britain, which are as good as possible, are only issued in a revised form every fifteen years, and the constant alterations and additions in a highly civilized area soon render the best work out of date.'[4]

At sea, charting of the coast was less systematic in 1803. The Admiralty Hydrographic Department had been founded in 1795, but it was intended to collate and assess the charts already in existence rather than commission new surveys. It had a whole world to cover, and for knowledge of the British coast sailors tended to rely on the experience of pilots. Important surveys had been completed by the Mackenzies, father and son, in the 1780s. Other naval officers, including Captain Bligh, of *Bounty* fame, had been employed to survey individual sections of the coast. Many more areas had been charted by private enterprise, by firms such as Imray and Norie.

In 1829 the Hydrographer Francis Beaufort began the 'Grand Survey of the British Isles' which was completed by 1855. Charts were to various scales, and one sheet might cover a whole ocean or a single port. They concentrated on sea features and showed the depth at low water in fathoms, but they would also show landmarks useful to the navigator, such as hills and church steeples. Unlike the Ordnance Survey, charts could updated regularly by reading the weekly *Admiralty Notices to Mariners*. The diligent mariner would mark in such changes as the movement of sandbanks, an alteration in the light characteristics of a buoy or new building of harbours and breakwaters. In wartime they also showed minefields and hazards, such as recent wrecks. The Germans could obtain copies through neutral shipping.

Neither the Ordnance Survey map nor the Admiralty Chart answered all the questions. Each was done from its own particular viewpoint of land or sea and did not pay much attention to beaches, where the first actions of a land invasion would take place. To assess the vulnerability of a particular beach it was necessary to know its gradient, and the nature of its surface, whether it could stand the passage of heavy vehicles or was too muddy for troops to pass over it. These could best be assessed by actual observation. In 1796, after Britain had lost her allies on the continent, General Sir David Dundas, the future commander of the Southern District was ordered to report on the coast and defences. The most detailed account of all was produced by General Dumouriez, an emigré Frenchman, in 1803–4. It considered almost every possibility in depth, including such unlikely ones as an invasion of Scotland. Its value was greatly augmented by the author's previous experience – he was able to provide considerable insight into past French invasion plans.[5] On a smaller scale, there were numerous reports on particular districts, especially by engineer officers. These were mainly about the state of fortifications, but they often included suggestions for local defence. In 1803, Colonel William Twiss, the main proponent of Martello Towers (see page 178), compiled detailed reports on the most vulnerable parts of the coast from a military engineer's point of view.

On the naval side, the most extensive survey was that conducted by Lord Keith in August and September 1803. Since Keith was already in command of the North Sea Fleet, the report was more concise than that of Dumouriez; he considered only the most crucial areas of his own command, between Selsea Bill and the Firth of Forth, and dismissed certain areas, such as the Isles of Sheppey and Wight, from consideration; but within these limits he produced a thorough report.[6] The Admiralty also had a supply of detailed and smaller-scale reports.

Officers in charge of the sea fencibles (see page 337), naval rendezvous and signal stations on the coast sent in reports on the manpower and defences together with rough maps of their areas, with comments on landing-places, local people, and how they might aid the defence, and any weak spots they might perceive.

In 1940, Admiral Sir Frederick Dreyer was appointed by the War Office to survey the beaches of the country. He was a distinguished, if rather controversial, gunnery officer who had devised the navy's main fire-control system in the previous war. He was a 'large man without much sense of humour' and 'one of the most outspoken of twentieth century admirals'.[7] He began work on 27 May 1940 when General Ironside ordered him 'to visit all the beaches in the United Kingdom and report to him on the possibility, from a naval point of view, of an enemy landing tanks and other armoured fighting vehicles (A.F.V.s) on them'. He set off by motor car with two staff officers, and they sent their first report by the 29th. By 18 June they had covered every beach between Lyme Regis and Berwick upon Tweed, before embarking on the rest of the country. Dreyer did not confine himself to the most likely areas but considered every possibility – he was imaginative to the point of paranoia and outspoken to the point of insubordination. For example, he produced a detailed case that the enemy might invade north-east England, about as far as possible by sea from his bases in Europe:

> As I approached from over the Morecambe sands to Barrow which has not even a Balloon Barrage over the Vickers Works, it seemed to me that Hitler might be greatly tempted to raid Barrow with sea-borne tanks, hoping to avoid our Naval and Air patrols in thick weather or to carry out the raid with very large forces of Infantry landed with light vehicles from Troop carrying Aircraft alongside Vickers Works on Barrow Island. Each attack to carry large quantities of demolition charges.
>
> The prize is a dazzling one – namely the achievement of a Naval disaster to us, by disrupting our Warship production by smashing Cranes and wrecking locks and docks and machinery. Especially destroying Gun Mountings from 15″ to 0.5″ and Fire Control Towers, &c., &c.[8]

With barely enough forces to defend the south and east, this was not what the authorities wanted to hear.

Dreyer consulted local experts everywhere he went, though usually establishment figures rather than fishermen and beachcombers, who might know the intimate details. He conferred with the marine surveyor of Mersey docks, with an admiral's daughter who was chief coastguard officer in north-east Scotland, and Dr Hogarth of Morecambe, the commander of the Wildfowler's Company of the Home Guard.

Dreyer appreciated that every beach had its unique characteristic and his individual reports were detailed, for example in south-east Scotland:

> LUCE SANDS – a good hard sandy beach some 6 miles long, well sheltered and suitable for tank landings and for landing of troop carrying aircraft.
>
> The beach is a very gently shelving one and landing craft would probably ground at a considerable distance from the shore if landings were attempted at High Water, or alternatively there would be a large expanse of open beach if landings were attempted at Low Water.
>
> The Western and Eastern ends of the beach have been covered with Anti-Aircraft stakes and some of the flat ground inland of the sand burrows.
>
> The beach is backed by sand burrows for a great part of its length rendering the passage of tanks extremely difficult.[9]

The health-giving and recreational values of the seaside had been discovered a few decades before 1803. The King regularly rested in Weymouth, the Prince of Wales made a fashionable resort out of the fishing village of Brighthelmstone [later Brighton], and the virtues of sea-bathing were being exploited at Margate, in competition with inland spas such as Bath and Buxton. But Eastbourne, Southend, Hastings and Folkestone remained small fishing villages while the Ordnance Survey map of 1811 showed 'Bourne Mouth' simply as the mouth of a river, with no sign of human habitation. Beaches remained unobstructed and were open to an invader.

All this changed in the course of the nineteenth and early twentieth centuries. In the Victorian age, steamships and then railways made the coast accessible to people of almost all classes, for day trips as well as longer holidays. Increased wealth and leisure augmented the demand for hotels, theatres and amusement parks. On a suitable stretch of coast, different resorts catered for the tastes and incomes of different classes. Torbay in the south-west had once been a great naval anchorage but it was no longer needed with the building of the Plymouth breakwater and the age of steam. Round its coasts, Torquay became a fashionable resort, Paignton catered for the working classes of the region, and Brixham continued as a picturesque fishing village. In the south-east, Margate was one of the oldest seaside resorts, originally affording sea bathing in privacy 'consistent with the strictest delicacy'. But it was closer to London than the others and became the brashest and most popular resort. Ramsgate combined a large artificial harbour with seaside facilities, while Broadstairs, situated between the two, was a favourite of Charles Dickens and was considered more genteel.

The seaside saw a good deal of development in the 1920s, much of it chaotic. The most notorious was Peacehaven, along the cliffs from Brighton, built soon after World War I (as its name suggests). 'Peacehaven has been called a rash on the countryside. It is that, and there is no worse in England ... Small plots (or stands), yet nothing semi-detached, let alone in terraces. Every man his own house, even if only a few feet from the neighbours.'[10]

The English seaside was preparing for a boom in the late 1930s, as recent legislation had made paid holidays compulsory for all workers. But the war intervened. By 1940 many hotels had been requisitioned for military purposes, and most beaches were covered with obstructions, barbed wire and mines.

Most seaside resorts had piers, originally used for steamer services but later for amusement arcades and small theatres. They might allow an enemy to land with comparative ease, which worried Admiral Dreyer during his visit to East Anglia. 'They thrust themselves into the sea like long arms, inviting tank-landing craft to go alongside them at their outer ends in deep water. And off them the tanks could drive straight inland on to good roads. Next day heavy detonations were heard from his promenade piers, followed by much wailing and gnashing of teeth from infuriated landladies with broken windows.'[11] Apart from that, seaside resorts were not ideal places to land. They were quite densely and solidly built up in their Victorian centres, so tanks and infantry were likely to be bogged down in street fighting at a time when they ought to be moving inland as fast as possible.

Britain is notorious for its variable weather, though extremes of wind or temperature are rare. It is subject to four main patterns – maritime polar air, which is cold and wet; continental polar air from northern Europe, which is cold and dry; maritime tropical air from the Atlantic, which is warm and wet; and continental tropical air from southern Europe, which is dry and warm. The weather is dominated by alternating areas of high and low barometric pressure (the jet stream had not yet been identified as an important determinant of it). A depression is a large area of low pressure that usually originates in the north-west Atlantic between the polar and tropical air fronts. It is many hundreds of miles across and contains air revolving anti-clockwise, with the barometric pressure declining sharply towards the centre and creating strong winds. It also has a system of fronts towards its southern end. The warm front comes first, preceded by lowering levels of clouds many miles in advance and increasing rainfall and winds veering gradually from southerly to south-westerly. The front itself creates a rapid change in wind direction to approximately westerly, a stabilization in barometric pressure, and the onset of a period of warm, humid weather with growing amounts of cloud. The cold front brings a much sharper change than the warm front, with heavy rain, a veering of the wind to north-westerly and a sharp drop in pressure. That is the simplest form of depression, but there are others in which one system of fronts is within another, and it was quite common for depressions to come one after another creating a long period of bad weather – which on the whole was good news for the defenders of Britain, bad news for the invaders. The English had long been told how the weather had dispersed the Spanish Armada and saved them from invasion in 1588.

In contrast there was the 'Protestant wind' a century later, which had kept King James's ships wind-bound and allowed William of Orange to land. That system was probably created by an anticyclone, or area of high pressure. This often extends from the Azores and brings light winds, sparse cumulus clouds, high pressure and good visibility. These conditions would have allowed Napoleon's fragile invasion craft to use their oars while the British warships were becalmed, and Hitler's barges and Stukas would have benefited too. Anticyclones often bring fog in the summer, as warm air passes over the sea which is still relatively cold and creates condensation. Churchill feared that too might benefit the invader: 'The gravest danger, in the opinion of the Prime Minister, was fog, as it would favour the infiltration tactics by which the Germans would most probably attempt to secure their lodgements ...'[12]

A high pressure area might establish itself over Britain for several weeks and bring a very good summer, like the one of 1940, to southern England. A typical weather report of 12 August read:

A large anticyclone extending from the Azores to the British Isles is increasing in intensity and spreading East. A trough of low pressure extending Southwards from Iceland is moving East. Weather will be fair or fine apart from slight rain or drizzle later today in the Northwest of Ireland and Scotland.[13]

The ability to forecast this was something that every commander of an invading force craved.

In 1805 there was no means of predicting the weather beyond what a later generation would call 'single observer' forecasting. There was no way of sending weather information fast enough ahead, especially from ships at sea, and of disseminating it to those who needed to know. The theory of weather was little developed, but over many centuries sailors and farmers had acquired their own systems, often remembered in rhymes. The well known 'Red sky at night, the shepherd's delight' was based on the fact that the redness indicated high pressure in the west, which usually meant that it was approaching Britain; red sky in the morning meant that the high pressure was moving away. 'Mares' tails' or cirrus cloud high in the sky could mean that a cold front was approaching, especially if it was followed by a deepening cloud base. Stratocumulus, or 'mackerel sky', could indicate some turbulence in the atmosphere. The rough state of the sea might also give indication of bad weather many miles away. Even as he lay dying at the Battle of Trafalgar, Nelson was able to predict a storm out in the Atlantic. For more scientific weather observations, the barometer was available and a rapid fall in the pressure would indicate the onset of bad weather.

Forecasting was much improved in the twentieth century by the use of radio, the development of theories of weather and the use of aircraft to make high-level observations. Since most bad weather came in from the Atlantic, the British had a natural advantage in 1940 in that they had more ships and aircraft in the region and could rely on reports from the United States, Canada and Newfoundland. Surface observations were obtained from British territories, Ireland and Iceland, as well as from Spain, Portugal and the Azores. Upper air observations were made from aircraft based at Mildenhall in eastern England, Aldergrove in Northern Ireland and Wick in Scotland. Balloons were sent up regularly from Lerwick, Liverpool, Larkhill (on Salisbury Plain) and Penzance. There were special weather reconnaissance flights from the north-west and south-west of the United Kingdom, and these proved very useful, though by their nature they could not provide the regular observations at fixed times that were essential. In peacetime the Admiralty had encouraged ships to send in weather observations by radio, but obviously that could not be done in war. United States reports were available in the area west of 65 degrees, and they maintained two weather ships between the Azores and Bermuda. But daily reports from seven key Atlantic areas were regarded as 'the only satisfactory basis of an Atlantic synoptic organisation', and ships passing close to these points would send in information. A specialized weather ship was fitted out in October 1940 but discontinued in July 1941 due to enemy action.[14] Meteorology was still an imprecise science, and the weathermen could claim with justification that they were working with barely adequate information.

As well as a variable weather pattern, the British Isles are dominated by unusually strong tides. A great volume of water is pulled in from the Atlantic by the moon and other heavenly bodies every twelve hours or so, then retreats. It is funnelled by estuaries and channels to create very strong forces. Tides have two main effects, one of which is the rise and fall of the sea level. The Bristol Channel has the third highest range in the world, around 40 feet, as the tide goes up a narrowing estuary. Even the English Channel, a far more likely invasion area, has a range of up to 25 feet at Hastings. This was important for an invader, for it was believed on both sides of the Channel that an army had to land around the time of high tide to get the maximum water for his landing craft and shorten the distance he had to travel over open beaches. That meant that he might only have as little as four hours out of the twelve to achieve his purposes. The time of high tide varies along the length of the Channel, so that high water at Plymouth is 5 hours and 36 minutes after that at Dover. If the enemy were to attack on a broad front, this might make it more difficult to coordinate his landing.

Secondly, tides create currents, which are at their strongest midway between high and low tide. This could affect the navigation of craft towards their landing area and was particularly important in the final approach. An hour or two before or after high water they might be pushing the craft sideways at a rate of one or two knots as they approached the beach. This could make a considerable difference to a vessel which could only do six or eight knots maximum. It needed a good deal of navigational skill and a certain amount of confidence to aim off by exactly the right amount so that one would land on the correct part of the beach. Sailors and bargemen used to the tideless Baltic or the canals did not always appreciate this, and their training periods were short. And even when he hit the beach, the barge coxswain's problems were not over. His bow was aground and his stern was afloat, so the tide might sweep his stern round to an awkward angle unless he was skilled in the use of the stern anchor. An invasion of Britain had many difficulties and hazards, not all created by the defending forces, and any commander attempting it would be well advised to bear this in mind.

THE INVASION BEACHES

In theory no part of the British Isles could be ruled out as a possible site of invasion. If the French fleet had gained temporary control of the seas, it might attack almost anywhere. In 1940 the Germans had the use of air power that could conceivably have defeated the RAF and then the Royal Navy and might open up even more possibilities for invasion sites. But in practice there were two considerations that limited the enemy options. Firstly, a blow away from south or east England would be far less devastating and would not lead to the immediate capture of London and defeat of the state. Secondly, the range of the French invasion flotilla was extremely limited. A fleet of transports could go anywhere, but the flotilla craft would be hard put to go more than 100 miles from their base. For the Germans, it was the range of their fighter aircraft that constrained them, though at first the British believed that they might strike anywhere on the English east coast.

An enemy invasion of Ireland was always on the agenda, but this was rather different from the invasion of mainland Britain. In 1803, the Irish people remained largely disaffected and would regard the invaders as liberators if properly handled. The Brest squadron was well placed for such an invasion. On the other hand, French victory in Ireland would not immediately lead to British national defeat – the British defences would be outflanked, and invasion of the mainland made much more likely, but another invasion would still be necessary for complete French victory. The invasion of Ireland was a special case, and not simply a variation on the invasion of England. An Irish invasion would be a combination of a colonial war and a war of liberation, not a blow at the British heartland. But it could create a very serious diversion, especially if it was supported by the Irish. The French made several attempts over the years: in 1796 Hoche's attempt at Bantry Bay was defeated by the weather, in 1798 Humbert was defeated at Castlebar and Ballinamuck, and Wolfe Tone at Vinegar Hill.

Ireland offered even more striking opportunities for the Germans in 1940. The great bulk of food, oil and goods imported for the British war effort came via Liverpool and the Clyde. A German conquest of Ireland would seal these off, and make it almost impossible for Britain to survive. The Irish government under Eamon de Valera resisted any British attempts to involve them in the war, but they could not be considered immune from invasion, in view of German actions in Norway. Memories of savage British repression were less than twenty

160

Above: An engraving of Nelson after Lemuel Francis Abbott's portrait.

Above: Napoleon as First Consul, an engraving after a portrait by Andrea Appiani the Elder.

Below: Hitler and his staff in his headquarters at the Berghof in July 1940, probably planning the invasion of Britain. Also in the picture are Field Marshal von Brauchitsch, General Jodl and Field Marshal Keitel. (IWM HU 75542)

Above: Unemployed men search for work in the newspapers in a public library. (Getty Images)

Below: Production at the Morris car works in Cowley near Oxford in 1930. (Getty Images)

Above: The Old Berkeley Hunt hold their first meet of the season at Latimer House, Chesham, Buckinghamshire, 1935. (Getty Images)

Below: The happier side of evacuation. Mrs Carter has Sunday lunch with the evacuated children Michael and Angela in Haywards Heath south of London in 1940. (IWM D 258)

Above: Children carrying gas masks enter the Anderson shelter in the garden of their home in Eltham south-east of London in 1940. (IWM D 778)

Above: Churchill inspects bomb damage in Ramsgate, Kent, in August 1940. (IWM H 3514)

Below: Evacuees on their way to safety. (CPL)

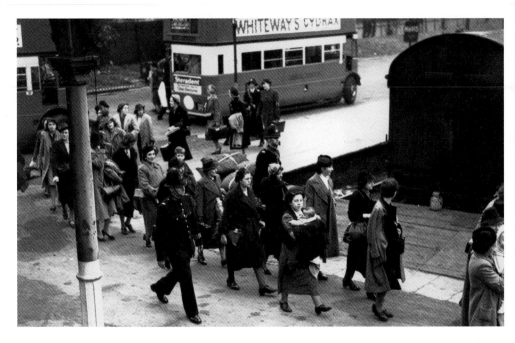

Above: Alien women and children are escorted to the railway station to be interned on the Isle of Man. (Getty Images)

Below: The Chiefs of Staff at the beginning of the war – Ironside, Newall and Pound. (IWM HU 59548)

Above: A photo reconnaissance view of Boulogne in September 1940. The successor to Napoleon's basin is near the top of the picture, with the channel leading to the sea, protected by breakwaters, to the bottom. (IWM C 2582)

Above: Parts of the defences on the beach at Sandgate near Folkestone, an obvious target for invasion in 1940 as in 1805. (IWM H 2187)

Left: Beach defences near Great Yarmouth. July–August 1940. (IWM H 2702)

years old, and in August 1940 Lord Louis Mountbatten (who would be killed by an Irish terrorist bomb in 1979) went so far as to claim that, 'Those who know Ireland really well maintain that if the Germans landed, say at Cork, the Irish would resist all help from England; in fact it is maintained that they would definitely resist any advance of British troops to fight the Germans.'[15] Churchill ruled out any pre-emptive action, partly because 'that might compromise our position with the United States of America ...'[16]

Scotland was not considered a likely area in 1803–5, and Dumouriez agreed. 'In no case does Scotland run much risk of a great invasion by Bonaparte.' It was far away from the French bases and the British capital; an army landing in central Scotland would easily be cut off; and 'the Scotch are the most likely soldiers in the British Empire to stop the French, thanks to their similar mode of fighting.'[17] Wales could also be ruled out, being 'so mountainous and so poor a country, that the enemy would never have sufficient motive for a descent, unless the possession of Ireland enabled him to recruit adherents in Wales ... The province is too distant, too difficult to march in; too denuded of supplies and transport, and its mountain ranges are too close and frequent.'[18] Likewise the west coast of England was not likely to be invaded. In practice, the likely targets were limited to the south and east coasts of England. Even here, the danger was limited to certain areas. Dundas remarked, 'It seems evident that the enemy's most desirable projects and advantage begin from the east of Kent, and diminish in proportion as they are obliged to land to the westward.' Dreyer was much more broadminded in 1940, and more sober voices did not rule out the possibility of diversionary attacks in the north, perhaps launched from Norway.

The south-west of England was always a possible site of invasion. British defences were quite widely stretched in this area, the whole coast of Dorset, for example, being guarded by a total of 43 serviceable guns in 1798.[19] But the natural defences of the area were strong. In general the coast west of the Isle of Wight is high and rocky, with few landing places. One of the best is in Torbay, which was 'an excellent roadstead, the whole coast of which is fit to be landed on with west or north west winds.'[20] The last successful invasion of Britain, by William of Orange, had indeed landed there in 1688. But Torbay was a main anchorage for the British Channel Fleet during the age of sail and was never entirely free of major ships of war. Any landing in the West Country would be threatened by ships from Plymouth and Portsmouth, and would be risky without full command of the sea. Furthermore, Cornwall and Devon are a long way from the main centre of power in London, and an army landing in the south-west peninsula might well be cut off unless it moved out very quickly.

Farther east, the Dorset coast offered no good landing places, though Portland might have provided a useful anchorage for a fleet with command of the sea. The Isle of Wight was quite well defended, and has high cliffs on its seaward sides. Furthermore, as Keith pointed out, 'I hardly think the enemy will land on an island like Wight, unless he had the superiority by sea, because it would not be easy to get off it to the main if we take common precautions. Besides there are a great number of ships and frigates at Spithead and a stationary force at St Helens.'[21]

Though the north of England was far from being the centre of either British or French plans, a landing there would cut the country in two and threaten the industrial and mining areas, on which British wealth depended. However, an army there would risk being cut off and having to fight on two fronts. According to Dumouriez, 'If they landed in Northumberland they would be shut up between the Tweed and the Tyne, and the [English] squadrons would cut off their retreat by sea and so compel them to lay down their arms.'[22] Landings farther south in Durham or Yorkshire would face similar hazards..

Nevertheless, Admiral Keith considered the possibilities of a northern landing. The River Humber was 'an object of much consequence, and I will have a ship of the line and at least one frigate stationed in it'.[23] There were possible landing sites at Bridlington, Filey and Robin Hood's Bay; but Newcastle and the Tyne were out of the question because the bar was 'so dangerous and so well defended that I think the river safe unless the enemy should land on the south side in fine weather, in which case he would command the river, but the length of voyage gives reasonable hope that our ships be on the coast before him.'[24]

In 1940, the possibility of a landing in the north of England seemed more serious, at least until the possibility of air cover could be disregarded. On 15 August the Luftwaffe sent 65 bombers and 35 Messerschmitt 110 fighters from Norway to raid the north of England. The new British radar chain was able to detect them in time to send up a strong fighter force. Eight German bombers and seven fighters were shot down against no losses by Fighter Command, and the bombing was ineffective. It was clear that the Germans could never get air superiority in that area.

The limits of the invasion area are difficult to define, but it is probably realistic to set them at East Anglia in the north, and Selsea Bill in the west. In 1940, far more than in 1803, a landing in East Anglia was considered highly likely. Admiral Dreyer discounted the Wash because of its flat beaches. 'Without daylight, clear weather and local knowledge, the risk of grounding would be great ... but if the day is clear enough for shore marks to be seen, the flotilla could be seen from the shore and surprise would be impossible.'[25] In 1803 the British naval base at Yarmouth made a landing north of that area unlikely, and one too close to it would be hazardous, but in 1940 Dreyer took it seriously. Weybourne on the north coast of Norfolk was described by the Port Admiral at Sheerness as one of only two beaches where barges could land at all states of the tide. That was not borne out by charts that showed several such beaches in East Anglia alone, but it was mentioned in a prophecy by the sixteenth-century self-styled prophetess Old Mother Shipton:

If Boney would old England win,
He must at Weybourne Hoop begin.[26]

Dreyer was less poetic but he found that on the stretch of coast from Blakeney to Winterton, 'the foreshore presents no serious difficulty to a landing, except just east of Cromer, where Foulness shoals extend a mile off shore and raise a high sea in strong winds'; but he could see no obvious military objective in the north-west of that area. A landing to capture the ports of Great Yarmouth and Lowestoft could be effected at Winterton. The coast off the two ports was difficult because of 'the shoals which from Yarmouth Roads obstruct direct approach to the town front', but it was possible to land between the two towns. The coast south of Lowestoft as far as Aldeburgh was also possible, and according to Admiral Keith in 1803, 'From Orfordness to Yarmouth it is an open coast and I think that landing there would be exposed and uncertain.'[27] In 1940, Dreyer thought, 'Though the exits from the beaches are limited, the hinterland gives good access inland without serious natural obstacles. An attempt to land on this part of the coast may therefore be a major operation, including the occupation of Harwich as a base.'

South of Aldeburgh the rivers Ore and Alde run parallel to the coast, and Dreyer was sure that these would 'prohibit advance inland except to infantry with collapsible boats'. The stretch of coast north of Harwich harbour is relatively straight and penetrated by the river Deben. According to Admiral Keith, 'The beach is good and within Bawdsey Sand may be landed upon, but in Hollesley Bay and towards Orfordness I doubt it, because I was there in fine weather with the wind from the land and yet there was wash upon the beach; beside it is a long peninsula of shingle running up to Orford Castle.'[28] The great natural harbour of Harwich, where the rivers Stour and Orwell join and enter the sea, was well protected in 1803 because it had once been a major naval base, and the fort at Landguard was the core of the defence. It had revived as a naval base by 1940 as the centre for North Sea escort forces, and their presence would probably deter a direct attempt at invasion.

Between Harwich and the River Blackwater, and east of its tributary, the Colne, is a coast that is today dominated by the resorts of Clacton, Frinton and Walton, but which was undeveloped in 1803. It was protected by an offshore bank, the Gunfleet, forming an anchorage known as the Wallet. Keith rather played down the danger here – 'The whole of the Wallet is a harbour and most of its coast is fit to land upon, but the water is so deep as to admit of ships sailing near the shore all over it'[29] – in other words, the shallow draught of the French flotilla craft would give it no special advantage. An attack up the River Blackwater itself was considered much more likely. Dumouriez recommended strong batteries to prevent this.

Attack south of the Blackwater was unlikely. Foulness Island, immediately north of the Thames estuary, had the disadvantages of all islands from an invader's point of view and was fronted by unusually wide sandbanks, which would have made any landing difficult. The Dengie peninsula, to the north of that, lies between the rivers Crouch and Roach. It too had very wide sandbanks on its seaward side, and its neck was rather narrow, so that an army landed there could easily be cut off.

In the past it had often been assumed that the Thames estuary was immune from attack because of the intricacy of the channels among its numerous sandbanks. With the advent of the shallow-draught invasion flotilla, these banks might be turned to advantage by the invader. The area was not threatened by the Boulogne flotilla but by the enemy possession of ports such as Flushing and Den Helder. Unlike the south-east peninsula, Essex is low lying, with few hills of any height, and is divided into a number of peninsulas, by several wide rivers.

The area south and east of London was always considered the most likely scene of an invasion in 1803–5, with good reason. It was closest to the French ports, especially Boulogne. It included much rich agricultural land, and many potential landing beaches. It was dominated by hills rather than impassable mountains, and its rivers were rarely wide or deep enough to impede the passage of a determined army for very long. It had seen the invasions of Romans, Saxons, Vikings and Normans, and had figured in the plans of Phillip II of Spain and of the Bourbon kings of France. It also offered a relatively short and easy march to London, and the prospect of a quick victory.

This area consists of the counties of Kent, Sussex and Surrey. It is bounded by the Thames and its estuary to the north, the English Channel to the south, and the North Sea to the east. It contains three main ranges of hills, each of which ends at the coast and forms a section of cliff, which makes landing almost impossible – the main invasion beaches were to be found in the gaps between the ranges. The chalk hills of the North Downs run south of London and end in the area of Dover. The South Downs are also chalk hills, running close to the coast and ending at Beachy Head. Between these are the clay hills of the Wealden

range, lower and less extensive than the other two, and ending at
Fairlight Head, near Hastings. There is another range just south of the
North Downs, then known as the Iron and Ragstone Range. It is 'lower
than the other three already mentioned. It ... presents a steep face to the
south, and slopes gently towards the chalk hills to the north.'[30] The four
ranges provided suitable positions for defence. In many places their
south-facing sides are quite steep and would be difficult for an army to
climb, especially when opposed; however, none presented an
insuperable obstacle.

The area has no rivers of great size, apart from the Medway and the
Thames itself. Above Rochester, the Medway cuts a deep valley through
the North Downs, which presented both advantages and disadvantages to
the defence – it would be difficult to cross, but easier to march along,
towards the dockyard at Chatham. The Medway widens at Rochester,
and after the bridge there it was very difficult to cross. Other rivers are
much smaller. The Stour runs through Canterbury and reaches the sea at
Sandwich. Never more than a hundred feet wide, it could be bridged by
pontoons. It cuts a valley through the North Downs, which might be used
to mount a rearward attack on Thanet. The River Darent runs northwards
to join the Thames at Dartford and also cuts a valley in the Downs.

The Kent coast forms the south side of the Thames Estuary.
Upstream of Whitstable the estuary is considerably narrowed by the Isle
of Sheppey. Keith considered an attack there unlikely, as the enemy
would not wish to be trapped on an island. A direct attack up the River
Thames was equally improbable. The north side of the estuary was
sparsely inhabited in 1803 and was dominated by marshlands and wide
sandbanks. It was not seriously considered as a place of invasion. After
Whitstable the coast is relatively straight and runs from west to east.
From Whitstable to Reculver a landing was quite possible. 'The coast
from Bishopstown [near modern Herne Bay] to Whitstable is good for
landing upon but the water is shallow. Boats of small draught may in
good weather land at half flood.'[31] However, the north Kent coast was
little defended, and Keith was concerned. He feared a pincer movement,
with one attack at Romney Marsh, the other at Whitstable. East Kent
would be cut off, Thanet could be taken from the rear, the anchorage in

the Downs threatened, and the rich resources of the county would be available to the enemy.[32]

In the north-east of the peninsula is the 'Isle' of Thanet, where the Thames Estuary ends. The former Wantsum channel, which had once separated it from the mainland, had been drained by the late Middle Ages. Ancient ports such as Sandwich, Sarre and Fordwich had been greatly reduced in importance. The easterly part was the area of the old channel: 'The coast from west by Reculver, to near Margate, is low and in many places inaccessible.' The former island was an area of higher ground, largely surrounded with cliffs on its seaward sides. In 1803, 'From Margate, where there is a battery, to Ramsgate, the shore is bounded by high cliffs, and in some parts there is a sandy beach under them, but on the whole, it may be deemed inaccessible.'[33] It had three useful ports, at Ramsgate, Margate and Broadstairs, all of which were already resorts in 1803.

Just south of Thanet is Pegwell Bay, which attracted some misgivings, and indeed featured in at least one Napoleonic plan.[34] Keith thought that it was 'too difficult and that it is protected by being in the immediate vicinity of the Downs.'[35] From Sandwich to Deal there are five miles of flat land and good beaches. This area was very close to the French bases at Boulogne and in the Low Countries; a landing there would allow quick access to Thanet, with its valuable ports. In 1803–5 it was protected mainly by Henry VIII's three ancient forts at Sandown, Deal and Walmer, but the area relied mainly on the fleet for its defence. A few miles off Deal were the Goodwin Sands, which formed a natural breakwater. Between them and the coast was the Downs, a great natural anchorage. It was much used by merchantmen waiting for a wind to take them up to London or down the Channel; it was also continually occupied by British ships of the line and frigates, in substantial numbers. Keith discounted an attack there. 'I think the Downs are secure, unless the enemy be superior at sea.'[36] The Downs do not seem to have been taken seriously as a candidate for invasion in 1940, perhaps because of the Goodwin Sands.

Dover is the nearest point on the British coast to France. It was not a likely place for a landing in 1803–5, though its capture afterwards would have done serious damage to British defence. The town nestles in a small valley cut by the River Dour, and is easily defended. The natural strength had been greatly increased by fortifications on the hills. Originally it had only a small harbour, but at the beginning of the twentieth century that was greatly expanded by the building of breakwaters. This made the town a much greater prize, and its capture was considered by the German paratroop General Kurt Student, though only after it was too late to execute it. Furthermore, capture of Dover would secure the German passage through the Strait. Sir Dudley Pound wrote:

> While it might be accepted on other parts of the coast that our coast defences are a 'crust' and the main body of resistance would be found further back, that rule must not apply to the Dover area where the coast-line must be held at all costs. Under no conditions could we accept that the Germans get any footing there at all.[37]

To the west of Dover, the cliffs continue for about five miles, and include the famous Shakespeare Cliff, 'a rocky coast, not open to descent'.[38] The first break comes at East Wear Bay, just east of Folkestone. Keith considered this a possible landing place in the right conditions, though Dumouriez believed it was 'impracticable'.[39] It has a narrow foreshore, but the cliffs soon ascend to provide a natural defence. The town of Folkestone was unlikely to be attacked, as the coast is fronted with cliffs. But just west of the town is Sandgate, which afforded possible landing places, also backed by higher land.

Three miles west of Folkestone the cliffs come to an end, and at the town of Hythe begins a long, flat stretch of coastline, forming the edges of Romney Marsh, another area of marshland, which had been reclaimed in medieval times. Ports such as Romney, Rye and Winchelsea had been separated from the sea by the reclamation of land. The marsh forms a kind of triangle, with two sides formed by the sea. The third side, to the north-west, is dominated by hills. This area was long regarded as the primary target for invasion in 1803–5. The marsh had two sides, so that the invaders could choose one or the other, to be protected from the winds. The marsh had risen from the sea relatively recently, so it had not been included in Henry VIII's scheme of defence. It provided a flat area on which the newly landed troops could regroup, and an easy route to London, or wherever Napoleon might wish to take his army. During the Napoleonic Wars it was to receive more attention, and expenditure, than any other area of the British coast. And to Admiral Dreyer in 1940, Romney Marsh was 'an exceptionally good landing beach'. He campaigned to have Romney Marsh flooded, but was told it was too valuable as agricultural land.[40]

From the sea the most easterly and most important part of the marsh is the area from Hythe to Dymchurch, forming a shallow bay sheltered from the west and north. According to Keith, 'In Hythe Bay, the beach is good, and may be landed on at half tides, with the wind off the land ... From Hythe to Dymchurch wall, the beach is good for landing at half tides.'[41] The second part was the tip of the peninsula, including the point at Dungeness. Here the British authorities were less afraid of a landing. According to Captain Bligh, 'Dungeness is probably the most extraordinary mass of pebbles ever seen, over which it is difficult to pass, that it is like a barrier to the country for full two miles. The beaches are steep, and a heavy sea rolls on them in bad weather, but landing can generally be effected on one side or the other of the ness point.'[42] According to Dundas, 'If an enemy were to attempt a landing on this part of the coast, the most likely place would seem to be near Hythe or Rye; for though the water is so deep off Dungeness that ships of any burthen can come almost close to the shore, yet it being next to impossible to move through the middle of the marsh lands, an enemy would be reduced to the necessity of advancing along the sea walls by Dymchurch ... or by the Jew's Gap and on towards Rye.'[43] On the west side of Romney Marsh is another bay, called Rye Bay. This is shallower than Hythe Bay, with no protection from the south-west winds, but it had suitable beaches and provided a quick route inland without having to cross the marsh.

After Rye Bay, the coast rises again at the cliffs around Fairlight. Then from Hastings to Eastbourne are fifteen miles of low land between the ridges of hills, with some landing beaches. In 1803 it was believed Hastings itself 'lacks sufficiently spacious a beach to admit of a landing

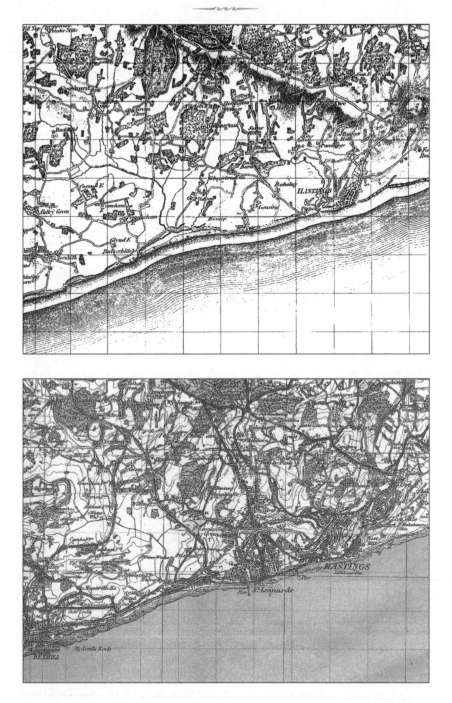

The Ordnance Survey map of the Hastings area, 1813 and 1920–1.

in force',[44] but Pevensey Bay provided good landing, as did the area round the modern resort of Eastbourne. After that the cliffs rise again, to a pinnacle at Beachy Head.

West of Beachy Head, the South Downs run parallel to the sea for some way and provide a natural defence; but then the cliffs 'become gradually lower at Brighthelmstone [Brighton], where they disappear, from thence, westwards to Chichester, the shore is everywhere flat, and the sea ebbs out a considerable way at low water.'[45] A landing in this area would provide the shortest route to London, albeit it over three ranges of hills; conversely, it was 60 miles or more from the French base at Boulogne and perilously close to the British fleet base at Portsmouth. The same was true of the coast west of Selsea Bill. By 1936 it was subject to a good deal of development, and Hilaire Belloc wrote:

> To-day the villages are linking up with the towns. Rustington has long been full of bricks. Rottingdean has now long been a suburb. A curious collection of bungalows has sprung up on the long pebbly beach which shuts out the Adur from the sea: and even upon the extremity of old Selsea a new settlement has risen. Seaford, which was saved for a time by its hills, fell into line. Bognor stretched out towards Littlehampton and now Littlehampton is preparing to meet Bognor.[46]

These were the natural defences of the country. The two great questions in 1803 and 1940 were: how could they be improved to keep the enemy out? And how far did the British assessment of the practicalities match what the enemy planned?

7

THE DEFENCES

DEFENCES AGAINST NAPOLEON

With its famous 'wooden walls' to defend its shores, Britain had little tradition of fortification in 1803. There was no native style of fortification, no British Vauban or Coehorn. The country had its share of Roman and medieval castles, built to show the authority of the state or a local baron, or as symbols of conquest in Wales. They were intended as protection during civil war, rebellion, conflict between the different countries in Britain and against general brigandage. Their high walls were easy to demolish with gunfire. Sometimes they had been modernized, like Dover; sometimes they were derelict and ruined, like Corfe Castle in Dorset. Some of its older cities were at least partly walled, like York and Canterbury, and there were more modern fortifications round Berwick upon Tweed, to keep the Scots out of England. Fast-growing cities like London and Edinburgh had outgrown their walls and almost forgotten about them, while the industrial and commercial ones like Birmingham and Liverpool had never had them.

The English navy had not always been strong. Henry VIII was faced with powerful enemies after he renounced the Roman Catholic Church in the sixteenth century, and he built the first systematic chain of coastal defence forts since the Romans had tried to keep out the Saxons more than a millennium earlier. Henry built two dozen defensive works, intended to deny the enemy the use of harbours after a landing. Ten of them, all on the south coast and in Kent, were major fortifications that survived through the centuries. The strongest ones were overlooking the anchorage at the Downs, in the Solent and protecting Falmouth Harbour in Cornwall. They were mostly low-built for protection against artillery, and all were designs based upon the circle. In the simplest form,

Calshot Castle, at the entrance to Southampton Water, was a high, round tower inside a much lower one, with a circular moat. Deal Castle on the Downs was also centred on a round tower with a tall watchtower inside it. Around this was a ring of six lower, round towers, then six more larger, but yet lower ones, all surrounded by a moat that reflected the shape of the work.

The weakness of the English navy, or more accurately of a divided political system, was shown in 1667 when the Dutch were able to raid the fleet in the River Medway and carry off the flagship, *Royal Charles*. Charles II employed the Dutch engineer Bernard de Gomme to build forts round the growing Royal Dockyards at Portsmouth and Chatham and protecting the entrances to the Thames and Medway. His greatest was the Citadel overlooking Plymouth Sound, though the area did not then have a dockyard of its own.

This was the period when Marshal de Vauban was building massive fortresses to protect France and when fortification was developing into almost a precise science. In Britain it was quite rare to find a fort in the purest form because of coastal geography. If an army was strong or rash enough to approach a fort directly, it would have to ascend a gentle slope of around ten degrees, called the glacis. The fort itself was kept as low as practicable, and its ramparts were only just visible, but the attackers would already be under fire from them. After a march of several hundred yards, the attacker would reach the first line of defence, a palisade of wooden spikes, lightly manned by the defenders. Having defeated that, the attacking army was now faced with the ditch, which was generally wide if it was filled with water as at Sheerness, or narrow if it was dry so that the attacker would find it difficult to get his guns to bear on the base of the masonry on the other side. The outer wall of the ditch was called the counterscarp revetment, and on the other side of it was a much higher wall, the scarp revetment. This, the main defence, was usually constructed of masonry and was almost vertical. Above it was a sloping parapet with a fire-step behind it, where the defending gunners and musketeers stood, and the wider terreplein behind that. Fort Amherst in Chatham has something like this classic cross-section, which can be seen where the modern road cuts through it.

The fort was also designed to create flanking fire in every direction. Its basic plan relied on straight lines; modern engineers were aware that circles created dead ground where attackers could hide. On flat land the pattern was usually a regular polygon, perhaps five-sided, as with Tilbury Fort on the Thames and Fort Cumberland near Portsmouth. It might be straight, as with much of the lines that protected Chatham Dockyard, or curved, as at Portsmouth. The contours of the coast might demand a more irregular shape, like De Gomme's Citadel at Plymouth.

The seaward side of a fort might well be straight to allow the maximum number of guns to bear on attacking ships, as at Tilbury. On the landward side, each corner was fitted with a strong bastion, carefully designed so that its guns could fire across the flanks of an enemy attacking the wall of the fortress or an adjacent bastion. Many European fortresses went much further than that and had numerous and complicated outworks, which were often reached by tunnel and gave a characteristic star plan to the fortress. Few British forts went as far as this, though many, including the dockyard defences, had triangular works known as ravelins, which were reached by covered way.

During the American War of Independence (1775–83), there was a serious threat of invasion, and the defences around the dockyards were strengthened with the building of Fort Amherst at Chatham and the fortification of Gosport, opposite Portsmouth. Batteries were built at many places, including Great Yarmouth and Lowestoft on the east coast.

Fortification was defined as, 'the art of fortifying a town or other place; or of putting it in such a posture of defence, that every one of its parts defends, and is defended by some other parts, by means of ramparts, ditches, and other outworks; to the end that a small number of men may be able to defend themselves for a considerable time against the assaults of a numerous army without; so that the enemy, in attacking them, must of necessity, suffer great loss.'[1] Fortifications could also buy time, but no fortress could hold out for ever. In the past the French had used elaborate systems of entrenchment and mining to attack them, but Napoleon was more inclined to by-pass them and let them fall later. Fieldworks were different from fortifications: the former were relatively simple to construct, usually in earth and built by the troops on the spot, with or without expert supervision from the Royal Engineers.

Military engineers had been employed by the British crown since Norman times, but it was only in 1716 that they were given a permanent form, and in 1757 they took on military rank. They became the Corps of Royal Engineers in 1787, an officers-only body. Manual work was done by troops from other units or by hired civilian labour until the Royal Military Artificers were formed in 1787. A company consisted of a hundred men, including carpenters, bricklayers, masons, smiths, wheelers, sawyers, miners, painters, coopers and labourers. But at home or abroad much of the work in building fortifications was still done by infantrymen or contract labour.

Each year about 300 potential officers enrolled as Gentlemen Cadets in the Royal Military Academy at Woolwich at the age of 14 to 16. Regulations demanded, 'No youth to be admitted until he is well grounded in vulgar fractions, writes a good hand, and has gone through the Latin grammar.' He was advised to have a good knowledge of French, in which most books on fortification were published.[2] Cadets learned a great deal of mathematical formulae, as used by a fortifications engineer, but according to Captain Charles Pasley in 1809, 'As to practical instruction, they had none; for they were sent on service without having seen a fascine or gabion, without the smallest knowledge of the military passage of rivers, of military mining, or any other operation of a siege, excepting what they might pick up from French writers ...'[3] In other words, they learned the defensive arts of fortification but not the more offensive ones of siege warfare and bridging. This was not so much of a problem in the defensive campaign against the invasion.

The Royal Engineers, like the Royal Artillery, were raised and organized by the Ordnance Board. In 1799 the Commander-in-Chief, the Duke of York, formed his own body, the misleadingly titled Royal Staff Corps, who were essentially combat engineers. They had rank and file as well as officers and were to assist the Quartermaster General 'in executing all Field Works, taking up of ground, choosing and surveying Military positions, conducting the different columns of the Army in the

Field, breaking up or repairing roads, bridges, etc., and in particular in directing the labour of Military working parties to advantage'.[4] Almost forgotten by history, they did much of the work on the new defences.[5] On the Royal Military Canal in 1805, civilian labourers were paid 5s. 6d. (27½ p) per day, while soldiers had two shillings (10p) in addition to their wages and rations.[6]

The work of fortification was overseen by the Royal Engineer Committee at the Tower of London, 'to which all Plans and Estimates for the Construction of New Works or Buildings, or for the Repair or Alteration of old ones were referred ...' It had not worked well in the past and for the moment it operated only on a temporary basis.[7]

Apart from Henry VIII's forts, the fixed defences of 1803 were largely concentrated around the Royal Dockyards and the major estuaries. The coast of East Anglia was little defended in 1803 apart from works around the natural harbour at Harwich. Since this coast faced directly on to the enemy-held bases in the Netherlands, it was considered vulnerable. The north bank of the Thames estuary was also devoid of permanent fortifications. Where the estuary narrowed at Sheerness, De Gomme's fort protected the dockyard there, the entrance to the Medway, the Nore anchorage and the Thames itself. The Thames and Medway were both protected by forts and batteries, carefully sited near the bends so that they could fire on the enemy when he was in the process of turning or tacking. But an invasion or raid up either river was extremely unlikely, unless the Royal Navy had already suffered a catastrophic defeat or the enemy had landed elsewhere and established a foothold. It was rather different on the north coast of Kent, which Admiral Keith considered very open, but no defences were planned there.

The Downs, off the east coast of Kent, was still a major naval anchorage, and perhaps that is why no new work had been done there since Henry VIII's three castles at Sandown, Deal and Walmer. Dover, to the south, was a special case. It had a huge castle, including a Roman lighthouse, a Saxon church and a Norman keep, enclosed in several concentric layers of wall that came to an abrupt end at the edge of the famous white cliffs. Dover Castle had been partly modernized during the mid-century wars between 1739 and 1748, by lowering the medieval walls and towers and digging ditches. Its strategic situation was vital, and no less an authority than Henry Dundas had claimed in 1798:

> Without Dover Castle the enemy can have no certain communication; and always supposing that on shore he finds no means to advance his purpose, the bringing up and placing sufficient artillery to reduce it is a work of slow process and would give time to relieve it.

If it fell,

> The possession to an enemy of Dover Castle and the opposite entrenched [Western] Height and of the town and port, fortified in the manner which he would soon accomplish and defended by 6 or 7,000 men would establish a sure communication with France and could not easily be wrested from his hands.[8]

Much effort was expended in its defence, mostly conducted by Lieutenant Colonel William Twiss, a very experienced Royal Engineer with a bird-like nose and receding forehead. He had far larger budgets than his predecessors, but he continued their work of reducing the medieval towers, and he built four outworks to command the slopes of the hills below. Archcliffe Fort was much lower down and was modernized to defend the town and harbour, while the hill opposite the Castle, already partly fortified as Western Heights, was greatly improved during 1804. With the much smaller Archcliffe Fort at lower level, the whole area was by far the strongest coastal fortification in England by early 1805.

The gap in the cliffs east of Folkestone was protected by Henry VIII's Sandgate Castle, which was in poor condition, and an extensive programme of modernization began in 1805. The highly vulnerable area of Romney Marsh was protected only by five batteries at Dungeness, two smaller ones on each side of the point and a huge 460-foot octagonal ring built in the shingle that was the only resource of the area. In 1805 its armament was upgraded to eleven 24-pounder guns.[9] The main hope was that the marsh could be flooded before the enemy had time to establish himself, but there was 'considerable doubt ... should the inundation be delayed till an enemy is on the point of sailing, whether a sufficient effect can be produced by the influx of the sea, previous to the moment when we are to apprehend that some of the principal sluices may fall into his possession ...' [10]

East of Dungeness, Rye was protected by Camber Castle, another of Henry VIII's forts. Due to changes in the coastline, it was now about a mile inland and had long been abandoned. There was no other permanent fortification until Pevensey Castle, more than twenty miles to the east, and built by the Romans. Apart from Dover, there was little in the way of fortifications to stop an enemy landing in south-east England.

In 1805 the government began to build the first large-scale beach defences, intended to stop the enemy army as it landed rather than stop it taking harbours afterwards. The idea of coastal towers came from the Mediterranean, where isolated square or circular towers were a common form of protection against raids by Barbary corsairs. Famously, the British Mediterranean Fleet had been put to a good deal of trouble in 1794 when it attempted to take Mortella Tower in Corsica, one of the witnesses to which was Sir David Dundas, now commanding the army in the Southern District. 'Mortella' was eventually corrupted to 'Martello', to give the towers their popular name. But it was the taking of Minorca in 1798 that provided a more direct inspiration, for the towers there were seen by Captain W. H. Ford, a witty and ingenious officer who submitted a plan by July 1803, when he was stationed at Dover. His towers were square rather than round, but he originated the principle that they should be set close together so that 'their defences cross each other at nearly point-blank distance'. This was taken up by his superior, William Twiss. The Quartermaster General's department also approved and outlined their tactical purpose:

> The advantage proposed by these towers is to keep possession of the coast defences to the annoyance of the enemy during the whole operation of his landing, and the probable prevention of his disembarking stores; and either to oblige his bringing artillery against them when he has landed or leaving us in possession of the bay or anchorage which they protect –

which would enable us to intercept all supplies which he might endeavour to follow the Armament.[11]

The towers broke the usual rules of fortification – they were round and high rather than angular and low, and they were dispersed along a beach rather than concentrated. They attracted a great deal of opposition from the Ordnance Board, which felt sidelined. Lieutenant Colonel Brown, the proposer of the Royal Military Canal, was not alone in thinking the towers an 'expensive and diabolical system'. Nevertheless they were approved at the highest levels after William Pitt had returned to office. Colonel Twiss became the main architect and toured the invasion areas in the autumn of 1804 to choose the sites. He wrote:

> My first object was to apply the general Principles of Fortification which the Committee of Royal Engineers had approved to the defence of the exposed line of coast and it occurred to me that the simple tower of about 29 feet diameter, arched over, and having on the top one heavy gun assisted by carronades or swivels would, (except in five instances which are hereafter enumerated, and where towers for four guns are recommended) apply throughout, placing them each 5 or 600 yards of each other in the most advantageous landing places and extending their distances as circumstances might render admissible.

This form of defence, he argued, 'had a decided preference over works of greater magnitude which after incurring greater expence must have much larger intervals'.[12] The standard tower was described in 1816:

> They are all of similar construction, built with brick, the walls of great thickness, and the shape that of an obtruncated cone: their height between thirty and forty feet. Those which are stationed upon the hills have their foundation laid at the bottom of a deep pit which being considerably larger than the base forms a dry ditch around the building; the entrance is guarded by a drawer-bridge, which, when raised, forms a double door, – the inner one, as also that which leads to the magazine within the lower storey of the tower, is strongly cased with copper. A large pillar rises in the centre from whose summit springs an arch which unites all sides with the exterior wall, and forms a roof which is bomb-proof, to which there is an

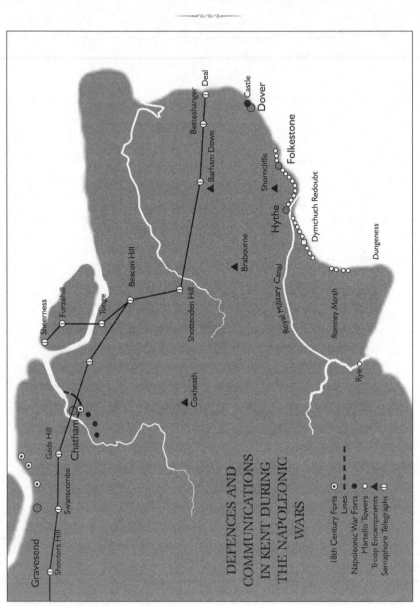

DEFENCES AND
COMMUNICATIONS
IN KENT DURING
THE NAPOLEONIC
WARS

18th Century Forts
Lines
Napoleonic War Forts
Martello Towers
Troop Encampments
Semaphore Telegraphs

Deal
Betteshanger
Castle
Dover
Barham Down
Folkestone
Shorncliffe
Dymchuch Redoubt
Brabourne
Hythe
Dungeness
Beacon Hill
Shottenden Hill
Royal Military Canal
Rommey Marsh
Furzehill
Tonge
Sheerness
Coxheath
Rye
Gads Hill
Chatham
Swanscombe
Shooters Hill
Gravesend

ascent by a winding staircase, and upon it a platform mounted ... with a long twenty-four pounder and on some of the towers a howitzer also.[13]

The chain of Martello towers started west of Folkestone with two towers. There were two more on the heights on the other side of the town, and in the valley below was the modernized castle of Sandgate, which now had a Martello-like tower as its centrepiece. There were three more on high ground east of Sandgate, then a gap before the chain resumed on the coast of Romney Marsh. A line of fifteen closely spaced towers protected the most vulnerable of landing beaches, including three larger ones known as Forts Twiss, Sutherland and Moncreiff. The line ended with the large, flat, circular redoubt at Dymchurch. There were three pairs of towers south-west of that, guarding Willop Sluice, Marshland Sluice and Globsden Gut. There was a gap in the chain on the southern end and eastern side of Romney Marsh, which Twiss explained as part of the scheme of flooding the area:

> From the harbour at Rye along the shore round Dungeness Point to the commencement of Dymchurch Wall, is about 16 miles, and in most parts affords a favourable landing to an enemy, but when on shore he cannot advance into the country except by a movement on his left towards Rye or advancing in front throughout the whole extent of Romney Marsh – or lastly by a movement on his right along Dymchurch Wall, it is presumed that the precautions already taken for destroying the sluices will render towers unnecessary to guard against the two first movements, and it seems only required to defend Dymchurch Wall so as to prevent an enemy landing on it, and ensure the opening of the sluices, whenever orders may be given for that purpose. To do this there is a tower on each of the three sluices, assisted by a tower for 4 guns at the north end of Dymchurch, and two single towers to take up the interval between it and eastward sluice appear necessary.[14]

As a result the chain did not resume again until three towers guarding the entrance to Rye Harbour. After that there was a close-spaced group of eight in front of the beaches at Pett Level, until the cliffs at Fairlight. Farther east there were 24 towers guarding Pevensey Bay. The chain ended just short of the cliffs of Beachy Head, at Eastbourne where a great redoubt, similar to the one at Dymchurch, survives to this day. The idea of towers had become so well established that another chain was approved in October 1805, on the east coast between Harwich and Aldeburgh.

Each of the Martello towers needed about a quarter of a million bricks, many of which had to be brought from London. Construction only started in October 1805, by which time the immediate threat of invasion had passed, and the south coast chain was not completed until 1808. Therefore the other great question of the Martello Towers was never resolved – who was to man them? During an invasion, an enemy force of perhaps 20,000 men would be concentrated on three or four towers, and it would have required good troops with steady nerves to stay in action. Several hundred invasion craft might be landing within range, but each was a small target, and it would have needed accurate gunfire to do maximum damage. If it was to prevent the enemy unloading as planned, each tower would have to hold out for hours and possibly days. Yet when asked about the manning, Henry Dundas merely blustered, 'Give us the towers and we will find men.' And perhaps the critics had a point when they spotted another vulnerable feature: that the guns were not protected from above. 'It is to be admitted that upon first landing of an enemy the tower is not to be taken by assault; but a few shells thrown by small mortars brought on shore ... might in a short time destroy the carriages of the guns on the platform on top of the tower and thereby render its effect as a sea battery useless.'[15]

Critics continued to rage against the towers for several decades, notably William Cobbett, an old soldier who did not understate his case. The fortifications of Dover were 'a parcel of holes made in a hill, to hide Englishmen from Frenchmen'. The Martello towers were 'pauper-making work' and 'incessant sinks of money; walls of immense dimensions; masses of stone brought and put into piles...'[16] Many of the Martello Towers remain today as monuments to the defence against Napoleon, though it is surprising how soon they were neglected – the first one was sold off by 1819 and some of the others were taken over by the coastguard.

There was another attempt to defend Romney Marsh by building a canal across its junction with the rest of England. The idea came from Lieutenant Colonel John Brown, a Scottish engineer. It was the great age of canal building, but this one was never connected to the main system and any commercial use was purely secondary. Instead, the Royal Military Canal was a 'great work of cutting a canal betwixt the Rother and the beach at Hithe Bay for the purpose of separating an enemy landed on the coast of Romney Marsh from the interior of the country...'[17] When completed it formed

> an indented line along the verge of Romney Marsh from Scot's Float, on the borders of Sussex, a distance of twenty-three miles. Its breadth is about thirty yards and its depth six; a breast work is thrown up throughout the whole line; the flanks are batteries enbarbette for cannon, and at several places there are embrasures in the faces of the work, to supply the want of flanks.[18]

The Royal Military Canal was only begun in 1804, but even the uncompleted work would have had some effect in stopping an enemy, and the very presence of so many soldiers might have helped the defence. Though it was to protect the same area as the Martello towers, it was not coordinated with them, and indeed John Brown was one of the fiercest opponents of the tower scheme. It is not surprising that it also incurred the wrath of William Cobbett – 'those armies who had so often crossed the Rhine and the Danube, were to be kept back by a canal, made by PITT, thirty feet wide at the most!'[19]

There was also another attempt to strengthen the defences around Chatham Dockyard, and at the same time protect the Medway crossing at Rochester, which might prove vital on the way to London. Fort Pitt was to be built on the hill above the town and Fort Clarence nearer to Rochester Bridge over the Medway. Again they were not finished in time to meet any real threat.

STOP LINES AND NODAL POINTS, 1940

Though the Martello towers soon fell into disuse after the end of the wars in 1815, it was not the end of coastal fortification. In the late 1850s naval technology was changing fast with the rise of steam power and armour, and with another Napoleon on the throne of France it seemed quite possible that the French might mount a sudden raid. A Royal Commission of 1859 recommended strong defences around the three main Royal dockyards at Chatham, Portsmouth and Plymouth, resulting in the building of 'Palmerston's follies'. These rings of forts were often impressive constructions and still dominate the landscape. For when war came in 1914, the German surface fleet was confined to the North Sea, and it was the new naval bases – Scapa Flow, Invergordon and the Forth – that were most vulnerable. World War I also created its share of invasion scares, and defences were built on the east coast, where it was feared an enemy might land. But coastal defences were neglected between the wars, with no new ideas emerging.

In 1940 the first line of fixed defences on the east coast was on sea rather than on land. In December 1939 the government declared the East Coast Mine Barrage, beginning some 30–70 miles offshore and about 60 miles deep. It was to join up the existing barriers to form a continuous line from the Thames Estuary to the North of Scotland. The first line of mines was laid at the end of 1939, but it was not until May 1940 that serious work began, deploying the converted merchant ships *Teviot Bank* and *Princess Victoria* as well as destroyers. When completed it numbered 35,000 mines. The barrage could stop German heavy ships approaching the east coast unless they were preceded by minesweepers, which would slow them down. It would do nothing against shallow draft vessels such as E-boats and landing barges, but these could not mount a full-scale invasion without support. In August 1940 another minefield was laid between Cornwall and Ireland specifically to prevent invasion there, but the English Channel was too deep for minefields along its coast, and those laid in the Dover Strait were not effective.

Land fortification was very unfashionable in 1940. Older soldiers remembered the years of horror and futility on the Western Front, and everyone knew how much money and faith the French had invested in the Maginot Line and how easily the Germans had ignored it. Nevertheless new fortifications were built, and very quickly. After the French campaign, Ironside was well aware of 'the catastrophic result which could be achieved by the armoured fighting vehicles operating through country unprepared for defence'. And it was essential 'to prevent the enemy from running riot and tearing the guts out of the country as had happened in France and Belgium'. He ordered three main elements in the land defence of the country – a 'crust' on the beaches, lines of anti-tank obstacles well inland and mobile reserves for reinforcement or counterattack.

Under Ironside's plan the beaches were outposts, 'to give warning of, to delay and break up the initial attack'. There were not enough resources to defend them all, so priority was to be given to those suitable for landing armoured fighting vehicles. These were to be equipped with naval guns to deal with the transport ships of the invading force rather than the troops. The land defence concentrated on the exits from the beaches that could be used by tanks. They would be blocked by concrete and covered by anti-tank guns if possible. If the beach was too open to block, it might be mined above the high-water mark. The beaches would also be covered with pill boxes mounting light machine-guns to attack infantry. Beach obstacles included lines of concrete cubes up to 7 feet high and scaffolding erected at the high-water mark.

The main defence was some distance inland, at the 'stop lines': 'The inland area will be divided into zones consisting of a series of "stops", culminating in a zone selected to cover London and important industrial centres.'[20] These were divided into two types, according to geographical features. The first included,

> a waterway or other efficient tank obstacle, such as steep hills. These portions must under the present circumstances [in June 1940] be lightly held in order to provide sufficient troops, especially artillery, for the remainder.
>
> It is essential that the fullest use of waterways should be made. Waterways at right angles to the general line of the front are of great value as they hinder lateral movement of the attack; they will always be included in the demolition scheme.[21]

Demolition was an essential part of the scheme. 'In order to make efficient demolition belts, successive lines of bridge demolitions, and cratering of important road junctions are essential.' Roads were also to be destroyed if absolutely necessary:

The destruction or restriction of road communications will form an essential part of the defence. A co-ordinated scheme is necessary to balance the conflicting requirements of movement and restriction of movement. If it is found that a bridge on an essential road is considered a necessary tank stop, the obstacle must be made by artillery defence and not by demolition.[22]

THE GHQ LINE,
JUNE TO JULY 1940

GHQ Line

Bridges were to be prepared for demolition, but the charges were not to be laid yet. Swing or lifting bridges would be left raised or opened and essential parts of the machinery removed.[23]

Railways were considered essential to the economic life of the country, and the enemy was to be denied their use by the removal of rolling stock: 'No railway bridges, tunnels or ancillary services will be destroyed except where a railway bridge affords an effective crossing of a waterway selected as an A.F.V. "stop".' Public utilities such as waterworks, gasworks and electricity supplies were not to be touched: 'The nuisance value to a hostile force, achieved by the destruction of these facilities, is negligible compared with the hardships which would be imposed on our own people.'[24] Fuel supplies, on the other hand, had to be given high priority for destruction, for it was well known that German tanks had filled up in French service stations to continue their attacks. Supplies were to be kept to a minimum in the most vulnerable areas.

The main defence, the GHQ Stop Line, ran from Richmond in Yorkshire through Newark and Cambridge to Canvey Island on the River Thames, using hills and waterways where possible. In the south, the line started south of the Thames and ran through Maidstone and Basingstoke to Bristol. These lines would protect the main industrial areas of the country, including Birmingham, Coventry, Derby, Manchester, Sheffield and the port of Liverpool. More northern towns like Newcastle and Glasgow were not regarded as liable to attack, nor was Wales; but the line would sacrifice great ports like Hull, Portsmouth, Southampton and Plymouth. In addition there were smaller stop lines in advance of the main one. Five of them crossed the flat lands in the great bulge of East Anglia, where a landing was considered highly likely. Three more crossed Kent and Surrey to the south, as the outer defences of London.

The concrete pill box was a product of the mechanical age, in which a machine-gun or even a few rifles could produce as much firepower as a regiment in former days. It first appeared as a fortification during World War I, usually circular and made of stone or brick, until concrete proved itself as effective and easy to construct. Some were built to defend the English east coast, while the Germans also built them on their side of the Western Front. Pill boxes were also an important feature of the now discredited Maginot Line.

As early as 20 May 1940, the War Office asked for drawings of new ones, to conform to three requirements – splinter and bullet-proof protection, no living accommodation and simple design for easy construction. These designs were ready within a few days and sent out to the chief engineers of the home commands. Where possible, existing buildings should be modified with loopholes in the walls. Siting was important: 'A good natural field of fire will be a vital factor in selecting defensive positions, and where this is obstructed out-buildings, hedges and other obstacles must be cleared at once.' Positions were to be protected by barbed wire at hand grenade range, or 40 feet, with more wire 60 feet away to protect against flame throwers. It was ordered that, 'Home defence preparations must now be given priority over all other works services.'[25]

Several designs were produced, of which the FW 22 and the FW 24 were the most common. Both were hexagonal, and the Type 22 had sides about 8 feet long and 15 inches thick, with loopholes on five of its sides. The Type 24 was larger, with walls 10 feet long and up to 3 feet thick. There was a great deal of local variety as Royal engineers and contractors built in brick or stone, or concrete faced with brick. Several types were designed specially for airfield defence, some of which could retract when aircraft were landing. All were very cramped and could be manned only for short periods except in an emergency.

The pill box protected the occupiers against fire from the ground and bombing from the air. It was reasonably cheap, using mass-production methods, but many officers were also aware of its disadvantages. It tended to restrict the defenders' field of fire. Reinforced concrete was 'not a fixed invariable material' and some would withstand shellfire better than others. The presence of a pill box would draw the enemy fire on to it, and they might use flame throwers as they had in France, to the terror of the defenders. Some even suggested placing dummy ones to draw the fire of the Stukas. And the large number of pill boxes might tie down large numbers of troops – one general complained, 'We are becoming pill-box mad' – more than half of his division would be used in a purely static role.[26]

As well as pill boxes, the defences relied on anti-tank obstacles. These included concrete pyramids known as 'pimples', or more dramatically as 'dragons' teeth', scaffolding on the beaches, and ditches. Sometimes the engineers adapted the defences of previous ages. Dover Castle was re-fortified yet again, a few Martello Towers near Bawdsey were adapted, and the line of the Royal Military Canal was fitted with pill boxes to contain a landing on Romney Marsh. At Pevensey Castle, the Roman fort had strongpoints incorporated in the ruins.

The Royal Engineers were responsible for fortifications, through the Directorate of Fortifications and Works in the War Office. The corps had developed vastly since 1805 and had initiated many new fields, such as telegraphy, mechanized traction and balloons, which eventually became branches of their own. By 1939 the Royal Military Academy at Woolwich had been closed in the interests of greater service unity, and potential engineer officers now did their basic training alongside those of other arms at Sandhurst. Then they went to the School of Military Engineering at Chatham for specialist training, but about half of the most academically-qualified spent much of the next two and a half years studying at Cambridge University. Other ranks were also trained at Chatham, in trades such as carpentry, bricklaying, mining, concreting, painting, plumbing and draughtsmanship. On the outbreak of war there was a vast need for expansion, largely met by the Territorials – more than 75,000 officers and men were added to the 13,000 regulars. This was still not enough to support the BEF in France, and officers and men were enlisted direct from building contractors, with a very small complement of experienced NCOs to maintain military standards. Meanwhile new officers with civil engineering qualifications were trained in OCTUs (Officer Cadet Training Units): 624 were under training at Shorncliffe and Aldershot at the end of May 1940. For other ranks, six training battalions were formed besides the one at Chatham.

The Royal Engineers consisted of 5,077 officers and 127,011 men at the beginning of July 1940, with 1,349 men added in the last week.[27] The Corps had many specialist units dealing with tunnelling, railways, airfield construction and surveying, and it would soon have to add bomb disposal. For operational purposes the most important units were the field companies. Three of these were attached to each infantry division, along with a field park company which did not have transport to carry all its stores and equipment. A field company was commanded by a major, with four other officers, a warrant officer and six senior NCOs. It had 231 other ranks including 153 skilled men of various trades known as sappers, plus transport drivers.

The Auxiliary Military Pioneer Corps was formed in 1939 using the precedent of a body in World War I. Traditionally a pioneer was a man who went ahead of the army to clear the way, but this formation (renamed the Pioneer Corps in July 1940) was intended to provide heavy labour for fortifications. Other units mocked the low educational standards of its members with aphorisms such as, 'sweating like a pioneer at a spelling test'. The Corps had 690 officers and 42,712 men at the beginning of July 1940, an unusually low proportion of officers. It had taken on 3,333 new men in the previous week, a faster expansion than any branch of the army except the infantry.

As well as the specialist engineering corps, the other troops of the army were expected to work on the defences. Private Staunton of the Wiltshire Regiment found it was hard work in Hampshire:

> The scaffoldings were quite large structures, clamped together on the beach and carried bodily out into the sea by twenty-five of us, when the tide was at its lowest ... When a long line of obstacles were carried out into the sea, all the tall men had to carry the shorter men out to join the sections together with further clamps and steel scaffolding. Sometimes the waves went right over our heads and it was indeed a very frightening experience to those of us who could not swim.[28]

But the great bulk of the work was done by civilian contractors, who often took on a particular stretch of the lines. Up to 150,000 men were employed on them during the summer of 1940. A. B. Kennell worked in Essex:

> I was on the defences of the coast; first on tide-work, erecting long iron spikes set in concrete on the beach at Jaywick. Being below the high-tide

190

mark, what a race we had to beat the incoming tide. Working all hours of the day and night, by moonlight often enough, to finish our section, with the youngest lads fifteen years of age to one glorious old-age pensioner of eighty-two, who inspired us all with his tireless energy, working in his bare feet and legs in the cold sea water and trousers rolled above his knees.[29]

Construction of pill boxes needed a considerable amount of material – two and a half tons of concrete for each, with more than two tons of steel reinforcement plus sand, aggregate and wood for shuttering. Financial control was largely abandoned, but the War Office was sometimes taken aback when the bills were sent in. Mr Hugh Cave built 24 pill boxes at Thorney near Peterborough and sent in an invoice for £2,852; the War Office had estimated the work at £1,211.[30]

Cuckmere Haven in Sussex was a vital spot on the south coast, where the River Cuckmere cuts a gap in the cliffs west of Beachy Head and the Seven Sisters range. In 1940 it was manned by troops of the 45th Division. There was a shingle beach half a mile wide, divided in two by the river. On the eastern side was a long line of scaffolding at high-water level, guarded by a pill box and a gun emplacement. Behind that was an anti-tank ditch with a minefield at the eastern end nearest the hills and four pill boxes on the lower slopes on a line running roughly north. The scaffolding and the ditch were shorter on the western side because of a bend in the river, but there were pill boxes at the scaffolding, at the ditch and on the slopes, with a command post in a high position facing out to sea. There were more defences a mile inland up the narrow valley and the bridge there was made ready for demolition.[31]

Weybourne Hope in Norfolk was another vital spot, both in legend and in fact – it was one of the few places where tanks could land at any state of the tide. The coast was much straighter and flatter here, with a narrow beach at high tide. Defended by the 5th Battalion the Norfolk Regiment, it relied much less on the pill box. Its outer defence consisted of a mile of scaffolding west of Weybourne Hope itself, protected by three gun emplacements close together, Vickers machine-gun sites and mines. An anti-tank ditch began at Weybourne Hope and headed inland for half a mile or so, then ran parallel to the coast. It was protected by three pill boxes just forward of it and gun emplacements close to the ditch itself.[32]

191

In view of the haste, it is not surprising that mistakes were made. On the coast of Dorset in October, Michael Joseph soon found that the pill boxes were poorly sited and constructed:

> One was several inches deep in water in wet weather and posed a nice problem for the storage of ammunition. Another was so exposed to view from both air and sea that it was impossible to camouflage and I for one would not have liked to be inside it in the event of trouble. But the prize specimen, which was being constructed when we arrived, was a hexagonal pill box with three loopholes. The front loophole had a field of fire of about twenty yards. The left-hand loophole enabled us to fire into a steeply rising bank of turf five and a half yards away (I measured it); and the third loophole offered as a target a few yards of trench which it was intended should be occupied by our own men.[33]

Critics accused Ironside of building 'A British Maginot Line', but there was not enough time to build defences on that scale, and it was never intended as an impregnable barrier. Despite its name, it was part of a defence in depth, rather than a single line. Nevertheless, as early as 26 June,

> The Vice Chiefs of Staff maintained that the idea of holding the coast with outposts and contemplating a main line of resistance after half the country had been overrun seemed nothing short of suicidal. The only policy, in their view, was to resist the enemy with the utmost resolution from the moment he set foot on shore. The Chiefs of Staff agreed that the balance of the defence leant too far on the side of a thinly held crust on the coast, with insufficient mobile reserves in the immediate vicinity of the points at which penetration might occur.[34]

On taking command of Home Forces on 20 July, Brooke was horrified by Ironside's plan:

> I visualized a light defence along the beaches, to hamper and delay landings to the maximum, and in the rear highly mobile forces trained to immediate aggressive action intended to concentrate and attack any landings before they had become too well established.[35]

At a conference on 6 August, Brooke proclaimed: 'The idea of linear defence must be stamped out; what is required to meet the dual threat of sea-borne and airborne attack is all round defence in depth with the maximum number of troops trained and disposed for a rapid counter offensive.' On beach defences he wrote four days later: 'Good progress has been made in the construction of defences on the most exposed beaches and I consider that the time has now come to concentrate primarily on maintenance and improvement of existing defences including concealment, and to release personnel and material as far as possible for other urgent work such as provision of winter accommodation.' The instructions issued to the area commands on the 7th were circumspect and tried to avoid admitting a complete change of direction. 'The policy for the construction of defence works has been reviewed in the light of the present situation. Owing to the progress of the work and the demands of other works of essential national importance, the absolute priority now enjoyed by defence work can no longer be maintained.' [36]

A prodigious amount of work had been done during the eight weeks of Ironside's command, especially in the most vulnerable areas. In Eastern Command 5,054 pill boxes had been completed out of 5,819; in Southern Command, 2,061 out of 3,242. In Eastern Command, 1,697 out of 1,842 miles of wire had been set up and 440 out of 483 anti-tank obstacles had been laid. [37] Many parts of the lines were virtually complete, including the east–west GHQ stop line between Bradford on Avon and Tilehurst, near Reading, using the line of the Kennet and Avon Canal.

> The obstacle, mainly a canal line, is complete. Nearly all the permanent defences are completed. The work as completed has 170 shell proof pill boxes, 5 miles of [anti-tank] ditch, 125 road blocks, 17 rail blocks, 15 armour piercing gun emplacements, etc. Approximate length 58 miles.

The command stop line heading south across the neck of Somerset and Devon from Bridgewater to Seaton,

> includes 379 shell proof pill boxes. 11 miles [anti-tank] ditch, 5½ miles [anti-tank] obstacles, 7 miles natural obstacle improved, 126 road blocks,

29 rail blocks, 23 [anti-tank] gun emplacements, 49 demolitions prepared. This line is approaching completion. Approximate length 47 miles.[38]

As well as mobile columns and strengthened beach defences, Brooke's new policy relied on fixed fortified areas known as 'nodal points':

Even in the flat country of Northern France, the German tanks did not willingly leave the roads, and returned to them as soon as possible. In S.E. England, however, the country is much closer, and the roads much narrower and less direct. Further, they nearly all converge on towns, small and large. The deduction made was that defence was best extended in depth inland by holding these towns, as they not only provided [anti-tank] localities, but also commanded the views of roads. The Home Guard were nearly all in such towns, and there were insufficient troops to hold a second or reserve line in strength. Any available troops, such as fighting personnel of [field ambulances], R.E. Field Coys, etc. with the local Home Guard under operational control, were accordingly organized into garrisons for these towns and villages, which were described as 'nodal points' or 'focal points'.

Not long afterwards the concept was expanded:

As defences became more organized, it was decided that each nodal point should have its keep made tank proof, by means of road blocks between houses, and that an outer ring of defences, usually on the outskirts, should be constructed. The expression 'fortress' came to be used to designate an inland town or village which was selected for fortification on these lines.[39]

The village of Sarre in Kent is situated in the former Wantsum channel, which once separated the Isle of Thanet from the mainland. It was considered a Category 'A' nodal point, for it could block the passage of troops landing on Thanet. The main defence was a ring of eight fortified house and defended buildings – one, at the junction of the A28 and A253 roads, was fitted with six firing positions covering its north and south sides. There were road blocks on the approach roads and pill boxes behind the village as well as slit trenches and weapons pits. A brigade headquarters was situated in tunnels in a disused quarry.[40]

The city of Worcester was defended on a much larger scale, though it was much farther from any possible sea-borne landing. With a population of 52,000 in 1931, it was able to produce a substantial Home Guard. It had an outer defence line that roughly followed the built-up area and consisted mainly of slit trenches and weapons pits. Inside that was the reserve defence line, which does not seem to have been well chosen or well fortified in practice. Inside that was the central defence sector, using the River Severn as its western boundary, with a tributary and a canal to the south and east. Inside that was the keep in the old city centre, mainly defended by fortified buildings.[41]

Vulnerable points were areas that had to be defended because of their intrinsic value, independent of any local defence scheme. They included airfields, bridges, gasworks, electricity generating stations, reservoirs and vital factories. At the beginning of August it was felt that 'sabotage is the main threat', and that paratroops could not be ruled out. The most vital points, such as aerodromes, experimental stations and wireless stations, were to be guarded by regular soldiers; less important ones, such as power stations and communication centres, were guarded by home defence battalions and the Home Guard.[42]

Coastal guns were rarely fashionable even within the Royal Artillery, except during an invasion scare, but the 1860s produced the 'disappearing gun' which could be lowered for loading and raised to fire over a parapet, though this led to a slow rate of fire. With the much more real threat of invasion in May 1940, it soon became clear how much coastal artillery had been neglected. Fortunately the navy had a large stock of guns left over from the previous war. On 19 May, the Royal Artillery branch of GHQ Home Forces and Captain Servaes at the Admiralty agreed by telephone that 150 of them would be allocated to coastal batteries and that the navy would man 22 two-gun batteries and the Royal Artillery would man 25. The guns were already mounted on pedestals for naval use. Distribution started on the 27th. They were transported by rail and road while the army supervised the digging out and concreting of sites. Civilian tractors and trailers were requisitioned for the final stage of moving the guns into place. The first six naval batteries were in service by 6 June, and 46 were ready for action six days later. After that, 635 smaller guns, mostly of 4-inch calibre, were supplied to the army. Among the 31 major defended ports, the Firth of Forth had a total of 29 guns including three old 9.2-inch and eighteen 6-inch, and Lowestoft had four 6-inch and two 12-pounders. Minor ports, such as Berwick upon Tweed, Ramsgate and Ardrossan, usually had a pair of naval guns, 6-inch, 4.7-inch or 4-inch. Their purpose was 'to extend existing fixed defences where such exist' and to 'guard the approach channels to ports, landing places and beaches against armed merchant vessels, transports, AFV. carriers and similar craft'.[43]

Ammunition was in short supply – only a hundred rounds were available for each gun. Aiming and fire-control systems were of the naval type, and parties had to be sent round to train the army to use them. Instructions were issued to hold fire until the enemy was within 6,000 yards, or less in fog. This would allow for the hasty training of the personnel, it would keep the battery concealed until the last moment, and it would be at a stage when the enemy had little sea room for manoeuvre. Camouflage was improved after Dunkirk veterans arrived to point out how vulnerable the defences were from the air, and dummy batteries were set up.[44] From 23 June the Admiralty began to press for the release of its personnel, but finding replacements put yet more strain on Royal Artillery resources.

Of course, the defences of Britain were never really tested. The key question was: were they an effective way of spending money and deploying scarce labour and materials? And would they have played a full part in keeping the enemy out, had he decided to come?

8

THE NAVY

THE NAVY IN 1803

The first notice the British public had that war was imminent was in March 1803, when the citizens of Portsmouth and Plymouth saw commotion in the streets as the naval press gangs went back to work. This did not mean that war was certain – there had been many cases where international disputes had been settled merely by the mobilization of the fleet – but it was obvious that the high hopes placed in the Treaty of Amiens were misplaced.

The right of the navy to press seamen into its ranks was grounded in the ancient prerogative of the King to call all his subjects into his service in a national emergency, but it gradually took on more importance through the centuries as the navy became the chief factor in national defence. Impressment applied only to seamen, though in a lawless age there were many cases where landsmen were taken up, and occasionally they were not released. Impressment was not abolished along with other royal prerogatives in the mid-seventeenth century, mainly because no one could find an adequate substitute for it. There were many attempts to replace it during the eighteenth century, but Parliament feared the kind of bureaucracy that would be needed for an efficient and fair system of conscription, while the seaman preferred one that gave him a fighting chance of escape.

Just before the King's message to Parliament on 8 March, St Vincent sent orders to the naval ports and ships in home waters, and press gangs were hastily formed from the crews of ships in commission and from marines in the barracks. At Portsmouth on 8 and 9 March, 'large parties of seamen from the different ships lying at Spithead and in the harbour, amounting to above 600, were ordered on shore late last night, for the purpose of impressing seamen for the fleet; and so peremptory were the orders that they took every man on board the colliers &c ... Early this morning the same bustle was repeated, and several gangs paraded the Point, and picked up a great many useful hands, whom they lodged in the guardhouse on the Grand Parade.'[1] By the 11th, there was no abatement: 'The order for impressing seamen is still continued with the greatest vigilance, and not a single vessel of any description, lying in the harbour, but what has been completely searched, and the men, and even boys, taken out. It is with the utmost difficulty that people living on the Point can get a boat to take them to Gosport, the terror of a press gang having made such an impression on the minds of watermen that ply the passage.'[2]

Naval ships landed parties to press men or sent boats to passing merchantmen to press their crews. The normal legalities were ignored, as John Wetherell found in a merchant ship off Shields: 'We ... clearly saw two frigates and several boats making towards us. Shortly after one of the boats fired at us. We hove to, they came on board, gave orders to send everybody aft. A grim looking fellow took up the ships articles. Turning to Nicholson, "Where is your carpenter?" "There Sir, at the helm." "Relieve him and put his things in the boat." "Why sir, he is protected." "That is the reason we want him in our carpenters crew. Coxswain, bundle his things into the boat."'[3]

Landsmen were also impressed. At Harwich on 1 April, John Wetherell (now part of a press gang instead of one of its victims) took part in a 'man plunder': 'The market house was to be their prison, where a lieutenant was stationed with a guard of marines, and before daylight next morning their prison was full of all denominations, from the parish priest to the farmer in his frock and wooden shoes.'[4] At Brixham on 6 May the catch included shipwrights, a fishmonger, coal-factor, grocer, cooper, ostler, shoemaker, constable, basket-maker and many more.[5] But all these men had to be released because they were not seamen.

St Vincent's orders created a maximum amount of disturbance in the seaports, but they were not a complete success. They added 10,000 men to the navy as voted by Parliament, but they tended to damage long-term relations between the seamen and the navy, and recruiting was slow for some time afterwards. Parliament voted for 100,000 men early in 1804, but only 84,000 were actually recruited; the following year it voted for 120,000 but got only 109,000.[6]

When the war began in 1803, the British navy was close to the peak of its power and prestige. In the war of 1793–1801 it fought five fleet battles, defeating the French (twice), the Spanish, Dutch and Danes. Each battle was more crushing than the last, until no British admiral was safe from criticism unless he annihilated the enemy. The great fleet battles were possible because an aggressive strategy caused the enemy to be trapped when he ventured to sea, and equally because of the skills and hard work of the dockyards and shipbuilders at home. The fleet also transported troops and carried out landings in many parts of the world. It provided convoys to protect merchant shipping. And it was as successful in small-scale single-ship actions as in fleet battle – it was reckoned that a British frigate stood an even chance against a French ship of fifty per cent greater force.

These naval triumphs had a darker side. Dockyards were often seen as a morass of corruption and malpractice. Seamen could be kept aboard ship for years without leave and often found mutiny and desertion their only ways out. To keep crews in order, flogging and hanging were used as deterrents, but, as on land, the draconian system of punishment was rarely effective. Sea battles were scenes of death and horror, but far more men died from disease, shipwreck and accident than from enemy action.

The sailing warship was the undoubted master on the high seas. It was stoutly constructed in wood and could carry a heavy armament, with firepower equal to a whole army in the field, or a large fortress. The largest ships, with two or three complete decks of guns, were the ships of the line, intended to fight in a single line of battle so that their firepower could be deployed to the best effect – though new tactics, especially those of Nelson, were beginning to alter this. The Royal Navy had 177 of them in 1803. They were virtually unassailable by smaller ships, which had much weaker sides and smaller guns; but they were expensive to build and difficult to man, with crews of up to a thousand men. The frigate, with a single deck of guns, was used for fleet reconnaissance, convoy escort, transmission of messages in battle and many other patrol and miscellaneous duties. Even smaller ships, known as sloops to the British and corvettes to the French, carried less than 20 guns and did most of the tasks of the frigates on a smaller scale, except fleet reconnaissance when they might have to take on the frigates of the enemy's reconnaissance screen. Other warships tended to be more specialized, either in function or in rig, such as bomb vessels for shore bombardment and cutters, which could sail much closer to the wind.

At sea as on land, the gun was the dominant weapon. Most warships were designed to carry guns as heavy as possible while retaining adequate sailing qualities. The standard gun of the ships of the line fired a ball of 32 pounds in weight. Even the smallest vessels, such as sloops and gunboats, now carried short, fat guns known as carronades, each firing a heavy ball over a short range. Shot was usually round, but it might be barbell-shaped for use against rigging, or consist of two round shots chained together, while grapeshot made up of numerous small balls might be used against personnel. Guns were invariably muzzle-loading and smooth-bored. They could fire at a range of up to 2,000 yards, but the effective and accurate range was much shorter, and Nelson preferred to get as close to the enemy as possible – 'No captain can do very wrong if he places his ship alongside that of an enemy.'[7]

Dependence on the wind was the greatest flaw in the sailing warship. All major warships were square rigged, with sails that were square with the line of the ship in their neutral position. They needed large crews to furl them in an emergency, and could sail no more than 67½ degrees into the wind – in other words, more than a third of the sea around them was inaccessible at any given moment. Of course, a ship could get to windward by pursuing a zigzag course known as tacking or beating, but then it would have to cover more that 2½ times the distance. If the tide was also against the ship, it would make no progress at all. If there was too little wind to give steerage way, a ship would anchor if the water was shallow enough, or it would have to drift. In these circumstances it was vulnerable to an oared warship. When there was too much wind the sailing warship could also find itself in severe danger, especially if it was being blown on to a lee shore and could not tack out. Another disadvantage was that virtually all the ship's strength and gun power was on its sides, and very little at its bow and even less at the stern, which was fitted with galleries and windows for the comfort of the officers. A ship could be 'raked' by attacking it end-on and firing a broadside along the length of its decks.

Oar-powered vessels had been in decline for more than two centuries, and even in its home in the Mediterranean the galley was regarded as extremely old fashioned. An oar-powered vessel needed a narrow hull, whereas a sailing ship had a broad beam to prevent it from heeling with the wind. Oars had to be kept low down, whereas a sailing warship tried to keep its decks as high above the water as was consistent with stability. A sailing warship was far stronger than a galley and had a much greater armament. Despite that, there was a move to revive the oared warship around 1800, but only for very small vessels, such as the boats Napoleon intended for his invasion. Their main armament could fire forward, which was an advantage in aggressive action. They could operate when there was little or no wind, though they would be in serious danger in gales. A sailing warship needed a large draft under the water to prevent it being blown sideways by the wind; an oared vessel did not, so it could go much closer inshore. The rowing vessel needed a large crew, but that was not necessarily a disadvantage in short-range operations when they did not have to sleep on board. They could be partly manned by non-seamen, including soldiers who would then land as part of the invasion force. Were these advantages enough to give the gunboat superiority over sloops, frigates and even ships of the line in certain conditions? This was one of the many questions posed by Napoleon's invasion fleet.

The British navy could deploy a total of 770 ships at the outbreak of war. The ships of the line carried from 64 to 120 guns, with complements of 500 to 850 men. The very largest were the three-deckers of the first and second rates, including the *Caledonia* of 120 guns, which was still on the stocks, and the famous 100-gun *Victory*, recently refloated at Chatham after an extensive rebuild. Second rates nearly all had 98 guns. Three-deckers were intended mainly as flagships and strong points of the line of battle, but the real strength of the line was made up of two-deckers of the third rate. There were eight 80-gun ships in the fleet, mostly captured from the French. There were 43 obsolescent 64-gun ships, but the main ship of the line was the 74, the ideal compromise between gun power, speed and seakeeping – there were 87 in the fleet.

Of ships too small to fight in the line of battle, the navy had a number of two-deckers of 50 or 44 guns, poor sailers, unable to run away from larger ships or catch smaller ones. The most effective cruising ship was the frigate, with a single deck of guns and good sailing qualities. The older ones had 32 guns, mostly 12-pounders. Since the early 1790s these had been replaced with ships of 36 or 38 guns, carrying 18-pounders. Ships of 30 to 44 guns were all rated as fifth rates. Sixth rates, mostly bearing 28 or 22 guns, were similar to the frigate in layout.

There were of various types of smaller, unrated ships. Some sloops were ship rigged with three masts, others were brigs with two. In all, there were more than 120 such vessels in the navy when the war began, and they would play an important role in preventing an invasion, as they were well suited to inshore waters. Yet smaller were the schooners, brigs (or brigantines) of around 150 tons. They had a powerful short-range gun armament in carronades, usually 18-pounders, and they could go close inshore to meet an invasion fleet on either side of the channel. Bomb vessels were intended to fire a high-trajectory mortar shell into an enemy position on shore. Cutters were small, fast vessels for patrols and dispatch-carrying.

Of all the personnel of the British navy, only the commissioned sea officers had their early training within the organization. To qualify for the rank of lieutenant, a man had to serve at least six years at sea. Often the well-connected could evade this and have their names borne on the books of ships from an early age without actually appearing. However, hardly anyone became a sea officer without a thorough training. Some officers came from the aristocracy. A few were from the lowest ranks of society and had risen from the lower deck. But the majority came from the younger sons of minor landowners, or from the professional and merchant classes. They entered at the age of 11 to 13. After at least three years a young man who stayed the course could become a midshipman, with a certain amount of authority over the crew. By the age of 20 he was entitled to present himself for the oral examination before three captains;

and if he passed he was eligible for a commission as a lieutenant, though he might have to wait for a vacancy.

Each lieutenant was assumed to have adequate knowledge of seamanship. navigation, man-management, fighting tactics, ship organization. He could take charge of a watch at sea or command a small vessel such as a schooner or gunboat. A ship had approximately one lieutenant for every 100 men, so that large three-deckers had eight, while third rates had five or six. The first lieutenant of a frigate or ship of the line had no watch-keeping duties but took responsibility for the organization and discipline of the ship.

For promotion, a lieutenant had to attract the notice of the Admiralty, either through family influence or by distinguishing himself in battle – the first lieutenant of any ship that did well in action was promoted at least to commander. The next promotion, to captain, was the most important. He was now eligible to command a frigate or a ship of the line, and further promotion was by seniority alone. After fifteen or twenty years he would automatically be elevated to rear admiral, though if he was old, incompetent, or had little sea service, he would become a 'yellow admiral', receiving half the pay appropriate to his rank and would not go to sea. Otherwise he would become a 'rear admiral of the blue', and would go on to the command of a group of ships, or to administrative duties as a port admiral.

In peacetime the majority of sea officers were unemployed on half pay, and old or incompetent men might remain 'on the beach' even in wartime. Naval officers were considered socially inferior to army officers, but they had been much more successful in battle in recent years. Their career offered the prospect of riches from prize money from the capture of enemy ships, promotion to the highest ranks and even a peerage through victory as a commander in a great battle. Many were killed through accident, disease or battle; others were worn out by the strains of constant watch-keeping or the need to preserve order among a mutinous crew. But the profession had no lack of potential entrants, for it was held high in the public esteem.

Warrant officers were mostly specialists and fell into four main groups. The wardroom warrant officers were almost equal to the lieutenants. The master was in charge of navigation and had often learned his trade in the merchant service. The surgeon was the head of the medical team. The purser, half supply officer and half sub-contractor, was responsible for stores and provisions and was often suspected of cheating the crew. The chaplain was expected to minister to the crew's spiritual needs, but few ships carried one.

Next were the standing officers, who stayed with the ship even when it was taken out of commission. The carpenter was responsible for the maintenance of the hull and woodwork, the boatswain for the rigging and the discipline of the crew, and the gunner for the armament, including the gunpowder. Warrant officers at the next level were mostly young men with hopes of rising in the service. The surgeons' mates were fully qualified surgeons; the masters' mates were young men working towards commissions; and the captains' clerks were potential pursers. The lowest group were equivalent to petty officers and lived among the crew. They included the cooks, veteran seamen who had been disabled in the service, sailmakers, armourers, coopers and other artisans. The master at arms was responsible for the policing of the ship; it was said that a soldier was better at this job than a seaman.

The seaman of 1803 was often regarded as a separate race, almost a separate species, from the rest of mankind. He had probably been brought up in a seafaring family and gone to sea at an early age, for a man had to start young to become an effective seaman; mature men who entered the navy as landsmen often did not progress any further. As well as his great skills in ropework, sail and boat handling and in working in the rigging, the true seaman had a very distinctive character. He had a vocabulary of several hundred words unrecognizable to the landsman. He was inured to hardship and had contempt for danger. He despised the landsman and regarded seafaring skill as the only worthwhile mark of status. Such men, if fairly treated and regularly fed and paid, would show true professionalism and make up crews that could beat any navy in the world. The seaman resisted entry to the navy, but once in he served it very effectively.

Less than half the crew of a typical ship was made up of professional seamen. The officers, marines, artisans and servants all had their role to play, and about a quarter of the average complement was made up of landsmen – adults who had been lured into the navy by one means or another.

The seaman was not always treated fairly by his officers or his government. There were a number of incompetent or tyrannical officers, who caused a few serious revolts in ships such as *Bounty* and *Hermione*, in which the crew displaced the officers. The seamen were badly and irregularly paid, and this led to the great mutinies at the Nore and Spithead in 1797; but such mass mutinies were only the tip of the iceberg – there were mutinies in which the crew of a single ship demanded certain rights, and were often granted them; mutinies of small groups of men, which were often put down with hangings and floggings; and probably dozens of small, unrecorded ones in which the men got their way, without a court martial or even an entry in the ship's log.

The seaman had another form of revolt – desertion. Nelson estimated that 42,000 men had 'run' in the war of 1793–1802. Pressed men constantly looked for an opportunity to desert, perhaps stealing ships' boats or swimming ashore. This had a profound effect on the way ships were run. Shore leave was rare because captains feared desertion, and the consequent atmosphere of imprisonment contributed to mistrust between the officers and crew. For all that, the seamen served the navy well. They provided the petty officers, such as boatswains and gunners mates, quartermasters and captains of tops, who formed the backbone of the navy. Despite his neglect by the authorities, the British seaman was the navy's greatest asset.

The marines had recently been given the title 'Royal' by St Vincent, who regarded them as an important means of preventing mutiny. Their main purpose was to provide the fleet with shipboard detachments, of up to 145 men on a first rate ship. On a ship of the line the detachment was commanded by a captain, with two or three subalterns under him. Some of the men did guard duty, but most worked alongside the seamen, cleaning the decks, hauling ropes and handling guns, though they could not be compelled to work aloft. Their messing and sleeping arrangements were deliberately kept separate from the seamen. The marines generally followed the policy of the army in uniform, equipment and training, but often some five years behind – chevrons for NCOs, for example, were introduced to the army in 1802, and to the marines in 1807.

On board ship, life was regulated by the watch system – four hours on and four hours off, except for the dog watches in the evening, which were two hours long and varied the pattern from day to day. The seamen slept in hammocks on the lower deck, with only fourteen inches width allotted to each man. The petty officers were allowed 28 inches, while the junior officers had cabins, mostly in the gunroom or wardroom. The captain alone had a large cabin divided into several compartments. The seamen ate at mess tables slung between the guns on a ship of the line. Their diet consisted of beef, pork, cheese, 'ship's biscuit' or unleavened bread, peas, oatmeal, butter, rice, raisins and such fresh vegetables as the purser could get hold of. Their most valued privilege was the drink allowance – eight pints of beer a day, or the equivalent in spirits, including half a pint of rum or brandy. The food was boiled in the galley stove under the forecastle. Since it had been salted and then stored in barrels for months or years, it was rarely enjoyable, though few seamen suffered from malnutrition. Mealtimes provided some of the few breaks in the ship's working routine and were much valued by the seamen.

There was no uniform for ranks below warrant officer, but the seamen's own clothes were likely to wear out over a long voyage, and eventually each man had to resort to the purser to buy slop clothing, which provided some uniformity.

Naval discipline was strict, and punishments, which reflected and perhaps exaggerated those ashore, could often be cruel – hanging was mandatory for eight different crimes in the Articles of War and optional for eleven more, but the most savage punishment of all was flogging round the fleet. An offender, usually convicted of desertion, mutiny or another serious offence, might be sentenced to up to 1,000 lashes; he was tied up in a boat and given 25 strokes opposite each ship in the fleet.

The navy had six Royal Dockyards in Britain – on the Thames, Medway and on the south coast – to build and refit the ships and keep them supplied with anchors, masts, boats, rope and dozens of other items. Deptford and Woolwich were far up the River Thames and concentrated on shipbuilding and long-term repair. Chatham was some distance up the River Medway and had extensive and modern facilities. It was the main rear base of the North Sea Fleet. Sheerness, at the entrance to the River Medway, was smaller but well placed to supply ships at the Nore anchorage. Portsmouth Dockyard was the most important. It was very close to the anchorage at Spithead and a few miles from the forward anchorage at St Helens Roads. The harbour was well sheltered, and facilities were situated on either side of the entrance. Plymouth was beginning to rival Portsmouth, but it had one grave fault – Plymouth Sound was far too open to provide a good anchorage, especially in southerly winds. Torbay was a very good anchorage in westerly winds, but it was 30 miles from Plymouth.

KEEPING NAPOLEON AT BAY

A squadron of French ships of the line could carry out an invasion by itself, loaded with troops and sent off to attack some ill-defended part of the British Empire – as it did in Ireland. However, an assault on the British homeland was much more likely to see the ships of the line carrying out their traditional role of disputing control of the sea. If a strong force of enemy ships of the line appeared in the Channel, having got rid of similar British forces by either evasion or battle, it could soon dispose of the frigates and sloops that patrolled off Boulogne and the Channel ports, and then cover the small flotilla craft as they crossed the Straits of Dover.

Strategic blockade was the main strategy of the Royal Navy. Its aim was to bottle up the enemy in his own ports, so that his fleet was unable to do any damage, or ensure that it would be engaged and destroyed as soon as it left port. The blockading forces were the first line of defence against invasion. Nelson's Mediterranean Fleet, stationed off Toulon and more than 1,700 sea miles from home, was making a vital contribution to the defence of the mother country – for the only practical invasion plan initiated by Napoleon involved the escape of the Toulon Fleet, and its doubling back from the West Indies having thus lured Nelson off station-to give the French command of the Channel. Such possibilities were always recognized by the policy makers. Despite its defensive strategy, the Addington administration had no hesitation in building up strong forces off Toulon, Brest and other ports, for it appreciated that enemy ships of the line, however far away they might be, were a threat to Britain's control of home waters.

There were two schools of thought about blockade. The most aggressive one, headed by St Vincent, believed that the main force should be stationed almost permanently off the enemy port, leaving only when extreme weather forced them off. The other school, led by Lord Howe in the previous war, claimed that this caused unnecessary wear and tear on ships and men, and allowed the enemy to choose his moment to attack. The main fleet would stay in its anchorages and the port should be watched by frigates, which would give warning of an enemy sortie and would pursue him until the main fleet could catch up. The close blockade has enjoyed the better press by far until very recent times. The most influential of all naval historians, Alfred Thayer Mahan, coined an immortal phrase to describe the blockade of Brest in 1803–5: 'Those far distant, storm beaten ships, upon which the Grand Army never looked, stood between it and the dominion of the world.'[8] Howe, on the other hand, was regarded as a 'once active officer', operating 'a system that was essentially bad'.[9]

But there were arguments in favour of open blockade. If the blockade were too tight, the enemy would never come out to risk destruction. He could remain in port for ever with a half-maintained and half-manned fleet, while the blockaders waited outside in the worst of the weather. Open blockade, on the other hand, might lure the enemy out to sea, and cause a decision in battle. Nelson's blockade of Toulon was described as open by some historians, and as close by others. According to one captain,

> Though Lord Nelson is indefatigable in keeping the sea, there are so many reasons that make it possible for the French to escape through the Mediterranean ... First, he does not cruise upon his rendezvous; secondly, I have consequently repeatedly known him from a week to three weeks,

and even a month, unfound by ships sent to reconnoitre ... thirdly, he is occasionally obliged to take the whole squadron to water, a great distance from Toulon; fourthly, since I came away the French squadron got out in his absence, and cruised off Toulon several days, and at last, when he came out, he only got sight of them at a great distance, to see them arrive at their own harbour.[10]

It was rather like a cat waiting at a mouse-hole and hoping that its prey would be lured out. This was appropriate in the Mediterranean, for the Toulon fleet had a long way to go before it could seriously damage British interests. The French fleet in Brest had to be watched much more closely, for as soon as it left port it could strike out for Ireland or the south coast of England.

The blockade of Brest was the cornerstone of British naval strategy, and the squadron there fulfilled two roles – to contain the French fleet and to guard the entrance to the English Channel. It was not until 1800, when St Vincent took command of the Channel Fleet, that close and continuous blockade was applied. At the time it was wildly unpopular with sea officers, though it was better established by 1803.[11] Brittany was one of the most difficult stations. To the north was the Gulf of St Malo, with some of the fiercest tides in the world; to the south was Biscay, notorious for bad weather. The coast was littered with rocks. The prevailing wind was from the west, so the enemy coast became a lee shore in the winter storms. The position of Brest offered many opportunities to an escaping French fleet – it could head for the English Channel, Ireland, India, the West Indies or North America. From the British point of view, a great advantage was that the westerly gales that could force the British off station would also prevent the French from sailing out through the Goulet Channel. The easterlies, which would help the French escape, would also aid the British returning from their anchorages on the other side of the Channel.

The blockade began in May 1803, when Admiral 'Billy Blue' Cornwallis arrived off Ushant in his flagship *Dreadnought*, almost at the same time as war began formally. By September 1804, twenty ships of the line were allocated to it, though it was expected that only sixteen would be available at any given moment. On service, the main body placed itself off the island of Ushant, a few miles north-west of Brest. This allowed the fleet to cover the entrance to the Channel and to retreat in westerly gales, but at the same time it was close enough to the entrance to Brest harbour to cover enemy movements. An inshore squadron was placed off the entrance to the Goulet. Its core consisted of some six two-decker ships of the line, chosen for their good sailing qualities. It was ordered to patrol the entrance to 'prevent the sailing of the enemy's ships or vessels from that port, or any considerable force, without my being apprised of it; and to cause the ships under your orders to be very vigilant in intercepting any of their homeward bound or coasting vessels which may attempt to get into that port.'[12] Even farther inshore was a group of frigates and smaller vessels.

Rochefort, the third and least important of the French fleet bases, was halfway down the French Atlantic coast and close to the sheltered anchorages off the Île d'Aix and the Basque Roads, but it was badly sited up the narrow, winding River Charente.

After war with Spain began in December 1804, a new British force was put together to blockade the powerful Spanish fleet in Cadiz. It was a slightly easier station than Brest, as it had fewer navigational difficulties and was close to the British base at Gibraltar. Its difficulties were described by one of the seamen involved: 'We were tacking or wearing ship continually, as the blockading service required us to keep as near the harbour's mouth as possible, and consequently when the wind was blowing on the land, we were obliged to beat off, and when it was blowing off the land, then to beat up to the harbour's mouth as near as we could, to prevent the escape of the enemy.'[13]

As commander of the North Sea Fleet, Keith was more concerned about the possible Dutch contribution to the invasion flotilla than their depleted and demoralized battlefleet. However, a force of ten ships of the line was allocated to watch the main base at Den Helder, situated on the channel between the mainland and the island of Texel. The British force was based at Yarmouth, and the Dutch could only escape during fortnightly spring tide. They could not get into the wider world without a passage through the well-guarded Strait of Dover, or round the tempestuous north of Scotland. A direct attack on the British mainland was unlikely with such a small force.

Close blockade was made possible by recent improvements in naval medicine, enabling crews to stay at sea longer, and in particular the virtual elimination of scurvy. The issue of lemon juice provided the best solution, but official parsimony substituted the cheaper, and much less effective, lime juice. Nevertheless the problem was largely solved. Around 1800 a new type of sick berth was fitted under the forecastle of most ships of the line, allowing the men a good supply of air as against their normal berth deep in the hull, and at the same time making it easy to isolate them from the rest of the crew. The calibre of sea surgeons tended to improve, though it was 1806 before they were given a wage rise sufficient to tempt more men into the naval service.

Blockade service offered great hardships. Captain Broke wrote of 'Another tiresome, useless week! The only variety, a little foul weather to tear our sails and make us swear at the wind.' The lower deck resented being called 'Channel gropers' by the public: 'One reason why they have a dislike of it is that they are open to the ridicule of seamen who might be coming from foreign stations, as well as by girls and people in the seaport towns, by cantingly telling them they would never have the scurvy, or that they might as well be by their mothers fireside and tied to the apron strings ...'[14]

Yet such service was not as passive as might be expected. The inshore squadron needed intricate navigation and skilful sailing to keep the ships clear of rocks, shoals and cannon-fire. The faster sailing ships in the main fleet were often detached to inspect passing merchantmen. The rest of them spent much of their time hove to, but they formed up regularly in line of battle for exercise. The immobility of the enemy was not total. Off Brest in August 1805 the gunner of *Caesar* recorded, 'we saw the enemy's fleet in the outer roads at anchor, all ready for a start to sea ... As an engagement was expected to take place next morning, every ship was prepared for battle ... early next morning we had the pleasure of seeing them all under way, 22 sail of the line ... But when the enemy got about a gunshot from our van ships their hearts failed them, for they turned tail and made the best of their way to the anchorage again.'[15]

If the ships of the Channel and Mediterranean Fleets were the long-range defence of the country, those of the North Sea Fleet, under Lord Keith, were the immediate defence, devoted to containing or destroying the most threatening force that France had assembled for many centuries. The men of the squadron off Boulogne were 'Channel gropers' even more than those of the Brest blockade, but they did not have the posthumous glamour that Mahan gave them – their ships were not 'far-distant' and most of the time they were not 'storm-tossed'. But at the time they were very much in the public eye, as the most obvious defence against invasion. They navigated among the sandbanks of the Channel and North Sea, and their raids and forays against enemy ports and gunboats were enthusiastically reported at home, as a relief from the monotony and gloom of most of the war news.

The Admiralty saw the defence of the 'narrow seas' as a two-tier operation; the policy was to have 'an active force on the enemy's coast for the purpose of keeping a vigilant and constant lookout on their proceedings and preventing as far as may be possible any considerable number of boats or craft from leaving their ports unmolested'. On the other side of the Channel, it was intended to 'fix such station on our coast as may be best calculated to operate against the enemy in case they should elude the vigilance of our cruisers on their coast, or put to sea in such force as to render the light cruisers incapable of making any effectual resistance against them'.[16]

Since Boulogne was the main centre for the French invasion fleet, the British force off the port was the key to the anti-invasion preparations – while a British force remained there it was highly unlikely that the invasion could ever be launched. The Boulogne force was merely a subdivision of the Downs Squadron, which was itself part of the North Sea Fleet. In gunpower it was far weaker than any of the squadrons off the great naval ports, and in October 1803 the Admiralty planned for a force of one 50-gun ship, four frigates, four sloops and 'as many brigs and cutters as could be appropriated'.[17] The 50-gun ship was the *Leopard*, later made famous (or infamous) in the novels of Patrick O'Brian. It served as flagship for the commander, a senior captain or a rear-admiral. Frigates and sloops were ideal patrol vessels, while cutters could sail closer to the wind than square-rigged ships. In addition, the squadron had the use of several bomb vessels for bombarding the enemy coast and the boats in his harbours.

The British force off Boulogne could find some rest by anchoring outside the Bassure de Bass sandbank, about four miles south-east of the enemy port.[18] Captain Argles wrote in May 1804, 'The view of the French coast is novel and interesting, we can see everything they are about and every person that is walking on the sands.'[19] But the position was dangerous in winds from the north or west, and some of the ships had to cross the Channel to Dungeness where they could anchor to either the east or the west side of the promontory, according to the wind. The ships needed to get back quickly with 'the first breath of an easterly wind', as this would allow the French to escape. The cutters went first, as they could sail closer to the wind and could be on station quickly.

There were constant scares when an intelligence report suggested that the invasion would come soon. On 21 February 1804, for example, it was reported that the enemy was in 'momentary readiness'. The Boulogne force was to be 'in constant readiness' to meet him.[20] In fair weather the French flotilla craft moved out of the harbour in large numbers, as on 21 March 1804, when 54 brigs and 64 gunboats were seen behind the Bassure bank, firing a salute. Two months later Captain Argles of *Trusty* reported, 'as I am writing 42 brigs and about 85 of their lugger rigged gunboats all moored in one line along the coast and all more at equal intervals, all with their colour flying and a broad pennant on one of them.'[21] The commanders on the spot sent constant reports to Keith about this, but it was difficult to judge when an enemy movement ceased to be an exercise or a taunt and became a serious threat of invasion.

A strong force was also planned off the port of Le Havre, though it never became quite as important as expected since the French did not choose to base major elements of the invasion flotilla there. The British needed larger vessels for this. In June 1804 the area was guarded by the frigates *Euryalus* and *Leda*, with orders to 'stretch to the westward upon the French shore, for the purpose of intercepting any of the enemy's vessels or cruisers'.[22] When blown off station by strong south-west or westerly winds, the Havre squadron was to seek shelter at Dungeness. With easterly winds it was expected to keep its station as long as possible, sheltered within the mouth of the Seine. If strong northerlies threatened to blow the ships on to the hostile shore, they were to keep well to the west of Cap de la Hève. They were discouraged from abandoning the vigil completely and ought 'never to proceed to Portsmouth unless absolutely forced to do so'.[23]

The flotilla craft at Vlissingen (Flushing) in the south of Holland were more of a threat than the Dutch ships of the line, for they could leave at any state of the tide. The first commander of the British force off the port was Commodore Sir Sidney Smith, who had become a popular hero with his defence of St Jean d'Acre in Palestine against Napoleon in 1799. A dashing figure, he was temperamentally unsuited to blockade service and very different from Keith, who wrote of him, 'I am so perfectly acquainted with that restless spirit and ungovernable vanity which renders it irksome to him to feel any superior.'[24]

The force off Vlissingen was recommended to consist of 'not less than a 50-gun ship, three frigates, four of the merchant ship sloops, and six smaller vessels'.[25] The duty demanded smaller ships than the Le Havre squadron, but was farther from bases than the Boulogne force, and Keith was doubtful about finding a suitable anchorage: 'I long ago thought of an anchorage in the estuary off Flushing, but it is nonsense; the first calm day and flood tide and [the enemy] would destroy any ship or gunboats on the Scheldt.'[26] But in March 1804, Smith found a position and wrote that the squadron 'has kept its station close to the entrance of Flushing by remaining at anchor, which although it cannot be said to be without some risk, is attended with less than cruising this season on a lee shore ...'[27]

The typical captain saw it as his duty to harass the enemy in any way possible. The French were constantly moving boats along the coast to Boulogne, covered by darkness and shore batteries. Attacks on them were a standard activity for the ships on the blockade, especially the smaller ones. On 20 February 1804, the cutter *Active*, with six guns and about 30 men, attacked sixteen French gunboats and transports off Gravelines. One was captured while the others sought the shelter of the shore batteries. Keith found it necessary to restrain his officers from attacking too close inshore. Captain Owen of the 40-gun frigate *Immortalité* had his foremast shot through in November 1803 and was ordered, 'to restrain your cruisers from being seduced by the appearance of the enemy's vessels and craft to attack them when under cover of batteries on the coast, when no opportunity can likely be offered of cutting them out or destroying them.'[28] Keith issued a general order 'directing the captains and commanders of HM ships and vessels not to suffer themselves to be drawn under the enemy's batteries on the coast, unless with a fair prospect of deriving some advantage correspondent on the risk.'[29]

Despite Keith's rebuke, Captain E. W. C. R. Owen was the hero of the force. Either alone or as leader of a flotilla, his *Immortalité* was constantly active and it was said that, 'Captain Owen kept the French coast in a continual state of alarm; and the *Immortalité* was well known to the inhabitants from the daring manner in which, in spite of banks and batteries, she approached their shores.' In September 1804, Owen escorted two bomb vessels to Dieppe, where their bombardment caused fires in parts of the town. In July of the following year the Boulogne flotilla craft were trying to get back into harbour on the onset of bad weather when Owen attacked with a small force and caused the loss of more than 400 French soldiers. On 25 August it was noted that there was 'an unusual degree of bustle' in the port. Napoleon himself had arrived to present decorations and inspect the troops and flotilla on exercise. *Immortalité* and her consorts disrupted the gunboats' manoeuvres, with some losses to themselves but greater ones to the enemy.[30]

It was activity like this that kept Napoleon's flotilla close to port and eventually convinced the Emperor that there was no real prospect of invading across the English Channel without gaining naval superiority.

THE NAVY IN 1940

Contrary to popular myth, the Victorian navy had no difficulty in embracing technological change. This was essential to maintain its supremacy, because over that period the warship developed beyond recognition. Steam power succeeded sail, wood was replaced by iron and then steel. Guns became breech-loading and were rifled, and armour plate was fitted to warships to counteract them. The torpedo was developed, so that a small warship could sink a large one; the Royal Navy answered this with the torpedo-boat destroyer, which became the destroyer. All this culminated in 1906 in the building of the battleship *Dreadnought*, able to outgun and outsail any warship afloat. The next few years were dominated by a race with Britain's new rival, Germany, to build as many of this advanced type of battleship as possible. Cruisers were also built to replace the old frigates in reconnaissance and escort work, while the battlecruiser emerged as a compromise between the two types, and the destroyer grew larger and became an independent warship.

The navy was geared up to a great fleet battle when war began with Germany in 1914, but that did not happen until Jutland, two years later. It proved a huge disappointment, as three of the mighty but under-armoured battlecruisers blew up, and the enemy fleet was able to escape without decisive damage. It did nothing to reduce the navy's obsession with capital ships, and its officers would spend the next twenty years refighting Jutland in exercises, reports and polemics. In the meantime, two new factors had entered the naval equation. The navy embraced air power, despite a shortage of concrete results, until the Royal Naval Air Service was taken away and merged with the Royal Flying Corps into the Royal Air Force in 1918. The submarine proved a more immediate threat, though mostly against merchant shipping rather than warships. The Admiralty had to be pushed into action against it before Britain starved, but a system of convoys was enough to save the country in 1917.

In the social sphere, the navy's record was far more ambiguous. Officer training became much more systematic and moved into HMS *Britannia*, an old warship at Dartmouth, and then to a college above that town in 1905. For the lower deck, change came in the 1850s as it became clear that the press gang was not acceptable any more. Ratings were now enlisted for continuous service of ten, and later twelve, years, trained as boys in old ships and issued with a standard uniform (though they still had to pay for it). New branches were founded for medicine and engineering, while the seaman developed new skills in long-range gunnery. The gap between officers and ratings increased. By the late nineteenth century it was virtually impossible for a rating to become an officer except by a very slow path – which meant he was probably on the verge of retirement by the time he was commissioned.

Admiral 'Jacky' Fisher and Winston Churchill worked hard to reform the navy before World War I, opening up new routes to commissioned rank for ratings and integrating the engineering branch with the rest of the officer corps. But the navy suffered savage financial cuts in the 1920s, and the changes came to nothing. Lower deck discontent was expressed by a short-lived but highly-publicized mutiny at Invergordon in 1931. The navy had lost its appetite for technological change and used its political energy fighting to regain control of it's own air force, which became the Fleet Air Arm. Its international prestige was curtailed by the treaties of Washington and London, by which it had to accept parity with the United States Navy. Only in the late 1930s, as it moved towards war with Germany, did the navy begin to get over its problems.

Naval officers of the 'executive' or 'seaman' branch were the real leaders of the navy; unlike engineers, marines and administrative officers, they were eligible to take charge of a watch on the bridge or command a ship or a fleet. The majority of them entered the navy around the age of thirteen after passing a highly competitive examination. They went to the Royal Naval College at Dartmouth for the equivalent of a public school education with a technical emphasis and were commissioned as sub-lieutenants at the age of twenty, after more than six years. It was a system that produced,

> a definite breed of fit, tough, highly trained but sketchily educated professionals, ready for instant duty, for parades or tea parties, for catastrophes, for peace or war; confident leaders, alert seamen, fair administrators, poor delegators; officers of wide interests and narrow vision, strong on tactics, weak on strategy; an able, active, cheerful, monosyllabic elite.[31]

The only other way to enter the navy as an officer before the war was by means of the Special Entry Scheme, which took young men at around eighteen and gave them a year and a half of training, after which they reached the same level as the Dartmouth entry, with the rank of sub-lieutenant. Many thought it was a better way to train the young men, but senior officers continued to believe that they had to enter at a very early age to become real seamen.

The British army of the day was a collection of regiments, but the navy was a collection of specialists – seamen, navigators, gunners, engineers, torpedomen, signallers, domestic and administrative staff, medical men, marines and many others. The seaman ratings were recruited young, at around fifteen, to go through a very strict training programme in shore establishments that still retained their original ship names. Tristan Jones joined one of the last boys' courses in the spring of 1940, and saw much of the pre-war system:

> Since I left *Ganges* I have been in many hellish places, including a couple of French Foreign Legion barracks and fifteen prisons in twelve countries. None of them were nearly as menacing as HMS *Ganges* as a brain-twisting, body-racking ground of mental bullying and physical strain ...[32]

Not everyone was happy with the early recruitment age, and a wartime Petty Officer wrote:

> Is our public aware that its young sailors are kidnapped into its senior service at the tender age of 15, and, to ensure that the sentence is binding, they have to sign or have signed for them a document stating that for 12 years, from the age of 18, their souls belong to the Admiralty. Imagine: 15 years signed away by children unaware of life's meaning.[33]

The seamen wore the 'square rig' uniform that had evolved in the nineteenth century, with bell-bottom trousers, a square collar and a round cap that was very uncomfortable if worn straight on the head as regulations demanded. It was very popular with the public, as Jones was told by an army veteran on the way to *Ganges*. 'Well, matey, at least you'll be all right where crumpet's concerned. They go for the navy blokes a lot more than the army, see? Can't go wrong in your little old navy-blue suit, Can you?'[34] Sailors themselves had mixed feelings: many were proud of it, but others complained about its inconvenience. One man wrote of his wartime experience, 'One has only to watch an A.B. dress to have pity on him, with a uniform consisting of tapes and ribbons and bits and pieces, and a blue jean collar which another person has to hold in place while the poor chap puts his overcoat on.'[35]

The better-educated of the boys in the training bases were selected to become signallers, either visual or by radio. The others eventually joined ships as boy seamen, where they were strictly segregated from male ratings. At the age of eighteen they could qualify as ordinary seamen, then as able seamen. In peacetime they might specialize as gunnery or torpedo ratings. Gunnery also included the whole military side of naval life, and members of the branch were expected to be experts in foot drill. The torpedo branch had a good deal to do with electricity, as there was no proper electrical branch until after the war. A few might specialize as physical training instructors, while the number of submarine detectors rose dramatically after the war started.

Seamen of the various branches made up about a third of the navy. The stokers made up the next largest branch. They joined as adults from the age of eighteen upwards. The title was obsolete, and very few of them actually had to shovel coal, since most modern ships were oil-fired. Instead they became semi-skilled mechanics working under the supervision of the engine room artificers, highly skilled men who had served apprenticeships inside or outside the navy and mostly had the rating of chief petty officer. Stokers tended to have a different culture from seamen and were kept apart on board ships.

The marines constituted the third largest group, and they served as much on shore as afloat in 1940. They too were recruited as adults, and as in 1805 they tended to follow army practices in training, uniforms, ranks and culture. Marine detachments still served in larger ships – battleships, cruisers and fleet aircraft carriers – but not on the destroyers and smaller vessels that would do most of the anti-invasion work.

The navy was trying to build up its maintenance personnel for aircraft carriers, but for the moment it still relied on the RAF for skilled staff. Other specialist branches included cooks, writers or clerks, stewards and stores assistants, all of whom wore the 'fore and aft' uniform with collar and tie instead of the seaman's square collar. This was not popular, and one wearer described it as 'a cross between that of a taxi driver and a workhouse inmate'.[36]

A seaman could pass his examinations for leading seaman, but in peacetime he might have to wait several years for a vacancy. This was not a desirable post, since it conferred little real authority, but the man was expected to keep order in the mess deck where he lived, so many men preferred to stay on and become 'three-badge' ABs, proud of the service stripes awarded after three, eight and thirteen years. Such men were described by Nicholas Monsarrat,

> either he hasn't the brain and energy to pass for Leading Seaman, or he doesn't welcome responsibility, or he 'likes it where he is', or for any other reason ... He may sound dull and stupid but he is rarely that; more often than not he knows it all ... Give him a job and he will work his way through it; not with any flash display of energy, like one of those jumped-up young Petty Officers, but at a careful and steady pace ...[37]

More ambitious men would rise from leading seaman to petty officer, where the pay differential was greater, they lived in a separate mess, and after a year wore a 'fore and aft uniform' with peaked cap and collar and tie. They could go on to become chief petty officers, the highest ratings on the lower deck.

Wartime expansion created a much greater demand for leading seamen and petty officers, promotion now being excessively fast rather than painfully slow. Before the war a crisis was already beginning to develop about the supply of senior ratings. New officers joining HMS *Hood* in 1938 were warned: 'Do not expect too much of your Petty Officers. We cannot expect that their standard shall be a very level one; large numbers are being made up and many are of very limited experience.' Fast-tracking promising men was not likely to succeed. 'It is well known that few men on the Lower Deck regard special promotion with any enthusiasm. Trade Unionism and an innate fidelity to their own kind limit their aim to one of general security, i.e., equal opportunity to rise steadily on a pay scale.' This could only get worse as the great wartime expansion programme outran the means to support it.

In addition to the regulars, the navy could call on three different groups of reservists. The most favoured by the Admiralty were those who had already seen considerable naval service but had left or retired. There were 8,500 retired officers on the emergency list, more than 14,000 seamen and marines of the Royal Fleet Reserve who had kept up some kind of training since leaving the navy, and nearly 30,000 naval pensioners under the age of 55. Such men were well used to naval discipline (though not all of them took kindly to having to return to it) and were a known quantity, but many of them were too old to go to sea. Their numbers were controlled by the needs of the navy ten or twenty years earlier rather than current needs, and very few of them knew anything about modern fields such as radar and aviation.

The Royal Naval Reserve, or RNR, had been founded in 1859 and offered merchant seaman of all types the chance to train with the navy and take naval ranks. The culture of the Royal and merchant navies began to diverge with the introduction of continuous service in that decade, and the RNR formed an essential link between the two. It included a special section of fisherman who would man trawlers and minesweepers in wartime, led by warrant officers with the rank of skipper, RNR. Most merchant seamen were unsuited to naval discipline, but those in the RNR adopted it willingly, and it became a very useful force, though it was quite small – 1,641 officers and 8,397 men in January 1939. It could not be expanded easily, for merchant seamen were needed in their own field.

The navy had been much less enthusiastic about the third group, the Royal Naval Volunteer Reserve or RNVR. It was formed in 1903 as a reaction to the invasion scare caused by the publication of *Riddle of the Sands*. The original idea had been to use yachtsmen, but very few had the time and energy to pursue a very active hobby and do naval training as well, so the great majority of members were landsmen and amateurs, whom the navy did not welcome on the decks of its ships. In 1914, Winston Churchill thought so little of their seamanship that he sent large numbers to the Western Front, where they fought and died as soldiers. There was cause to regret this later as the German submarine menace increased, and the RNVR proved very useful for inshore patrols. The navy took them a little more seriously after that, but they remained a small force, with 809 officers and 5,371 ratings in January 1939, plus 2,000 more in specialist wireless and sick-berth reserves.

By calling on all three of its reserves, the Royal Navy reached an active strength of 180,000 officers and men in September 1939, plus 1,600 in the newly revived Women's Royal Naval Service, or Wrens.

By June 1940 the navy had expanded by another 50 per cent to 271,000 officers and men, and by the end of the year it would have almost doubled its size, with 333,000 men. It did this mostly by taking on men for 'hostilities only', or HOs, whether volunteers or conscripts. New training bases were set up, often in converted holiday camps. An officer in one of these described what he hoped had been achieved as his men prepared to leave:

> Each could look after himself and his kit; whatever his category, each could swim, and pull and sail a lifeboat; each knew enough about fighting a ship not to be a nuisance at sea. And, above all, they had a sense of belonging, a rock-bottom foundation for living together, in preparation for the time when they would be locked together for months on end in a steel box far from land.[38]

For temporary wartime officers, the navy had no intention of promoting its ratings in large numbers. If it was occasionally considered appropriate, the officers in charge had to take care to be discreet. 'For permanent long-service ratings, therefore, who are candidates for permanent commissions, a suitable reticence should be maintained on the subject ...'[39]

The navy turned to experienced yachtsmen, mostly men who had joined the Royal Naval Volunteer (Supplementary) Reserve when it was formed in 1936. Ewen Montague was one of those who were attracted:

> To my joy, the Admiralty formed the R.N.V.(S.)R. – the supplementary reserve. This was simply a list of people who had some knowledge of seamanship, boat handling and navigation, and who were ready to be called up on the outbreak of war and who the Navy felt, with training, might make officers. There were no drills or periods of annual training, a factor of importance to me with a busy junior practice at the Bar.[40]

These men were called up in batches at the beginning of the war and sent to HMS *King Alfred*, an improvised training base in a leisure centre at Hove. Early courses lasted as little as ten days before the men were sent into the world as temporary sub-lieutenants, RNVR. By May 1940, 1,700 men had been commissioned in this way. They were to be found in shore bases and increasingly in ships at sea, and some had already seen action in the 'little ships' of Dunkirk. But naturally the Supplementary Reserve scheme was limited in numbers, and officers would have to be found in other ways.

The navy adopted the army policy of insisting that all potential officers, apart from those with specialist qualifications, should serve on the lower deck before being selected for training, and this led to the CW scheme, named after the Commission and Warrant Branch of the Admiralty which administered it. Men would do their normal naval basic training then go to sea for at least three months as ordinary seamen before being selected for a three-month course at *King Alfred*. The stated aim there was,

> to instil in every man the alertness, enthusiasm, broadmindedness, sense of responsibility, conscience and good humour (as well as a basic knowledge of technical subjects) which centuries of Service experience have shown to be necessary if a Naval Officer is to carry out his normal duties.[41]

The first course for ex-CW ratings had already passed out by the end of May 1940, and about a hundred men were entering every week, so several thousand more joined the fleet during the rest of 1940.

In mid-1940 the Royal Navy remained undefeated and immensely proud of its achievement in rescuing the army at Dunkirk. It was still largely a professional force, for it had expanded less quickly than the army and the air force. It had many good quality leaders at the top but a good deal of snobbery in the lower officer ranks.

NAVAL OPERATIONS AGAINST INVASION, 1940

Traditional admirals tended to regard the capital ship, the successor to Nelson's ship of the line, as the final arbiter of naval power. There were far fewer than in Nelson's day, because each one was far more expensive.

Rodney and *Nelson*, the most powerful, could fire nine 16-inch shells, each weighing 2,048 pounds, over a distance of 37,500 yards or 21 miles. The five new ships of the *King George V* class were not yet in service, and several of the older ships had been damaged, so the navy had eleven battleships and three of their faster cousins, the battlecruisers. Three or four them were serving with Admiral Cunningham in the Mediterranean, though they were not there on quite the same mission as Nelson's fleet in 1803–5, because no one seriously expected the Italian fleet to break out in support of an invasion of England. Another force, centred on the famous battlecruiser *Hood*, was based at Gibraltar to operate in the Mediterranean or Atlantic as required. Those in British waters were part of the Home Fleet, the navy's main striking force and usually based at Scapa Flow in Orkney, where they could be safe from air attack but ready to stop a German breakout into the Atlantic. They were under the command of Admiral Sir Charles Forbes, who was as sceptical as Churchill about the possibility of an invasion, and wrote on 4 June, 'there is little likelihood of the enemy being able to or being so confident as to try to invade England, Scotland or Wales by sea',[42] though he did not rule out an attempt on Ireland. Therefore there was no point in weakening the Home Fleet to counter it.

Forbes was possibly right, and not just about the likelihood of invasion. The battleship was not ideal for destroying an invasion fleet, for its great guns could only engage a limited number of targets at once, while it was vulnerable to bombing and to torpedoes launched by aircraft, submarines, destroyers or E-boats. Its best use would have been in attacking shore positions after the invasion had landed, perhaps destroying any ports that the navy had failed to immobilize. Certainly in extremis a group of powerful battleships could have turned the tide, and this is perhaps the situation that Churchill envisaged for them.

Cruisers were the successors to Nelson's frigates, used in reconnaissance and convoy escort. In fact, aircraft and later radar took over much of reconnaissance, while convoys were now threatened by submarines, which called for smaller, cheaper ships to fight them, so the role of the cruiser was in flux. This and the need to keep to treaty limits explained the confusion in British cruiser design over the preceding two decades. Essentially there were two types. The heavy cruisers, carrying 8-inch guns, were only built between 1924 and 1930, and they had limited deck armour against dive-bombers, so they were based on the Clyde during the invasion scare, only to be brought south as a last resort. Light cruisers, with 6-inch guns, were more common and came in several types. Some were small, like the *Leander* and *Arethusa* classes with only eight and six main guns respectively; larger ones of the *Southampton* and *Newcastle* classes had twelve guns. Smaller cruisers of the *Dido* class were designed largely for anti-aircraft work and had 5.25-inch guns.

Destroyers were the most versatile ships of the surface fleet and had the leading role in preventing invasion. By 1939 the biggest ones were as large as the light cruisers of a generation earlier. British destroyers had their faults – they were designed for short-range operations – but that was not a problem in anti-invasion work. Ship for ship they were inferior to German equivalents, but since these were few in number that was not a grave problem. More seriously, they were short of anti-aircraft armament. They had a high speed of around 36 knots, as fast as any normal surface ship, they carried powerful torpedo armaments of up to ten tubes to attack enemy cruisers and transports, with 4- or 4.7-inch guns to engage smaller vessels. They had sophisticated fire-control systems for their guns, unlike smaller vessels, and they had depth-charges and asdics to deal with submarines. Their captains were often the élite of the navy. Admiral Cunningham wrote:

> I have always maintained there is more real discipline in destroyers than big ships, and of course we are always so much more in touch with our men. The skipper of a destroyer gets soaked to the skin on the bridge just the same as any sailor, but his opposite number [in a battleship] walks dry-skinned from his luxurious cabin where he has been sitting aloof from all goings on, to an equally luxurious bridge.[43]

The typical destroyer captain was a lieutenant-commander in his thirties, experienced enough to make decisions but young enough to be daring. Rather than long-range gunnery, he preferred to be in the thick of things using his own initiative to the full.

Destroyers were in great demand precisely because of their versatility, The newest ones were serving in the Mediterranean, where a naval war with Italy was just beginning, or as the anti-submarine screen of the Home Fleet. More were needed in Western Approaches Command, based in Liverpool, for, apart from trawlers and the new but unstable corvettes, they were the only ships available to protect convoys from the U-boats. The ones allocated to the anti-invasion commands – Nore, Dover and Portsmouth – tended to be of World War I or 1920s vintage. Those of the 'V' and 'W' classes had been built towards the end of the war and each carried four 4-inch guns. The 'A' to 'I' classes, built between 1927 and 1937, were equipped with four larger 4.7-inch guns. They were good ships and incorporated most of the experience of the last war but were rather short of anti aircraft armament.

As soon as the threat of invasion became serious, each of the southern C-in-Cs issued orders to deal with it by means of destroyer patrols. Since the Nore Command was considered the most vulnerable, it was allocated four destroyer flotillas early in June, 'in all a force of 32 ships – on paper' as the War Diary commented. But many destroyer crews were on much-needed leave after Dunkirk, and their ships were being repaired. In fact the average number available to the Command at that time was six, and the C-in-C begged for at least three more. Nevertheless, destroyers based at Harwich carried out night patrols between their base and Smith's Knoll off Great Yarmouth. The situation began to improve, and some ships were lent from Western Approaches, depleting convoy escorts. By 30 June there were 22 in the command, and 30 by the middle of July. Patrols between Flamborough Head and Sheringham in the northern part of the Command were added, while the Harwich destroyers went out nightly to Brown's Ridge, and two of them spent each night anchored off Margate ready to slip at instant notice. The Command also had to provide escorts for east-coast convoys. This was done mostly by sloops and corvettes, but sometimes the destroyers had to give support, leading to a very exhausting life. On 5 August a division of the 5th Flotilla was ordered to join the Home fleet at Scapa due to losses among the heavy ships, and the Flamborough to

Sheringham patrol had to be suspended. On the 13th came reports that German troops were embarking all along the coast of Norway, and all ships were ordered to raise steam and be at half an hour's notice for sea.

Offensive patrols were also carried out. Sam Lombard-Hobson was first lieutenant of the destroyer *Whitshed*, under Commander Conner, on the night of 30 July when she was off the coast of Holland with *Ambuscade* and *Wild Swan*. Nothing was found, and Lombard-Hobson was on the bridge as the ships were just about to head home before daylight.

> There was suddenly a tremendous, thumping noise under the forecastle; and a great column of water, which I distinctly remember looked black in core, shot up in the air and the bows of the ship crumpled downwards. With difficulty I clutched hold of the compass binnacle, to stop myself going upwards, only to be knocked down by what seemed a tidal wave of water which cascaded on to the bridge, sending everyone sprawling. I hit my head on something and was momentarily dazed because I though I was in the sea.

The ship had hit a mine. The bows were seriously damaged, and men off watch were trapped in the bows. Accepting the risks of bomber attack in the growing daylight, *Wild Swan* towed *Whitshed* stern-first back into Harwich, and eighteen men were buried at sea on the way over.[44]

At Dover the anti-invasion role was complicated by the need to protect convoys going through the Strait under heavy air and E-boat attack. In 12 June, before the dust of the Dunkirk operation had settled, Dover Command began what were called OD patrols, with one group off the North Goodwin Light Vessel, another off the South Goodwin, and a third off Dungeness. Their first aim was to prevent minelayers and submarines operating in the convoy routes, and they would report and attack any enemy vessels encountered. They were also to act in support of the small craft forming anti-invasion patrols closer inshore. The commanding officers on the spot were given discretion to carry out more offensive operations to interrupt enemy traffic along the French coast. Like all Commands, Dover had to react to the alerts when invasion seemed most likely, and when the 'First Degree of Readiness' was taken up on 3 July, all available destroyers were 'at sea on special patrol'. This was Patrol OE, with three or four ships operating east of Dungeness and four more to the west. They were to leave harbour at dusk and operate outside the shipping routes, looking out especially for E-boats, which tended to lurk near lighted navigation buoys. The object was 'having ships at sea in a most favourable state of readiness for dealing with any invading forces entering the Straits of Dover. Such effort could not be kept up for long without exhausting the crews, and on the 11th they were reduced to the second state of readiness, 'In order to give as much rest as possible to officers and men, and to enable minor repairs to be carried out.'[45]

But Dover was soon to suffer from a shortage of destroyers. The 1st Flotilla had just worked itself up to full efficiency when three of the G-class ships were taken away, to be replaced by escort destroyers with much inferior armament. There was disaster for the flotilla on 20, 25 and 27 July when *Brazen* and *Codrington* were sunk by air attack and five others were damaged, leaving only *Bulldog* and *Fernie* in service. Dover was proving too dangerous as a destroyer base, and the 1st Flotilla was withdrawn to Portsmouth, leaving only a sub-division of two ships at Dover. Six days later they too were withdrawn. The surviving ships of the flotilla continued patrols off Dover but were only at sea during the hours of darkness. Meanwhile, the attempt to escort convoys through the Strait was abandoned, and now they had to go the long way round or unload at western ports. But by the second half of August, the destroyer situation was even worse:

> Owing to the shortage of destroyers at Portsmouth, six only being available, and the calls made on their services it was agreed with Commander in Chief Portsmouth that these ships should be held available for operating to the eastward of Portsmouth instead of maintaining a patrol, unless the situation at the time clearly demanded they should be on patrol.[46]

By the end of September, destroyers from Portsmouth were operating off Dover on alternate nights, but this was ended on 6 October as the forces at Portsmouth were reduced. After that, C-in-C Nore was instructed to provide 'an intermittent patrol of two or three destroyers on two nights a week and whenever weather conditions and intelligence suggested the enemy might be encountered'.[47]

Destroyers could also carry out offensive patrols closer to enemy territory. By the end of June it was clear that the enemy was moving craft down the Channel towards Cherbourg, and Admiral James decided to try and intercept them. Each patrol consisted of two or three destroyers, which were to leave the Solent at dusk. Patrol JC West was to arrive eight or ten miles off Cherbourg then head slowly east ten miles off the coast, using their asdics set on 'hydrophone effect' so that they would hear the noise of any passing E-boats. A three in the morning, probably close to Le Havre, they would turn north and head home. Patrol JC East was to arrive ten to fifteen miles off Cap de la Hève near Le Havre, then sweep towards Dieppe.[48] By the beginning of August, however, the authorities were beginning to believe that enemy movements might be a feint, and new orders to the JC patrols gave them a more general area of operation, while establishing a new aim, 'To have available destroyers favourably disposed as striking forces to attack the flank if enemy forces attempting invasion in the Portsmouth and Dover Commands.' They were given elaborate orders on how to react if the enemy was reported outside the regular patrol area.[49]

Offensive patrols in the Dover area yielded poor results, and the successes of Captain Owen in the area 135 years earlier were not repeated. In a reversal of the procedure in the previous century, the enemy tended to move his ships by day rather than by night so that they could enjoy fighter cover and support from shore batteries.[50]

Nore Command's orders of 4 July give some idea of what might have happened had the destroyers needed to confront an invasion fleet. If possible they were to allow the enemy to cross the east coast mine barrier and attack him just to the west of it, as it would allow him little room for manoeuvre. Furthermore, it would make it possible for a strong fighter cover to be provided, assuming the RAF had not been defeated by that time. The sea battle would be Nelsonic, for ammunition supplies were not unlimited, and 'Close action must be the general rule, so that the biggest percentage of hits may be obtained with every outfit of ammunition'. The commanders on the spot had to decide whether to attack in ones or twos, or wait to form up divisions of three or four, which would give them an advantage if an enemy destroyer force was close, but it increased the risk of collision in poor visibility. If destroyers on passage sighted enemy transports they were to engage them; if they saw them trying to enter a port, they should attack them at all costs. If possible the destroyers should get between the transports and their naval escort, so that the torpedoes could hit the larger vessels. They were to aim especially at vessels that might be carrying tanks. The destroyers could also engage medium-sized ships with their guns and smaller ones with pom-poms and machine-guns. If they ran out of ammunition they should go as fast as possible to a port to replenish, but even then they were not out of action:

> In fog or short visibility destroyers and other vessels can usefully ram any warship larger than themselves. The best position to ram is from amidships aft to the propellers. Capture by boarding is recommended if circumstances permit but careful preparation is necessary if this is going to be done. Such attack on warships should be considered only if all transports have been dealt with.[51]

There is no doubt that destroyer sailors, the élite of the navy, would have carried out the attack with great skill and spirit, and the invading force would be lucky to survive without heavy losses. But there were never enough destroyers to guarantee security, and Mountbatten wrote in February 1941: 'It seems likely that there are going to be available many more transports than can be sunk by the warships available in the Channel ...'[52]

Another craft with potential use against an invader was the motor torpedo-boat, or MTB. During the previous war the Royal Navy had developed a small, fast craft with a planing hull, which could launch one or more torpedoes and possibly sink a ship of a hundred times her value. That concept had little appeal to the battleship admirals of the 1920s and 30s, and the thread of development was lost. Hubert Scott-Paine's British Power Boat Company at Hythe, near Southampton, produced its own designs, which were taken up by the navy in the late 1930s, while a dozen mixed craft which were building for foreign navies were taken over at the beginning of the war. It was soon found that the 60-foot BPB prototype was too small, and 71-foot boat was developed by their rivals Vosper. Some of the boats were fitted out as motor gunboats or MGBs with 20mm guns in place of torpedoes. Meanwhile the Germans had spent the inter-war years developing the Schnell or S-boat, usually known to the British as the enemy or E-boat. It had a speed of up to 40 knots, a hull of steel rather than wood, diesel engines, whose fuel was far less inflammable than the petrol of British boats, and it was big enough to carry guns and torpedoes at the same time. Fortunately, there were not many of them in service in 1940.

The MTB was fast enough to move into the invasion area in time to interrupt the landings. It had a shallow draft to let it pass over the minefields, and its torpedoes would be valuable against the transports, while the guns of the MGB could damage the barges. These coastal forces, as they became known, were initially based at Felixstowe on the east coast and Portsmouth on the south. They were still mostly commanded by regular naval officers early in 1940, but RNVR officers began to take command of them from that summer. Numbers were increased as 56 motor launches came into service in the second half of 1940.[53]

In the case of an invasion on the east coast, MTBs might be used inside the British minefield, where they would have an advantage because of their shallow draft, and fire their torpedoes without much risk of hitting friendly vessels. They should 'use their torpedoes to the best effect; they should endeavour to destroy the largest transport ship they can get at. Torpedoes should be fired at short range to ensure hits. When the torpedoes are expended, M.T.B.s should make the best use of their machine gun armament by attacks on small craft, including enemy "E" boats.'[54] They made contact with the enemy ten times during the second half of the year, mostly brushes with E-boats off the Netherlands or Calais. They claimed six small enemy transport vessels, but lost four MTBs to enemy action and accident, and two MLs.[55]

Behind the destroyers were two further levels of patrol. In the Dover area there were 'Listening patrols of asdic trawlers about 4 miles off-shore to detect the approach of the enemy, to report and attack him'. These trawlers would use their asdics, not in the usual anti-submarine role, but with the transmitter switched off so that they could listen for the engine and propeller noises of enemy vessels. Next came the 'Inshore patrols of drifters and motor-boats to report and attack the enemy'.[56] These formed the Auxiliary Patrol, which consisted of fishing boats and large yachts, sometimes manned by fishermen of the Royal Naval Reserve. It had served well against submarines in the previous war, but now its main function in anti-invasion work was to report the enemy, at a time when the potential of radar was not yet realized. It was often referred to as part of 'coastal forces', a title which was later taken over by the fast and glamorous MTBs and motor gunboats.

> Owing to their diverse nature, many different forms of armament are to be found in vessels of the coastal forces. Insufficient supplies of regular armaments to go round exist today but initiative and ingenuity may go far to make good the lack of the more orthodox forms of armament.[57]

The Auxiliary Patrol had 242 large yachts and 450 motor fishing vessels and motor-boats between Portsmouth and the Tyne early in July. They were expected to spend two nights out of three at sea, so that more than two thirds of them were out on 3 July.[58] Admiral James at Portsmouth was sceptical: 'I put no faith at all in this patrol. If the Germans decide to try invasion they will sweep up these unarmed boats on any suitable night beforehand.'[59] In fact, their main function was information, for which some of them were equipped with radio transmitters, only to be used 'to report enemy surface forces, submarines or large numbers of aircraft; to report distress or any suspicious occurrences or to give any other vital information'. They were to use one five codewords: 'Blackbird', meaning 'I have sighted enemy ships'; 'Mustard', to report 'I have sighted suspicious vessels which I think are probably enemy but I am not sure'; 'Apples', meaning 'I have sighted a large number of aircraft believed to be enemy flying towards the shore'; and 'Finish', denoting that it was no longer possible to maintain the patrol. 'Blackbird' and 'Apple' would be reinforced by fireworks, which were the main means of communication for vessels without radio transmitters.[60]

In addition, there were river patrols by armed motor-boats such as those operating in the Thames, Medway, Crouch, Colne, Blackwater, Deben, Orwell and other rivers on the east coast. The independent Member of Parliament A. P. Herbert was a water enthusiast, and in 1938 he had enrolled in the semi-official River Emergency Service with his cabin cruiser *Water Gypsy* in order to help protect the Thames in the event of war. When invasion threatened he and his boat were taken over more formally, but not entirely to his satisfaction:

> When we hoisted our first White Ensign (an enormous flag it was) I might have been Admiral Jellicoe himself. The first patrol orders we received were addressed to H.M.S. *Water Gypsy*, and I have the staggering document still. That, you may imagine, did not last long. We came down to 'H.M. Patrol Vessel': and in the end we were reduced to a 'Naval Auxiliary Boat' (the mean fellows). They reduced us grudgingly from Second Hand to Petty Officer to Petty Officer (Small Craft Only).[61]

Mines could be lethal to both sides in the shallow waters of the North Sea. Both sides carried out offensive mining, laying them off the enemy's ports and shipping channels, and defensive mining. The largest example of the latter was the East Coast Mine Barrage laid by the British between the coast of Kent and the Moray Firth. It was intended mainly to protect the shipping lane against submarine and surface-ship attack, but it would serve to stop an invasion on the east coast as well. Shallow-draft barges could get over it at high tide, but it would have to be swept clear for transport ships and large escorting warships to cross it.

The Germans would undoubtedly use mines to protect the flanks of their invasion forces, and the British would have to build up a fleet of minesweepers able to clear paths through them, probably in the most dangerous conditions. The Germans had developed the magnetic mine, which an aircraft could drop in shallow water where it would be set off by the magnetic field of a ship. The first task of the British was to spot them, and in December Nore Command reported:

> Aircraft mining more determined than usual took place in the Thames

Estuary on the night of the 11th–12th; and during the 12th–13th night the most intensive attack of the war so far took place also in the Estuary. Some 45 mines in all were seen to drop, and it is concluded that many more were laid unobserved.[62]

The navy also had to develop means to counteract the magnetic mine. Eventually the LL sweep was perfected, able to detonate mines by means of an electrical discharge between two ships. Minesweeping became a far more scientific business, and the fishermen of the RNR who had manned the vessels in the early days were largely superseded by young men of good education. At the end of September 1940, Dover Command had eleven 'Oropesa' trawlers to sweep for conventional mines and four LL trawlers for use against magnetic mines.[63]

In late June in Nore Command area,

A large new minefield was revealed when 'Clan Monroe' and 'Moidart' were mined on the 29th and it is significant that suspected minelayer was sighted by M.T.B. 28 in the early hours of the 30th ... 26 mines were swept in this area between 27th and 31st. Some of these mines were of a smaller type weighing approximately 1,000 lbs. which might have been laid by E-boat. Twenty-eight magnetic mines were exploded during the period, nine in the Humber area, eight in the Harwich area and ten in the Sheerness area.[64]

The mining war had elements of a game of chess, as one side tried to predict the other's movements. On 30 August, Dover Command reported,

There are indications that the channel between the Outer-Ruytingen and West Dyck banks is being swept which would provide a route southward of the main barrage. In certain circumstances in the event of invasion it may be the enemy's intention to attempt the use of Dover harbour for his transports, and to cross the channel by taking a departure for Dover from a position 360 degrees, Calais 6 miles or from Calais No.1 buoy. To counter this it is proposed that two lines of surface mines should be laid as follows ...'[65]

Minesweepers of different types were stationed in all the ports where naval vessels might operate, because it was feared that just before an invasion the Germans might try to mine the ships in. This was particularly important for naval ports: Portsmouth had ten active minesweepers in July, while Dover had sixteen.[66]

One of the greatest fears in the early stages of the invasion scare was that the enemy would take a port by surprise, and use it to land his panzers – for there were very few tanks in Britain to meet them. Most ports were defended poorly, if at all, and there were dozens of possible disembarkation sites between Peterhead in the North and Swanage in the west. A port might be taken by ships forcing a way in against weak defences or by paratroopers taking it from the rear.

The navy took responsibility for making sure that the ports were

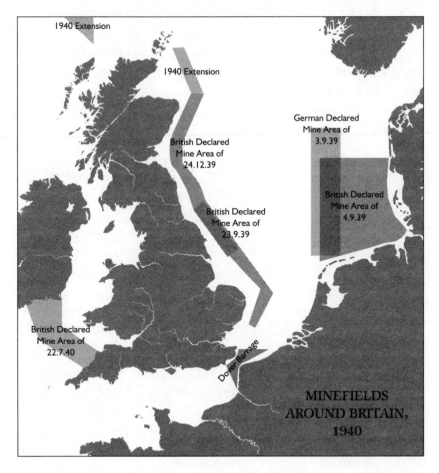

MINEFIELDS AROUND BRITAIN, 1940

rendered useless should one or more be taken by a sudden coup. The Admiralty issued its first orders on the subject on 20 May and elaborated on them over the following few days. The aim was 'to deny the invader any facilities to exploit his initial schemes, particularly in regard to landing armoured fighting vehicles and the transport and movement of troops by mechanical vehicles after landing'. The port authorities and locally based naval officers went to work on this quickly and with surprising enthusiasm, with separate schemes to immobilize the port for seven to ten days, and for longer periods. They proposed sinking blockships across the entrance, demolishing piers and cranes, and blocking roads in and out. At Blyth in the north-east it was planned to drop half a million tons of coal to fill the harbour and immobilize the railway. At Harwich it was intended to remove the leading marks into the harbour. At Ramsgate a wooden pier was to be set on fire with petrol, which would serve the additional purpose of destroying stocks that might be useful to the enemy. At Poole an old tug and two old hoppers, *Tweedledum* and *Tweedledee*, were to be sunk to block the narrow entrance. The authorities at Folkestone planned to immobilize the port for seven to ten days by 'the demolition of all cranes, cut off railway communication with the port by the demolition of railway viaduct over the inner basin, blocking of all exits by erection of railway barricades or by dropping of ironwork and masonry'.

By 6 June, however, the Admiralty had begun to see that many of the schemes were going too far. At Southampton, for example, it was planned to sink two dozen blockships across Southampton Water off Hythe pier. This was unnecessary as the port was well inland and could only be brought into use after the enemy had already captured Portsmouth and the Isle of Wight. It was made clear that 'these plans for destruction should be limited to material, plant and structures which would be of immediate use to the enemy in consolidating a foothold obtained in this country; there was no necessity to make arrangements to destroy oil fuel installations, range finders, or spare parts for ships.' This did not totally curb the excesses, and on the 25th it was noted that the Flag Officer in charge at the River Humber planned to 'release thousands of tons of fuel into the river and set it alight – at the moment selected by him. Such a conflagration, with a westerly wind, would create a smoke screen which would effectively prevent any offensive action being taken by our military forces.' The officers of Chatham dockyard wanted to remove all stores, which would have tied up vital transport and made them unavailable to ships that needed them. They would destroy plant and equipment, which might 'render the port useless for a matter of years – that is to say, *we* are doing what the Germans would like to do if they had the chance.'[67]

On 26 August the Nore Command issued general orders on how to deal with an invasion and again the echoes were Nelsonian – 'No captain can do very wrong if he engages enemy transports at close action range.' On receipt of the signal 'Purge', all ships were to come to instant readiness for battle and be ready to execute the general orders without any reference to the C-in-C. Once they had left harbour, the senior officers in charge of groups of cruisers, destroyers and MTBs would 'use their initiative and judgement according to the circumstances and the information that reaches them'. All ships would proceed immediately to the attack, preferably west of the mine barrier unless there was very early intelligence or the C-in-C ordered otherwise. Ships that sighted the invasion force would regard it as their first duty to report it by any means available. Smaller craft, including corvettes and the Auxiliary Patrol, should operate close inshore, destroying enemy landing craft, engaging aircraft attempting to drop paratroops, bombarding the landing grounds and beaches and helping to transport counterattacking troops across waterways, which were quite common in East Anglia.[68] It was just the kind of attack the navy had always loved, and there is no doubt that they would have created havoc among an invading force.

9

THE ARMY

THE ARMY IN 1803

The British army was not a greatly successful force in the opening years of the nineteenth century. It could look back to great leaders such as the Duke of Marlborough (an ancestor of Winston Churchill) almost a century earlier, and since then it had fought its wars principally in distant lands, with very limited involvement in the European theatre, where its performance had been poor. Parliament had a very long memory and mistrusted it, for collectively it remembered the days, almost a century and a half previously, when, following the Civil Wars, the New Model Army had dominated politics. Unlike other European countries, the navy was the first line of British defence and the army was often seen as a barely tolerated luxury.

The basic weapon of the early nineteenth century, whether by land or sea, was the smooth-bore, muzzle-loading gun, firing a non-explosive metal shot. Industrial change was well under way in Britain, while the American and French Revolutions were transforming man's vision of society. Military and naval strategy were being revolutionized by great leaders like Napoleon and Nelson, but the technology of war was still the same as that of a century or more earlier.

The battlefield was dominated by the light or medium cannon, firing a ball of 12 pounds or less, and the combined muskets of the infantry. Almost alone among contemporary fighting men, the cavalry relied on their sabres or lances more than their carbines or pistols. Compared with modern weapons, the firearms of 1803 were inaccurate, slow to load and had limited destructive power. Breech-loaders were almost unknown, and the rifled gun was a specialist weapon because of its slow rate of fire. Explosive shells were used mainly for bombarding towns but were notoriously inaccurate and dangerous to use. Colonel Shrapnel had already invented his 'spherical case shot' for bombarding infantry with a mass of small pellets, and red-hot shot was used by shore batteries against wooden ships. Otherwise, projectiles were of cast metal. A cannon could fire a solid ball, or a large number of smaller balls known as grapeshot.

The British army still used the 'Brown Bess' musket, which had been in service since 1715. Well-trained troops could fire at a rate of three rounds per minute, though with some loss of accuracy. It fired a ¾-inch lead ball, and it was not reckoned efficient at ranges of more than 80 yards. Because of the inaccuracy of an individual weapon, guns were usually fired en masse. Even so, it was estimated that only one man was killed for every 250 rounds fired. Conventional infantry fought with men drawn up in straight lines and very tight formations, partly to maximize the effect of their shot and partly to make retreat or desertion more difficult. They were usually in three lines, with at least one ready to fire while the others reloaded. The British army was beginning to train its own riflemen, rather than employing German or American hunters. The first British light infantry units were also being organized under Sir John Moore. As skirmishers, their discipline was not as tight as for ordinary (line) infantry, and even private soldiers were trained to use their initiative. The volunteer regiments would perhaps have added another mode of fighting, between light infantry and guerrilla warfare, but they were never tested at home.

Artillery 'in a general sense, signifies all sorts of great guns or cannon, mortars, howitzers, petards and the like'.[1] It was classified according to the trajectory at which its ball was fired. The cannon, by far the most common type, had a relatively flat trajectory, whereas howitzers and mortars fired a ball or shell higher into the air, either to give it longer range or to lift it over fortifications or one's own troops. Artillery could also be classified by its mobility. Fortress artillery was not intended to be mobile at all in battle. It used relatively heavy guns such as 24- and 32-pounders mounted on truck carriages with small wheels. Siege artillery included heavy mortars and howitzers, which were used to batter down walls and fire shells over them. Field artillery was by far the most common, and it had relatively light guns, firing rounds of 12 pounds or less, drawn by teams of horses. Horse, or 'flying', artillery was even more mobile, for the gunners were also mounted, and they could ride in support of the cavalry or gallop to a critical section of the battlefield.

Edged weapons were not totally obsolete, since guns were relatively inefficient. The infantryman still fixed his bayonet at the onset of battle, for use when his musket was unloaded or to form part of a solid wall against cavalry. Artillerymen carried swords for self-defence, while the traditional weapon of the cavalry was the sword or sabre. The lance, the main weapon of the medieval knight, had survived in Poland and had recently been taken up by the French army, though not yet by the British. Nor had they introduced the other type of central European cavalry, the Hussars. Instead the British army had three main types. There were three regiments of Household Cavalry, the 1st and 2nd Life Guards and the Royal Horse Guards, all used as bodyguards to the sovereign but employed with the army in the field when required. There were 21 regiments of heavy cavalry, which found their main role as shock troops during battle charges. The third type was the eleven regiments of light dragoons, who carried out reconnaissance, patrols and skirmishing. The British cavalry was comparatively small in numbers, and more fashionable than most infantry regiments. It was generally well mounted, for fine horses had been bred in Britain for sport and transport as well as war, but there was no central supply organization as in most armies.

Benjamin Silliman witnessed the cavalry in Liverpool in 1805:

The English light horse ... must be admirably calculated for celerity of movement. The horses have slender limbs, with great muscular activity, and are very quick and high spirited ... The men are also rather slender, and very active, and most of them young. Their dress is blue, exactly fitted to the body and limbs ... They have high helmets, and their broad swords, which are sheathed in bright steel scabbards, are of such enormous length, that they drag behind them on the pavement as they walk, unless they carry them in their hands, which they often do.[2]

The prestige of the rank and file of the army was very low, and this affected recruiting. Adam Smith wrote that 'The son of a creditable labourer or artificer may frequently go to sea with his father's consent; but if he enlists as a soldier, it is always without it.'[3] A soldier was normally enlisted for life, he was poorly paid, there was little provision for him to marry and support a wife, and he might well be sent to an unhealthy station such as the West Indies, where death rates were enormous. On the other hand, the army offered a glamorous uniform and regular employment – it is significant that many recruits came from trades affected by social and technological change, such as farm labourers and weavers. Recruiting was nominally controlled by the War Office, but in practice it was done by small parties sent out by each regiment. The dominant figure was the sergeant, with a drummer to attract attention. He was paid for every recruit and resorted to public houses and market places to find his men. His tricks were legendary. He exaggerated the benefits and prospects of a military career, the abundant food and extensive leisure. He might try to get his man drunk and then swear he had enlisted by 'taking the King's shilling', or one day's pay, though he would have to establish the point before a magistrate. Such methods did not produce a high quality of recruit, and numbers were barely adequate. Globally the British Empire used many recruits from poorer regions such as Germany and India; at home it had disproportionately large numbers from Ireland and the highlands of Scotland.

The British army relied heavily on its non-commissioned officers, often from middle class families with better education than the privates. They were only given their chevrons officially in 1802, four for a sergeant major, who was the senior NCO of a regiment, three for a sergeant and two for a corporal. The lance corporal or 'chosen man' had worn a single stripe for some time. An infantry company had an establishment of four sergeants and four corporals for 100 men. NCOs supervised the men at their training and in battle the sergeants would stand behind the line to rally them and prevent retreat.

Regular officers were separate from the men in their recruitment and lifestyles. They lived in messes largely funded by their private means, and only met the men in training and in battle. Officers were usually members of the upper and upper-middle classes, and a rank-and-file soldier had little chance of a commission except as a quartermaster or paymaster. In the engineers and artillery the initial appointment was after training at the Royal Military Academy at Woolwich, and further steps were by seniority. Promotion was very slow, and men of quite junior rank served in positions of great responsibility.

In the cavalry and infantry, an initial appointment might be gained by 'recruitment for rank', by recruiting a number of men to the service and then taking command of them. Occasionally there were 'promotions by brevet' in which specific groups of captains or majors were promoted en bloc even if there were no appointments for them. Individuals might even be rewarded for good or heroic service by promotion to particular vacancies. But in general an appointment and promotion as a cavalry or infantry officer was by means of the purchase of a commission. Officially a scale was laid down for prices, ranging from £450 for an ensign of foot to £6,700 for a lieutenant colonel in the foot guards – but rules were often broken in those days and much higher prices might be sought and paid.

It seems an extraordinarily inefficient and unjust system to modern eyes, but contemporaries were prepared to justify it. It provided the officer with an investment, for he could sell the commission when he left the army. It allowed young men to reach high rank, including the command of regiments in the field, quite quickly. And, most important from the ruling class point of view, it ensured that virtually all officers were men of substance, who were not likely to use the army to overthrow the established order. It was credited with preventing any modern British tradition of military coups or direct interference in politics.

The regiment was the focus of loyalty and tradition, both for officers and rank and file. It had a Colonel, usually a general who had a financial stake but rarely served with it. Its real commander was the lieutenant colonel. The number of troops varied according to success in recruiting, but the standard was ten companies of about a hundred men, each led by a captain with two lieutenants and an ensign under him. Regiments were usually known by a number and regional title in the Army List, such as the 'Fifteenth (or the Yorkshire East Riding) Regiment of Foot' or the 'Seventy-Fifth (Highland) Regiment of Foot'. Lowland Scottish infantry, such as the 'First (or the Royal) Regiment of Foot', wore the same dress as English troops but the Highland regiments wore kilts for training and battle as well as for parade. Local affiliations were growing but were not yet fixed, and it was only in 1806 that the War Office allocated definite recruiting areas:

> Regiments of infantry are to send their recruiting parties to those counties of which they bear the name; by which means it is hoped that they will acquire a local interest that may ultimately assist them in obtaining men. The regiments of cavalry, the royal regiments of infantry, and such as do not bear the name of any particular county, will apply to the inspector general of the recruiting service, to be permitted to recruit in such place as they think most advantageous.[4]

Permission might also be granted to send parties into the great manufacturing centres, where large numbers of bored or unemployed men might be found.[5]

The militia was the 'constitutional force', ready to protect the state against a standing army that might overreach itself. It was popular in parliament if not among the general population, who were liable to be conscripted. The militia was largely under the control of the local gentry rather than officers appointed by the central government. It was cheap in peacetime as its members were part-time, but it was mobilized or 'embodied' in war. In peacetime a militia officer was expected to have a certain amount of landed property in the country, but these rules were waived in wartime. According to Charles James,

> The regular way of obtaining a commission in the militia is by application to the Lord Lieutenant of the county, riding, or place. The names of the several gentlemen are sent by him into the Secretary of State's office to be laid before His Majesty. At the expiration of fourteen days, the different commissions are made out by the clerk of the county, &c. to such gentlemen as the King has not disapproved of.[6]

The militia was almost equal in numbers to the army at home – 90,000 of each in Britain and Ireland in June 1804, for example. In wartime most of them marched away from their home counties to forts and camps closer to the coast. Militia troops were often regarded as superior to these recruited to the regular army, and militiamen were given the option of transferring to the regulars. This proved an effective way of improving the army – Benjamin Harris wrote, 'My father tried hard to buy me off, and would have persuaded the sergeant of the 66th that I was of no use as a soldier, from having maimed my right hand (by breaking a forefinger when a child) . The sergeant, however, said I was just the sort of chap he wanted, and off he went, carrying me (amongst a batch of recruits he had collected) away with him.'[7]

A new soldier for the regulars or militia was issued with his uniform, with a red tunic for the infantry and most of the cavalry, blue for engineers and artillery. New clothing regulations were issued on the eve of war in April 1803. Each infantryman was to be issued once every two years with 'a lackered felt cap, with a cockade, and a feather or tuft.' This was the standard shako, a tall black hat. In addition he was to have annually, 'a jacket lined, but not laced, the sleeves unlined; a kersey waistcoat, with serge sleeves; a pair of blue pantaloons, made of cloth of the same quality as the jacket; and a pair of military shoes ...[8]

Militia and regulars trained in the same way, and in those days training drill was the same as battle drill. According to the 1803 *Rules and Regulations*, the instructor was to be kind and understanding.

> He must allow for the weak capacity of the recruit; be patient, not rigorous, where endeavour and good-will are evidently not wanting; quickness is not at first to be required, it is the result of much practice ... The recruit must be carried on progressively; he should comprehend one thing before he proceeds to another ... Recruits should not be kept too long at any particular part of their exercise, so as to fatigue them and make them uneasy.[9]

According to William James,

> A non-commissioned officer is to attend strictly to every circumstance of a soldier's conduct and behaviour in his quarters, and to make it his business to discover the different shades of character, so as to satisfy his commanding officers on every point of enquiry.

Every non-commissioned officer must be perfectly acquainted with the duties of a battalion, be master of the manual and platoon exercises, &C. and know how to write in a clear and expeditious manner.[10]

At the end of his career a soldier might look forward to a place as a pensioner in Chelsea Hospital, but Silliman was not impressed with the prospect when he visited it in 1805.

But, the life of a common solder is, in every part of it, deplorable. His pay is a song, his service is severe, his privations are great, his dangers frequent and imminent, his death undistinguished and unlamented, and, if he survive, his old age is dependant, vacant and miserable.[11]

The Army in Defence, 1803

In the age before mechanical transport, the soldier moved as he had always done, using his own legs. Cavalry could, of course, go somewhat faster, but it did not operate as an independent arm. Therefore the speed of an army's progress was limited to that of the soldier carrying his musket, ammunition, rations and equipment. Fifteen miles a day was reckoned a reasonable rate, though averages are not always useful when dealing with a military genius like Napoleon, who might perform great feats by means of forced marches. For the British soldier in his homeland, the pace was much more sedate, partly because his progress was controlled by the office of the Secretary at War. Even moving a regiment from one posting to another was a complicated process. An order would arrive prescribing the exact route and where stops of more than one day should take place. A quartermaster sergeant was appointed, along with 'two sober, intelligent privates', who would go ahead and find suitable billets for the overnight stops, in inns and private houses. Meanwhile the officers would prepare their men for the march.

The regular complement of a soldier may be carried with ease, but while bits of cord and packthread are allowed to supply the deficiency of proper straps, and the men are suffered to let their knapsacks rest upon their pouches, galled shoulders and oppressed loins must unavoidably ensue. Sore feet and corns will likewise be prevented by a strict attention to the soldiers' shoes and stockings. New shoes should not, on any account, be worn on a march; and soldiers ought to have it particularly recommended to them to wash their feet every day after a long march.[12]

The colonel had to remember that if he was passing though the City of London the colours had to be furled and the men's bayonets unfixed, unless he happened to be with the 3rd Regiment of Foot, which had originally been raised in the City. If passing through Oxford or Cambridge he was expected to pay his respects to the Vice Chancellor of the University. In humbler towns he might meet with local hostility or indifference:

the constable of Dartford, in Kent, refused to issue out the billets until he had counted off every man himself. This happened on a market day. The consequence was, that the companies were under the necessity of remaining upwards of thirty minutes in front of the George Inn, amidst droves of cattle, broken and deformed by the perpetual passage of wagons, carts, and horses; an inconvenience which must have been obviated, had the constable either trusted to the serjeant's route and state of the division, or have given himself the trouble of meeting it one mile from the town.[13]

In the event of an enemy landing, all these procedures would go by the board, as a War Office order of July 1803 recognized, even it if understated the amount of chaos and urgency that a landing would entail.

In the first hurry of assembling the troops on the landing of an enemy, it may be impossible, in all cases, to prescribe positive routes, and to prevent crossing, crowding, and interference, in the march of so many bodies, moving from distant places, and tending to the same point. The prudence and arrangement of the commanding officers must, therefore, as far as possible, provide against these unavoidable difficulties.

It was possible to move troops by ship, and the navy had a whole department devoted to the hiring of transport vessels, subject to the vagaries of the wind. Another scheme during the invasion scare was to have volunteer units brought closer to the action by means of requisitioned wagons and coaches. This might have worked well over friendly territory, and the roads of Britain were now adequate for it.

Conventional military tactics were linear, especially for the infantry. According to the 1803 *Rules and Regulations*, 'All great bodies of troops are formed in one or more lines.'[14] The initial formation was in 'Parade of Exercise', in which most of the preliminary work was done by the NCOs:

> The Regiment parades Three deep with Ordered Arms, standing at Ease, and in Open Column of Companies, with the Right Wing in Front, unless ordered to the contrary by the Commanding Officer. The Covering Serjeants take up correct Distances for their Companies on the Left or Pivot Flank; the Second Serjeants are to see that the Pivot Men cover with exactness, in Line with the Camp Colours, and that the Ranks are at close Order and dressing by the Left. They are to tell off their Companies (those of the Battalion having been equalized by the Serjeant Major) into Subdivisions or Half Companies, and into Sections or Quarter Companies, unless from Deficiency of Numbers, the Commanding

Unglamorous views of infantry on the march, showing supply wagons and camp followers. The figure on the bottom right with a halberd is a sergeant. From Pyne's Microcosm.

Officer should order each Company to form only Three Sections. In this Situation, the Companies are in charge of their respective Covering Serjeants, who take post on the Left, covered by the Second Serjeants, the Third of each Company being in the rear, and seeing the Ranks well closed up. The Flugel Man is advanced Forty Paces, nearly in the centre of the Regiment

After several more manoeuvres, the adjutant took charge of the parade, after which the other officers went to their situations:

The Colonel and Lieutenant Colonel (being both dismounted) place themselves, the former at Nine Paces. The latter at Six Paces, before the centre, the Major (on horseback) Six Paces in the Rear of the Third, and the Adjutant (also mounted) Six Paces in the Rear of the Sixth Companies.

Company officers also took up their stations, 'Captains (or those commanding) placing themselves before the Second Files from the Right, and the next Seniors before the Second Files from the Left, and the Juniors before the Centre; the two senior ensigns or those appointed to carry the Colours, to go to the Centre of the Regiment.'[15]

Troops up to battalion strength exercised in nineteen different manoeuvres, including close column, march in open column, countermarch by files, retreat in line, retiring and filing to the rear, echelon change of position and forming closed and open squares against cavalry. In the case of the latter, the commanding officer would give the caution, 'The Regiment will form a Hollow Square upon the three centre companies, viz., the fourth, fifth and sixth. Those companies will stand fast. The remaining companies in the Right Wing will wheel backwards Four paces on the Left, and those on the Left Wing will wheel backwards Four Paces on the Right.' The word of command was given: 'By Companies, on the inward Flanks backwards wheel.' On the order 'Quick March', each of the affected companies went diagonally into its position. Then it was up to the officer commanding each company to wheel it into line as part of the square and dress it. The officers and sergeants were inside it, with the regimental headquarters and colours in the centre.[16]

These were the formal tactics much favoured by Sir David Dundas, but there was another school that saw light infantry as the way forward. It was not a new idea when Major General Sir John Moore took it up in the camp at Shorncliffe, near Folkestone, in 1803. It had already been used with one company attached to each infantry regiment, and on a larger scale by the French. Moore took three ordinary infantry regiments and trained them to use their initiative in the forefront of the battle. He needed officers of dedication and human sympathy, while dilettantes were encouraged to transfer out by the hard work involved.

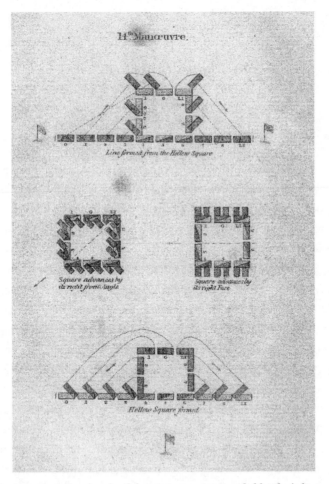

Forming square, showing the elaborate manoeuvres needed by the infantry.
(*From H. Dickinson,* Instructions for forming a Regiment of Infantry ..., 1803)

Power was delegated to the company commanders, and officers and NCOs were made to understand that it was their duty to prevent crime, rather than punishing it by flogging. The intelligence of the individual soldier was developed, not repressed. A review in October 1803 before William Pitt gives some idea of Moore's tactics, involving cooperation between several arms:

> the Major General having taken the command, the rifle corps was ordered to advance and skirmish in front, where the enemy was supposed to be concealed in a valley. The field pieces advanced at the same time to support it, and a brisk fire was kept up for a considerable time. The columns then formed the line, and advanced until they arrived at an opposite hill, where the line halted. Here the 52nd, being a light infantry battalion, extended, together with the rifle corps, and kept up a brisk fire to cover the line, which was ordered to retire, having first formed in close column again. When they regained their former ground, the line was formed again, and the light infantry and rifle corps retired, keeping up a sharp fire, and disputing every edge, until the close was surrounded, when they rapidly formed in line with the other regiments.[17]

Moore's troops were in the front line of any possible invasion and would have fought well against the French; they would show the effectiveness of such tactics when they fought under Wellington in the Peninsular War a few years later.

Napoleon wrote that 'Infantry, cavalry and artillery are nothing without each other.'[18] The infantry was likely to form the great majority of any army, especially in an invasion of Britain, for the British were rather weak in cavalry, but that was not necessarily a disadvantage as the French would have had great difficulty landing them in large numbers. Thus in June 1804 the forces for the defence of Britain constituted 82 per cent infantry (including militia but not volunteers), 12 per cent cavalry and 4 per cent artillerymen. Infantry could not attack without a preliminary bombardment by artillery. Cavalry was not likely to succeed in a frontal attack on a line of infantry, though it might be devastating against the flanks and rear. To guard against this, the infantry battalions formed into squares when cavalry attack seemed likely, which could leave the defenders ill-prepared for a subsequent infantry attack. Cavalry was also needed for reconnaissance and for holding off the enemy cavalry. After the battle, it could harass a retreating enemy.

In the previous war, around 1800, General Sir Charles Grey of the Southern District had drawn up a plan showing regular lines of defence, starting with the coast from Selsea to Deal. Then there was the 'line to retire upon from the coast' while covering evacuated livestock, followed by an inland line from Petworth to Canterbury. There were first and second lines for the defence of Chatham and the Medway, where the dockyard had to be protected and the river crossing denied if at all possible; then a third line to protect Gravesend and communication across the Thames with Essex; and a fourth line from Boxhill to Wrotham, exploiting the natural defences of the hills. Behind that was a 'half line' to defend the Dockyards at Deptford and Woolwich, and finally a line from Wimbledon to Blackheath for the final defence of London. An individual unit might have its line of retreat marked out, for example from Worthing and Angmering, to Steyning, Mock Bridge, Charlwood Green, Cockshead, Reigate Hill and Streatham near London.[19] Such detailed planning would probably not have survived long in the face of battle.

In June 1804, as the second summer invasion season began, the Southern Command had a strong and balanced force inland at Canterbury, with artillery, the Royal Horse Guards and 2nd Dragoons and the Radnor, Derbyshire and Warwick militias. The artillery was based at Chatham, along with two battalions of foot guards, and the cavalry had a depot at Maidstone. Apart from that, the defences of east Kent were mostly on the coast, with an army of the reserve battalion and an artillery battery to guard the dockyard and entrance to the Medway at Sheerness, a militia regiment at Margate, militia and dragoons at Ramsgate and two battalions of militia at Walmer. Dover Castle was defended by four battalions of militia, and Moore had four regiments of regulars, possibly the best infantry in the army, at Shorncliffe, with the local East Kent Militia guarding and observing from Dungeness. There was a separate force of light dragoons nearby at Hythe. Farther inland there were regular troops at Ashford and militia at Brabourne Lees, closer to Dover. On the south coast there were troops at Playden, near Rye, and at Winchelsea, both a very short distance inland from the coast. Infantry battalions at Hastings and Bexhill were backed up by more in the barracks at Silver Hill and Battle, those at Pevensey and Eastbourne by two regiments at Hailsham. West of Beachy Head, troops were stationed in Brighton and Shoreham, with an inland line from Ringmer and Lewes to Steyning, Arundel and Chichester. [20]

That July the region was greatly reinforced as the authorities became aware of the threat to the south. Large bodies of troops were stationed inland in Kent as reserve forces. A camp for up to 5,000 regulars was set up at Barham Downs, ten miles north-west of Dover, and guards regiments were marched in from Chatham, while others were brought in by sea from Leith, Sunderland and York to disembark at Ramsgate. A militia camp for up to 11,000 men was also set up at Coxheath, south of Maidstone. Troops were brought in from Essex, crossing the Thames at Tilbury Fort.[21]

In 1803, Dumouriez recommended some places where the country could be defended inland. He considered specific lines of advance for an invading army and where they could be countered, for example, the enemy, seeing the impossibility of forcing the hills on his right and not daring to attack Oxney camp, would try to cross the river at Rye to penetrate into Sussex by Winchelsea in order to turn the two camps he had not dared to attack. In this case the Kent army would prolong its march as far as Goudhurst, and the division assembled there would take up the excellent position of Tunbridge Wells. The western divisions would march along by the left, and so make for Hampshire and Sussex to prevent the enemy's turning aside to Portsmouth, which he could not hope to succeed in capturing with no heavy artillery nor time for a siege. This French army would find itself at a distance from the sea, without hope of reinforcements, and would soon be lost.[22]

If the enemy could penetrate farther, Dumouriez recommended the defence of 'the two great chains of hills west and south of Maidstone ... In this third line of defence everything would be a military position, and there would not be a single height remaining undisputed to damp the ardour of an enemy, that incurred fresh losses every day without hope of retrieval.' Then there was another line among the rivers a few miles east and south of London, 'on the heights ... by the Medway and Darent valleys. Between these two rivers are such a number of excellent positions, as also between the Darent and Cray, and the Cray and Ravensbourne, that a foolhardy enemy penetrating so far would undoubtedly be crushed by the assembled forces of England.'[23]

THE ARMY IN 1940

The British army saw no more service in Europe after Waterloo until the Crimean War against Russia in 1853–6. It is chiefly famous for 'The Charge of the Light Brigade' and 'The Thin Red Line', both symbolizing the bravery of the rank and file, while the Charge of the Light Brigade also gave the public an exaggerated idea of the incompetence of some of the officers. Reform was clearly necessary, but even in an increasingly democratic age, the purchase of commissions survived until 1871. Edward Cardwell, Secretary for War from 1868 to 1874, greatly reinforced the local associations of the infantry and cavalry regiments. Each was to have two regular battalions, one serving overseas in the empire, one in the depot for home defence and to provide replacements for the other battalion. Mergers produced a force of 46 regiments in England, ten in Scotland, eight in Ireland and three in Wales. Regiments were now closely associated with counties, where each had its recruiting area. The two regular battalions were supplemented by two or three of militia and volunteers. It worked well, for local pride was a feature of Victorian society, both in town and country – the other focus for rural loyalty, the County Cricket Championship, was set up in the 1870s. There were city regiments, such as The Manchester Regiment and The Royal Fusiliers (City of London Regiment), but it was generally agreed that countrymen made the best infantry and cavalry, and recruitment was aided by a high level of rural unemployment for the rest of the century.

Each regiment had its nicknames from past campaigns. The Argyll and Sutherland Highlanders were the original 'Thin Red Line' after the formation they adopted at the Battle of Balaclava. The Middlesex Regiment was 'the Diehards', the East Yorkshire Regiment was 'the Snappers', for they had once run out of ammunition and used their gun locks to mislead the enemy. Each regiment had its colours with a list of the battles it had fought in. It had an honorary colonel-in-chief, usually royalty or a distinguished military figure. It usually took its title from its county, sometimes with other features, so that the 40th and 82nd Foot became The South Lancashire Regiment (The Prince of Wales's Volunteers). A recruit expected to serve his whole military career with the regiment and regarded the rest of the army as inferior copies of it. Battalions from the same regiment rarely served together, and because of this isolation the individual battalion was often referred to as 'the regiment', even in official publications.

Meanwhile the militia declined and became little more than a recruiting agency for the regulars, while the volunteers were mostly social clubs. The yeomanry was a force of part-time farmers who trained as cavalrymen and was another focus for local loyalty. In 1908 another reforming Secretary for War, Richard Haldane, replaced the militia and volunteers with the Territorial Force (later the Territorial Army) as the main reserve. It strengthened the regimental associations, but it could not be sent overseas – a provision that was altered by statute when a major war actually began. It provided many thousands of men for the army in World War I, though the great bulk of recruits came from the New Armies raised by Lord Kitchener, which by-passed the territorial organizations.   This was the army that fought the war from 1914 to 1918. Despite the horrors of the trenches, the regimental system was immeasurably reinforced, as large-scale volunteering followed by conscription brought in a far wider range of men than the regulars and territorials had ever done. A single regiment might send out up to sixty battalions, in a war dominated by infantry.

Otherwise the army's reputation was severely damaged by the war, and particularly the Western Front. Warfare had been transformed in the century since the last great European conflict, but British generals did not always accept reality. Long-range exploding shells replaced smooth-bore solid shot. The repeating rifle and machine-gun provided a rapidity and accuracy of fire that gave a great advantage to the defence and to men protected in trenches. Cavalry was useless, and movement towards the battlefield was by railway, which meant that the defenders could bring in reinforcements to a threatened sector while the attackers were still trying to advance slowly and bloodily on foot. There were four years of stalemate, with many futile attacks, such as the Battle of the Somme in 1916, in which 20,000 men were killed on the first day. No generation was ever more crushingly disappointed than those who went to war willingly in 1914 and returned, if they did return, crippled or traumatized. War memoirs appeared in the 1920s and 1930s, such as Robert Graves's *Goodbye to All That* in 1929. Every young man had a father, uncle or schoolmaster with memories of years of filthy 'troglodyte' existence, interspersed with lethal battles. Many were too traumatized to talk, but a few did, for example to Ken Kimberley, who avoided the army because, 'Old Murray's Friday afternoon lectures down at Balaam Street had put me off the Army for ever. His reminiscences of life in the trenches in the First World War, freezing mud, bayonets, barbed wire and what have you, gave me the creeps.'[24]

The army officer's reputation suffered worst of all, and the legend of 'lions led by donkeys' persisted throughout the peace. It was reinforced by David Low's 'Colonel Blimp' cartoons. In fact the title character was never seen outside a Turkish bath, where he made fatuous and self-contradictory comments about the political situation – 'Gad, sir. Lord Bunk is right. The govt. are going over the edge of an abyss and the nation must march solidly behind them.' But his very title made his name symbolize the pig-headed officers who had sent thousands of men to a pointless death in the last war, and were allegedly still running the army in the present one.

In peacetime a potential infantry or cavalry officer was usually aged eighteen and just out of a public school when he went to the Royal Military Academy at Sandhurst for an eighteen-month course. The syllabus had less horsemanship and more strategy than in the past. There were 120 hours of instruction in military drill and 129 hours on mathematics and science, while civilian schoolmasters taught general subjects such as geography and history, with special stress on the British

Empire, where most of them would serve at one time or another. It could be a tough life, especially in the early stages.

> We were called 'Gentlemen Cadets'. The officers and non-commissioned officer instructors were the pick of the whole British Army and the drill instructors were exclusively, the pick of the Brigade of Guards. Knowing you were due to become an officer in eighteen month's time, the N.C.O.'s could call you anything they liked provided they prefaced it with a 'Mr. So-and-So, Sir.' ...
>
> It was very hard and exhausting – for the ten weeks on the square, we never stopped running, saluting, marching, drilling, climbing ropes, riding unmanageable chargers and polishing and burnishing everything in sight ... boots, belts, chinstraps, buttons and above all our rifles ... 'the soldier's best friend, mind'.[25]

There were other ways of becoming an officer, through the Special Reserve or militia, or direct from university. Promotion from the ranks was easier than in the navy, and selected young NCOs were trained for commissions at Sandhurst,[26] but the young ex-public school entry included most of the men who would reach high rank and set the tone for the army as a whole.

The rank and file were not held in much respect either. Despite massive unemployment in the early 1930s, joining the army was seen as a desperate last resort by the urban working classes. Many of them were involved in trade unionism or left-wing politics, and they had not forgotten how the army had been used to break the General Strike in 1926.

Even after Britain began to rearm in 1935, the idea of a land campaign in Europe was rejected, and the resources went to the navy and air force. This was only reversed in February 1939 when the government committed itself to a 32-division force, which would be ready by 1942. Thus the army of 1940 was far less prepared than the other services, with serious shortages of equipment and thousands of half-trained men.

The Territorial Army barely survived the cuts after World War I, sandwiched between War Office indifference and anti-militarism in the population at large, though its annual camps proved popular in an age of deprivation. There was a great surge of recruiting with the Munich crisis of 1938, and for a short time the TA became the best hope for national defence. In March 1939 the War Minister, Leslie Hore-Belisha, announced that its strength was to be doubled. It was not difficult to find men in the climate of the times, but the training facilities were overwhelmed. It was worse the following month when it was decided to introduce a limited form of conscription. Men of the age of twenty would be called up for six months of training in a revived militia, followed by three and a half years of service with the territorials.

The first 34,000 militiamen started training in mid-July, but it had not got very far when the war began in September, and a much broader system of conscription was introduced. Five territorial divisions had been sent to France by April 1940, followed by three less well trained ones intended for labouring. All of them were involved in the fighting after the Germans attacked, and the 51st (Highland) Division was eliminated at St Valéry-en Caux. A German report offered some praise: 'Certainly the Territorial Divisions are inferior to the Regular troops in training, but where morale is concerned they are equal.'[27] The conscripts who followed them into the ranks saw them differently: 'we in the ranks heartily despise most Territorial officers, and Territorial N.C.O.'s too. They try to copy the Regulars, and so imperfectly: they are so obviously inferior to the god-like, awe-inspiring Regular officers and sergeants who trained us in our impressionable first month in the Army.' They were 'so peculiarly constituted that they enjoy Army routine for its own sake'.[28]

Even after conscription was introduced for all, an individual could still volunteer for the service of his choice before his turn to be called up arrived. During 1940 the RAF had more volunteers than conscripts, the navy slightly less. But in the army, conscripts outnumbered volunteers by more than three to one, 858,000 against 252,000.[29] The navy and the air force could still pick and choose its men among the conscripts, and the navy only took on about a third of the men who ticked it as a preference. The army had to take practically everyone who came up to the basic medical standards. Within the army, men with trades or good educational qualifications went into the technical corps, leaving the infantry for those who had nothing specific to offer. According to Major

General Utterson-Kelso, the infantry was 'the legitimate dumping ground for the lowest forms of military life'.[30]

Yet there were many who were happy to go into the army. It offered life on land, a more familiar environment. It had lower eyesight standards than the navy or the flying branch of the RAF. Some may have thought it was easier to get a commission than in the more technical navy and RAF. Most important of all was family tradition, fostered by the regimental system, for many men had fathers or uncles who had served in infantry regiments in the last war. Not every infantryman was there against his will.

In 1940 as in 1803, the army had low status and was tainted by its defeats in Norway and France. However, Army Training Memoranda suggested that they had actually not done all that badly in the war in Europe, and hinted that the main fault had been with the French.

> The B.E.F. in Flanders was compelled to undertake a series of withdrawals to conform to the movement of allied forces on its flanks, but it is noteworthy that, in spite of the enemy's superiority in material, on no occasion was the B.E.F forced to relinquish a main position by frontal attack ... Two of the lessons that emerged were, firstly, that the British soldier is man for man at least the equal of if not better than the German and, secondly, that our tactical conceptions of the defence have on the whole stood the test, though modifications may be necessary to suit the very wide fronts which are likely to become normal in future.[31]

The Training Memoranda also provided a fund of inspirational stores from the campaign:

> The extreme right section of a certain battalion was heavily attacked. Its task was to cover a partially demolished bridge.
>
> Every man in the section, except the commander, was killed or wounded. The platoon on the right was heavily shelled and withdrew.
>
> The section commander stuck to his post, prevented the enemy from crossing the bridge by using his Bren gun, and enabled the battalion on his right to re-establish its position on the right of the bridge.
>
> Lesson – Defence must be absolute. Unless direct orders for a withdrawal are given, it is the duty of the individual to remain at his post

until killed or captured. The devotion of an individual may prevent disaster to a whole company or battalion.[32]

In theory the new army officers were now recruited on a far wider basis. In 1937 it was decided that extra officers should be appointed from men who had served in the ranks. Hore-Belisha, the Secretary for War, presented a rosy picture of a new meritocratic force:

> In this Army the star is within every private soldier's reach. No one, however humble or exalted his birth, need be afraid that his military virtues will remain unrecognised. More important, no one, who wished to serve in the Army need consider his status minimised by starting on the bottom rung of the ladder.[33]

In the summer of 1940 the army was a long way from living up to this. Many young men who held the Class A certificate of the public schools Officer Training Corps, or the Class B certificate of a university OTC had been recruited direct as officer cadets, nearly all from the upper and upper middle classes. Other potential officers needed the recommendation of their battalion commanders, often 'old-school' colonels with their own prejudices. It was not formally based on education, but that certainly had an effect. 'Nowadays he cannot hope to find Eton and Oxford among the recruits. So he acts on the principle of accepting the second best. If he cannot get Eton, he will get a good Grammar School. If he cannot have Oxford, he will get a graduate of a provincial university.'[34] It was not until 1942 that a more 'scientific' system was set up, in which men were tested for several days under the eye of psychologists and military men.

Even worse, some COs were suspected of hanging on to efficient NCOs because the unit needed them. The War Office was well aware of the problems by May 1940, when it urged existing officers:

> The responsibility for spotting suitable men and bringing them to the notice of commanding officers rests largely with junior commanders. If they adopt the selfish and short-sighted policy of hanging on to good men, the future of the Army will be jeopardized. Alternatively, to recommend a man because he is the best of a poor bunch may be no more than an error of judgement; but to recommend an indifferent man merely to fill somehow a unit vacancy is criminal.[35]

This could be taken too far, and it is reported that one commander of a pioneer battalion was asked to nominate a specific number of potential officers. He replied that most of his men were 'of the labourer type, wholly unfitted by education, upbringing or experience to hold a commission or command troops'. He was ordered to provide the names anyway.[36] Some men did not put themselves forward because 'I remained happily in the ranks, partly because I preferred the company there, and partly because I know I would make a very bad officer, and there are enough bad officers in the Army already.'[37]

Selected men went to the Officer Cadet Training Units for four months, or longer for engineers and signallers. There were 29 of these in 1940, including two for the Royal Armoured Corps, four for the artillery, eight for the infantry and five for different branches of the Royal Engineers. On 6 August they had 9,281 cadets under training.[38] An infantry officer who did the course late in 1940 pointed out the faults. They never saw, let alone fired, weapons such as mortars and anti-tank guns. They learned nothing practical about armour, artillery or the air force, while 'A great deal of time was wasted in improving the rifle and squad drill of the cadets ... and upon polishing buttons and equipment.' None of the instructors had any experience in the present war, and they were mostly sergeants who acted as if they were dealing with 'unwilling and stupid learners who required to be driven to work'. The course was sometimes accused of training 'the perfect private soldier' rather than instilling the qualities needed in an officer.[39] It was always recognized that a green second lieutenant still had a good deal to learn on the job before he became useful, but that was even more true in 1940, and much depended on the intelligence and character of the individual. Furthermore, the modern platoon leader was not just a junior officer under the eye of the company commander, but the leader of a well-equipped fighting group in its own right.

Another source was from ex-officers from World War I, who joined through the Army Officers Emergency Reserve, but they resented having to start again as second lieutenants, and found their experience was undervalued: 'any N.C.O. or man who evacuated at Dunkirk, is ipso facto an infinitely more worthy subject for commissioned rank, than one who was demobilised in 1919, after 4 years of commissioned active service in France or some other theatre of war.'[40]

In 1938 the army had tried to cover the shortage of junior officers by using warrant officers as platoon commanders. Unlike his naval namesake, an army warrant officer was more like a senior NCO than a junior officer. He lived in the sergeants' mess and usually had a title like 'sergeant-major' or 'quartermaster sergeant'. He had invariably risen from the ranks and had seen long service. The most prominent ones were the sergeant-majors, well known for their parade-ground manner, fierce discipline and intimate knowledge of military administration. A regimental sergeant major was the senior non-commissioned member of a battalion and was a Warrant Officer Class I; a company sergeant major was Class II. The new idea was to create a Class III, of platoon sergeant majors, but they were actually to command the platoons, with sergeants under them. This tended to cut across the traditional army structure:

> The old ideal of the officers of a company living and working as a team under the Company Commander, learning his thoughts and absorbing his spirit, is impossible of attainment when some of his platoon commanders (the W.O.IIIs) live with the men, and cannot mix on equal terms with their commander and his officers.[41]

Within the platoon, the sergeant was used to dealing with an officer with a good education, and what the numerous snobs called 'breeding', not with a warrant officer who was little different from himself. 'A young soldier promoted to W.O.III has a far harder task than if he were given a commission. As a W.O.III he lives with the men, who regard him as one of themselves, and discipline is difficult. Moreover, his position vis-à-vis the W.O.II (not treated as a trained or pseudo officer) is invidious.'[42] In any case, once the war had started, conscription provided a larger proportion of men who were suitable for commissions, and everyone started off in the ranks anyway. In France it was found that a unit tended to fall apart once it had lost its commissioned officers. Churchill agreed that, 'Every platoon should have an officer without the slightest delay.'[43]

Everyone knew that the warrant officers and non-commissioned officers were the backbone of the army. The sergeant major of a company or a battalion was a fearsome figure, almost as dreaded by junior officers as by privates. A sergeant in the infantry was the second-in-command of a platoon, often left in command when there was a shortage of officers, or bearing great responsibility in guiding a young and inexperienced lieutenant fresh from OCTU. In the artillery he might command a gun, in the armoured corps a tank. The sergeants were separated from the men under them, living in a comfortable mess with the warrant officers and enjoying much better pay.

In the artillery an NCO with two stripes was known as a bombardier; in the armoured regiments a corporal was usually a junior tank commander. In the infantry, the corporal was in a unique position. Unlike the sergeants and sergeant majors above him, he was in sole charge of his sub-unit, but he had no specific training in leadership. He fell in with the men on parade, and he lived with them in barracks with no particular privileges. The RAF allowed its corporals single rooms and separate spaces in mess halls, while the United States army promoted its squad leaders to sergeant, but the British army was not prepared to dilute the ranks of its senior NCOs by promoting large numbers of corporals.

The lance corporal or lance bombardier, with a single stripe on each arm, was in an even more awkward position. He held an 'appointment' rather than a rank, so he could be demoted at any time. In the infantry section he was the second in command and in charge of the Bren gun, providing the bulk of the firepower. In appointing new lance corporals, officers were advised to impress on them that, 'It is the duty of every N.C.O. to set a very high standard and example of loyalty, behaviour and turn out.' He was to look after the interests of his men and help any lame ducks. On receiving an order he was to make sure that he understood it completely before replying, 'Very good, Sir.' He was to make his own orders clear, and specific to individuals. He had to remember that his men's lives might depend on his decisions, and 'It is his bounden duty on taking his stripe to do his utmost to make himself fit for the job.'[44]

NCOs were promoted within the battalion or regiment at the discretion of the CO to fill places in the official 'establishment' as laid down by the War Office. A standard infantry battalion was allowed 31 sergeants and staff sergeants, 53 corporals and 650 privates, of whom up to 40 might be lance corporals. Technical and administrative appointments had certain rules about educational qualifications and length of service, but in other cases the battalion CO had a free hand. With little guidance apart from the advice of his subordinates, he took into account the candidate's seniority, leadership, character and general reliability.

The army had just over a million and a half men in the homeland in July 1940, plus 22,000 from Australia, New Zealand and Canada and 37,000 women in non combatant roles. About one in five men had recently been evacuated from France, while the majority of the others were untrained and ill equipped. On taking over the Southern Command in July, General Brooke found, 'Untrained men, no arms, no transport, and no equipment. And yet there are masses of men in uniform in this country but they are mostly untrained, why I cannot think after 10 months of war.'[45]

THE ARMS OF SERVICE, 1940

If it is true that the army with the grandest uniforms always loses the war, then the British had a natural advantage. The red tunics were put aside in wartime and even guardsmen outside Buckingham Palace paraded in battledress. This was in khaki, a nondescript light brown colour, which the army had adopted in India towards the end of the last century. The standard army uniform was the 1937 pattern, based on a mechanic's overall and uncompromisingly functional. The blouse stopped at the waist, as it was believed that anything below that level would restrict the soldier's movements. Orders claimed that 'Men can look smart in battle dress if it is worn correctly and the necessary trouble is taken', but had to admit that 'a slovenly man can look like a tramp'.[46] It was often ill-fitting and far less attractive than the Service Dress of the last war.

In battle, training, exercise or on leave, the fully equipped soldier wore stout black lace-up boots, which were an obsession of military life:

> Despite all the ballyhoo about the Army being mechanised now ... the British High Command still clings to the view that an army marches on its feet. We were issued with our boots on the day of our arrival before anything else, and warned to start wearing them straight away so that our feet could get used to them before we went on the square. They were our absorbing interest during our first fortnight in camp.[47]

The soldier wore a canvas belt and braces over his uniform. He had a pack on his back, the size of which varied according to the operation in question. Above that was a rolled cape for protection against mustard gas attack. Ammunition pouches were suspended in front, specially designed to carry magazines for the Bren gun, as well as other weapons. His gas mask was hung on his chest, his bayonet slung on his left hip, with a small entrenching tool over that, and a water bottle hung over his right hip. Equipped like this, a soldier was expected to survive for up to two days without replenishment or support.

For normal dress the soldier wore a forage cap, an inconvenient garment worn tilted to one side, which gave little protection from the rain unless its flaps were lowered to cover the ears. It did however carry a regimental badge giving the unit its clearest sense of identity. In battle he wore the circular steel helmet as issued to all the adult population for use in air raids. It was designed in the previous war mainly for protection against shrapnel, and gave far less lateral cover than the well-known German helmet.

The infantry, the 'poor bloody infantry' of the last war, were no longer dominant in numbers. On 6 July 1940 the infantry, including the Brigade of Guards and men enrolled for home defence only, consisted of a total of just under 600,000 officers and men, nearly 40 per cent of the men in Home Forces. But as Major General Utterson-Kelso wrote in 1941, 'Infantry is the principal arm. It bears the decisive weight of battle. It suffers the heaviest casualties. All the other arms support it.'[48] This was especially true because of the weakness of the other services. The Royal Engineers, the Royal Army Service Corps and the Royal Army Ordnance Corps, among others, all fulfilled vital roles but were not expected to fight the enemy except in extreme circumstances. The Royal Armoured Corps was small, with just under 40,000 officers and men in July 1940. The Royal Artillery had 350,000 officers and men, but nearly two-thirds of them were in the anti-aircraft batteries, mostly defending the great cities and not intended for the land battle.

The smallest infantry unit was the section of seven men led by a corporal. It was now being increased to ten, though initially it was intended that only seven of them should go into action, this number being 'the most that can be controlled by a section leader'.[49] Its most powerful weapon, 'the principal weapon of the infantry',[50] was the Bren light machine-gun. Fired from a bipod, it had a rate of fire of about 120 rounds per minute, allowing for time to change magazines. Its 30 rounds were held in a characteristically curved magazine mounted above the gun, and the other members of the section carried Bren magazines in their ammunition pouches – an infantry section could carry 300 rounds in this way.

Apart from the Bren gunner, the members of the section were equipped with the Lee-Enfield rifle, which fired the same .303-inch round as the Bren. It fired single shots from its 10-round magazine, but the rifleman could reload by lifting the bolt-action while still keeping his aim on a target. Later the section leader would be given a .45-inch calibre Thompson submachine-gun, 'the gangster gun of the American films. Its light weight and ease of handling make it very suitable for engaging opportunity targets at short range.'[51] Each man carried hand grenades, including the well-known Mills bomb, and a bayonet that was still 'an excellent fighting weapon' according to the latest instructions.[52] The section commander had a variety of weapons at his disposal and had, or should have had, at least as much tactical initiative as a company commander in 1805, for his Bren gun could provide fire and the rest of the section provided movement, the essence of infantry tactics.

Three sections were combined into a platoon, led by a lieutenant or a warrant officer with a sergeant as second-in-command. The platoon also had a batman and runner and men to operate a small mortar and a light anti-tank gun, making a total of 36. The next level up was the company, headed by a captain or major. It had three platoons and a headquarters consisting of a company commander and a second-in command, a sergeant major and a quartermaster sergeant plus ten other ranks, making a total of 122 officers and men. Four companies were grouped into a battalion, which also had a headquarters company including specialist platoons dealing with signals, light anti-aircraft guns, mortars, Bren gun carriers and pioneers. The battalion was commanded by a lieutenant colonel, invariably known as the 'the CO' or 'the colonel'. When a man in Michael Joseph's company wrote 'The C.O. is a Barstard' on a wall, no one had any doubt who he meant.[53] The battalion had a major as second-in-command, a captain as adjutant, an intelligence officer, quartermaster, quartermaster sergeant and the fearsome figure of the regimental sergeant major. A medical officer and a chaplain were attached, bringing the total according to the war establishment of April 1940 to 779 officers and men. It was the basic operational unit of the infantry. Companies and platoons might be reorganized quite casually, and a battalion might be transferred for another division in a different part of the country, or overseas, but it was rare to tamper with the personnel of the battalion itself unless officers and men were promoted out of it or became casualties.

A new army had to be reconstructed out of those rescued from Dunkirk and recent recruits. Gerald Templer found a unique way of deploying the Dunkirk veterans:

> Someone told me that the gymnasium was full of regular soldiers of the regular battalion back from Dunkirk, and nobody was doing anything about them. Somewhere I picked up a Sergeant Major by the name of Pack, and we sent to the gymnasium and saw them all – I suppose about a hundred – filthy, tired, covered in oil and lying on the floor. I told Pack to fall them in, which he did with a voice like the bull of Bashan, and I told them that I was raising the new 9th Battalion of their Regiment. I wanted non-commissioned officers, and if they came to me I would nearly kill them with overwork, but as from that moment I would give every NCO one more stripe than he had already got. I also wanted some good private soldiers to fill the rank of Lance Corporal. I then said, 'Now anybody who is prepared to take this on, and it is going to be a pretty hard stint, take one pace forward.' Every man did so ...[54]

When a batch of recruits arrived to join the 9th Battalion of the West Kent Regiment at Maidstone, there was no uniformity:

Our two hundred recruits had arrived in civilian clothes of a remarkable variety. Some wore suits of an overpoweringly elegant cut which were usually accompanied by pointed shoes of an aggressive yellow; the majority were more soberly dressed, some with collars and ties, others without. There were raincoats and hats of all kinds, caps, felt hats, bowlers, even a straw boater, while many had no hats at all. When this variety of garments was exchanged for the uniformity of battle dress and side caps, individuality disappeared and it was no longer possible to distinguish between the bank clerk and the bricklayer.[55]

An official pamphlet of September 1939 outlined the priorities in training recruits: 'The first step in the training of the soldier is the inculcation of discipline. This is done through the medium of drill, physical training, mental training and the inculcation in the man of pride in his unit and himself.' Physical training was 'valuable for the development of physique and for the attainment of quickness in hand and eye'. Mental training was designed to teach the man 'to think for himself and to act intelligently in the field when thrown on his own resources'. Obviously he had to be highly skilled in the use of his weapon and maintaining it in difficult conditions on the field of battle.[56] 'Fieldcraft', or concealment and the use of cover, were relatively recent parts of the soldier's training, for as pamphlet of 1940 told him,

On a modern battlefield, the close formations of the past cannot survive; dispersion is therefore essential ... The offensive power of modern small arms depends almost entirely on concealment and surprise ... It is the art of the hunter and includes concealment, silent movement, knowledge of his prey and skill with his weapons.[57]

According to Michael Joseph,

The day was divided up into nine periods. Drill, with and without rifles, bayonet practice, fire orders, tactical formations, instruction in the use of the Bren ... judging distance, use of ground and cover, and practice in the use of respirators and gas capes, alternated with lectures on various subjects. In addition to talks on the regimental history, military law, discipline, and so on, all of which were part of the curriculum.[58]

Infantry training placed a great deal of emphasis on foot drill, though that was no longer as relevant to actual fighting as it had been in 1805. 'On my third day in the Army they taught me to salute. On my thirteenth day they taught me to shoot. This time lag between saluting and shooting represents fairly accurately the relative emphasis placed in my training on drilling and fighting.'[59] Infantry instructors were told in 1940,

> The basis of morale is discipline, which is the foundation of all military success. It is a reserve which comes into play in a crisis, but will not be there when required unless it has been first instilled by close-order drill, and subsequently maintained by a rigid insistence by officers and N.C.O.s of a smart and soldierly bearing by their men and meticulous attention to detail, turn out and saluting.[60]

The army placed much emphasis on obedience, little on initiative. Moreover the training did not do enough to prepare men for battle. Manoeuvres were held when time and space permitted. The umpire, usually an experienced officer not personally involved in the exercise, had a vital role here. The rules he interpreted, and the weight he gave to different types of firepower, for example, would have a decisive bearing on how tactics evolved. In addition, he was expected to create the atmosphere of a real battle though his verbal descriptions. 'A good umpire should combine the functions of an actor, a sports commentator, a war correspondent, and a thought reader.'[61] But he would have needed uncommon literary and acting skills to carry it off well. 'Battle schools' in which men were surrounded by explosions and regularly came under live fire, were not set up until 1941. There was a serious gap in the very heart of infantry training, which did not add up to a real preparation for battle.

The British had invented the tank in the previous war to batter through the trench system of the Western Front, but development lost focus after that, even though Basil Liddell-Hart, Major General J. F. C. Fuller and Percy Hobart developed the theoretical basis for tank warfare, which Guderian acknowledged had contributed directly to the success of his panzer divisions in France.

The Royal Armoured Corps had been formed recently out of two very different elements. The Royal Tank Corps had been created in 1923 from the remnants of the forces that had fought on the Western Front. Several times they were on the verge of gaining acceptance, until financial cuts or a change of policy led to frustration. The inter-war leaders were now outcasts – Fuller had a history of supporting fascism, and Hobart was regarded as 'impatient, quick-tempered, hot-headed, intolerant'.[62]

The other element was the old cavalry regiments, which were converted to armour on the eve of war. This maintained the regimental spirit of the old units and found a role for officers who had learned aggressive and daring action, though mostly in polo or fox-hunting rather than in battle. Some of the cavalry regiments were amongst the most snobbish in the army. They loved their horses and despised the oily and eccentric technicians of the Tank Corps, none of whom would ever take command of a ex-cavalry regiment. The two elements of the RAC did not work well together, though territorial and yeomanry regiments converted to tanks were more successful. According to General Horrocks, 'In spite of mechanisation they have retained that independent, self-reliant outlook which was the hall-mark of their ancestors, the yeoman-farmers of this country. They were largely composed of young men with a gleam in their eye, who took to mobile warfare as ducks take to water.'[63]

In 1936 the War Office decided to concentrate on two main types of heavy armour. The infantry tank was to go forward with the foot soldiers; it had heavy armour and low speed, the latest models, the Mark II and III, travelling at 15mph with armour 78mm and 65mm thick. The Mark II, the Matilda, had proved the most effective British tank in France and had led an effective counterattack near Arras. But, like all the infantry and cruiser tanks of the period, it was armed only with a 2-pounder, 40mm gun. This compared very unfavourably with the 75mm of the Panzer IV. The main infantry tank on the production lines by the middle of 1940 was the Mark III, the Valentine, which had a smaller turret and lighter armour than the Matilda, but it was more reliable. Most tanks had a crew of four – a commander, gunner and loader in the turret plus a driver. The Valentine had only room for two in its turret, so the commander helped with the loading.

The Mark I cruiser tank had a speed of 30mph but only 14mm of armour and two very cramped machine-gun turrets in addition to the 2-pounder. The Mark IIA was originally intended as an infantry tank with extra armour bolted on to it, making a thickness of 30mm. The armour was considered inadequate for infantry support by 1938, and it was reclassified as a cruiser, though its speed of 16mph was very low. The Cruiser Mark III was based on the American Christie chassis, whose large wheels allowed a speed of 30mph. Its hull and turret were redesigned to make the Mark IV.

The smallest tracked vehicle was the Bren Gun Carrier, which weighed only four tons compared with eleven for the lightest infantry tank and carried a crew of three equipped, as its name suggests, with a Bren gun. At 30mph, it was not fast. Its 12mm armour could keep out machine-gun bullets, but its top was open and it was vulnerable on a downward slope. Ten were issued to each infantry battalion, and experience in France appeared to show that it was of 'inestimable value in every type of role, including many for which it was not originally designed'.[64] It was to prove very useful in reconnaissance, message-carrying and miscellaneous tasks. Apart from that, the British army had few of the vehicles the Germans had found essential in support of a tank attack. It had no command vehicles, no half-tracks or other vehicles to go forward carrying infantry over rough terrain, and no self-propelled artillery.

The greatest part of the armoured force consisted of light tanks, mostly the Mark VIB, which had only 14mm of armour and one heavy and one light machine-gun. They were the latest version of a design from 1928 and were suitable only for reconnaissance. Also useful in this role were armoured cars, with wheels rather than caterpillar tracks. British design had finally moved away from standard car chassis, including the famous Rolls Royce, to four-wheel-drive assemblies that could get over most kinds of terrain. The most successful was the tiny Daimler Scout Car, equipped only with a Bren gun, which could use its manoeuvrability and its high speed of 55mph to escape from more powerful enemy forces. Armoured cars were also improvised in many ways, official and unofficial. One of the best known was the Ironside, aptly named after the commander-in-chief at the beginning of the invasion crisis. In the emergency they reverted to the idea of using a standard car chassis with 12mm armour, a machine-gun or anti-tank gun and an open top. They were issued to armoured units until suitable tracked vehicles became available.

There were not enough tanks to deal with a massed attack. Very few had come back from France – the 1st Armoured Division had taken more than 600 and returned with nine. As a result there were 110 infantry tanks and 103 cruisers in the United Kingdom in June 1940, along with 618 useless light tanks and 132 obsolete 'medium' tanks, mostly in training camps. In effect there were only 200 tanks that were in any sense capable of meeting the enemy.[65] Churchill was concerned about this shortage, and tank production was put almost, but not quite, on a par with aircraft production. Whereas Beaverbrook achieved much with his Ministry of Aircraft Production, Herbert Morrison at the Ministry of Supply was not able to concentrate on a single task, and tanks competed for factory space and skilled labour with the aircraft industry. The Defence Committee (Supply) had hoped for 167 infantry and cruiser tanks in August 1940, 194 in September and 222 in October; in fact it got less than 60 per cent of the target.[66]

As a result, there was a huge amount of improvisation. The 21st Army Tank Brigade was formed to defend the Gloucester, Cheltenham and Cirencester area in west-central England in July. Its commander was ordered:

> While continuing its training, your Brigade will prepare, with such resources as it has, to co-operate in emergency with 3 Div. if so ordered by G.H.Q ... You will form all battle-worthy A.F.V. into a composite unit, suitably organised for the possible tasks ... All A.F.V. that can be gunned will be included. In addition, such of your transport as remains will be utilised to carry any surplus armed personnel who will be organised into a suitable unit.[67]

British tank doctrine was also faulty. The infantry tanks were misused by splitting them up into 'penny packets' rather than concentrating them for a decisive blow. It was always tempting for soldiers to want to shelter behind several inches of steel armour, but, as with battleships, this only encouraged the enemy to find ways to penetrate it and destroy a dangerous and prestigious target. The German 88mm gun was used in large numbers and could easily penetrate a tank's armour. Furthermore, the weaknesses of the tank were not fully allowed for. It was high and noisy and very difficult to conceal, unlike a machine-gun or an anti-tank gun. Its crew had very limited vision and an even worse problem hearing above the noise of the engine. These were faults the Home Guard spotted before the regular army. They could be dealt with by having the infantry work very closely with the tanks, for the foot soldier had advantages as well as weaknesses – he could see and hear everything around him, he could change direction quickly and dive for cover as soon as he was in danger. The German blitzkrieg had the infantry sometimes moving just ahead of the tanks, sometimes just behind, sometimes riding on top of them, whereas British doctrine had the two forces operating separately.

Artillery was the most efficient arm, and the others often relied on a heavy barrage to help them advance or get them out of trouble. Certainly they had the numbers, a total of 356,331 officers and men in July; but two thirds of them were in coastal or anti-aircraft artillery, and the great majority of these were allocated to the air defence of the great cites and would take no part in any land battle. The 7,547 officers and 122,571 other ranks of the field artillery were well trained, but there were significant gaps in their armoury. The 25-pounder field gun was coming into service in 1940, a classic design –it could fire its shell for a range of 13,500 yards, or 7.6 miles, and it could serve as a low-trajectory field gun, an anti-tank gun or a howitzer. Its trail was not split as with most guns but formed in a single piece, so it could be deployed quickly. More important, it had a large horizontal wheel that could be placed under its road wheels so that it could be rotated very quickly, a great advantage in the anti-tank role. At the end of May, Eastern Command, the most likely to face an invasion, had a total of 87 of these guns, spread unevenly among its eight divisions – the 48th Division had 48, out of an establishment of 72. The situation improved. They were produced at the rate of 35 per month and rising, and by September 194 new guns had been issued, while 231 more had been converted from other calibres.[68]

The Royal Artillery had very little that was both modern and effective above and below the 25-pounder, for heavy artillery had gone out of fashion since 1914–18, so the army had to dig out old 8-inch howitzers and line them to a calibre of 7.2 inches, while supplies of more modern guns were obtained from America. In anti-tank artillery, the main weapon was the 2-pounder as also used by British tanks. Like many British weapons, it came too soon: its design seemed advanced when it was approved in 1936, but it was soon overtaken, and its range and penetrating power were inadequate by 1940. Nominally it had a range of 8,000 yards, but it was regarded as ineffective at more than 500. However the 2-pounder was kept in production because the factories were equipped to make it and the troops were familiar with it.

Officers complained that training was often interrupted by other tasks, including helping with the harvest. No. 224 Infantry Training Depot at Maidstone, serving the Queen's Own Royal West Kent Regiment, found its men sent away to guard aliens when they were rounded up in June. They had to provide defence for several of the RAF aerodromes in the area. They sent out parties to guard crashed aircraft from souvenir hunters, and a lance corporal accidentally fired the guns of one, fortunately without casualties.[69] Churchill himself noticed that thousands of men were being diverted to construct beach and other defences during June and observed, 'At the present stage they should be drilling and training for at least eight hours a day, including one smart parade every morning. All the labour necessary should be found from civilian sources.'[70]

DEFENDING THE HOMELAND, 1940

To some, the army was the least important of the services in the defence against invasion. It would probably be the last to be engaged, for the navy and the RAF would have harassed the invaders on the way over and perhaps defeated them. Indeed on 5 August 1940, Churchill implied that it was merely a decoy: 'The land defences and the home army are maintained primarily for the purpose of making the enemy come in such large numbers as to afford a proper target to the sea and air forces above mentioned, and to make hostile preparations and movements noticeable to Air and other forms of reconnaissance.' But at the time he was still thinking of an invasion across the North Sea, which would have given plenty of warning with the radar chain now in place.[71]

As invasion seemed almost imminent, General Ironside was well aware of the difficulties facing his forces: 'The coastline is terrific in length and we may be attacked at any point of it, owing to the fact that the Germans may start from Norway, the Baltic, Holland, Belgium or France. They may also take Ireland first and so extend the possibility of landing still further to the west.' He knew that air landings were also possible and that most of his troops were untrained or ill-equipped, especially in anti-tank weapons. He decided that it was impossible to hold all the possible landing sites strongly, and the defence of beaches should form only a 'crust'. The troops there were 'to beat off minor enterprises, to keep a watch for, and to report immediately, German invasion attempts, and to break up, delay, and canalize penetrations'. LDVs would man road blocks farther inland, set up anti-tank obstacles and harass the enemy in any way they could. The main defences were the 'GHQ Stop Lines' of pill boxes and gun emplacements to prevent the enemy from capturing London and the main industrial cities.

Sudden and apparently pointless moves were the lot of the infantryman in 1940, as defence needs changed. Now there was no need to get the permission of the Secretary at War, as in 1803, and most movements were carried out largely by train. The orders issued by the 9th Battalion of the Buffs for a move from Marlow on the banks of the Thames to Plymouth were typical of many. The night before, all the bell tents would be taken down and the men would sleep in the dining tents. Sandbags would be emptied, but the slit trenches for defence would not be filled yet. Kitbags carrying the equipment that a man could not carry on his person were put in stores, marked with the details of companies and platoons. The men were roused by bugle call at 4.30 next morning, had breakfast and rolled their spare blankets into bundles of ten for onward transport. At 6.00, 'A' Company marched out of the main gate of the camp, followed by 'B' Company, each man carrying a steel helmet, a slung pack and haversack rations. They arrived at Marlow Station at 6.20, where they were allocated places on a special train. There was an NCO in charge of each carriage and a second lieutenant in charge of the train. As the train set off, men relaxed and took off their kit, and at around 11.30 the train stopped at Taunton for light refreshment. As they approached Plymouth the bugler sounded the single note 'G' to tell them to get dressed, and two 'G's to warn them that they were about to detrain. On arrival, they marched off to their quarters, while a party unloaded the baggage into trucks. 'C' and 'D' companies followed the next day with a slightly easier schedule, as reveille was at 6.00.[72]

The army now had plenty of barracks for its peacetime needs and supplemented them with wartime accommodation including the corrugated-iron Nissen hut. But the barracks were mostly situated to meet training needs rather than the sudden demands of an anti-invasion force, so the men often lived in bell tents during the summer, or in requisitioned church and school halls or even private homes as their ancestors had done. The 1st Battalion of the King's Shropshire Light Infantry moved to a chain of villages twelve miles inshore from the Lincolnshire coast in July, transported by bus. The headquarters was in West Keal Hall, 'A' Company in the village of Old Bolingbroke, 'B' Company in Windbrush Poultry Farm and East Keal Rectory, 'C' Company in Manor House Farm and 'D' Company in the village of Halton Holegate. Their tasks were to deliver an immediate counterattack on any forces that succeeded in penetrating the Brigade's forward defence line and to destroy any paratroop landings in their own area. Each company was allocated two trucks to get them to the scene of the action. One company and a section of carriers was always to be ready to move out and deal with paratroop landings with the least possible delay, and links were forged with the Local Defence Volunteers, who were to defend certain vulnerable points, man road blocks and report any suspicious activity.[73]

Evelyn Waugh was not impressed on arrival at his new billet:

We went to Haverfordwest. Our departure was planned with customary unnecessary haste. The battalion was shaken out of camp at 4 am and then left standing about until noon ... A long journey and late arrival. Marched in the dark to unlit billets; all settled in with the utmost gloom.[74]

But he was pleasantly surprised with the accommodation. 'Daylight revealed a town of great beauty, full of people eager to be hospitable. Billets were cleaned and redecorated. D Company secured the drill hall and were the best housed of the battalion. Training came to an end and we settled down to a delightful ten days.[75]

On taking over a sector of the coast of Dorset in October, Michael Joseph was horrified at the lack of progress that had been made with the defences during the summer, though perhaps he was too influenced by his experiences of the Western Front in the previous war, where every inch of territory was fiercely defended.

I had pictured a strongly fortified zone, with abundant wire, pill boxes, trenches, and well-organized communications. There certainly was wire, but what little there was looked limp and neglected. There were a few pill boxes, 'not much use,' I was told. There were trenches and weapons pits, some of them containing several feet of water, and others abandoned because they were falling to pieces. One or two bedraggled camouflaged nets were lying about. There was one telephone line linking company headquarters with one of the platoons, but all other communications were by means of Don IIIs, and these field telephones were so old that they often failed to work.[76]

Furthermore his men were spread very thinly:

An infantry company, even if it is up to strength, does not go very far in a six-mile sector. Long stretches were supposed to be of unscaleable cliffs, but a number of vulnerable gaps was known to exist and there might be others. I simply could not believe that we were taking a chance. Surely every inch of the coast had been reconnoitred? Then there was the question of minefields. No one seemed to know very much about them; whether they existed, and if so, where they were.[77]

The situation was helped by the arrival of Brigadier Gerald Templer, 'one of the most inspiring and efficient senior officers I had come across'. He issued a series of 'Questions for all Officers Having Beach Responsibilities', including:

> Does every man know his action station? Has he been rehearsed in finding it in the dark?
>
> Has someone been told off to close every gap in every wire obstacle? Has he been practised? Is the necessary material ready?
>
> Can each man who is allotted to a fire position in a trench really use his weapon in that position? Is the height of the parapet correct? Is there an elbow rest? Have the men tried their fire positions?[78]

As well as training his men, each commander on the spot had to think of every eventuality for maintaining morale and defeating the enemy. He had to produce a plan of defence for his own area. The 2nd Armoured Division had one for the Lincolnshire coast in June, though it was questionable whether such a mobile force should be tied down to defending the beaches, and it was eventually moved farther east. There were 80 miles of coastline to be defended, but the 25 miles between Gibraltar Point and North Haven were likely for landing, and obstacles were to be constructed there. Road blocks were built at the entrances to all small towns where troops were billeted, round large towns and on the defensive lines between the River Ancholme to Boston and the River Trent to the River Witham, as well as round the larger towns of Boston and Grimsby. It was a low-lying area, but flooding was not to be allowed – on the contrary, the troops had to stand by to prevent the enemy from flooding areas on his flanks.[79]

In addition, every unit had to consider the possibility of aerial landings by parachute, glider or aircraft, and the 2nd Armoured's orders recognized, 'Apart from aerodromes there are suitable areas where aeroplanes can land all over Lincolnshire.' The Isle of Wight was less flat but still very vulnerable to paratroops, and the 2nd Royal Fusiliers' orders demanded, 'All tps will act immediately with the utmost vigour against any airborne attack in their vicinity taking into consideration only the situation at the time as regards seaborne attack. All tps will be particularly vigilant against airborne attack from 0500 – 0700 and sentries will be posted accordingly.'

Vulnerable points also had to be specially protected against saboteurs, especially aircraft factories. According to an Eastern Command instruction of 1 August,

> Certain V.P.s such as aerodromes, experimental stations and wireless stations must be guarded by soldiers, field force troops being employed as necessary. Points of secondary importance such as power stations and communication centres will be guarded by Home Defence troops as far as they are available, and by Home Guards.[80]

Each area worked out a plan of what essential facilities had to be demolished in the event of a major landing. In Eastern Command generally, no demolitions were to take place that would take more than seven days to repair, but charges were to be prepared for other places to use as needed, and chambers were to be cut in the works to receive them. In 2nd Armoured Brigade's area in Lincolnshire, destruction was to be confined to a limited number of road and rail bridges. Forms were prepared for issue to the officer or NCO in charge of a particular point, either allowing him to demolish a road or bridge on his own authority, or on the written orders of the divisional commander.

On the coast of Norfolk and Suffolk, Admiral Dreyer conferred with General Le Fanu about the demolition of piers. It was agreed that the first warning of enemy attack might be when a ship arrived off the pier in a fog, and it was necessary to demolish a span in the framework above the high water mark now, and be ready for total demolition later if necessary.[81]

One of the problems that exercised the military mind most during that summer was what to do about enemy tanks. Every effort was to be made to destroy potential tank-carrying aircraft and ships, but there was always the chance that they might land in substantial numbers. Each infantry platoon had its Boys anti-tank rifle, firing a .55-inch round. It had the great advantage of being concealed easily, but its effective range was only 500 yards. The authorities remained both cautious and optimistic. Officers were told that 'No obstacle must be regarded as proof in itself against tanks', but at the same time its effects were largely moral, and the enemy tank crews suffered from 'fatigue and noise, the limited field of view, blind spots, the danger of fire, maintenance requirements and dependence on petrol supply'.[82] The commanders were setting up parties to 'hunt, harry and ambush enemy tanks with determination'. In Eastern Command, instructions were issued for the use of the new 'Mollitoff bottle' filled with petrol, tar and kerosene oil ('buy locally and submit bill').[83]

Another problem was gas, which had been used by both sides in the preceding war. Everyone in Britain, including babies, was issued with a gas mask, known as a respirator, and the armed services devoted a good deal of time to training while wearing them. The authorities were confident that they could deal with any likely gas attack if everyone was prepared, but even then there might be many casualties. There were several types of gas to be considered – those that caused choking, those that affected the nose, tear gas and blister (or mustard) gas. Gas bombs dropped by aircraft were considered less effective than explosive bombs dropped in the same way, but blister gas might easily be sprayed, and capes were issued as protection. Artillery and mortar shells might be used, but their gas content was low, while in favourable winds it might just be released into the air to drift on to the lines. It was impossible for men to wear capes and respirators without suffering a great deal of discomfort and losing efficiency, so they had to be ready to put them on at the first warning, and officers were told, 'Troops must be made to realize that the first time they fire their weapons on these shores in defence of their own land, they may be wearing respirators. If these respirators fit badly, they may soon be dead men.'[84] It was also possible to use gas in defence of the homeland. But that would involve a breach of the Geneva Convention, and in theory that would only be done if the Germans used it first.

The unit commander on the spot had to consider the logistics of his force, when any part of the infrastructure around him might be collapsing, or in enemy hands. Most plans were rather mundane in this respect and largely confined to the issue of rations for the next few days. In the 2nd Armoured each man in the AFVs was to have three days' rations, on the scale of 9 ounces of preserved meat, 8 ounces of biscuits, ½ ounce of tea, 2½ ounces of sugar and 1½ ounces of tinned milk per day. Early in July no one seemed to know if it was possible to carry this in the tanks available inside standard containers, and methods were sought of carrying it outside. A month later it was clear that this was difficult in light tanks, and the amount issued was left to the discretion of brigade commanders.[85] Meanwhile GHQ began to set up a system of supply depots throughout the country, doing its best to cut across the usual red tape surrounding the issue of stores.

No. 8 Main Supply Depot began operations in Hereford on 3 June. Part of the cattle market was requisitioned, along with a nearby car park, while two meadows outside the town were taken over for fuel dumps. The War Office sent fourteen store sheds to a total of almost 90,000 square feet, but only six of them could be erected on the site. The depot had an establishment of more than 100 officers and men, but it needed more troops from the Central Base Depot and civilian labour to unload the 120 lorries that arrived every week. When fully equipped, the base had supplies for half a million men, including 125,000 pounds of preserved meat, 230 tons of flour, 78,125 pounds of cheese and twelve million cigarettes. There was several days' supply of most items, but twenty days of tea and seven days each of sugar and canned milk. Hospital supplies included arrowroot, anchovy essence, taste-removing tables, and remarkably, 8,400 bottles of stout, 84 of whisky and 168 of champagne.[86] Ammunition depots were set up on the same terms, and fuel dumps were established, each holding 500 tons of fuel in cans with quantities of oil and lubricants. [87]

There were numerous alerts when it was believed that invasion was particularly likely. The first came on 12 May when the War Office, in fear of a sudden parachute attack, issued this telegram:

WARNING ORDER STOP EVERY SEARCHLIGHT, ANTI-AIRCRAFT GUN AND LIGHT-GUN STATION WILL BE REINFORCED BY FIVE MEN STOP THESE MEN WILL BE FOUND FROM THOSE DUE TO COMPLETE TRAINING ON 15/5 AT ALL CAVALRY, GUARDS, INFANTRY, MACHINE GUN AND MOTOR TRAINING CENTRES STOP ... FOLLOWING WILL BE TAKEN PER MAN STOP THREE BLANKETS, PALLIASSE, WATER-PROOF SHEET, MUG, PLATE AND UNCONSUMED PORTION OF A DAY'S RATION.[88]

At the beginning of the next month as the troops came back from Dunkirk, the commander of the 2nd Armoured Division was concerned about the vulnerability of his men to a parachute attack and ordered, 'In general it is desirable that individuals and a proportion of all parties travelling for whatever purpose in country districts should be armed.' Three weeks later he told his senior officers, 'Whilst the Div has no operational role in the present area a situation might arise when enemy parachutists or airborne might land in the immediate vicinity of the Divisional Billeting Area ... Under such conditions Regtl Comds will act on their own initiative with up to 10% of their strength.'[89]

The most serious alert began on 7 September, when the moon and tides seemed to be in conjunction for an invasion. The codeword 'Cromwell', which meant that invasion was believed to be imminent and that all troops should go to battle positions, was issued for Southern and Eastern Commands, all leave was stopped, and men already on leave were recalled. In the Plymouth area, the 9th Battalion of the Buffs prepared for an attack:

> Companies manning the line will hold it during the night with Bren Guns and such men as [officers commanding] Companies consider necessary to provide sufficient double sentries, patrols and listening posts, always on the alert to warn them of enemy activity. The remainder of their Coys will be allowed to loosen their equipment and go to sleep provided they can get rapidly into position in the event of an alarm.
>
> Coy in reserve will have their equipment on and post sentries, but the remainder of the men will be allowed to sleep with their boots off, equipment loosened, rifles by their sides ... the whole battalion will stand to one hour before dawn and will stand-down as soon as the morning mists clear.[90]

The alert lasted until the 19th, when the authorities relented. Southern Command ordered a new state of readiness:

> Beaches will be patrolled during the hours of darkness and troops will stand to at dawn. In foggy weather very active patrolling will be carried out and sentry posts will be increased as necessary. Defences will be manned on scales to be laid down by Corps Commanders and Area Commanders

having operational control. Training in Training Units which have an operational role will be interfered with as little as possible consistent with the necessary degree of readiness ... Seven days leave for five per cent at a time, officers and other ranks, will be reinstituted on receipt of instructions to be issued later.[91]

Since 'Cromwell' was a rather clumsy procedure, new orders were issued. 'Stand To' would indicate 'conditions peculiarly favourable for an invasion'. Troops would come to a complete state of readiness, all posts and road blocks would be manned 100 per cent, and the command reserve would be at three hours' notice to move. The next stage was 'Action Stations', on which the reserve would come to one hour's notice. After that, specific orders would come from command headquarters.[92]

Unlike the navy and the air force, the soldiers of Home Command had no means of striking back at the enemy, and they were often stuck in out-of-the way places for weeks at a time, so boredom was a major problem. Army Training Memoranda recognized this in July:

From time to time complaints are heard that young officers – and sometimes older ones – have not enough to do and are bored. There is no excuse for this. The United Kingdom is for the first time a theatre of war. The more knowledge officers have of the area in which they may have to fight the better ... If officers have troops to command, there is and always must be something to do – either training, or preparing for training, or getting to know the area.[93]

It was not difficult for troops to become demoralized during static defence, and perhaps Captain Evelyn Waugh did not help with his own doubts while on the coast of Cornwall in August: 'Our task is the defence of Liskeard. None of us can quite make out why anyone should want to attack it. Even the CO says he cannot rid himself of a sense of unreality.'[94]

They might arrange competitions among the men, preferably with some relevance to the work in hand, and in the 2nd Royal Fusiliers, 'A prize of £2 for the best camouflaged position in the Company was given by Major D. W. G. Ray, commanding "X" Company, to Sergeant Brown of 10 Platoon, for a section at ROCKEN BAY 9295. A prize was also won by L/Sergeant Mitchell of 11 Platoon for the best array of trip-wires.' Later the unit organized a concert, dominated by impersonations of the popular stage and screen character Old Mother Riley, with a sketch called 'The Road Block', the 'Miss Spitfire' song-and-dance routine and concluding with community singing of *Land of Hope and Glory* and *God Save the King*.[95]

However, the authorities recognized that the problems were very difficult to solve, especially with men who had never wanted to be soldiers in the first place, who had only had a minimum of training and whose families were often subject to bombing and all the disruptions of war at home:

> There is no conceivable remedy for preventing a man from 'looking over his shoulder' in the domestic sense of the phrase. The only palliative is for the officer – who, it is perfectly well realised, may well have pressing domestic problems of his own – to share with the men the burden of their domestic worries – and thereby help to assuage his own.[96]

It was the duty of every leader, from lance corporal upwards, to keep his men alert and trained for the day when the long wait was over.

How well would they have done if the enemy had landed? It might be a desperate gamble or a gross miscalculation by the Germans, in which case they would have been harassed by land, sea and air and would almost certainly have been defeated heavily. But more likely they would delay an invasion until the RAF had been defeated and the Royal Navy was either defeated or could be evaded. In these circumstances, there is little doubt that the section or platoon guarding each beach or landing field would have fought hard and well, backed by a leadership that would not countenance surrender. But they might well have been crushed after heavy losses, and then the army's real test would come. Could it get its men to the scene of the action in time to launch a devastating counterattack? And if the enemy had become established and had been able to land its panzers in some numbers, would the relatively feeble British armoured units have been able to defeat them? There is no doubt that British forces, including the army, Home Guard, naval and air force troops and even some civilians, would have resisted them at every stage. But where was the killer punch to destroy them if things ever went that far?

STRATEGY AND MOBILITY, 1940

General Montgomery's 3rd Division was one of the few effective units in Britain in June 1940, for it had been building up before being sent to France. Now it was stationed in a key area along the south coast. Brigadier Brian Horrocks commanded one of the units within it and found the task daunting:

> My first task was to defend the south coast of England from Rottingdean to Shoreham – one brigade of some 3,000 men was stretched in a thin line along ten miles of densely-populated coastline. We wouldn't have stood much chance against a well-organised invasion, but even so this probably was one of the most strongly defended parts of Britain, because we were a well-trained and experienced regular division, complete with war equipment.[97]

Churchill visited the division early in July and was rather shocked by the lack of mobility. Over dinner in a hotel overlooking Brighton pier, Montgomery told him,

> The main thing which seemed curious to me was that my division was immobile. It was the only fully equipped division in England, the only division fit to fight any enemy anywhere. And here we were in a static role, ordered to dig in on the south coast. Some other troops should take on my task; my division should be given buses, and be held in mobile reserve with a counter-attack role. Why was I left immobile? There were thousands of buses in England; let them give me some …

This produced a classic Churchillian memo, and perhaps contributed to the replacement of Ironside:

> Considering the great masses of transport, both 'buses and lorries, which there are in this country, and the large numbers of drivers brought back from the BEF, it should be possible to remedy these deficiencies at once. I hope, at any rate, the GOC 3rd Division will be told to-day to take up, as he would like to do, the large number of 'buses which are even now plying for pleasure traffic up and down the sea front at Brighton.[98]

Within three days of taking command of Home Forces, Sir Alan Brooke was questioning Ironside's plans. He had no intention of giving up almost a third of the country without a serious fight, and with his bitter experience of the blitzkrieg he could see that far more offensive tactics were needed:

> much work and energy was being expended on an extensive system of rear defence, comprising anti-tank ditches and pill boxes, running roughly parallel to the coast and situated well inland. This static rear defence did not fall in with my conception of the defence of the country.[99]

He had formulated a plan by 6 August and outlined it forcefully to his area commanders:

> Mobile offensive must be the basis of our defence. The idea of linear defence must be stamped out; what is required to meet the dual threat of sea-borne and air borne attack is all round defence in depth with the maximum number of troops trained and disposed for a rapid counter offensive.
>
> Armoured formations should be employed in the van of every attack with the object of creating situations which could be exploited by motorised infantry.

He elaborated on this to Eden a few days later:

> It is not possible to be strong everywhere on the many hundred miles of coastline of Great Britain, and at the numerous places where the enemy may attempt to land troops from the air. Reliance has, therefore, to be placed mainly upon mobile columns trained and equipped to take vigorous and rapid counter-offensive action against any enemy who may succeed in setting foot in this country.

He told his area commanders of the defects that had to be remedied – higher standards of motor and foot mobility were needed; all groups to be trained offensively; a higher standard was required in anti-tank weapons; and bolder methods were to be be used in training.[100]

Mobility was easier to describe than to achieve, since nearly 64,000 vehicles had been left behind in France. British main roads had largely been covered with tarmac since the advent of the motor car at the turn of the century, but apart from that they were largely unimproved since the turnpikes. Armour and field artillery, of course, had their own mobility, though they relied on supplies of fuel and cover from the air. There were three ways of moving large bodies of infantry. They could march as they had always done, but they were not likely to be fast enough over a long distance in the age of the blitzkrieg. For the better part of a century they had moved longer distances by train, but rail services might well be disrupted or overwhelmed in an invasion and could not be depended upon. Otherwise they relied on motor transport, which came in several forms. Army lorries, of 3-tons capacity and over, were designed with a certain amount of mobility across country and could carry men in bulk. The army had not done much to develop four-wheeled drive between the wars, and the most common vehicle was the 15-hundredweight truck, built by several makers including Austin, Ford, Bedford and Commer. According to the war establishment of April 1940 each infantry battalion had 14 motorcycles, a staff car, nine 8-hundredweight light personnel carriers, 31 15-hundredweight trucks (including one per platoon) and 13 30-hundredweight lorries.[101] They were intended for the movement of officers and their staffs, and stores and equipment, rather than bringing the troops themselves into battle. Because of shortages it was decreed at the end of August that static and training units should only have 25 per cent of their complement, and operational units should have half. Often it was much less than that. At the end of August the 9th Battalion of the Buffs was down to one staff car and a utility truck.[102] Even the beach divisions needed some vehicles of their own for their battalions, as most of them were stationed in out-of-the-way beaches and coves. The 14th Royal Fusiliers, based in Westward Ho! in North Devon, had only nine vehicles in mid-June.[103] The army's mobility would have to come from other sources.

The Royal Army Service Corps was responsible for providing the 'second line' transport of the army, beyond that needed by the individual battalions. It had 150,000 officers and men in the United Kingdom in July 1940, in eight ambulance car companies, four bulk-petrol transport companies, six forward bakeries and two field butcheries, and 26 reserve motor transport companies.[104]

Since many lorries had been requisitioned on the outbreak of war and then lost in France, bus transport was the next best available. The country had 53,000 buses and coaches in 1938.[105] Many of these were double-deckers, which were too high for army work, and others had to keep up essential services. Nevertheless, the Home Command went ahead with forming Motor Coach Companies within the RASC. A company should have had a total of 60 32-seater coaches, each capable of carrying a reduced platoon. They were organized in three sections of twenty, allowing for eighteen on operations and two spares. Each company was also allocated 24 motorcycles and six other vehicles. It was recognized that the motor coach companies were inferior to troop carrying companies, which used lorries with cross-country ability and could get much closer to the battlefront, but by February 1941 there were only twelve of the latter in Home Command, compared with 37 motor coach companies. Buses, it was agreed, should be 'retained for their intended role and not used for cross country runs or even on bad roads'. In Western Command, 20-seater coaches were preferred in some areas because the roads to the beaches were so narrow.

Many were hired short-term from commercial companies. As early as 20 July the 4th Division had to surrender 33 buses on a promise that they would be back again in an emergency. There would be delay in doing this, and the Corps Commander pointed out, 'the length of the fronts involved may well make it impossible for reserves to intervene in time.' Even after Brooke's mobility policy was adopted, it was some time before vehicles were available and Major General Gammell of the 3rd Division complained on 13 August,

> I am very concerned about the fact that no Troop Carrying Company or Coach Company has yet been allocated to 7 [Guards] Brigade.
>
> This brigade has a most important role if we are employed to the South, to the South East or to the South West and it obviously cannot carry out its job unless it is provided with mechanical transport for its battalions. I know it is possible, if we do move for 24 hours, to provide it

with a Coach Company after the flag falls, but this is not really satisfactory and might easily break down when the emergency occurs.

Even when vehicles were allocated, they were often in poor condition:

> I think you ought to know that the state of these 'Bus Companies is far from satisfactory, technically, and Woolmer's Company had 13 buses off the road each day of the past fortnight. This is a serious matter and represents nearly one Company per Battalion immobilised.

Regulations forbade the use of military vehicles for leisure and sporting purposes, which made it very difficult for troops stationed on isolated beaches and other positions to get any recreation. Early in August one staff captain complained that,

> since the arrival of No. 7 Motor Transport Company in the Cotswold Area, eight coaches have been used at least two evenings per week to bring numbers of men into Cheltenham for purposes of recreation, and until very late hours the vehicles were parked in various parts of the town. During the evening of the 3rd August, I observed two coaches, parked in the Promenade and left unattended.[106]

Requisitioned vans also had their faults:

> Only one company vehicle was capable of negotiating the rough road which led to one of the distant platoons and the other two trucks looked as though they might fall to pieces at any minute. Molt was coping valiantly with transport difficulties and did miracles of juggling with the few trucks at the disposal of the battalion, helping the companies out with the loan of an extra vehicle when it was urgently needed. These old crocks of tradesmen's vans and antiquated horse boxes somehow stood the strain.[107]

The 141st (London) Infantry Brigade worked out detailed plans for its transport into battle. A reconnaissance party of five cars, 21 trucks and 24 motor cycles was sent ahead to find the debussing point and guide the troops in. Meanwhile the men of each unit could be embussed simultaneously, but that provided a large target for air attack and was difficult to control, so it was better if buses or lorries drew one by one

Above: An anti-tank ditch near Farnham in Surrey, part of the stop lines, in July 1940. (IWM H 2473)

Below: Army gunners training on an ex-naval 6-inch gun at Felixstowe in Suffolk. (IWM H 3293)

Above: An RNR lieutenant and warrant officer, probably ex-fishermen. They are part of the Boom Defence Service that protected naval and merchant harbours. (IWM A 937)

Below: Seamen on the crowded messdeck of a destroyer. (IWM A 1247)

Above: The destroyer *Brazen* sinking after an attack by Stukas on 20 July 1940, with crews still manning the 3-inch anti-aircraft gun. (Commander Sir Michael Culme-Seymour, RN)

Below: Militia men called up for training in July 1939. (IWM HU 103463)

Opposite page, top: The unsuccessful Handley Page Hampden bomber, being used as part of an Operational Training Unit in July 1940. (IWM CH 707)

Above: A Westland Lysander on Army co-operation exercises, flown by No 225 Squadron in Wiltshire in August 1940. (IWM CH 1194)

Left: Men of the Green Howards defend a beach at Sandbanks near Poole in Dorset at the end of July, 1940. (IWM H 2669)

Below: A three-rotor Enigma machine.

Above: Learning to drive across country with the army in 1939. (IWM H 401)

Below: Two cruiser Mark IIA tanks, a Valentine and two Matildas in August 1940. (IWM H 3086)

Above: Pilots of No 257 Hurricane Squadron with their leader, Bob Stanford Tuck at Martlesham Heath in 1940. (IWM CH 1674)

Below: A Spitfire of No 19 Squadron being refuelled by bowser at Fowlmere, Cambridgeshire, in September 1940. (IWM CH 1357)

Above: Training the LDV early in July 1940. (IWM H 2005)

Below: The airfield at Charmy Down, built in 1940 as a satellite of Colerne for the defence of Bristol and Bath, showing the perimeter track and the three crossed runways. (IWM HU 93042)

to a single point where the men would get on – a trained platoon could be embussed in 30 seconds. An officer or senior NCO sat beside the driver and was in charge of the vehicle. Military policemen helped plan the route and were stationed along it to guide the vehicles. When moving and properly spaced, the brigade would take up 34–36 miles of road – each unit commander had a motorcyclist attached, to ride up and down the column and ensure the correct distances. Broken-down vehicles would be pushed off the road with a 'pass' sign attached, and the column would not stop for anything except dive-bombing in a defile. In that case the men would all get out and fire everything they had at the attackers, 'with the object of filling the air with shot and bringing down in flames the aeroplane attacking the col[lum]n. Half measures are useless.' As they got within 300 yards of the debussing point, the drivers would see a red board with a white 'D' on it. The company sergeant major would be waiting there to tell them to get ready, and the company commander would instruct them exactly where to get out. In a lorry, the officer or NCO would jump out of the cab and run to the back to take charge, while the men got out in around fifteen seconds. If it was a bus with two doors, they were expected to get out in 30 seconds. It was hoped that the reconnaissance party would have arrived back, and they would instruct the men in how to deploy. Normally the companies would advance with the individual sections in columns and the Brens in the rear. The commander had to ask, 'Is the attack to be noisy or quiet? There can be no hard or fast rule. In either case careful co-ordination of artillery and M.G. fire is called for.' Then the men would move forward to enter the battle of their lives.[108]

10

THE AIR FORCE

Air Power

It might seem strange to consider air power within the context of Britain in 1803–5, and certainly it had no effect on the French invasion plans. Yet there were far-sighted ideas that gained some support as means of harassing the enemy in his own ports. The most extreme was sent to Lord Keith by Charles Rogier, who proposed to bombard Boulogne by floating 32-foot balloons over the harbour. Each would carry '8 cwt. of spiked rockets, shells, etc.', which would be released by a clockwork timer at the right moment. According to the inventor,

> The fuse explodes the rockets and lights the fuse of the shells, which drop by means of the clockwork. The last ignition to the gas by means of the matches annihilates the whole. Now, if the enemy should attempt to prevent the operation by striking the balloon with spiked rockets, it will fire the gas from which matches 5 and 6 will communicate to the combustibles and bring them on their own head. But if the balloons be sent in at night the enemy will not perceive them till the moment of their operation.[1]

Though he anticipated both night bombing and anti-aircraft fire, Rogier's suggestion was not taken up. He was not the last air enthusiast to underestimate the difficulty of hitting the target.

William Congreve's plan for rocket attack was slightly more practical. Admiral Keith was sceptical, as always: 'Mr. Congreve, who is ingenious, is wholly wrapt up in rockets, from which I expect little success, for Mr. Congreve has no idea of applying them professionally.' An attack was launched on the night of 19/20 November 1805, but in bad weather the rockets failed to reach the target.[2] They were used more successfully on other occasions, against Copenhagen in 1807 and Washington in 1814.

The American Robert Fulton's schemes for submarine attack were rejected by both sides, while plans to sink blockships at the entrance to Boulogne were carried out by 'some sapient blockheads' but failed.[3] Steamships were meanwhile under development on both sides of the Atlantic, and it is remarkable how many of the weapon systems that flourished in the twentieth century were anticipated in 1805.

Practical aviation remained a dream throughout the nineteenth century, and it took a few years for the effects of the Wright Brothers' successful flights of 1903 to reach Europe from America. Louis Blériot's flight across the English Channel in 1909 was a symbolic moment for British defence, and soon army and navy set up their own air arms. Raids on Britain by airships and aircraft during World War I had a great moral effect, and an independent force was proposed for the bombing of Germany. The Royal Flying Corps carried out reconnaissance and spotting on the Western Front, while the Royal Naval Air Service was getting close to successful aircraft carriers and torpedo bombers by 1918.

The Royal Air Force, formed on 1 April 1918 by a merger of the Royal Flying Corps and the Royal Naval Air Service, was the first independent air force in the world. There were drastic cuts when the war ended suddenly seven months later, and the new service had to struggle for its identity and its existence. It regarded Marshal of the Royal Air Force Lord Trenchard as its founding father. Known as 'Boom' because of his extraordinarily loud voice, he was a man of great strength of character but rather blinkered vision. Winston Churchill had some kind of role as a stepfather at least: after the war ended in 1918 he was appointed joint Secretary of State for War and Air, and it was left open whether he treated the army and air force as two services or one. Only a man with Churchill's capacity for work could run two departments at once, and he helped the RAF establish its identity. It adopted the blue-grey uniform that was eventually taken up by air forces throughout the world. He devised the system of officer ranks, largely based on naval titles as used in the RNAS. But the descriptive titles soon proved misleading. By 1940, a pilot officer was not necessarily a pilot, a squadron of multi-seat aircraft was usually headed by a wing commander rather than a squadron leader, and a group was never commanded by a group captain.

The Air Ministry remained independent of the War Office to run the RAF. It was also responsible for civil aviation and aimed to foster 'air-mindedness' in the general public – the idea that flying was both an exciting adventure and a practical means for travel as well as fighting wars. The RAF's flying displays at Hendon, north of London, were among the highlights of the year in the 1920s and 30s. When it founded the University Air Squadrons, its aim was to foster an awareness of air power in future leaders rather than just train pilots. The Ministry's campaign was greatly helped by the publicity surrounding the great pioneering flights of the age – Alcock and Brown, Amy Johnson and Francis Chichester from Britain, and Charles Lindbergh and Amelia Earhart from the United States made sure that flying was rarely out of the headlines.

Britain regarded herself as a world power in 1939, and a strong aircraft industry, able to supply all the country's needs, was a vital part of that. There was much heart-searching in 1938 when it was proposed to fill a gap by buying Lockheed Hudsons from the United States. There were fourteen British firms capable of designing aircraft, mostly founded by the pioneers around the time of World War I, and some were still in their hands. Sir Frederick Handley Page was still managing director of his company and had a strong tendency to interfere; Sir Geoffrey de Havilland designed many of the aircraft that bore his name. Other companies were parts of much larger armaments groups. Vickers controlled the Supermarine Company, which designed the Spitfire. Hawker Siddeley controlled several companies including Armstrong-Whitworth and Avro. Aircraft design was in the hands of small ad hoc teams led by men who had often started off quite humbly as apprentices, such as Sidney Camm at Hawker and R. J. Mitchell at Supermarine.

The Air Ministry encouraged a diverse industry and used competitive tendering for new aircraft. This usually began with the Ministry issuing a specification briefly describing the aircraft, its role and its projected speed, armament, etc. It would be taken up by firms that specialized in that type of aircraft – Hawker and Gloster for fighters, Handley-Page and Vickers for bombers, Fairey and Blackburn for naval aircraft, and so on. Several designs were produced, and a prototype of each was built and tested. If successful, production orders would be placed. In peacetime the design process was slow, and it took nearly seven years to get the Wellington and Hampden bombers into service. It could be truncated by dropping competitive tender and dealing with a single firm, by ordering 'straight from the drawing board' without a prototype, or cutting out the development stage. Sometimes the initiative came from the manufacturers. The De Havilland Mosquito, which entered service in 1940, was a private venture in which the design was produced without any intervention by the Ministry. Others were more complex, and both the Spitfire and Hurricane were products of interactions between the Ministry and the industry.

All the design firms built their own aircraft, and often those from other companies. In addition a system of shadow factories got under way in 1936 – famous names from the motor industry such as Daimler, Humber, Rover and Austin, who already had experience in mass production of mobile metal machines powered by internal combustion engines. Many of the factories were concentrated in the Midlands, but a major one was built at Speke near Liverpool. Ideally a shadow factory should be close to an airfield where the finished products could take off, but it was possible to move the parts by road and carry out the final assembly on an airfield. Underground factories were also set up, notably at Corsham near Bath.

Supplies of aircraft were boosted when the hugely dynamic Lord Beaverbrook was appointed Minister of Aircraft Production in 1940. He brought in experts from industry and his own newspapers. He appealed to the public to send in aluminium pots and pans, though that turned out to be futile. He encouraged public subscriptions to buy aircraft, of which the Spitfire was by far the most popular. He eschewed civil service methods with his slogans 'Committees take the punch out of war' and 'Organisation is the enemy of improvisation'. He by-passed the air marshals (apart from Dowding of Fighter Command) by having new planes delivered directly to the squadrons. Traditionally the RAF had preferred quality to quantity, but Beaverbrook turned that on its head, and he gave priority to fighters rather than bombers. All this had a down side. The production of other items, including weapons for the army, was dislocated. And Beaverbrook preferred established designs rather than new ones, which might interrupt the flow. But he was successful, and by the autumn of 1940 the RAF was short of pilots rather than aircraft.

There had been a great revolution in the design of aeroplanes in the five years or so before 1940. In 1935 the Bristol Bulldog, the standard RAF fighter, had a speed of 178mph and an armament of two machine-guns. By 1938, the Hurricane and Spitfire were entering service with an armament of eight machine-guns and speeds of 316 and 355mph. Several interrelated changes had happened to make this possible. The most obvious was the substitution of the monoplane for the biplane. This had been pioneered by civil airlines, mostly in the United States, who needed speed for their mail contracts. Air forces continued to believe that two wings, braced together by a system of wires, were needed to give the aircraft manoeuvrability and strength in combat, until the internally-braced cantilever wing had proved its worth. Faster aircraft had higher landing speeds and needed longer runways, though the use of flaps was very helpful. Older aircraft were made in wood covered in canvas, which was clearly unsuitable at higher speeds, so new alloys were developed, first of all for the frame and then for the skin of the faster aircraft. Drag-producing fixed undercarriages were made retractable. Enclosed cockpits were also necessary at higher speeds and greater altitudes. Radios were now standard, and aircraft were altogether far more complex than they had been a few years earlier.

Behind all this were the increasing power-to-weight ratios of aero engines. The most innovative British companies were Rolls Royce and Bristol. The former's speciality was the Vee engine, which needed liquid cooling; Bristol made radial engines with the cylinders arranged in a circle round the crankshaft. This allowed air cooling and was lighter, but it tended to create more drag. Engines were now fitted with superchargers for high flying and used alloys to reduce weight. The Bentley BR2 Rotary, which had powered the Snipe, the RAF's standard fighter for much of the 1920s, had developed 230 horsepower. The famous Rolls Royce Merlin, the power plant of the Spitfires and Hurricanes, was capable of 1,030 horsepower in its early versions.

In 1933, with new and much faster bombers in prospect, it was believed that an attacking fighter could only hold one in its gun sights for two seconds. A much greater intensity of fire was needed, and the RAF looked at several possibilities. The .5-inch gun was largely untested and had rather a slow rate of fire, so it was rejected. The 20mm Hispano cannon, which was being developed by the French, had a much greater destructive power, but it was felt that it needed a more rigid mounting than could be provided in the new fighter aircraft. Meanwhile tests with eight of the well-established .303-inch machine-guns seemed to show that they were adequate, so that armament was adopted for the new fighters. This was unfortunate: the 20mm eventually proved more effective and was fitted from 1940. The Spitfire (apparently named after the young daughter of the managing director of Vickers) did not spit quite enough fire until then.

Traditionally the air gunner of a multi-seat aircraft had operated a single or twin Lewis gun; but he was exposed to the slipstream, and this could not continue as aircraft got faster. Captain Fraser Nash observed a fully-enclosed, power-operated turret in France and developed it as a private venture. By 1940 twin or four-gun turrets were fitted to bombers such as the Whitley and Wellington and were far in advance of anything the Germans had, but this was not a powerful enough armament for the RAF to operate self-defending bomber formations. Meanwhile another use was found for the four-gun turret, in the Boulton-Paul Defiant fighter, intended to attack bombers from their vulnerable sides; however, the Luftwaffe soon found that the Defiant was slow and vulnerable from underneath, and its days as an effective fighter were soon over.

The RAF's long-range bomber force was dependent on three types. The Handley-Page Hampden, like the Wellington, was developed to Specification 9/32. It was an unconventional aircraft by any standards, for its very narrow fuselage had a deep forward section where all of the four-man crew operated, and a thin tail boom, which earned it the nickname of 'the flying pencil'. Initially it was described as a 'fighter-bomber', but it soon became clear that it had neither the speed, the manoeuvrability, nor the armament for the first of these roles. It had a single forward-firing machine-gun operated by the pilot, and one upper and one lower machine-gun in the rear fuselage. This soon proved grossly inadequate in action, while the narrow fuselage restricted crew movements and caused fatigue. Twin machine-guns were eventually fitted on the rear-firing positions, but it was impossible to fit rotating gun turrets, so the Hampden was vulnerable to fire from the side, which the Luftwaffe soon discovered.

The Armstrong-Whitworth Whitley was ordered as a night bomber, and in early versions its speed was very low, at 184mph, though the fitting of Merlin engines increased that to 222mph. The Mark I carried one-gun, hand-operated turrets and a ventral turret underneath the fuselage. The armament was later upgraded by fitting a four-gun power-operated turret in the tail to cover the main point of vulnerability. The Whitley also had an odd appearance. Its designer had not understood the use of flaps, and he set the wing at a very high angle of incidence, so that at speed the fuselage tended to angle slightly downwards. The maximum depth of the fuselage was right forward and it tapered slightly towards the stern. This, combined with a prominent bomb-aimers position in the nose, gave the appearance of an outsize chin. It was a difficult aircraft to love.

The Vickers Wellington was the most conventional in appearance, with a streamlined fuselage rather like a slightly squashed cigar. It had a turret in the nose and another in the tail. Its unique structure, known as geodesic construction, was designed by the great engineer Barnes Wallis of 'dam-busters' fame. This was made up of diagonal metal members forming a frame, and covered with canvas. It gave a structure that could stand considerable battle damage and was easy to repair. The Wellington had the best performance of the three aircraft, with a speed of up to 255mph in the Mark III.

If the Whitley and Wellington were barely adequate, the RAF's light bombers presented greater problems. The single-engined Fairey Battle had seemed very advanced when it was first shown to the press in 1936. But it used the same Merlin engine as the Spitfire and Hurricane, though it carried twice the crew and weighed around 30 per cent more. Its only defence was a machine-gun firing forward and a hand-operated one in the rear of the cockpit. It had suffered heavily in the Battle of France, losing 40 aircraft out of 71 during a single raid. But it filled a gap and was used against invasion barges in the summer of 1940, meanwhile holding out the possibility of some kind of dive-bombing role if the enemy landed.

The twin-engined Blenheim light bomber was only slightly more successful. It came in two versions, the Mark I, with a short nose in which the pilot and observer sat side-by-side behind a glass windscreen, and the Mark IV, with a longer nose covered in Perspex for the observer. In either case the cockpit was very cramped – one pilot is said to have exclaimed, 'What a horrible place in which to die!' A gunner completed the crew, in a single-gun dorsal turret. The Blenheim had been developed from a civil machine, Lord Rothermere's 'Britain First', and it was considered fast in 1937 with a speed of 260mph. It was eventually converted into a stop-gap night-fighter.

If the RAF was unlucky in the timing of its bombers, it was far more fortunate with its fighters, the Hawker Hurricane and Supermarine Spitfire. Both had originated a decade ago in Specification F7/30, the first for a monoplane fighter. Sidney Camm and R. J. Mitchell both found that the terms of that specification were impossible, but they began to look at other ways, and with the Air Ministry they worked out Specification F5/34, which added a retractable undercarriage and deployed Rolls Royce's new Merlin engine. Camm's Hurricane design was conservative, based on a long line of light bombers, and it still used an internal structure of metal girders rather than stressed skin. Mitchell based his aircraft on the experience of designing winners of the Schneider Trophy for seaplane racing. He developed a unique elliptical wing to minimize induced drag, and this became one of the aircraft's most recognizable features. It had the new monocoque construction in which the metal skin was a part of the strength of the airframe, and every part was carefully calculated.

The Spitfire was a beautiful aircraft to fly, once one had got over the initial shock of having so much power:

After a few minutes cruising round I realized that this fearsome beast was perhaps not quite so formidable as I had thought in that first breathless minute, so I decided to try a landing. This came off reasonably satisfactorily, and I took off again, feeling much more sure of myself. So I climbed up to a good height and played about in the clouds in this superb new toy and did a few gentle dives to 400 m.p.h., which gave me a tremendous thrill. Altogether I was almost light-headed with exhilaration when I landed at the end of an hour's flight ...[4]

The Bristol Beaufighter arrived in the squadrons in August 1940. It was a twin-engined fighter, based on the wings of the less successful Beaufort torpedo bomber, with a speed of 333mph, which put it on a par with day fighters, so it was an ideal replacement for the Blenheim. It was less spectacular than the Mosquito, which entered service soon afterwards, but it was a solid aircraft with a powerful armament of four 20mm cannon and six machine-guns.

Coastal Command had its long-range aircraft, such as the Short Sunderland flying boat, which were not relevant to defence against invasion. It also had several squadrons of Avro Anson twin-engined general-purpose aircraft, among the first monoplanes to be adopted by the RAF. In 1940 they flew the bulk of the anti-invasion patrols that might have been the first to spot the enemy, along with the Lockheed Hudsons, which were faster and had a much longer range.

Airfields are the other main material requirement of air power. The RAF kept on a few selected ones after World War I and opened more with buildings to a high specification in the 1920s. In 1934 it began a great expansion scheme that would add about a hundred stations, often with many design features in common, and these were mostly in use by 1940. Fighter Command's airfields were in a ring around London, with 'arms' spreading to the north and west. Bomber airfields were all in the east by mid-1940, with five separate groups based respectively in East Anglia, north Norfolk, south and north Lincolnshire and the East Riding of Yorkshire. Training airfields were spread more evenly, often near the main centres of population to cater for the Auxiliary Air Force and the Volunteer Reserve. Operational airfields came in two types – sector stations and satellites. Thus, in Fighter Command, Biggin Hill was the

Sector Station for Sector C, south-east of London, with full operations room, servicing and accommodation facilities, while West Malling, fifteen miles farther east, and Lympne close to the Channel Coast, were satellite stations.

Despite the use of the term 'aerodrome' to dignify them, most RAF stations were really just fields – there were only nine places in Britain with hard runways in 1939, the rest being grass. The sites were carefully chosen, and most had good drainage, but bad weather was a problem – for example, at Hawarden in Cheshire, which became waterlogged in the rain.[5] Moreover, it took time for a new grass surface to become hard enough to use, and it was often quicker to lay concrete, which was preferred to tarmac because it was easier to produce and supervise. The first runway building programme began with twelve stations in May 1939. Each was to have two runways 800 yards long and 50 yards wide, crossing in the middle and with a 50-foot perimeter track round them. From February 1940 new bomber airfields had three runways set as near to 60 degrees to one another as possible and 1,000 yards long.[6] Some efforts were also made to convert existing airfields. RAF Kenley, an important fighter station just south of London, was closed from July 1939 until the end of the year to have two runways laid.[7] Most fields, especially those in Fighter Command, were still grass when the invasion crisis began.

With the growing threat of attack from the air, dispersal of aircraft and facilities was vital. Kenley was built with nine rectangular 'pens', reached by concrete tracks from the perimeter track, each holding three aircraft. Other airfields had circular standings 125 feet in diameter and reached by slightly longer tracks, but it was found that too much dispersal could lead to problems in maintenance and access. The older aerodromes had most of the facilities close together, except the bomb store. In those built during the expansion schemes of the later 1930s, accommodation and technical facilities were usually put in a space that fanned out behind the very prominent hangars. Those built in wartime were more dispersed, with accommodation in groups of 250 or 400 men separated by at least 200 yards.

In the stations built in the 1920s the officers lived in elegant but often overcrowded messes. Those built during the expansion programme of

1935–9 were also to a classical pattern approved by the Arts Council. It had improved single accommodation, better serving facilities and a more intimate 'club' atmosphere, perhaps a little too intimate if numbers increased. The sergeants' mess was like a simpler version of the officers' mess, but it was placed under great strain as increased numbers of sergeant aircrew began to move in, and annexes were added to cater for them. The airmen lived in various designs of barrack block with an 'H' plan, usually with two stories. In the war-built stations they usually lived in huts. The airmen also had the use of a large mess hall, with eating and games facilities and separate accommodation for corporals. Peacetime stations had married quarters, but in operational areas these were emptied of families when the war began.

The station headquarters was usually quite a dignified building, housing the office of the group captain in charge and various administrative functions. Detailed control of flying in the immediate vicinity was carried out from the control tower. After 1934 it was usually an almost cubical two-storey building with a balcony in front and sometimes a turret on top; but air traffic control was an underdeveloped art in the RAF of 1940. The most important control centre was the operations room. Fighter and Bomber Command Headquarters were situated away from airfields, at Stanmore and High Wycombe respectively and naturally had the most elaborate operations rooms. The individual groups also had separate sites. Winston Churchill described a visit to the Fighter Command operations room of No. 11 Group in September 1940:

> The Group Operations Room was like a small theatre, about sixty feet across, and with two storeys. We took our seats in the Dress Circle. Below us was the large-scale map table, around which perhaps twenty highly-trained young men and women, with their telephone assistants, were assembled. Opposite to us, covering the entire wall, where the theatre curtain would be, was a gigantic blackboard divided into six columns with electric bulbs, for the six fighter stations, each with their squadrons having a sub-column of its own, and also divided by lateral lines. Thus the lowest row of bulbs showed as they were lighted the squadrons which were 'Standing By' at two minutes notice, the next row those at 'Readiness', five minutes, then at 'Available', twenty minutes, then those which had taken off, the next row those which had reported having seen the enemy,

the next – with red lights – those which were in action, and the top row those which were returning home. On the left-hand side, in a kind of glass stage-box, were the four or five officers whose duty it was to weigh and measure the information received from our Observer Corps. Radar was still in its infancy, but it gave warning of raids approaching our coast, and the observers, with field glasses and portable telephones, were our main source of information about raiders flying overland. Thousands of messages were therefore received during an action.[8]

Each of the main operational airfields also had its own operations room. In Bomber Command it was often linked to station headquarters by a tunnel; in Fighter Command it was some distance away and protected by 6-foot-high earthworks.

From a distance, the most prominent feature of the typical airfield was its water tower, followed by the great hangars. The most common during the expansion period was the Type C, 300 feet long and more than half as wide with more than 35 feet of headroom under its gabled roof. It had internal gantries to lift aircraft parts and workshops and stores along the sides, which were in reinforced concrete to resist blast. The six-part main doors were ballasted for protection and needed a good deal of labour to open them. A crescent of four or five hangars was a common feature on expansion-programme airfields, and their shadows must have made them easy to pick out from the air. In war-built stations the hangars were more dispersed, and simpler types such as the Bellman could be constructed more quickly.

Kenley had underground storage for 35,000 gallons of aviation fuel, 8,000 of motor fuel and 2,500 gallons of oil, as well as a million and a quarter rounds of small-arms ammunition. A station needed a guardroom at the gate and a barbed-wire fence to protect against sabotage, which was regarded as a very real threat in 1940. It had an improvised airfield defence, perhaps with pill boxes and armoured cars. It had buildings for simulators, including the well-known Link trainer for teaching night flying, as well as places where crews could practice shooting, navigation and bomb aiming. The station needed sophisticated radio operation and repair facilities, as well as workshops for engines and instruments. It had garages for its motor transport, crash rescue and fire-fighting vehicles, stores for every kind of goods and a parachute store. It needed very good drainage on its runways, and concreting alone did not always solve the problems. It also needed sewage and central heating, and links with the outside world, mostly in the form of road transport. Each air station was a small town of perhaps 2,000 men and women. With luck, it might be close to a village with a good pub or have bus links to a town where cinemas and dance halls were available. Fighter Command tended to be best off here, with many airfields grouped around London.

AIRMEN

Trenchard's new air force was similar to the older armed forces in that it had three levels of status – officers, NCOs (or petty officers) and men – but it was to be different in many other ways. In the initial scheme every officer, apart from a small minority of chaplains, doctors and accountants, was to be a pilot. There were no specialist navigators, or any other kind of aircrew. As in the navy, selected officers would specialize in subjects like navigation, engineering and signals. Officers who trained in the College at Cranwell expected a full career in the service. Trenchard, who had spent a long time as a junior officer himself, saw that the RAF would need a large number of officers in its lower ranks with little prospect of promotion, so he removed this blockage by taking on large numbers for short-service commissions. They were recruited straight from civilian life and taught to fly, to serve for ten years in the RAF with the possibility of transfer to a permanent commission. Three-quarters to two-thirds of pilots were officers, the rest were sergeants promoted from the ground crews and expected to revert to their original trades after five years.

The bulk of the ground crews, the highly skilled men who would keep the aircraft flying, would be trained as apprentices in the RAF schools at Halton and Cosford. This was partly modelled on the navy's artificer scheme, but it took far larger numbers and promotion was much slower. At the bottom of the heap were the aircraft hands (general duties), recruited with no particular qualifications – but even they felt themselves far superior to army privates. T. E. Lawrence (Lawrence of Arabia) served in the ranks of both services in the 1920s and observed, 'The fellows at Uxbridge had joined the RAF as a profession – or to continue at their trades ... These fellows (Soldiers) have joined up as a last resort, because they have failed and were not qualified for anything else.'[9]

Trenchard's attitudes to class were rather ambiguous. He expected to recruit many of his apprentices from the middle classes, and up to six of them could be awarded cadetships at Cranwell every year, while slower promotion to officer ranks was to be quite common for more experienced men. At the same time, he was anxious to increase what he called the RAF's 'dining-out power', its appeal to the upper and middle classes. Despite his low budgets, he employed Sir Edwin Lutyens, the architect of New Delhi and the Cenotaph in Whitehall, to design officers' messes. For parade, officers and men were dressed like cavalrymen, with puttees and knee breeches. For formal occasions officers wore a full dress uniform with gold braid on the sleeves and a fur busby that vaguely resembled a flying helmet. Most of this would disappear in the 1930s as Trenchard's successors prepared for a major war.

The campaign for respectability was not entirely successful, at least at the most snobbish end of the educational ladder. At Eton, Tim Vigors was discouraged by his teacher:

> Mr. Roe had always been violently opposed to my idea of joining the RAF ... He referred continually to RAF officers as 'a lot of bloody mechanics!' and told me that by trying to join their ranks I was wasting all the experience of mixing with 'gentlemen' which my father and he had provided.[10]

Class was also prevalent in another of Trenchard's creations, the Auxiliary Air Force. A part-time reserve was a natural development, though it had to wait until Churchill had left the Air Ministry – he had failed twice to learn to fly in his spare time and said to Trenchard, 'Weekend fliers, Boom? Never!'[11] Twenty squadrons were formed, all numbered in the 500 and 600 series but with geographical designations attached: 501 (County of Gloucester), 504 (City of Nottingham), 600 (City of London) and 602 (City of Glasgow), for example. 'Johnnie' Johnson, later one of the RAF's most successful pilots, tried to join in 1938 and was interviewed by an unimpressed officer:

> his flagging enthusiasm revived a little when he learnt that I came from Leicestershire and that my home was at Melton Mowbray. 'That's a jolly good thing,' he said. 'I know the country very well as I hunt there a lot. Tell me, which pack do you follow?' When I tactfully explained that all my spare cash was devoted to flying, not hunting, the interview was speedily ended ...[12]

The Auxiliary Air Force required a good deal of commitment – 'Tennis, golf, rugger, going away for week-ends – we had to cut those out entirely and concentrate instead on loops and rolls, formation flying and fighter tactics, armament and engines.' Every member was also liable to serve for fifteen days as part of a unit.

> Summer camp was always good fun. Grand flying in glorious weather, basking lazily in the sun between flights, all packing into cars in the evening and racing between Tadcaster and York, pleasant friends and lively company – what more could anyone ask of life? Altogether we had an enjoyable, if somewhat hardworking, fortnight.[13]

Every applicant for flying duty was subjected to a strict medical:

> In all eight different doctors prodded and poked me in places I had never been prodded or poked before. It was winter time and more than a little chilly as I stood in their various offices and examination rooms, removing my shorts or dropping my trousers depending on which medical specialist I found myself in front of. I was ushered from room to room, while the doctors bombarded me with endless questions about the state of my health.[14]

New pilots had their initial training in civilian flying schools, a dozen of which had opened by the end of 1938. Mr Arnold, who taught Jimmy Corbin, was a typical instructor, a former flight sergeant pilot with twelve years' experience:

Many people can fly, but teaching others is a skill that few can master well. As he was my instructor I kept a respectful distance from him and always addressed him as Mr Arnold, but, despite our formal relationship, Mr Arnold was such a friendly person that I instantly warmed to him. His approach to teaching was based on encouragement and praise, which I responded to as I was determined to perform well for him because I liked him and not because I was frightened of him.[15]

Successful men went on to Flying Training Schools, where they would learn more advanced techniques. The skies over Britain would become very crowded in wartime, and plans were made to train pilots overseas in Canada, South Africa and Rhodesia (now Zimbabwe), but these did not come to fruition until after the war had started. In September 1939 the schools in Britain were renamed Service Flying Training Schools, and the course was reduced from six months to sixteen weeks. The RAF was now planning for 20,000 new pilots a year compared with 300 in 1934. This created a huge demand for instructors, and in August 1940 it was decreed that half the new ones would be pilots who had just completed the SFTS course.

Meanwhile the Royal Air Force Volunteer Reserve was founded in 1936 for training individual pilots on a part-time basis in peacetime. According to Jimmy Corbin who joined it in 1938,

The idea was to open up the RAF to all different kinds of people and not just the upper classes who had dominated its ranks since its inception, as they were the only ones who could afford to entertain the idea of becoming a pilot and had the money to turn it into reality. Then as war approached the Air Force suddenly woke up to the idea that talented pilots could come from any social strata. Besides, if they confined themselves to recruiting from the upper classes, the pool of pilots would soon dry up.[16]

By September 1939, Volunteer Reserve training was taking place at 46 centres. Successful applicants were enrolled as sergeant pilots under training:

I examined my uniform at close quarters. On my sleeve were three white stripes denoting my rank of sergeant, which made me feel immensely proud, especially as poor old Ken went into the Army Reserve as a private. The coarse material of the uniform was blue-grey in colour and identical to the regular RAF uniform in every respect except one. On my shoulder was a small brass plate with the letters VR – the Royal Air Force Volunteer Reserve.[17]

Many sergeants were commissioned at some stage in their career. It was all done on the commanding officer's recommendation to the Air Ministry; there was no particular interview or course, and a man might find himself eating in the sergeants' mess one day and the officers' mess the next.

Most pilots had their initial training on the De Havilland Tiger Moth, a two-seater biplane with open cockpits and a fixed undercarriage. Some started on the Miles Magister, 'a single-engined monoplane, which had been specifically designed for the RAF to use as a basic trainer ... Its main drawback was that it was non-aerobatic and any attempts at aerobatics were forbidden.'[18] Few people had flown in civilian airliners in those days, and for most the first flight in the RAF was a revealing and memorable experience:

> The bumping stops. We must have left the ground or something equally horrible. A quick look out as if I really don't want to believe what I am afraid I am going to see. We are flying.
>
> The ground recedes and once in the air all sense of speed vanishes. The view that unfolds enthrals me; it is absolutely beautiful. A voice down the speaking tube asks 'How are you feeling? Not too bad, is it? Nice day for it.'
>
> 'Wonderful'
>
> 'Good, then how about starting to earn your pay and getting down to a bit of work? I'm going to demonstrate the effect of controls; follow me through on the stick and rudder.'[19]

A pilot's first solo flight was just as memorable:

> I taxi for a few yards, check I'm pointing the aircraft dead into wind and without more ado open the throttle. Stick forward, the tail comes up and away we go. On take-off I manage to keep her as straight as a die. I get round the circuit tidily, throttle back and glide at seventy crosswind. Turn in for the final approach about now; just right. So far, so good. The hedge

comes underneath and there's a moment of concern as the ground appears to come closer very rapidly indeed. Check her, for God's sake, check her again, now stick back, wait for it, and we arrive on the ground. A small bump, but only a small one. Anyway, no matter, we are down in one piece, nothing broken. I have flown an aeroplane on my own, no matter what happens. I have soloed.[20]

During the long peace, operational squadrons had to train crews fresh from the schools, but this would be very difficult in war, so in November 1938 it was agreed that the pools attached to each group should give 'interim' training before the men were allocated to squadrons. In February 1940 those in Fighter Command were renamed Operational Training Units or OTUs, followed by those in Coastal and Bomber Command. All OTUs were in the United Kingdom so that the aircraft and partly-trained crews could be called out on operations in an emergency, and it was hoped that pilots would now join squadrons ready for operations:

The following three weeks at Aston Down were filled with flying, interspersed every day with lectures on fighter tactics and gunnery. Aerobatics, cross-country navigation, formation flying, and practice gunnery filled the days ... For me everything went pretty smoothly, apart from gunnery practice. Although I felt in total control of the aircraft and seemed able to get it into the right position for shooting at the right time, for some reason I continually missed the target drogue being towed by its aircraft.[21]

But again, resources were limited. There was a shortage of modern aircraft to train on, and in May 1940 the Fighter OTU course was only two weeks long.

The RAF's pilot training was generally very efficient, and David Crook commented,

I possess now a great admiration for the flying training given to pilots by the R.A.F. I don't think there is any training system in the world to touch it for thoroughness, and it also seems to impart to many of the pupils those qualities of initiative and dash which we seem to produce to our great advantage over the German Air Force, who are not half such good individualists.[22]

The main flaw in the fighter pilot's training was in gunnery. As 'Johnnie' Johnson observed,

> The majority of our fighter pilots could fly reasonably well. They were trained sufficiently to hold their own in a dog-fight, but when it came to the ultimate test, judging the range and deflection angle of their opponents, the average pilot failed, and this was because we paid too little attention to the science of air gunnery ... the average pilot could knock down a 109 when he overhauled it from dead line astern and hose-piped his opponent with two cannons and four machine guns. But give him a testing deflection shot of more than a few degrees and he usually failed to nail his opponent.[23]

Although Johnson had been turned down for the Auxiliary Air Force for showing too little interest in the traditional country sport of fox-hunting, he found that his experience in another – shooting – was much more useful in the air.

The RAF was far less effective when training non-pilot aircrew, largely because Trenchard rejected the experience of World War I, which showed the need for trained specialists such as observers. In the 1920s pilots did their own navigation, which usually consisted of following railway lines, a practice known as 'Bradshawing', after the well-known timetable. The only other people who flew regularly were the air gunners, aircraftsmen of the ground trades who were allowed a certain amount of time in the air and learned gunnery within the squadron.

In 1934 the RAF grudgingly recognized the need for some kind of 'back-seater' to assist the pilot on longer flights or in bad weather and began to train observers in navigation, gunnery and signalling. As corporals they were too junior to argue with the pilot, and indeed they were regarded as 'pilots' servants', plotting courses on a board but taking no decisions. In 1937 they were given their badge, the 'flying O', revived from the last war, but it was difficult to recruit enough men from the service, as part-time conditions were not good:

> For example, an Air Observer (Fitter) would be told to change the engine on an aircraft. When he informed the Flight Sergeant that he was to go on

308

a six-hour flight, the answer would be, 'Ho, Cpl, scrounging off flying again, eh?, right, you can work all night on it when you come back'[24]

Part-time service in more than one trade gave flexibility in peacetime, but it did not survive the test of war. There was no point in training a skilled fitter and then having him spend half his time on other duties or, worse still, going on a dangerous mission and being lost. Furthermore, it was impossible to build up coherent teams to crew bombers. The part-time concept was abandoned in May 1938 when observers were given full responsibility for navigation. More were recruited by direct entry from civilian life. From early in 1939 all were to graduate as acting sergeants. In view of the neglect between the wars and the reluctant acceptance of the observer, it is not surprising that the RAF's navigation was very poor when war started.

The other aircrew category, the air gunners, had an even slower rise. Most were wireless operators and combined the two duties in the air, but in 1937 their training in the squadrons was found to be inadequate, and it could certainly not cope with the new powered gun turrets. Six armament training schools had been set up by mid-1939. The final stage came when they were all promoted to sergeant in June 1940.

All this caused great stress in the sergeants' messes, originally the home of a few dozen older men. When Bill Magrath visited an RAF station, he was refused a drink when a senior warrant officer intervened saying, 'We don't serve whisky to boys.'[25] It was even worse when the larger numbers of air gunners were allowed the privileges of the mess. As one of them observed,

> Like all changes, it took some getting used to, particularly among senior NCOs in ground trades who might well have served fifteen years before advancing to the same rank as that handed out to an eager eighteen-year-old after only six months in the service. But they soon realised that it was unfair to bear grudges; most of the new sergeants did not live long enough to justify a grudge.[26]

Volunteers for flying were sought in other branches of the armed forces. Early in 1941 Gunner Spike Milligan came before a selection board (though we do not have to accept that his account of the interview was literally true):

> 'What would you like to be?'
> 'A pilot, sir.'
> 'Want to go out with the pretty girls, eh?'
> After a stringent physical examination they told me, 'Sorry, your eyesight isn't up to what we need for a pilot; however we have a number of vacancies for rear gunners.'
> 'No sir, I don't want to be in the back, I want to drive.'[27]

No selection procedure is perfect, and by the end of September the Air Ministry was becoming concerned about those who, 'though not medical cases, come to forfeit the confidence of their Commanding Officers without having been subjected to any exceptional strain of operational flying'. The term 'lack of moral fibre' was used to describe such men, who had to be weeded out before they put their comrades in danger. In such cases an officer would have his commission terminated, and an airman would revert to his original trade, if any. Squadron Leader Stanford Tuck had to deal with two sergeants who peeled off from the formation as they went into the attack. He decided to give one another chance; the other was court-martialled and reduced to the ranks. He was later seen cleaning the steps in an airfield control tower, still wearing his pilot's insignia but no other badges.[28] Despite the stresses and dangers, there were always plenty of applicants for aircrew duty, because of the glamour of the service and the privileges awarded to aircrew.

On the Ground

Only about one in ten of RAF personnel flew regularly, but those on the ground were just as vital. Cooks, policemen and clerks could be trained and often taken from people with civilian experience, but the men and women who serviced the aircraft were even more necessary if the force was not to suffer an unacceptable rate of accidents or have too many of its aircraft grounded because of lack of maintenance or repair of action damage.

In the original Trenchard scheme, the maintenance of aircraft was done by the highly-skilled products of No. 1 Technical Training School at Halton, who had served three-year apprenticeships. In 1932 riggers and fitters were merged so that both would be skilled in airframe and engine work, and mates were introduced to give them some semi-skilled assistance. This was not a success, for the mates had only two months' technical training and could not cope with the increasingly sophisticated aircraft coming into service – 'with the new types, especially where stressed skin was concerned, there was no part of an aircraft which could be entrusted to an unskilled man, without danger of damage.'[29]

The answer was to create a new class of flight mechanics, specializing in airframe, engine, instrument repair, radio or armament. The Air Mechanic (E) was selected from suitable aircraft-hands and sent on a 22-week course to 'train airmen and naval ratings to undertake minor routine inspections, cleaning, simple anti-corrosive treatment and simple adjustments on initial equipment aircraft and engines'. The Air Mechanic (A) was similar but knew less about engines. He learned about the principles of aircraft construction, components of aircraft, the use of tools and minor repairs, the handling of aircraft and aerodrome procedure.[30] According to the recruiting plan for 1939–40, 27,061 men would be taken on for the ground trades and nearly half of them, 12,590, were to be trained as Flight Mechanics and Flight Riggers.[31] Already there were signs of stress in June 1939 when Bomber Command complained that it was 20 per cent short of NCO fitters, 80 per cent of instrument makers and 85 per cent of electricians. The Air Ministry decreed that men who had completed 75per cent of their training courses and appeared to be up to standard could be sent on to squadrons, by which it was hoped 4,000 men would be added immediately.[32]

Tiny bits of status were important during and after trade training, and men's motivation increased when they actually got near an aircraft on an operational station:

As mechanics' mates, we are proud that we now have an official designation. At 'A' Flight we get our first close-up of a 'Spitfire', in which is seated a flight mechanic. He asks us whether we would like to help him run-up. Wishing to create a good impression we lean on the tail as he instructs.

Next moment we are in the grip of a tornado the like of which we had never known before. It tears the breath from our bodies and we are subjected to much the same feeling as a fly may feel in proximity to a vacuum cleaner.[33]

When the war began the RAF had capacity for 6,350 recruits and 35,978 men under trade training, over periods ranging from one week to 2½ years. The recruits underwent a four-week course at Uxbridge, Cardington and Padgate, rather like the army and navy:

The first few months of service life in uniform, square-bashing, learning how to drill and to march and to do without privacy and swallow the basic principle of 'if it moves salute it, if it doesn't move, paint it' was an educational experience, and not all of it unpleasant; only parts of it were … ritual humiliation … service language … I had never in my life heard such a concentration of profanity and obscenity.[34]

The start of the war brought a considerable increase in numbers. More than 96,000 new men joined during the remainder of 1939, followed by more than 276,000 in 1940. The RAF had no trouble in attracting volunteers, who mostly joined early to avoid conscription and to have a better choice of service – 158,000 of the new men volunteered for the RAF during 1940. Among conscripts, almost twice as many men chose the RAF as the navy during most of 1940, rising to three times by the end of the year.[35] As a result the RAF was largely able to pick and choose its men, and most of them were highly motivated.

All these men needed training. One way of speeding up supply was to increase the number of specialized trades, so that each would need shorter training. In June 1940 alone, 29 new trades were added to the list, including Link Trainer Instructor, Radio Mechanic, Grinder and Meteorologist.[36] The ratio of instructors (mostly civilians) was reduced from 13:1 to 15:1. Meanwhile more instructors were found by ordering base and squadron commanders to seek out men who might have suitable skills and offering them promotion to acting corporal.[37]

The trade groups had largely been watertight in peacetime, but now commanding officers were ordered to seek out talent within their units.

> It is of primary importance that those airmen mustered in a Group II trade who, by reason of their skill and experience either in the service or in civil life, are capable of remustering to the corresponding Group I trade without the necessity of undergoing a conversion course, should be afforded all possible facilities to do so.[38]

The RAF was also considering the best way to organize its maintenance crews. Traditionally a fitter and a rigger had been attached to each aircraft, but that tended to be wasteful of labour. The other extreme was to employ the 'garage' system, by which all aircraft were serviced in central facilities; but that tended to reduce the connection between the man and an aircraft, with bad effects on morale. Most stations used a compromise between the two, with routine servicing, arming, refuelling and so on carried out by mechanics and aircraft-hands in the flights, while more extensive repairs were carried out by fitters in the station workshops. In addition the RAF created a third level of maintenance by which seriously damaged aircraft could be put back into service, and a specialized Maintenance Command was founded in 1938.

Most squadrons had a traditional organization in 1940, based on the Flight of around six operational aircraft. The Flight Sergeant was a dominant figure, known as 'Chiefy', because of his origins in the chief petty officers of the Royal Naval Air Service of the last war. Each aircraft still had its own Fitter and Rigger. Bob Stanford Tuck was introduced to his on taking command of a squadron in 1940. The fitter was 'a shambling, grinning Cockney named Hillman who had a flattened nose, chopped teeth, a head shaggy as a hearth-broom and hands huge and ungainly as bunches of bananas'. According to 'Chiefy' Tyrer, he was 'the scruffiest type on the station' but the best Engine Fitter.[39]

When an aircraft had landed it was guided in by its Rigger on the port wingtip and the Mechanic to starboard. It was refuelled right away in the open air, partly to prevent condensation inside the fuel tanks, and the air force used a large number of tankers or 'bowsers'. Each aircraft had a regular pattern of inspection recorded on Form 700, the Aircraft Maintenance Form. It was inspected before each flight, after 30, 60 and 240 hours' flying time, and daily, when the Flight Rigger, Flight Mechanic, Armourer, Wireless Operator, Electrician and Instrument Repairer worked as a team moving anti-clockwise round the aircraft. If faults were found they were passed on to the NCO in charge to arrange maintenance. If not, the aircraft was ready to fly again.

In the past the Fitters had largely been allowed to get on with the maintenance themselves, supervised by their pilots, who obviously had a vested interest in the matter. There were a few specialized technical officers, chosen from among the general duties officers and given a two-year course. Allen Wheeler was delighted to be appointed to 'a magnificent course of instruction' at RAF Henlow, where he would learn both the theory and practice of air engineering.[40] Many were less happy, seeing engineering as a diversion from flying, which they had joined the RAF to do. There was no coherent group of engineering officers until April 1940, when the Air Ministry set up a Technical Branch composed of those who had already passed the course at Henlow and could be spared from flying, warrant officers who would be commissioned as engineer, signals or armament specialists, and engineering graduates from civilian life. Again, the part-time principle was overtaken in war.

The RAF had certain advantages in the employment of women. The majority of its members were employed on non-military duties on the ground, whereas everyone in the navy was expected to be ready to go to sea, and everyone in the army to fight – roles that were forbidden to women. Flying was considered glamorous even by association, and the uniform was far more attractive than that of the army. The Women's Auxiliary Air Force was founded at the end of June 1939, based on the Women's Royal Air Force, which had been in operation from the foundation of the RAF to 1920. It was headed by Jane Trefusis Forbes, a formidable businesswoman and dog breeder. The WAAFs had 1,734 women when the war started, and there was a sudden but rather incoherent expansion programme. Women had to be found separate accommodation on or near the air bases, but for the moment they often had to be billeted out, and in April 1940 the Director complained that they sometimes had to sleep two to a bed. This led to a programme to build separate WAAF quarters in air stations. There were nearly 9,000 WAAFs by the beginning of 1940 and nearly 20,000 by the end, a higher proportion than in the other services.

Initially women were recruited for the traditional roles of administration (especially typing), cooking and domestic duties, and more than half the 15,000 women in the service in September 1940 were employed on these. A growing number (nearly a thousand) were already working on aircraft servicing and maintenance, with slightly more on medical or transport duties, and driving soon became a popular trade. The largest group, apart from domestic and administrative staff, consisted of the 2,685 women in ground signals, including those working in radar stations and operations rooms. By August 1940 women were employed in eighteen trade groups, compared with six at the beginning of the war. Separately, women pilots formed the Air Transport Auxiliary, which delivered aircraft from the factories to RAF stations. Its most famous member, the pre-war aviation pioneer Amy Johnson, disappeared after baling out over the Thames Estuary early in 1941.

In 1936 it was decided to set up a balloon defence around London and other major cities. Tethered balloons had been used during World War I but mostly as observation points over the Western Front. Now they were to be deployed unmanned, and it was intended that their cables would obstruct and possibly damage aircraft in their tracks. Four hundred and fifty were needed for London, in a ring seven miles in radius around the city. They were spaced at nine balloons per mile, which it was calculated would give an aircraft with a 60-foot wingspan a one-in-ten chance of striking one. They were to be run by the RAF because of the need to cooperate with Fighter Command in deciding when to raise and lower them. Barrages were also set up in the other major cities, and also at the main naval bases, but they could not be sited anywhere near an airfield, and there were not nearly enough to give any kind of cover over invasion beaches. Even over cities their utility was doubtful. They did something for civilian morale and they might have forced attackers to fly higher and lose their aim, but it had to be admitted that the number of enemy aircraft destroyed by them was 'infinitesimal'. Even worse, Sir Charles Portal wrote in January 1941, 'in practice they have proved almost as successful in bringing down our own aircraft as enemy aircraft.'[41]

The Observer Corps was founded in 1925, composed of ground-based men, and later women, who would observe the movement of aircraft over British skies. Until 1939 its members were enrolled as Special Constables and wore the black-and-white police armband when on duty. The first observers were confined to south-east England, the Midlands and the industrial north, but in 1936 they were extended so that only Cornwall, west Wales, the west and far north of Scotland and Northern Ireland were left uncovered. The Observer Corps took in an unusually wide range of people from many different occupations. It adopted a uniform in RAF blue and became more tightly disciplined, though it was never fully militarized.

The radar chain did not remove the need for the Corps, for it faced outwards and the RAF still relied on the observers to report aircraft as they moved inland. Their duties were:

> To report the position of aircraft continuously to the [Observer Corps] Centre and co-operate in this duty with those Posts on the same telephone circuit ...
>
> To 'Tell' required tracks of friendly aircraft and all hostile and unidentified aircraft simultaneously to a Fighter Group or Sector Operations Room. The reporting of crashes and other unusual incidents to the Groups and Sectors was also the responsibility of the Centre.

Each aircraft or group of aircraft was given a number as it was spotted and tracked from one place to another. At first the observers were reluctant to supply information on height, as they could see the possibility of error, but in July 1940 it was decided that they would provide estimates to the nearest 5,000 feet. The Corps took on various new responsibilities as the war progressed, including reporting the fall of bombs and parachute landings, whether of small numbers of shot-down airmen, or mass attacks.

Chain Home Stations ●
CHL Stations ○
Observer Centres ▲
....
Boundary of
observed area
Unobserved tracts
within observed area

Shetland
Islands

Sunburgh

Fair Isle

● Caitnip
○ Nether Button

● Thrumster

Rosehearty ● Hillhead
○ Doonies Hill
▲ School Hill
Aberdeen
○ St Cyrus
● Douglas Wood
Dundee ▲
Anstruther ○
Dunfermline ▲
Cockburnspath
▲ Glasgow ○ Drone Hill
Galashiels ○ Bamburgh
▲

○ Cresswell
Ottercops Moss
▲ Carlisle Durham
▲ Shotten

● Danby Beacon
▲ Lancaster
▲ York ○ Flamborough Head
▲ Leeds
○ Easington
▲ Manchester
Stenigot ●
Lincoln ▲ ○ Ingoldmels
▲ Wrexham
▲ Derby West Beckham
● Happisburgh
Shrewsbury ● Norwich
▲ Coventry Stoke Holy Cross ●
▲ Bury St Emunds ○ Dunwich
Strumble Ho High Street
○ Haycastle Gloucester Bedford ▲ Cambridge Bramley ● Bawdsey
St Twynells ▲ ▲ Uxford ▲ Colchester ▲ ○ Walton
Warren Watford ▲ ○ Conewdon
Cardiff ▲ ▲ Bristol Dunkirk
Maidstone ▲ ▲ ○ Foreness
Winchester Horsham ○ Dover
▲ Yeovil ▲ Truleigh Rye
Exeter ▲ Poling ○ Fairlight
● Hawks Tor Worth Ventnor Beachy Head ○ Pevensey
Carnanton ○ ○ Rame Head
○ West Prawle
○ Drytree

THE OBSERVER CORPS
NETWORK AND THE
RADAR CHAIN, JULY 1940

The Corps was divided into two types of member: those who spotted the aircraft and those who manned operations rooms that fed information to the sector stations and group headquarters. Initially it was not the Corps' duty to identify aircraft – that was the job of the RAF staff. There was no formal training in aircraft recognition, but members set up the 'Hearkers' Club' in November 1939. Books of aircraft silhouettes were issued, often years out of date, and it was found that these alone were not enough. It soon became a national sport, with best-selling books by Peter Masefield and Francis Chichester among others.

Anti-aircraft artillery was run by the army under the control of the RAF. This was a huge organization, with more than 140,000 officers and men in April 1940, under Lieutenant General Sir Frederick Pile. The great majority were hastily trained Territorials. Its main heavy weapon was the 3.7-inch gun which first entered service in 1937 and fired a 28-pound shell to a maximum ceiling of 41,000 feet. But supplies were limited, and only 1,544 had been produced by the end of 1940. The gap was even more serious concerning light artillery. The navy and the air force used 20mm guns in their respective elements, but there was no mechanism to self-destruct the vast majority of shots that missed, so they were not judged safe for land use. The best weapon was the Swedish 40mm Bofors gun, which could fire a 2-pound shell to a maximum height of 23,600 feet at a rate of 120 rounds per minute, five times that of a 3.7-inch. The British government arranged manufacture under licence in 1937, but supplies were slow, and only 1,233 were available in December 1940. The deficiency had to be made up with obsolete 3-inch guns, and with machine-guns.

Radar could be used to detect aircraft as they approached the country, but as yet it was of little help in aiming the guns. For heavy artillery this was done by means of simple mechanical computers known as predictors. Light artillery was aimed by eye, using deflection shooting. Searchlights were used at night, and there were 4,310 of these in service in September 1940. Anti-Aircraft Command was focused on the defence of cities and towns against strategic bombing, though later it moved some of its light units to RAF airfields. It had not studied the problems of tactical mobility, and anti-aircraft guns were not likely to be available in large numbers to defend troops against dive-bombers. Even in its core role of defence of the cities, it was severely challenged by night bombing. A heavy barrage could do much to keep up civilian morale, but during the winter and spring of 1940–1 it brought down 169½ enemy aircraft (including some shared with the RAF). This was not a great total for such a huge force.

FIGHTING TACTICS

To justify its independence after World War I, the RAF adopted the view that strategic bombing of enemy cities was the only way to deter a future war. It tended to neglect the fighter arm, and this got the support of Stanley Baldwin, the dominant political figure between the wars: 'I think it is well for the man in the street to realize that there is no power on earth that can protect him from being bombed. Whatever people may tell him, the bomber will always get through.' The only answer was to build up an even stronger bombing force as a deterrent. For many years the RAF had planned, rather vaguely, for a war with France. There was no particular quarrel with that country, but Germany was defeated and the United States and the Soviet Union were isolated for very different reasons, and she seemed to be the only other world power to rival Britain. An air war with France was just about credible with the means available – Paris was only 150 miles from the English coast.

This belief that the bomber could not be stopped was literally an article of faith, with no particular evidence to support it. Much was made of the effect on civilian morale of a German attack on the exposed coastal town of Folkestone in 1917, but no account was taken of what could be done with air-raid shelters and other civil defence measures. No exercises were carried out beyond bomb-aiming practice, and there was no dispassionate study of the subject. The RAF's only practical experience, of bombing defenceless rebel villages under the clear skies of Iraq and Somaliland, had no relevance to the air over France or Germany. However, the belief that 'the bomber will always get through' was largely reversed in the late thirties, and Fighter Command had become a very efficient arm by 1939. None the less, the RAF as a whole maintained its faith in bombing.

Bomber Command soon proved ineffective on its first missions into enemy territory. Both sides were careful not to escalate the 'phoney war', and direct attacks on civilian industry were out of the question, but naval forces were fair game. Then came a turning-point, with two raids on units of the German fleet at Wilhelmshaven in December 1939. On the first occasion half of a force of 12 Wellingtons was lost; on the second, 15 out of 24 were shot down with no real damage to the enemy. If the best bombers in the RAF could not succeed against a coastal target, there was no chance that they could penetrate inland in daylight. There were three more specific weaknesses. Firstly, there was the speed of the fighters. Often during the 1920s and 1930s the RAF's bombers had actually been faster than the fighters, but the recent dramatic increases in speed had applied much more to fighters than bombers, and the maximum speed of a Messerschmitt 109 was more than 100mph greater than that of a bomber. Secondly, the fighters were armed with cannon, which had a greater range and hitting power than machine-guns, while the hopes placed in powered gun turrets were misplaced. Thirdly, the Germans had an early form of radar that allowed them to direct their fighters to meet enemy bombers.

There was also the possibility of bombing by night, though the RAF had practised this very little and it had not developed navigation by radio. Bomber Command spent most of the winter of 1939/40 dropping 27 million leaflets, and absolute accuracy of aim was not essential in this. An early night raid in March 1940 on the naval base at Hörnum did not augur well when one crew bombed neutral Denmark by mistake, and the other aircraft inflicted little damage.

After the fall of France the RAF found itself in a very difficult strategic position. Berlin was a long way away and very difficult to find in the middle of Germany, and there was no point in bombing Paris instead – that would only alienate neutral opinion and inflame the French even further after the crippling of their fleet at Mers-el-Kébir. London, on the other hand, was less than a hundred miles from German bases in France and easily identifiable by means of the River Thames.

And if the Germans wanted to bomb other towns and cities, they had radio navigational aids that were well beyond anything used by the RAF.

Bomber Command was confused by different objectives during the crisis of 1940. At the end of May, as the Battle of France went on, it was ordered to concentrate on trains and marshalling yards, but the lack of moonlight precluded accurate attack at long range; five days later it was to make plans for an attack on enemy oil resources and his aircraft industry. By 20 June the targets listed were the aircraft industry, communications, oil and the destruction of crops and forests. On 4 July they were to attack ports and shipping, mostly the large warships and naval bases but also Rotterdam and other Dutch ports. The medium bombers were to concentrate on 'the attack of barges and small craft on the canals and ports in Holland and Belgium'. As the air battle over Britain intensified, the main target was the Luftwaffe and the German aircraft industry, though Air Marshal Portal pointed out that this was not likely to have any immediate effect. On 21 September the anti-invasion operation had a clear priority over everything else.[42]

Despite the hard lessons of the first few weeks of the war, Bomber Command operations were still very amateur early in 1940:

> We could choose our own route; we could bomb from any old height; sometimes we could carry whatever load we wished; we could go off at any time. We were individuals, but to tell the honest truth we were not very efficient, and out of the total tonnage of bombs carried by A.3 that night I would say that the actual amount which fell on the target might have been at most ten per cent.[43]

Attacks on barges and the means of getting them to the ports were most direct means of defeating the invasion of Britain by Bomber Command. One of Bomber Command's most notable raids was on the night of 12 August, when the Hampden commanded by Flight Lieutenant R. A. B. Learoyd succeeded in putting an aqueduct over the Dortmund–Ems Canal out of action for ten days, for which he was awarded the Victoria Cross. Meanwhile, the concentrations of barges in the invasion ports were growing, and serious raids began early in September. Most of the Command's Blenheims raided the Channel ports on the 5th and 6th and Hampdens and Battles joined in on the following night. Ninety-one sorties were flown on the 13th, and 84 barges were sunk or damaged at Dunkirk on the 17th.

Attacks were a little better organized by this time:

> These raids on the invasion ports were organised to destroy as many barges as possible. Each squadron was given a port which was to be considered its own particular port and the pet baby of all concerned; each crew was given a basin; in each basin there were so many barges, sometimes 200, sometimes even 400. Bomb-loads were organised so that the maximum amount of damage would be done per aircraft. Many small bombs were carried, even hand-grenades, which would, at least, do the job if they hit the right spot.[44]

In all these raids claimed 214 barges, 21 transports and five tugs, about twelve per cent of the German force.

Coastal Command was another of the home commands founded in 1936, but it did not have the glamour and urgency of Fighter Command, nor was it considered the RAF's raison d'être like Bomber Command. The ship-borne aircraft of the Fleet Air Arm had been a bone of contention between the navy and the air force until they were put under naval control on the eve of war. However, the RAF retained the shore-based aircraft operating over the sea, and these were grouped together in Coastal Command. The very title suggested a rather limited aim of patrolling the waters close to the shore, and it was by no means as well equipped as other parts of the RAF. It would be well into the war before it could play its decisive role in winning the Battle of the Atlantic.

Of the Command's three groups, No. 15 was equipped mostly with long-range flying boats and was concerned with the developing battle against the U-boats in the Atlantic. No. 18 covered eastern Scotland and north-east England, and faced the possible invasion ports of Norway and Denmark. No. 16 Group was based in the south and east between Flamborough Head and Lyme Bay and looked out to the enemy-held coasts of the Netherlands, Belgium and northern France. The Coastal Command Groups were already setting an example of inter-service cooperation, for joint maritime and air headquarters had already been

set up at Pitreavie in Fife for No. 18 Group, and Chatham for No. 16
Group. Coastal Command had many duties, including anti-submarine
patrol, convoy protection on the east coast, cover for the fleet at sea and
even flying over London to check if the blackout was effective.

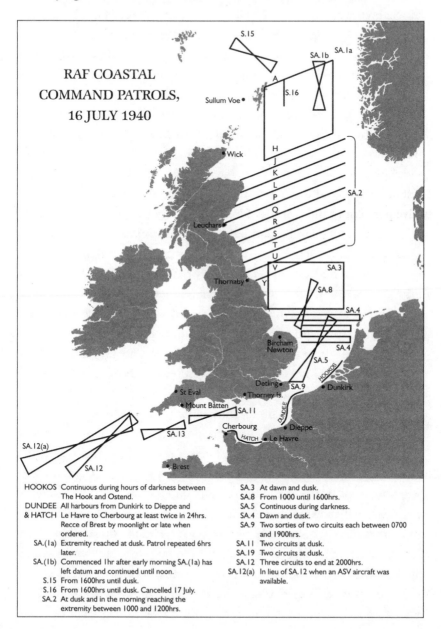

RAF COASTAL COMMAND PATROLS, 16 JULY 1940

HOOKOS	Continuous during hours of darkness between The Hook and Ostend.
DUNDEE & HATCH	All harbours from Dunkirk to Dieppe and Le Havre to Cherbourg at least twice in 24hrs. Recce of Brest by moonlight or late when ordered.
SA.(1a)	Extremity reached at dusk. Patrol repeated 6hrs later.
SA.(1b)	Commenced 1hr after early morning SA.(1a) has left datum and continued until noon.
S.15	From 1600hrs until dusk.
S.16	From 1600hrs until dusk. Cancelled 17 July.
SA.2	At dusk and in the morning reaching the extremity between 1000 and 1200hrs.

SA.3	At dawn and dusk.
SA.8	From 1000 until 1600hrs.
SA.5	Continuous during darkness.
SA.4	Dawn and dusk.
SA.9	Two sorties of two circuits each between 0700 and 1900hrs.
SA.11	Two circuits at dusk.
SA.19	Two circuits at dusk.
SA.12	Three circuits to end at 2000hrs.
SA.12(a)	In lieu of SA.12 when an ASV aircraft was available.

As the Dunkirk evacuation was completed, Coastal Command received orders that the total effort of 16 and 18 Groups was to be devoted to anti-invasion patrols, and the system of anti-submarine patrols was modified to cope with this. The number of patrols was doubled ten days later. No. 18 Group operated various patrols between Norway and Shetland, mainly to intercept raiders and protect the naval base at Scapa Flow. It continued to run a series of ten parallel patrols running from south-west to north-east. The first aircraft on each set off at dawn; the second sortie was timed to end at dusk so all the patrols were in daylight. South of that, No. 16 Group originally operated a square search at dawn and dusk, but later it had three patrols that were literally in parallel with No. 18's efforts. South of that it first operated a patrol that zigzagged between the Dutch and East Anglian coasts between dawn and dusk until it was replaced by a series of patrols in complex triangular patterns. 'Hookos' were patrols operating directly off the coast of Zealand around dawn and dusk, except when there was good moonlight, when they operated all night. There were figure-of-eight patrols in mid-Channel in the early days, replaced by 'Moon 1', '2' and '3', which flew at dusk and remained there while there was still a possibility of seeing anything. 'Hatch' patrols operated immediately off the coast of Normandy once every 24 hours, as did 'Bust' patrols off Brest; 'Dundee' patrols were between Dieppe and Dunkirk. Patrols could be dangerous. On 27 June, 235 Squadron carried out a reconnaissance of the Zuyder Zee and lost four aircraft out of six.

Aircraft were not yet fitted with radar, and Coastal Command's manual, last revised in 1938, was not optimistic about the possibility of finding an enemy without prior intelligence, especially at night. The best patrol height was 3,000–6,000 feet, lower at night. In a clear sky and bright moon it was possible to pick out ships below, but often only by their wakes. If the ships were sailing at less than twelve knots, as most invasion barges would, then sighting would be far more difficult. A Coastal Command aircraft should also be able to attack, but Ansons carried a very light bomb load of 360 pounds, and there was as yet no effective bomb sight for use against a moving ship. Coastal Command's record of attack was not impressive during 1940 – it sank only six vessels, totalling 5,561 tons, and damaged 14 more, while it lost 158 of its own aircraft. It was not impossible that on a dark night an invasion fleet might slip through undamaged or perhaps even unreported by the patrols of Coastal Command.

Even weaker was the army cooperation organization, which highlighted the differences between British and German views on the subject. The Germans had used the Stuka with decisive effect in support of their armies. The RAF had turned down the idea of a dive-bomber, though it continued with some experiments during the late 1930s. During its expansion phase after 1935 government policy was directed towards a sea-and-air war against Germany, so army cooperation was neglected. The main aircraft was the Westland Lysander. With its diamond-shaped wing and protruding fixed undercarriage it looked just as odd as the Stuka, but it was designed mainly for reconnaissance and spotting for artillery rather than attack. It had a maximum speed of 219mph at 10,000 feet, compared with the Stuka's 255mph. It could carry a total of 500 pounds of light bombs under struts projecting from the undercarriage, but these reduced the aircraft's speed by 15mph, and this was less than a quarter of the load carried by the Stukas. It could only drop them in level flight or in a shallow dive. Its armament of two forward- and one rear-firing machine-guns was inadequate, and the five squadrons operating with the BEF in France had lost 50 aircraft. Army cooperation aircraft would soon go off in two different directions: light, low-performance aircraft would carry out reconnaissance and spotting at low level and under fighter cover, while high-performance, fighter-like aircraft would carry out attacks on enemy tanks and concentrations, using bombs or rockets. The Lysander was trying to carry out both roles and doing neither well. In the summer of 1940 there was one squadron attached to each army command, an inadequate number of an inadequate aircraft.

In many ways Fighter Command was the best organized part of the RAF in 1940. It had been built up under political pressure since 1936, with excellent aircraft and an efficient ground organization supported by the newly invented radar. The squadron was a tactical as well as an administrative unit in Fighter Command, more so than in Bomber and

Coastal Commands, where the aircraft often operated individually. The rank of Squadron Leader was truly appropriate in fighters, his main job being to train his men and lead them into battle. A squadron was expected to send up twelve aircraft, for which purpose it had sixteen as its 'initial equipment' and three-to-five more as 'immediate reserves', to allow for damage and maintenance. In theory a squadron had 26 pilots, including some spares, though these were in short supply by the end of the summer of 1940.

Of the four groups in Fighter Command, No. 11, based at Uxbridge near London, was clearly the most important, covering London and the whole of England between Dorset and Essex. On 9 July it had seven sector stations, each with a number of satellites. A typical station had three squadrons of Spitfires or Hurricanes for day fighting, and some had a squadron of Blenheims for night work. No. 12 Group, to the north, was next in importance, with six sectors, mostly with two squadrons in each. It would cover part of the possible invasion coast in East Anglia, protect the vital industries of the English Midlands and reinforce No. 11 Group if needed. No. 13 Group covered the north of England and Scotland from five sector stations, while No. 10 Group in the west of England was the weakest, with only three stations and four squadrons.

'Johnnie' Johnson found it very difficult to get to know anything about fighting tactics at an Operational Training Unit in August 1940. The syllabus concentrated on learning to fly the aircraft, and experienced pilots were unwilling to talk about fighting. He found some friendly Czech pilots, who told him that formal tactics, as taught before the war, were useless:

> The book laid down various techniques whereby fighters attacked bombers from various positions, including dead astern, directly below, below and astern, from the beam and ahead. Various formations were adopted by the fighters as they manoeuvred for the correct tactical position and the leader gave several orders when they swung into a precise, co-ordinated attack. These types of textbook attacks called for accurate flying and lots of time. Time! This was the key to the whole business. For the presence of the aggressive hard-hitting [Messerschmitt]

RAF FIGHTER COMMAND
GROUPS AND PRINCIPAL
AIRFIELDS

Turnhouse • Drem

Prestwick •

• Aldergrave

Acklington •

Usworth •

NORTH SEA

No 13 Group

Catterick •

IRISH SEA

Leconfield •

Church Fenton •

Ringway • Kirton-in-
Lindsey •

Digby •

Ternhill •

No 12 Group

Coltishall •

Wittering •
Callyweston •

Duxford •

Debden •

Martlesham •

Pembrey •

North Weald •

London

Hornchurch •

West Malling •

Filton •
Colerne •

Hendon •
Northolt •

Rochford •

Croydon •
Biggin Hill •
Kenley •

Gravesend •

Manston •

Middle Wallop •
Boscombe Down •

No 10 Group

No 11 Group

Hawkinge •
Lympne •

Exeter •

Warmwell •

Westhampnett •
Tangmere •

St. Eval • Roborough •

ENGLISH CHANNEL

Fliegerkorps I

LUFTFLOTTE 2

LUFTFLOTTE 3

Fliegerkorps IV   Fliegerkorps VIII

109s would not permit our fighters the time necessary to carry out elaborate manoeuvres. Tactics must be simple. Surprise if possible, and a straight-in attack – from the sun. Always with your number two guarding your tail. Always keep your head turning. It takes about four seconds to shoot down a fighter – so look round every three![45]

In peacetime the six-aircraft flight had divided quite naturally into two 'vics', or 'V' shapes, of three each. Keeping this tight formation distracted the pilots from the more important task of looking out for the enemy, and the unit did not split up easily in action. It was soon found that the basic unit was two aircraft, a leader and his wing-man who would protect his tail as he attacked. Squadrons formed up in groups of four in line-astern, but this was hard on the 'tail-end Charlie', who was often the least experienced pilot and was likely to be lost if the enemy 'clobbered' them. Some squadrons were beginning to use a line-abreast formation, with the aircraft arranged like fingertips, the 'finger four' – this gave the best views above and below, and kept the basic principle that the unit should be able to split into groups of two.[46]

In battle, fast reactions were needed:

Throughout it all the radio is never silent – shouts, oaths, exhortations and terse commands. You single out an opponent. Jockey for position. All clear behind! The bullets from your eight guns go pumping into his belly. He begins to smoke. But the wicked tracer sparkles and flashes over the top of your own cockpit and you break into a tight turn. Now you have two enemies. The 109 on your tail and your remorseless, ever-present opponent 'g', the force of gravity. Over your shoulder you can still see the ugly, questing snout of the 109. You tighten the turn. The Spit protests and shudders, and when the blood drains from your eyes you 'grey-out'. But you keep turning, for life itself is at stake. And now your blood feels like molten lead and runs from head to legs. You black-out! And you ease the turn to recover in a grey, unreal world of spinning horizons. Cautiously you climb into the sun. You have lost too much height and your opponent has gone – disappeared.[47]

The great debate within Fighter Command was whether to send single squadrons and flights up piecemeal to deal with raiders, or to mass a greater force for a devastating counterattack. Keith Park of No. 11

Group was in the front line, and he favoured the piecemeal approach, arguing that there was no time to get a force larger than a squadron together before the enemy dropped his bombs, and that the 'big wing' might be lured out to a feint raid. He was supported by Dowding, the C-in-C, but Leigh-Mallory of 12 Group to the north wanted his share of the action, and he was supported by the heroic figure of the legless fighter leader Douglas Bader, who was prepared to by-pass normal military authority to get his way. Even though Fighter Command, more than any other branch of the services, was fully involved in the campaign against invasion in 1940, the issue was never fully resolved, and both sides have their protagonists to this day.

11

THE CITIZEN SOLDIERS

THE VOLUNTEER MOVEMENT, 1803

The idea of voluntary part-time service in national defence was not a new one, but it took on a modern form early in the wars against the French Revolution. Henry Dundas first called for volunteers in 1794, partly to deal with radicals at home. The force turned out to be very different from what he had envisaged. He had planned them as a supplement to the militia, but in fact most of them were independent companies. He expected them to be rural, but most were in the towns and cities. And the force was less political than expected, becoming a focus for national unity rather than repression. It revived in 1798, with the threat of invasion becoming more of a reality, and reached a strength of 100,000 men by 1800. One reason for this was that serving as a volunteer exempted a man from the militia ballot – so by no means were all the volunteers motivated by patriotism alone.

Despite the obvious patriotic sentiment and a good deal of popular support, the volunteer movement was slow to revive after the declaration of war in 1803. It was boosted artificially by the Levy en Masse Act, which was passed on 27 July. This decreed that all fit men between 17 and 55 were liable for military training and to be called out in an emergency. The act allowed that if a number of volunteers could be enlisted in the district equivalent to three-quarters of the men in Class 1 (unmarried, childless and under 30) then the district would be exempt. This gave an incentive for the local authorities to support them morally and financially. As a result, offers of volunteer corps began to flood in towards the end of July. In the county of Dorset alone, on the 23rd the parish of Symondsbury and Bridport offered to form corps of infantry; two days later there were offers from Beaminster and Stocklance; from the port of Poole on the 28th, Weymouth on the 30th, Wimborne and Wareham on 1 August, Piddletown on the 3rd and a rather belated one from Shaftesbury on the 20th.[1] In Scotland the volunteers were popular, unlike the militia, which was reviled because of its compulsory element.

In one village twelve miles west of London, the volunteer force began to revive on 28 July, the day after the Levy en Masse Act was passed. There was a 'numerous and respectable meeting of the inhabitants of the Parish of Ealing, in the vestry assembled'. Feelings were running high against 'the Corsican usurper and his blood stained legions', and it was quickly agreed that 'we will, one and all, with the utmost readiness and alacrity, give our assistance to repel the common enemy'. Volunteers would be paid out of parish funds, and posters were issued in which Napoleon was quoted as saying, 'The spoil must be immense – their wives and daughters will fall within our power – and every French soldier will have an Englishman as his slave.' The inhabitants of Ealing and the neighbouring parishes of Hanwell and Brentford were invited to a meeting on Monday the 8th in the Chapel in Old Brentford. Lieutenant Colonel Drinkwater took the chair, and Thomas Macdonald rose to speak. 'Stand forward my friends, and rally round the pillar of your country's safety! Our sovereign calls, and who can brook the thought of one moment's delay?' It was resolved unanimously 'to form a volunteer corps of the inhabitants of the said parish and township'. There was to be a subscription of three guineas ($£3.15$), and it was to take the arms of the old Brentford Armed Association. The unit would consist of up to 300 men, in six companies of 50 men each under a lieutenant colonel. In September it was agreed to increase this by 60 men. Colours were produced for the corps and blessed by the Chaplain in Ealing Church:

> In the temple of God, whose altar is menaced by an unprincipled infidel, I shall have the honour to deliver the banners into your hands ... Rather die! and let these colours precede you to the grave, than surrender them to an atheist and a regicide.

It was decided to adopt a corps banner in the form of a target, and members were asked to produce slogans for it – 'Let your efforts never cease, till our country's at peace', 'This will proclaim that right you aim' and 'If we aim well our shot must tell'. The corps held a shooting competition on 24 November, firing by squads of one sergeant and fourteen men. Later it exercised an advance in line, fire by wings, halt and fire by battalion and form an open column in rear of the right or left hand direction. By the end of January they could muster 326 men, and in April they paraded on Wimbledon Common with men from Isleworth, Twickenham, Fulham, Chiswick and Kensington, to a total of 620 – a little disappointing as the units had a combined establishment of 1,498.[2]

Regulations were produced in December. There would be an annual subscription according to means, from one to 25 guineas. There would be four line companies and one light company, commanded by a lieutenant colonel, a major, five captains, five lieutenants and five ensigns, with an adjutant, a chaplain and a surgeon. The dress was prescribed in detail:

> A uniform scarlet regulation jacket, blue cuffs and collar, no lapels, uniform buttons and lace – blue pantaloons ornamented with scarlet worsted in front, and buttons at the ankle – black cloth half gaiters, edged on the top with scarlet – uniform cap, ornament and feathers, Sergeants' to be white with red tops, corporals', drummers', privates' white with red buttons – black velvet stock and hair powder.

There were to be fines of a shilling (5p) for improper uniform on parade, uncleanliness, lateness and talking in the ranks. Discipline would be supervised by a committee seven officers and six other ranks – an egalitarian structure compared with the regular army, where only officers could sit on courts-martial.

Volunteer corps were formed by different professions, especially in London. The Law Association Volunteers were quickly nicknamed 'The Devil's Own'. Their colonel, Thomas Erskine, was so incompetent that he needed a card to recall the words of command.[3] The portrait miniaturist Thomas Lawrence got the support of Benjamin West and the Royal Academy to set up an Armed Association of Artists, but was turned down by the government as there were too many corps already.

Instead Lawrence enrolled alongside his fellow Scots in the Loyal North Britons.[4]

The government was reasonably satisfied with recruiting during the summer of 1803, and in mid-September the Secretary at War wrote, 'the volunteer corps and companies which have been accepted by His Majesty in consequence of the loyal and spirited offers which have flowed in from every part of Great Britain are already very numerous and daily becoming more efficient.'[5] By 16 December more than 380,000 men had enrolled, almost four times as many as in 1800. There were 3,976 infantry companies, 604 cavalry units and 102 artillery companies.[6] In Kent, the towns of the Cinque Ports were separated from the others, and their volunteers were led by the Lord Warden, none other than William Pitt himself. They included 26 corps, a large number of which were artillery and manning the numerous coastal batteries in the area. The rest of Kent had 56 infantry units including six of riflemen and one of messengers, 24 cavalry units and one of mixed cavalry and infantry, six artillery companies and two of watermen, on the Thames and Medway. Units were signed up for different conditions of service, which was to bedevil the organization of volunteers; some were to serve locally only, some in the military district, and some could be sent anywhere in the country.[7]

Most volunteer corps were infantry and wore red tunics according to the regulations of June 1803. They were allowed a certain amount of individuality by adopting different colours of facings, and they might design their own badges. Uniform could be quite expensive, and the Roxwell company near Chelmsford in Essex paid a total of more than £182 in February 1804 for items which included £15 worth of officers'

uniforms, a set of NCOs' uniforms for £20, 'fine pants' for nearly £50, privates' uniforms for £91 and 40 pairs of gaiters at 2/6 (12½ p) a pair. In addition the aristocratic Captain Cheveley bought three sets of gold bullion 'wings', or extended epaulettes, on yellow cloth from Messers Blatchford, 'Gold and Silver Lace & Thread Manufacturers' of London.[8] Artillery units wore blue tunics, while rifle regiments had green for better concealment in their role as snipers. The Yeomanry was a force of volunteer cavalry that originated, as its name implies, among small- to medium-sized farmers but spread to the cities and to other classes in society. A member had to be able to ride, so it was more exclusive than the infantry volunteers, and in some cases he had to provide his own horse, which raised the bar still higher.

The social composition of the volunteer force was very different from both the regular army and the militia. Many corps had subscriptions, so it was difficult for the very poor to enter. Aristocracy and gentry were comparatively rare in the volunteers, except as patrons. Not everyone approved of this. Joseph Farington wrote of the St Pancras Volunteers, 'This evening 7 candidates for the Rank of Captain were nominated – a Mr Le Jeune is appointed Major. He is a Stock Broker. The whole of the Military business of the Parish appears to be in low hands.'[9] In Sussex, the Lord Lieutenant reluctantly agreed to sign an ironmonger's commission: 'I should have preferr'd an Independent Gentleman, but as there is none to be got, we must be content with Mr. Wimble.'[10] But there was no body of experienced soldiers to take command of the units, as another friend of Farington's complained. 'Halls called – He belongs to the St. James's Volunteers & speaks very well of the Corps, but that their officers want experience.'[11] Colonel Hanger thought that this was a crucial fault:

> they will be found, in many degrees, inferior to a British regiment of the line which has been a considerable time completed; and why are they? It is owing to their officers not having had a military education, and practised for years, as the officers of the line are, in all military manoeuvres. But take the officers of a regiment of the line who are experienced and perfect in their duty, and put them to command a volunteer corps; with that knowledge of duty which the volunteers already have, in a month or six weeks that volunteer corps will be perfect, and capable of performing every requisite duty that can be required from a regiment of the line ... Every officer on half-pay should be called forth, and distributed among the volunteer corps.[12]

The volunteer force tended to appeal to the middle ranks of society – professionals, clerks and artisans. Often it was ruled by a committee without regard to military rank. In St Pancras this consisted of three officers and twelve privates, with a private for president. In the Loyal

Lambeth Corps the right of electing the officers was vested in those who had equipped themselves at their own expense.[13] It had a much more egalitarian system of discipline. In Bath in September 1803, a drunken private quarrelled with an officer of another company and was dismissed for refusing to apologize. His fellow privates demanded his reinstatement and resigned en masse when it was not granted. The issue reached the Secretary of State before it was resolved in the officer's favour.[14]

Meanwhile the government was trying to bring the volunteers under control. Two lieutenant colonels were appointed as inspecting field officers for the London Area in September 1803, with orders 'to be continually employed in visiting and superintending the drill and field exercises of the several corps of yeomanry and volunteers within the London District'. Early the next year they were given definite objects for inspection:

> That the utmost silence prevail in the ranks and that in marching in line not even an officer shall speak except the commanding officer of the regiment.
> Each volunteer should be taught to take his lock to pieces, to put it together, and to clean his firelock himself.[15]

An act of June 1804 subjected them to the Mutiny Act while on permanent duty. Officers were allowed to refuse a day's pay to men who misbehaved, or even to put them in custody while the corps was under arms. Rules and regulations for new corps were to be sent to the Secretary of State for approval.[16]

Benjamin Silliman watched a review in Manchester in 1805:

> They are composed principally of mechanics and manufacturers, but gentlemen of the highest rank and first fortune, equally with the lowest of the people, join these military associations. Their appearance at the review was such as to do them much credit, though they are far from being such perfect machines as regular soldiers. The review was on a Sunday, because this day does not interfere with the work of the artists.

He speculated that there was a new Commandment, 'Six days shalt thou labour, and the seventh shalt thou train.'[17] Going on to London, he found that the volunteers were the only topic of conversation at a dinner party, but he had doubts when he saw another review in Hyde Park: 'By many this system of volunteer defence is regarded as a national palladium, and by others as a mere pageant, calculated to amuse the country into a false sense of security.'[18]

The artist Joseph Farington found that regular officers did not have a good opinion of the volunteers, and one officer was just as scathing:

> I asked him what he thought of our regiment of City Light Horse. He said he had seen them, and was of opinion that they wd. do verily to relieve the Regulars by taking care of Prisoners, – Baggage – and keeping the people in order but were not fit for military duty against an Enemy, their charge being loose & irregular, & their disorder upon being moved such as to expose them.[19]

Volunteer officers tended to ape the regular army, both in their uniforms and in the 'Prussian' system of discipline, with the men drawn up in regular ranks firing their muskets by volley on order. The eccentric Colonel George Hanger, a country sportsman himself, praised the volunteers' marksmanship:

> A company of volunteers, some short time past, seventy only in number, fired at the figure of a man painted on a board … each man fired three shots at one hundred and twenty yards, and they put into the body of the figure one hundred and thirty balls. Can any one company, the same in number, in a regular regiment of the line do as much?[20]

Hanger wanted the younger men, making up two-thirds of the average corps, to train as light infantrymen, in open order and firing into the enemy from all points while the remainder formed a solid body in more conventional fashion. He addressed the regular officers with their contempt for the volunteers:

> Supposing … that ten thousand of the enemy be landed , and that we have but the same number of regulars and militia in that district at the moment of time before reinforcements can arrive, and you are ordered to attack the enemy … But candidly tell me gentlemen, how much more satisfied you

would be to view twenty, or even only ten thousand Volunteers ... most of them excellent marksmen, hovering over both flanks, nay, even in the rear of the enemy, and pouring in, in all directions, from all sides, fire on the enemy. Do you think, gentlemen, that the enemy would consider them a rabble, to which no opposition was necessary.[21]

Charles James, another regular officer, was even more radical in his tactical views and anticipated guerrilla warfare:

From the first moment of a landing being made, the great object of the irregular troops must be to harass, alarm, and fatigue an enemy. Nothing can more effectually contribute to this object than the operations of small bodies of men, who will approach and fire upon the advanced posts of his army, without ever engaging in serious action, or hazarding themselves, in any situation where their own natural intelligence and watchfulness do not ensure them the danger of being cut off.[22]

The Sea Fencibles were another volunteer movement, the naval equivalent. They took their name from the organizations of 'fencibles' or 'defensible men' who were supposed to arm themselves in defence of the state but were largely defunct by this time. The Sea Fencibles were recruited among seafarers such as ferrymen and fishermen, who were not liable for the press gang, though that claim was often doubted – at Start Point in Devon, for example, it was said that, 'The Sea Fencibles in this bay ... amount to forty-six, the greatest part of these are clearly liable to the impress, as they are all fishermen in boats which do not allow more than one man being protected.'

The Sea Fencibles were

expected not only to serve, against an Enemy attempting to land upon the Coast, but also to watch the Beaches, whenever the Wind and Weather shall be favourable for the Enemy to attempt a landing; to perform any services which may accelerate the progress of our Army, or retard that of the Enemy, if he should effect a landing; but also to embark on board any Gun Boat, or other Armed Vessel, for the protection of Merchant Vessels when any Armed Vessel of the Enemy shall be in sight.[23]

At the end of 1803 there were 941 men enrolled between Emsworth and

Beachy Head on the south coast, 'all perfect in the boat and great gun exercises', with 59 boats. At Bigbury in Devon, 'The Sea Fencibles in this place are 146, they are mostly bargemen who are employed in open boats to dredge for a particular sort of sea sand for the purpose of agriculture.' Unlike the volunteers on land, the Sea Fencibles were under regular naval officers, one of whom was the author Jane Austen's brother Frank, who used his time in Kent to court and marry Miss Mary Gibson.

There were more specialized forces off the coasts, including the Trinity House Volunteer Artillery, which was sponsored by the body that maintained the lighthouses and carried out charitable work for seamen. It was formed at a meeting in the London Tavern on October 1803 attended by William Pitt, who was honorary Master of the Corporation. The diarist George Rose recorded, 'the sight was really an extremely affecting one – a number of good and exceedingly gallant old men, who had, during the best part of their lives been beating the waves, now coming forward with the zeal and spirit of lads, swearing allegiance to the King, with a determined purpose to act manfully in his defence, for the protection of the Capital.' They were able to recruit 1,200 officers and men, from 'seamen, landsmen, volunteers, pilots, lascars, Harbour volunteer Marines, River Fencibles, Greenwich Pensioners, Trinity Pensioners and East India Company Pensioners'. For ships they were allowed two Royal Yachts and eight old frigates, including *Retribution*, once *Hermione*, which had been the scene of a notoriously bloody mutiny in 1797 and was recaptured from the Spanish by HMS *Surprise* two years later. The ten ships were anchored across the Thames in Lower Hope reach. The crews were given detailed instructions on what to do if the enemy came: they were to move ships to close a gap in the middle of the line, and heave all the ships round so that they could bring their guns to bear. Boarding nettings were to be rigged and guns manned.[24]

Numbers of volunteers declined as the threat of invasion receded and the government asserted its control over it. There were only 68,000 by 1812, 30,000 below establishment. The idea of a part-time military force set up by local initiative was revived in Victorian times, when in 1859 it was feared that the French were planning a surprise invasion. The volunteer units formed after that became part of the army regimental system and made up significant feature of Victorian local activity. Some of them volunteered to fight in the South African War in 1899–1902, but on the whole the numbers that came forward were disappointing, and the volunteers became part of the Territorial Army in 1908.

THE HOME GUARD, 1940

The army and the navy dated from time immemorial. The RAF began on a specific day, 1 April 1918, though most people were too involved in the war to pay much attention. But almost everyone remembered the exact moment when the Local Defence Volunteers, later the Home Guard, came into being. Anthony Eden, the Secretary of State for War, broadcast to the nation on 20 May 1940, as the Blitzkrieg tore its way through France and no one knew where it would stop:

> We want large numbers of such men in Great Britain who are British subjects, between the ages of seventeen and sixty-five, to come forward now and offer their services in order to make assurance doubly sure. The name of the new force which is now to be raised will be the Local Defence Volunteers. The name describes its duties in three words. You will not be paid, but you will receive uniforms and will be armed. In order to volunteer, what you have to do is give your name at your local police station, and then, when we want you, we will let you know ...

Before the broadcast had finished, thousands of men were already queuing outside police stations, where Eden had told them to report, though the bewildered constables had not been warned. A quarter of a million men gave their names within 24 hours, with far more to come. The Local Defence Volunteers soon became a national phenomenon, with nearly a million-and-a-half ill-equipped men by the end of the month. Basil Boothroyd wrote in September 1940:

> For some reason or other the press has taken us to its fickle heart. We take precedence over the R.A.F., Mr Churchill and Gracie Fields. We appear in every other headline. The penny papers have special articles telling us how to take cover behind trees and how deep we ought to dig our

trenches. *The Times* has light leaders about our neckties and whole columns of correspondence about whether we're worth one-and-sixpence a night or not.[25]

One platoon commander told his men later:

Hitler apparently imagined that it would be quite impossible for England to mobilise a sufficient force to withstand his contemplated invasion without completely and utterly paralysing our industry and productive powers. That in itself would have spelt defeat. But Hitler was wrong. What seemed to him an insuperable problem was solved almost overnight by the creation of the L.D.V. – in a few days, in a few weeks, at any rate long before he could organise and formulate his plans ... It must have sounded like a miracle to Hitler.[26]

There is no evidence that Hitler thought anything of the kind, or paid any attention to what he would have regarded as a bunch of ill-disciplined and poorly armed civilians.

Articles on Home Guard tactics were to be found in periodicals as diverse as the *The Times*, *The Illustrated London News*, *Modern World*, *The Pictorial Review* and *Picture Post*. At least two dozen books had been published by the end of 1940, mostly in a very small format to save paper and be carried in the pocket of a battledress blouse.

In the meantime the force had to be organized. It was established by a statutory order under the Emergency Powers (Defence) Act. Members were not to be liable for full-time service, to be called upon to live away from their homes or to serve beyond 'the present emergency'. They were allowed to resign by giving two weeks' notice, which became known as 'the housemaid's clause'. They were put under the control of the Territorial Associations, which had little to do now that most of their original men had been mobilized. The legal status of the LDVs was defined:

As members of His Majesty's Forces, L.D.V.s have military rights and military obligations, and are subject to law when carrying out their duties. In case of need, Local Defence Volunteers being 'Forces of the Crown' have the legal right to arrest and detain for 24 hours suspicious persons, but during the 24 hours the police must be informed and the suspect handed over to them.[27]

Much of the work of organizing the units depended on local and often self-appointed individuals. The new LDVs had the advantage that thousands of men had served in World War I just over twenty years earlier. They knew nothing about modern warfare beyond what they read in the newspapers, but they had plenty of experience of military discipline and the use of arms, and their experience in the trenches might still be useful in a dogged defence.

There were several types of unit, according to geography and function. The idea of factory units appealed both to employers and workers, and it was widely, if erroneously, believed that German paratroopers might target individual factories. It was very wasteful of manpower to have so many men in static roles, and this caused friction with local Home Guard commanders. By orders of September 1940, factory units were to guard against sabotage, espionage, ground attack and air attack. It was quite clear from the detailed instructions that the units were seen as militarized security guards in the first two roles, controlling visitors and guarding fences. For the other two, schemes of defence were to be prepared including observation posts and gun positions.

In towns the Home Guard's role was less clear, for it was obvious that the enemy would try to avoid them as far as possible, and most units were committed only to their local area. This did not make them any less active. The West Sussex Home Guard was photographed staging mock battles on the streets of Worthing with one side wearing steel helmets and the others forage caps, to the bemusement of holidaymakers and residents.[28] Inland, the 1st Worcester Battalion was initially responsible for Perdiswell Airfield, then part of a line along the River Teme using a large number of trenches and weapons pits. Then it manned an anti-tank island within the city of Worcester itself.[29]

The real milieu of the Home Guard was in the countryside and small towns, where men often had an intimate connection with the land. The author and broadcaster J. B. Priestley went on an LDV patrol and told the nation on 16 June,

Ours is a small and scattered village, but we'd had a fine response to the call for volunteers; practically every able-bodied man in the place takes his turn … I think the countryman knows, without being told, that we hold our lives here, as we hold our farms, upon certain terms. One of these terms is that while wars still continue, while one nation is ready to hurl its armed men at another, you must necessarily stand up and fight for your own … I felt too up there a powerful and rewarding sense of community; and with it too a feeling of deep continuity. There we were, ploughman and parson, shepherd and clerk, turning out at night, as our forefathers had often done before us, to keep watch and ward over the sleeping English hills.[30]

The basic structure was described in a Training Memorandum of July. The men would be organized in sections of about 24 men, the leader of which wore the three chevrons of a sergeant on his arm. Up to four sections were grouped into a platoon under a leader with a single stripe across his shoulder straps, platoons came under a company commander with two stripes, and up to four companies made a battalion whose leader had three stripes. It was accepted in a huge understatement that this would 'vary, however, to meet local circumstances'.[31] The use of stripes instead of the pips and crowns of the army side-stepped the question of whether the commanders were officers or not. This was modified slightly by an Army Council Instruction of 15 August. Zone commanders and group commanders were added above the battalion commanders, while the squad commander, with two chevrons, was to operate under the section commander. It was not until the spring of 1941 that the ranks and badges of the army, from brigadier to lance corporal, were introduced.

According to Brigadier Green in his *Home Guard Pocket-Book*, 'The Platoon is the essential unit in the Home Guard and the Platoon area is the essential administrative subdivision of the county.'[32] In the regular army a platoon commander was traditionally a green young second lieutenant, constantly under the eye of his captain and colonel. In the Home Guard he was a mature man, and often a significant figure in the local community. 'Contrary to what happens in mobile armies, the Home Guard is never intended to operate in Battalions or Companies manoeuvring in a formed body; nor, as a general rule, is it likely that anything larger than a Platoon will act as a formed body for a specific operation.'[33]

Churchill criticized the name of the new force. He inspected various units on 26 June and wrote to Eden, 'I don't think much of the name "Local Defence Volunteers" for your large new force. The word "local" is uninspiring. Mr. Herbert Morrison suggested to me to-day the title "Civic Guard". But I think "Home Guard" would be better.'[34] Thousands of brassards had already been printed with the letters LDV, but Churchill insisted that the name be changed.

The role of the force was something that emerged through time. The original idea was inspired by fear of paratroopers, and they were known as the 'parashots' in the press. In a sense they were rather like the Observer Corps, but reporting parachutes rather than aircraft; however, the Observer Corps could do nothing about bombers except report them, whereas a Local Defence Volunteer could attack a paratrooper. Indeed it was recognized in the LDV's training memorandum of June 1940 that, 'The parachutist is most vulnerable just when he alights and before he has had time to release his parachute and harness, re-adjust his belt outside his overalls, and open the container and get hold of his real weapons.'[35] It was logical that the LDV should be an armed force.

The next task was to deal with fifth columnists. According to General Ironside, during the invasion of Holland, 'Servant maids, who had been working in the country and had gone back to Germany, landed by parachute and guided the people to the places they wanted to go.'[36] This was reflected in the first 'Instructions regarding role and status' in June 1940: 'It will be seen how important the Local Defence Volunteer organization is from the National aspect. Indeed it is the first, and perhaps the most important, defence against enemy parachutists and "Fifth Columnists".'[37] This was to prove the most controversial and in some ways damaging of the Home Guard's roles, as over-enthusiastic and ignorant volunteers impeded the war effort or put the public in danger.

More ambitiously, the Home Guard was to deal with the other elements of the blitzkrieg. Tanks could be stopped by traps and road blocks. Offensively they could be attacked by a few brave men. The Home Guard could provide guides for the regulars, being men who knew their area intimately. This gained the respect of General Horrocks: 'The more I saw of the Home Guard the more I came to respect their keenness. Their greatest asset was local knowledge and operating against them on exercises was like hitting a pincushion.'[38]

General Ironside addressed some of the leaders on 5 June, just as the Dunkirk evacuation was completed, and some of them seemed rather mean and argumentative.

> QUESTION: I live in a rural area and I have been trying to get farmers to give us information if they see parachutes arriving in the early morning. I may say that I have arranged to do so but can they have authority from the Post Office to send through the message without payment?
> GENERAL IRONSIDE: We will reimburse him, tell him to put the twopence in and he shall get it back.
> QUESTION: But he has no money.
> GENERAL IRONSIDE: I am sorry but he must have twopence. I cannot do anything on that. All sorts of people could come in and give false messages.

He told them his ideas for their role:

> Now the two main duties of you L.D.V.s are static defence and information. I put them in that order. Each one of the localities from which you come must be secure. ... Now in France the picture that we have just seen was of a great army cowering behind obstacles, waiting to be attacked and the guts of the thing being torn out while they were waiting and doing nothing. There was no organisation in France at all to stop this fighting force which pushed its way through and rushed over the country absolutely unhindered ...
>
> The other thing is information ... If we have not got the right information in a country like this where the attack may come not only from the air, which allows the enemy to land where he likes, but from the sea, it is essential that the news, the information, should come in quickly to the central authority, in order that we can know if it is a big attack or only a small one, and so we know where to put our big stuff in.[39]

General Ironside had considerable faith in the volunteers. He wrote at the end of May:

Anyway, we shall get these L.D.V.s going. Static defence in every village by blocks, and information going out from there. And thousands of Molotoff cocktails thrown down from the windows of houses. That might well settle tank columns. We just want the courage of the men. Nothing else matters. No defence is any good if the men behind it leave it and run away. The old L.D.V.s won't do that.[40]

General Brooke was less enthusiastic and asked, 'Why do we in this country turn to all the old men when we require a new volunteer force?' He had even less faith in Beaverbrook's ideas for factory Home Guards: 'The whole thing was fantastic. How could individual factories have held out, and what part could they have played once the main battle for this country was lost?'[41] He wrote to Eden in August:

Priority should now be given to the regular forces and steps taken without delay to prevent diversion of resources to the Home Guard at the expense of the former.

The role of the Home Guard has been clearly defined as that of local and static defence on a voluntary, part-time basis; there is a tendency to go beyond this and to employ Home Guard on full time duties prior to invasion which necessarily involve questions of pay, administration and transport.

According to Brooke, anyone who had time to do this and was fit enough should enlist in a home defence unit of the army.[42]

Priorities changed over the months, and one Home Guard poet wrote:

The Brigadier we had last spring,
    Said Static roles are not the thing;
As mobile as a midnight flea
    Is what the Home Guard ought to be.

He went; another came instead
    Who deemed mobility quite dead,
And thought the Home Guard, on the whole,
    Far safer in a static role.[43]

The Home Guard was not a political force – less so than the early volunteer units of William Pitt's day – and it rejoiced in being an expression of national unity. But not everyone was happy with it. George Orwell wrote: 'The Home Guard swells to a million men in a few weeks, and is deliberately organized in such a way that only people with private incomes can hold positions of command.' It was,

> the most anti-Fascist body existing in England at this moment, and at the same time is an astonishing phenomenon, a sort of people's army officered by Blimps. The rank and file are predominantly working class, with a strong middle-class seasoning, but practically all the commands are held by wealthy elderly men, a lot of whom are utterly incompetent.

The leader of the campaign to turn the Home Guard into a people's army was Tom Wintringham, a journalist who had led the British Battalion against the Fascists in the Spanish Civil War. He was now estranged from the Communist Party because of his private life, which left him free to throw himself into the continuing struggle against the Fascists and Nazis. His success with a Home Guard training school alarmed the authorities, but they were careful not to over-react in view of popular feeling. They took his school over by stages and gradually replaced its instructors, while setting up more amenable schools of their own; by the spring of 1941, Wintringham's organization had largely been by-passed.

Eden's broadcast of May 1940 had referred specifically to 'men'. Although there were women's auxiliary units in the regular services, the government resisted attempts to set up one for the Home Guard. But this was opposed by Dr Edith Summerskill, Labour MP for West Fulham, and Women's Home Defence was set up in December 1940 with the aim,

> to train every woman in the Country to be of the maximum use in the event of an invasion. This does not mean that they will be issued with rifles – the combatant services must have the first call on all weapons – but it is essential that they shall be proficient in certain forms of defence.

The idea of fighting women was far too radical for the Churchill government, though women helped with administration and domestic duties in local Home Guard units.

The Home Guard uniform never had the visual appeal of the red volunteer uniforms of 1803. At first the men had to make do with armbands (or brassards as they were known) with the letters 'LDV' and later 'HG'. Some wondered if the brassard was enough, and whether they could be shot as franc-tireurs or irregular combatants if captured by the Germans – knowing what we do about Nazi ruthlessness, there is little doubt that they would have been.

Uniforms arrived eventually, in the form of denim overalls as issued to regular troops for fatigues. Basil Boothroyd described it in *Punch*

'I'VE LAID YOUR UNIFORM OUT, MY LORD.'

Baker's cartoon is a gentle satire on the early lack of equipment and clothing for the Local Defence Volunteers. (Punch)

magazine:

> The evening's parade was one of mingled embarrassment and pride. We were embarrassed because the little boys ran after us, delightedly reading the sizes from the tickets on our backs and our trousers, and expressing pardonable surprise that Mr. King, at four feet ten, wore size nine-and-a-half, while Mr. Benn the butcher (six feet tall and practically square) had chosen size three, medium ... Yet we were proud, though none of us would perhaps have admitted it; for we were wearing the King's uniform, even if it did fit our functions rather than our physique.

Boothroyd describes what happened next:

> The nights are growing cold and the winds whistle freely over the open spaces; the frost steals upon us in the small hours, and even behind his greatcoat-collar the teeth of the sentry can be heard chattering in the darkness.
>
> Recognising these things, Mr. Anthony Eden (or was it Sir Edward Grigg?) has promised us uniforms of khaki serge, just like the real soldiers wear, and appreciation of this kindly thought has been voiced on all sides; our denim overalls, so recently our joy and pride, can scarcely be called weather resisting, and their mysterious redolence of linseed oil seems to hang over them like a pall. But there has also been voiced, by thinking Volunteers, a suspicion that these luxury garments may only arrive with the warmer weather of 1941.[44]

THE HOME GUARD AS FIGHTING FORCE

Formally, Home Guard training was controlled by the 'Instructions' issued by the War Office, and these give some idea of the priorities during the hectic summer and autumn of 1940. In May there were hints on how to set up road blocks, and in June there were memos on the role and status of the Home Guard, and on German paratroopers. In July there were instructions on training policy and elements of training, relations with civil defence and similar bodies, the construction of field defences, tank destruction and grenades. In August the instructions on road blocks and Home Guard status were superseded, and there was a miscellaneous set of instructions including ear protection during air raids and the use of dogs for Home Guard purposes, followed by a memorandum on factory defence. The Home Guard drill book was issued in September, along with programmes of winter training as the invasion season drew to a close. There was a note on common German military expressions, which seemed to assume that the enemy would surrender easily, and men were told that 'Hands up!' could be translated as 'Hände hoch', which was pronounced 'Hender hoch'. There were notes on sighting rifles, care of weapons and anti-aircraft training, but, despite Churchill's well-known claim that 'We shall fight on the beaches', there was nothing about beach defence or the problems of engaging landing craft as they discharged their loads.[45]

There was clearly a need for a more general form of training for the specialized needs of the Home Guard, and it was Tom Wintringham who stepped into the gap here. In July he met the Edward Hulton, the wealthy left-wing proprietor of *Picture Post* magazine and its editor Tom Hopkinson. Over dinner they decided to set up a Home Guard training school in the grounds of Osterley Park. Wintringham gathered like-minded men as instructors, such as Hugh Salter from the International Brigades, Peter Wyatt-Foulger from a more conventional army background, Stanley White from the Boy Scouts, Wilfred Vernon, an aircraft designer and expert on bombs, and Roland Penrose, a surrealist artist and camouflage expert. The school filled a gap where the authorities had failed, and it was widely publicized in *Picture Post* and other magazines. Naturally it moved away from the static roles that the War Office preferred to impose on the Home Guard, towards outright guerrilla warfare, and it had much to teach on the key tasks of defeating the tank and the dive-bomber.

In planning his tactics, the Home Guard commander at every level had to consider the weapons available to him and the local topography, as well as cooperation with other forces. Michael Joseph visited the local Home Guard Commander in Maidstone in Kent to coordinate defensive plans for the first time:

> at a glance his map showed me that our respective defence schemes bore no relation to each other. We had sited a large number of road blocks, and so had the Home Guard, but they were fatally unco-ordinated. I did not care to think what would have happened if we had suddenly been confronted with trouble.[46]

The commander also had to consider the character and fitness of his men. Not all the members of the Home Guard were suitable for the most active roles, and in his book *Total War Training* Matthew Armour hinted at some of the problems:

There are several DON'Ts connected with the choosing of men for

guerrilla units:–
Don't include a man with defective vision or glasses,
Don't use a man who is a victim of Hay Fever.
Don't use a man who cannot do without a cigarette for several hours
without discomfort.
Don't use a deaf man, but you can use a dumb man if he is not already
deaf.
Don't use a man who has a bladder weakness.
Don't use a man if he is at the time unfit physically or mentally.
Don't use a man who has proved unreliable in any way.[47]

As for the others, Brigadier Green offered a grim prospect in his *Home
Guard Pocket Book*:

we must have Sections (10 to 12 men) fit for any kind of military duty.
We must also have Sections of men, not so fit; Sections which specialize
in team weapons; Sections organized, armed and equipped like a Battle
Drill Section in the Regular Army; some Sections which can only sit on
their backsides and shoot and die, reluctantly but venomously.[48]

George Orwell's general in the London Home Guard was even more
gloomy – 'Our job, he said, was to die at our posts.'[49]

On 17 June, Anthony Eden had to agree in Cabinet that the Home
Guard was 'a broomstick army' until supplies of weapons could be
arranged. The standard army Lee-Enfield was issued in limited
quantities, but the army had lost a large number at Dunkirk, and
thousands of new recruits had to be equipped, so supplies were limited.
Often they had to be spread very thinly – one unit had six rifles for 400
men in the early days. Improvisation was the order of the day, and
shotguns and other weapons were found through official and unofficial
sources. Some men did indeed drill with broomsticks, and a cartoon
showed a man about to reattach the head to the stick with the caption,
'At the command "Fix Bayonets" …' Large stocks of rifles were found
in the USA and Canada, and, as the bulk of them came over in a single
ship, Churchill worried that it might be sunk. It was not, and 100,000
American and 75,000 Canadian rifles became available for distribution.
The P14 and P17 were both American and based upon the Lee-Enfield

design, but the P17 Springfield used American .300-inch ammunition. It was painted with a red band across its muzzle to distinguish it. The Canadian Ross Rifle had a straight pull-back action on the bolt, which was quicker to operate but jammed easily in mud. It was more accurate than the Lee-Enfield but longer and heavier and more difficult to load. Units that had their Lee-Enfields replaced by Ross rifles were disappointed in it.

Wintringham looked back as far as the American Civil War and the Russo–Japanese War at the beginning of the century to show that the bayonet was useless: 'Against automatic weapons and against hand grenades men with bayonets are useless.' With rather deeper military experience, Brigadier Green could see more point to them: 'The Bayonet is an additional weapon which H. G. ought to carry, not merely for "bayonet-fighting," but because it is a good tool for breaking open doors, windows, etc., and for getting through obstacles and other purposes.'[50]

Another American weapon was the Browning Automatic Rifle, or BAR. It had a 20-round magazine and could be set for short bursts of automatic fire, but that led to loss of accuracy and, with ammunition in short supply, was not recommended for the Home Guard. Instead it was used as a single-shot automatic rifle, which meant that the firepower of a Home Guard section was much less than that of the regular infantry, with the fully automatic Bren gun. The favourite Home Guard automatic weapon was the Tommy gun, as also used by the army, but this was rare in the Home Guard until well into 1941. Older Vickers and Lewis machine-guns were used when they could be found. At the end of September 1940 the force was estimated to have 847,000 rifles, 47,000 shotguns and 49,000 automatic weapons for 1.682 million men, so nearly three quarters of a million of them had no firearm.[51]

The Home Guard also deployed vehicles of all kinds for patrols or to take them into action, including horses and carts and bicycles, as well as motor cars. Armoured cars were improvised locally, along with a type devised by the Ministry of Aircraft Production for the defence of its factories and known as the Beaverette, after the minister. It was built on a standard car chassis with 0.35-inch armour plate, this at the front backed by 3-inch oak and armed with a standard light machine-gun or anti-tank rifle. It had a 45-horsepower engine but could only make a top speed of 24mph.

The tactical debate at the essence of the Home Guard was: were they guards or guerrillas? It was the same question that had surfaced with the volunteers in the days of Pitt, but with extra emphasis in an age of Blitzkrieg. Tom Wintringham regarded foot drill as pointless, and he devoted no less than four pages of *New Ways of War* to condemning it:

> to take perfectly good young men and give them weeks on end of barrack-square, knocks out of them not only any 'instincts' for fighting they may have, but also their ability to think about all orders received and to use their own judgement. Independence, initiative and intelligence are all ground out of the recruit at the average training depot ... Drill teaches straight lines and use of the smoothest available ground. In war all straight lines are suicidal ...[52]

In practice, most of the Home Guard's work would consist of sentry duties and routine patrols. In July 1940, after several unfortunate incidents, instructions were issued on how to conduct sentry duty 'in order to minimize the danger to civilians and friendly persons'. A man guarding a vulnerable point was to issue the challenge, 'Halt, who goes there!' He was to be certain that his challenge had been given 'in the loudest manner possible – so that even those who may be dull of hearing can have the chance of responding'. If the suspect did not stop, the sentry called out, 'Halt or I fire!' and repeated it. If there was still no reaction and no other way of stopping the suspect he could open fire, 'aiming low to hit but not to kill'.[53] The Home Guard spent many thousands of hours on fruitless patrols, but it did have the satisfaction of capturing Hitler's deputy, Rudolf Hess, when he made an unauthorised flight to Scotland and landed by parachute in Renfrewshire in May 1941.

The Home Guard was designed in response to the blitzkreig and attempted to find answers to its main elements. It patrolled against the fifth column with an enthusiasm that was often deeply misguided. During the height of the scare in June 1940 there were several cases of

Above: Junkers Ju 87 Stuka dive-bombers. (CPL)

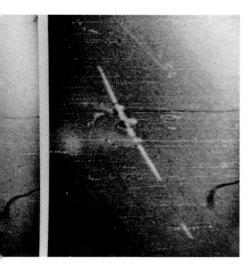

Left: A sequence of camera gun shots showing the destruction of a Messerschmitt Bf 110 by a British fighter in the summer of 1940. (IWM C 2433)

Opposite page, below: Spitfires of No 610 Squadron flying in formation over Kent in July 1940. (IWM CH 740)

Below: A sailor in conventional uniform stands beside one in a hybrid army/navy dress, with naval leggings. He is ready to defend his base against enemy attack. (IWM A 1821)

Above: Officers and a communications rating on the deck of a battleship, with aircraft silhouettes to aid identification. (IWM H 3722)

Below: Naval gunners man a machine-gun on HMS *Royal Eagle*, having claimed the destruction of a Stuka. (IWM A 1804)

Above: A Miles Magister does its best to imitate the attack of a Stuka for Home Guard training. (IWM H 4757)

Below: An invasion craft with a very cumbersome ramp lowered by a gantry. (Kugler Archives)

Opposite page, top: A German tank is lowered into the sea for its run to the shore. (Kugler Archives)

Above: A Heinkel 111 is hit by shots from Flight Lieutenant J. H. G. MacArthur's Spitfire during a raid on Bristol on 25 September 1940. (IWM CH 1823)

Left: Londoners shelter from bombing in Aldwych underground station in October 1940. (IWM HU 44272)

Above: Troops constructing the ramp of an invasion barge. (Kugler Archives)

people being shot for failing to stop at Home Guard road blocks. Members of the armed forces and even policemen were often stopped by patrols, convinced that the Germans would use disguises during an invasion. The Commissioner of the Metropolitan Police complained that

Home Guards training against dive-bomber attack at Osterley Park.
(Illustrated London News)

the force was a menace to lawful policing and implied that none of his men had been killed only because the Home Guard were poor shots. And in Glasgow the Chief Constable had an open dispute with the military authorities about the boundaries of Home Guard power. [54]

Paratroops were the original raison d'être of the LDV, and extensive measures were taken to prevent them landing. Again, there were excesses when friendly airmen were shot at, and the problem was compounded by the strange accents of many foreign airmen serving with the RAF. Since no Allied aircraft normally carried a crew of more than seven, only larger groups of parachutes should be fired on. But if real enemy paratroops did land, action had to be swift. According to his training instructions:

> The parachutist is most vulnerable just when he alights and before he has time to release his parachute and harness, re-adjust his belt outside his overalls, and open the container and get hold of his real weapons. For the space of about 30 seconds, therefore, he is not a very formidable enemy as he is unlikely to have weapons except two or three hand grenades and an automatic pistol with limited range.
>
> As soon as the men have opened the containers and retrieved their weapons they become very formidable opponents.[55]

This argued for constant patrols over a wide area, though the Home Guard did not recognize that paratroops were expensive to train and would only be dropped in key areas, not indiscriminately across the countryside. Spies, of course, were another possibility, but in practice most of them would be landed by sea, and all would be identified.

Road blocks were a form of passive defence against the tank, especially if sited in a village or a defile on a country road. The very first training instruction of the Local Defence Volunteers told them to site blocks where the approaching vehicles would not see the obstacle until they were very close to it, so that there was no room to turn around or drive off the road. They could be made with barbed wire, vehicles filled with stones, farm implements or felled trees as a last resort. But it was important not to obstruct normal business or impede one's own forces: 'blocks should take the form of two overlapping fixed obstacles with a gap of size sufficient to allow the largest vehicles to negotiate it at walking speed.'[56]

As to more active defence, it was Wintringham who expressed most clearly the weakness of the tank, which had seemed all-powerful on the battlefields of France:

If the question is asked about any sort of tank, 'What is its weakest point?' the answer that should be given is always 'The minds of the men inside it.' They are men like ourselves, subject to fear and fatigue, they are half-stifled, they cannot see well, hostility is all round them. Anything new or strange within their field of vision checks them or spurs them to a mad rush. They cannot drive their desperately uncomfortable vehicle continuously at high speeds. They can be fought at any time, when moving fast or when moving slowly; when at rest they should be hunted. A tank at rest is a target for men stalking it; a tank moving is something to be trapped and ambushed.[57]

Finally, if all else failed, the Home Guard had to be prepared for guerrilla warfare behind the lines. Naturally this appealed to the left-wing element, and Wintringham wrote:

I could not help thinking how alike these two armies were: the Home Guard of Britain and the Militia of Republican Spain. Superficially alike in mixture of uniforms and half uniforms, in shortage of weapons and ammunition, in hasty and incomplete organisation and lack of modern training, they seemed to me more fundamentally alike in their serious eagerness to learn, their resolve to meet and defeat all the difficulties in their way, their certainty that despite shortage of time and gear they could fight and fight effectively.[58]

And he offered some practical advice on how to fight behind enemy lines:

Guerrilla war is best carried out by parties of two or three men moving concealed and not obviously carrying weapons. They should use their imagination and turn every possible means they come across to the disadvantage of the enemy. And where possible the destruction they should do should be invisible. It is better to sink a barge than to burn it ... If you burn it, troops for miles around will be warned that you are out and active ... If the Nazis seize an English county we must make it impossible for them to send dispatches about that county without a heavy escort of armoured cars. We must make it impossible for their staffs and generals to be safe, even when sentries are all around them. Therefore be audacious; but at the same time always give yourself some way out of the trouble that you are causing ... A live guerrilla is much more use to your friends than a dead hero.[59]

Even as they sidelined his views, the authorities took over some of these methods. In September 1940 plans were made for the coming winter, and commanders were told: 'Time must not be wasted in attempting to train for roles for which the Home Guard is neither organised nor intended; this however should not debar elementary training in guerrilla warfare which, indeed, may be an important part of the defence of a locality.'[60]

How would the Home Guard have fared in action? The German equivalent, the Volkssturm, had no real effect when the Allies invaded their country in 1944–5, but the Germans had no tradition of irregular warfare and tended to treat it very harshly when used against their own men. Guerrilla tactics worked far better in the Soviet Union. Possibly the British would not have been quite so fanatical or careless of their own lives as the Soviets were, but it seems quite likely that the Home Guard would have put up a stout resistance as far as it was able.

12

WORKING TOGETHER

ARMY AND NAVY COOPERATION

An invasion of Britain could be defeated at any one of several stages. The enemy might fail to establish air superiority and prudently decide not to advance without it. His landing force might be defeated at sea, by naval or air power. But if the enemy landed, or even came close to British shores, then all the services would have to fight together as never before to defeat him.

The British armed forces have often had difficulties with combined operations. In the age of sail, the army and the navy were very different organizations, with different personnel and customs, and the sailor was a very different animal from the soldier. According to Admiral Patton, who served on the Board of Admiralty in 1804–6,

> Seamen cannot be made the object of an admiring crowd and are, from their previous education and changes of situation from merchants' to the King's service, and from their country's to the service of trade, incapable of being modelled so as to imbibe military ideas. Or, if these ideas could be introduced, it is impossible they should prevail without destroying the enthusiasm of the seamen, who must always be less exposed to danger from the enemy than from the inconstancy of the atmosphere and the instability of the ocean.[1]

According to Captain Glascock, 'The sailor of our wars with France had so much esprit de corps for his own branch of the national service that he genuinely and heartily – not to say unreasonably – despised all that pertained to soldiering and pipeclay.'[2] Even Marines, who were trained within the navy but using army methods, were radically different from sailors:

No two races of men, I had well nigh said two animals, differ from one another more completely than the 'Jollies' and the 'Johnnies'. The marines are ... enlisted for life, or for long periods as in the regular army, and, when not employed afloat, are kept in barracks, in such constant training, under the direction of their officers, that they are never released for one moment of their lives from the influence of strict discipline and habitual obedience.[3]

The sailor was a hero to the general public, the saviour of his country against countless attempts at invasion. Yet what the public actually saw of him, particularly in the naval ports, was a kind of holy fool, generous to the point of extravagance, spending his hard-earned wages and prize money in a drunken orgy as soon as he could get some shore leave. The sailor tended to see the land as a perpetual holiday, an excuse for merriment, with all his work and skills on board the ship now forgotten. They had all been trained in the use of arms, but there was a general feeling that sailors, often victims of the press gang, could not be trusted ashore, especially in their native land, where they might be tempted to desert. They did have their uses in colonial expeditions, for example: during an attack on Martinique they manhandled guns over difficult obstacles with great enthusiasm, and it was observed, 'A hundred or two of them with ropes and pullies, will do more than all your drayhorses in London.'[4] They might also have made very useful guerrillas after an invasion, but their real value was afloat, with an essential role in maintaining British sea power.

Soldiers, on the other hand, might spend a good deal of time at sea. Since much of the war was fought on foreign or colonial stations such as India, the West Indies, the Mediterranean, South Africa and later Spain, they had to get there by troopship. As well as their purely passive position on transports, soldiers had also served as part of the complement of many warships in the last war, due to shortages of proper marines. But St Vincent did not regard that as a happy precedent, for the army officers resented naval discipline and were unenthusiastic about their men performing shipboard duties such as hauling on ropes and scrubbing decks, which marines did as a matter of course. St Vincent put much effort into building up the marines during his term at the Admiralty. Army artillerymen continued to man the main weapons of bomb vessels for bombarding the enemy coast, but off Le Havre in 1804, the gunners 'refused to do any other duty than simply that of attending mortars in time of action, and keeping them prepared for service; their officers supported them in this determination ...'[5] The Admiralty responded by forming the Royal Marine Artillery to take on the job.

The launching of an invasion needed far more inter-service cooperation than stopping one. Landing craft would have to be designed around the needs of the soldiers, ideally to accommodate self-contained units with a proper mix of infantry, artillery and cavalry. The sailors would have to show great consideration for the seasick soldiers and find a landing place that was suitable, not just for disembarking the troops, but for them to proceed inland with the minimum of interference and casualties. The French had a military system that could cope with this at the highest level, for Napoleon had full powers over both services and could be expected to exercise them. He had already organized and led the expedition to Egypt in 1798, though that did not have a happy result.

Inter-service cooperation was slightly less important in defending against an invasion in those days, and there were not many opportunities for it. Guns had very short ranges, so it was rarely possible for one on shore to hit a ship at sea, unless the ship came very close inshore. It was even more difficult for a ship-mounted gun to hit a target on shore, with the exception of the bomb vessel, which was specifically designed to fire one or more high-trajectory mortars into an enemy fort or town. Unlike a normal naval gun, it fired explosive shells rather than solid shot. The French could have used them to neutralize Martello towers by bursting shells over them and keeping the men from their guns. Keith considered their use to attack the flotilla in Boulogne but was not encouraged by Captain Owen, who wrote that,

> I consider the range of a shell to be at all times uncertain, and though it is possible to throw them into a town or any considerable space, I consider it requiring much more practice than can be obtained afloat to make them bear upon any one object, and ships passing under sail cannot, in my opinion, injure the vessels within the pier by shot.[6]

It would be very difficult for the navy use its gunpower against an enemy on the beaches, as its heaviest ships could not come close inshore. It might be possible for specially designed shallow-draft gunboats. The navy had 70 of these when the war began, and many more of the *Archer* class were ordered early in 1804. Keith had 42 of them in his fleet in the autumn of 1804, including ten in the Dungeness Squadron alone. They were intended to operate between there and the French ports and would have been useful if any enemy forces had attempted to land on the Dungeness peninsula, though there is no sign that they had any specific training in cooperation with the army.

Gunboats were some use on open beaches, but it would be difficult to concentrate them in time to prevent a landing. They could be more useful in narrow estuaries, such as a particularly shallow one about which General Sir James Craig wrote to Keith in October 1803:

> We have at present a gunbrig and one gunboat in the mouth of the Blackwater. This is a point that I am exceedingly anxious to have secured, because if the enemy lands at Clacton beach, and while we are opposing him there, if he was to send a force of any magnitude up the river in question, to land upon either of its shores, I will not conceal from you that he would embarrass us considerably. The mouth of the river is near two miles over, in which extent there would be room for operations of such a number of gunboats as I fear would be more than match for the four [sic] now there, while the tide of flood with which they must go up the river would render it impossible for the gunbrig, which is in the Colne, to be of any assistance. Another brig or vessel of that description would set my mind much more at ease.[7]

In the 1740s there had been an attempt to equate the officer ranks of the two services, with a naval lieutenant equal to an army captain, a naval captain to a colonel and a rear admiral to a major general. This was a matter of protocol rather than command, and there was no provision for an officer of one service to take charge over one of the other. When an expedition was sent out, everything depended on agreement between the army and the navy commander, for there was no possibility of reference to a higher authority. Sometimes this went very badly, as in the 1740s when Admiral Vernon and General Wentworth attempted to take

Cartagena on the Spanish Main. Relations deteriorated, and Vernon later spent much of his retirement publishing diatribes against Wentworth. Lord Keith had some difficulties during his numerous amphibious operations – a failed attack on Cadiz in 1799 was 'most sadly botched'. On the other hand, his landing in Egypt in 1800, conducted against serious opposition, was successful partly because he and the army commander, Sir Ralph Abercrombie, worked together very well. There is a suspicion that Keith cooperated better with fellow Scots, which might have augured well for a campaign with Sir David Dundas in the event of an invasion of England. He had fairly regular but rather formal contact with the general, and a little more with Sir James Craig, in charge of the Eastern District, but Keith's meticulous filing system had no specific section for relations with the army, and they did not figure high on his agenda.

There was a certain amount of cooperation at a lower but vital level. Since 1795 the Admiralty had maintained a chain of signal stations, on headlands and heights every few miles round the coast. Much of their work was in spotting enemy privateer movements and warning shipping in the area by means of signals, so each was commanded by a naval lieutenant with a midshipman and two seamen. But they might also give the first warning on shore of an approaching invasion fleet, so each station had two dragoons attached, to carry messages to the local army and militia commanders.

Cooperation between the services did not develop well in the Victorian age. The naval ratings were given uniforms and a military training, so that the sailor became more like the soldier, which led him to believe that he did not need his military colleague. The navy developed into a mobile and largely self-contained police force for the empire. A colonial governor who feared trouble would use the electric telegraph and ask the navy to 'send a gunboat'. On arrival, the ship would land some of its men, seamen as well as marines. The army would arrive much later, if at all, in troopships. Either the trouble was over by that time, or it would develop into a much longer war. Admiral Sir John Fisher ended all this in the 1900s by withdrawing his men to build up the fleet at home, but the war that followed saw little cooperation between the forces. The landings at Gallipoli in 1915 were a disaster and led to a belief that amphibious operations were almost impossible in the days of mass armies and long-range guns. A raid on Zeebrugge in 1918 was not completely successful and was mostly a propaganda victory.

However, the potential for army and navy cooperation was greater than ever, because the navy's long-range guns could fire quite accurately over many miles. Either the ships could stand some way off and bombard a coastal position, or they could come closer inshore to hit strongpoints several miles inland, using heavy guns that could not be transported easily on land. The navy had neglected shore bombardment before World War I but had to use it during the Gallipoli campaign. It was found that naval guns could frequently out-range the Turkish forts but had to keep manoeuvring to avoid their fire, which made aiming difficult; and that only a direct hit would put an individual gun out of action. Later the navy shelled troops and positions on the Belgian coast to some effect. Special vessels, known as monitors, were designed for this. They had the maximum weight of heavy guns on the smallest possible hull, and a shallow draft for going close inshore. There were three of these in the navy in 1940, carrying 15-inch guns.

The navy had more practice in 1923, ironically in the Gallipoli peninsula while it was still under occupation pending a post-war settlement. It also trained on the large army range at Shoeburyness at the mouth of the Thames, but the land was too flat for realistic practice in a varied landscape. A new range opened at Cape Wrath in the north of Scotland in 1932. Each capital ship, cruiser and destroyer was to carry out shore bombardment training once during a commission, which might last three years. Sloops and gunboats were to practise once a year.

All of this, however, was designed to support British troops landing on an enemy shore, not to attack enemy forces landing in Britain. Naval bombardment could be dangerous to one's own side if it was not used properly. Naval guns had flatter trajectories than army howitzers, and it was risky to fire over the heads of one's own troops. Naval artillery was generally less accurate but more powerful than army artillery, and it was not recommended to aim within 1,000 yards of one's own men. This demanded accurate knowledge of what was going on ashore, which was provided by army artillerymen known as Forward Observation Officers, but it was assumed that they would only be used in operations planned well in advance. 'It is essential for the success of the Naval bombardment that F.O.O.s should have previous contact with the Gunnery Officer of the bombarding ships as this is not likely after the start of the expedition.' Nor was this likely to be possible during the chaos that might follow an invasion. Moreover, the Commander-in-Chief of the Home Fleet resisted any attempt to move his force south unless large German warships were supporting the invasion, so he made no specific plans for army liaison. Bombardment by naval gunfire might have been used against the Germans on the invasion beaches, but it would have been improvised and would not have got the best out of the resources available.[8]

In one sense cooperation was easier than in the past. The seaman of 1940 wore a uniform, was drilled in military manoeuvres and was able to fire a rifle; and he was no more likely to desert than a soldier. There were always thousands of sailors on shore in Britain, under training, awaiting allocation to a ship or from ships under repair or in port. It was not difficult to organize them in platoons and companies to fight on shore, and those in basic training bases such as *Ganges* at Harwich and *Collingwood* near Portsmouth were part of the local defence scheme.

There was no provision for a supreme commander with authority over all the services, a role that did not emerge until Mountbatten was appointed to take charge in Burma in 1943, largely following American practices. It was something that seriously worried Brooke:

> There was, however, one point above all others which constituted a grave danger in the defensive organisation of this country, there was no form of combined command over the three services. And yet their roles were ultimately locked together. Who was deciding the claims between the employment of destroyers against hostile landing craft, as opposed to anti-submarine operations on the Western Approaches? Who would decide between the conflicting calls of the Army for bombers to attack beaches, as opposed to the Navy wanting them for attacks on hostile fleets? ... It was a highly dangerous organization; had an invasion developed I fear

that Churchill would have attempted as Defence Minister to co-ordinate the actions of these various commands. This would have been wrong and highly dangerous, with his impulsive nature and tendency to arrive at decisions through a process of intuition, as opposed to 'logical' approach. Heaven knows where he might have led us.[9]

This is not unrealistic – Churchill was always a military commander manqué, who would have relished the role. He might not have been as bad as Brooke feared, but the weaknesses went a little deeper than that. A serious invasion attempt would have required coordination between different commands, not just different services.

Brooke also envisaged the three chiefs of staff taking joint charge in the event of an invasion, but that prospect was no more encouraging. The General attended one of their meetings on 30 September and was not impressed: 'This organisation works surprisingly slowly considering there is a war on! We seem to meander along, and there is no snap about it.'[10] It is difficult to see how 'Dilly-dally', the narcoleptic Pound and the inadequate Newall could have found the dynamism and daring to lead the defence.

Churchill had set up a powerful inter-service organization, Combined Operations, within weeks of the fall of France, but it was not quite what was wanted for repelling an invasion, for it was focused entirely 'outwards' in characteristic Churchill fashion, towards renewing the attack on the enemy. At first the Chiefs of Staff had appointed the Adjutant General of the Royal Marines to head it, but Churchill wanted something 'far more extensive than is at present foreseen'[11] and took on Admiral of the Fleet Sir Roger Keyes, who had led the Zeebrugge expedition of 1918, one of the few amphibious operations that was considered successful. Combined Operations studied ways of getting forces back on the continent, either in the form of raids or, eventually, a complete army. They may have offered some insight into the difficulties the Germans faced, but there is very little sign that it was used. A paper in Southern Command's files on invasion contains a lecture by an unnamed naval officer on the 'Naval Aspect of a Combined Operation'.[12] L. E. H. Maund, an early pioneer of Combined Operations, was invited to a conference early in 1941, but otherwise the growing knowledge and experience of Combined Operations was not called on for the defence against invasion.

There can be little doubt that the services would have cooperated together on the ground once an invasion had started, and relations between troops and officers on the spot were nearly always better those between their masters in Whitehall, until well into 1940 at least. But a little more advanced planning of such matters as shore bombardment might have prevented the risk of death by what later became known as 'friendly fire' and have got a little more from the resources available to make victory more certain.

NAVAL–AIR COOPERATION

Early in the twentieth century air power arrived to (literally) add a new dimension to warfare. It might have forced a measure of cooperation between the services. Aircraft can intervene as easily over the sea as in the land battle, and no modern commander could afford to ignore their effect. But the Royal Air Force adopted the doctrine of 'the indivisibility of the air', so that all military flying machines should be concentrated in its hands. It went on to argue that bombing of cities could win the next war alone, or better still deter it, without any help from the army and the navy except in the passive defence of its bases. In a period that saw fierce rivalry between the services for limited funding, powerful Chiefs of Staff like Trenchard of the RAF and Beatty of the navy were barely on speaking terms for most of the 1920s. Even the issue of relative ranks, settled between the army and the navy almost two centuries earlier, was revived when the RAF pointed out that an RAF flight lieutenant had to do much more service before his promotion than a naval lieutenant; the issue was settled in the navy's favour in 1924.[13]

The biggest source of conflict was over the control of naval aviation. During World War I the Royal Naval Air Service had been a highly innovative service, combining the best of naval discipline with the inventiveness of temporary officers. It had originated several of the weapons systems to be used in the next war, including the tank, the strategic bomber, the airborne anti-submarine patrol and the aircraft carrier. In 1918 it was merged into the RAF, and its identity was lost after the war ended. By a compromise of 1922, the navy was to provide 70 per cent of pilots for the shipboard and carrier-borne aircraft of the Fleet Air Arm, and all of the observers. But not enough naval officers volunteered for training, and the navy wanted to draft in ratings. This, according to the RAF undermined one of the purposes of the scheme, to provide the future senior officers of the navy with air experience. When the issue was re-opened, even the supposedly dispassionate RAF staff history could not conceal the bitterness of feelings:

> Shocked by the resurrection of this bitter controversy the Air Ministry retaliated by saying that the Trenchard Keyes Agreement had only been achieved by wholesale abandonment of their real convictions in the cause of inter-service peace and that in reality they could run the Fleet Air Arm with the same and even better efficiency at far less cost if they had never departed from their original scheme of allowing only 20 per cent of posts to be filled by Naval pilots.[14]

Though dual control seemed to work reasonably well on the decks of aircraft carriers, it caused dissension in Whitehall, and eventually in 1937 it was agreed that the navy should have full control of all shipboard aircraft. This was not immediately relevant to the threat of invasion, which would, of course, take place within range of shore-based aircraft while the carriers operated on broader waters. But its shore-based reserve aircraft might have helped with home defence – except that they were nearly all of poor performance in 1940. The only British dive-bomber, the Blackburn Skua, had been obsolete when it came into service, attempting to combine the roles of fighter and dive-bomber and doing neither well. It had had some success in sinking the cruiser *Konigsberg* off Norway, and it operated over the beaches of Dunkirk, but numbers were short and they were nearly all sent off to join the carriers, mostly in the Mediterranean. The main torpedo bomber was the Swordfish, a biplane that would soon have spectacular success against the weaker Italian navy and in the open oceans where there was no aerial opposition; but it would be terribly vulnerable in British waters.

The other half of the 1937 compromise was that shore-based maritime aircraft should remain part of RAF Coastal Command, and this did necessitate inter-service cooperation. Joint air and maritime headquarters were to be set up at Plymouth, Chatham and Pitreavie Castle near the dockyard at Rosyth in Fife. This last turned out to be the most developed one by 1940, but it was farthest from the likely scene of invasion.[15]

There were plenty of joint exercises in the years before the war, with 29 in the eight months of peace in 1939 alone. These tended to follow the standard belief that there were two main purposes in maritime war – to destroy the enemy battlefleet and to defend merchant shipping against surface raiders and submarines. The final and largest joint exercise took place as late as 15–21 August and involved eleven RAF squadrons in the northern approaches, testing navy and air force organization in searching for enemy surface ships breaking out of the North Sea.[16]

If the invasion was launched, Bomber Command and Coastal Command would both attack barges and their escorts at sea. During the 1930s joint exercises had tried to establish the best ways to attack and defend warships. The RAF had started off with the premise that the battleship was obsolete, but it came to believe that its heavy armour could protect it against most air attack in north European waters, where high-level bombing was likely to be restricted by the low cloud base.[17] Cruisers and destroyers were considered more vulnerable. High-level attack on ships was soon shown to be inaccurate. Midshipmen Terence Lewin and Roderick Macdonald were detailed to stand aft on the bridge of HMS *Valiant* during attacks off Norway. '"Bomb doors open, sir." Then "Bombs away!" He then put the wheel hard over one way or another. It always worked, as the explosions and columns of water erupted where we would otherwise have been.'[18]

Dive-bombing, as developed by the Luftwaffe, was as effective at sea as on land, for the bomb was more accurately aimed, at closer range, and allowed the ship little time to dodge it. Its velocity helped it to penetrate armour. Its effectiveness had been realized during the 1930s. In exercises of 1934 dive-bombers could obtain 22 per cent hits on the old battleship *Centurion*, compared with a maximum of seven per cent for level bombing from 10,000 feet. However, the RAF and navy continued to believe that the speed of the bomb on impact did not constitute sufficient penetrating power – but this was partly because they had used obsolete Hind biplane bombers at a diving angle of 45 degrees, whereas the German Stuka had higher speed and twice the diving angle.[19]

The experience of Dunkirk soon showed what dive-bombers could do. Of six British destroyers lost, four were victims to air attack, though mostly in the confined waters of the harbour and beaches. One of the most dramatic losses was HMS *Keith*, as reported by one of her gunners, Ian Nethercott:

> I was blazing away at the Stukas diving on us from three different directions, coming in from ahead, the port beam and from astern. Captain Berthon, on the Keith's bridge, had worked up to about 30 knots and was throwing the ship round to dodge the bombs. Unfortunately, at that time we were in the deep-water channel with sandbanks on either side and there was little room for manoeuvre.[20]

If British destroyers were to operate against an invasion fleet, they would need some protection against such counterattack. Their own anti-aircraft defences were already known to be inadequate, as the gunners of the *Keith* had shown:

> After almost continuous firing, our 3-inch high-angle gun ran out of ammunition. Our main armament of four 4.7-inch guns couldn't be elevated more than about 65 degrees so was completely useless against aircraft. That left us with our two quadruple pom-pom guns, both of which were rapidly running out of ammunition. The continuous noise of battle, the screaming dives of the Stukas, every available anti-aircraft gun of several destroyers firing almost without pause, was deafening.

Even if the guns and ammunition were available it was still very difficult to hit a target as fast-moving as a dive-bomber:

> The violent swinging from side to side made it very difficult to keep my gun lined up on the diving Stukas, so I just fired fused shells at 2,000 feet

and hoped that would divert them. I then tracked a Ju 87 right across the ship. A large bomb then exploded about 25 feet from our starboard side, half drowning us in seawater. More dive bombers were on the way down and it became increasing obvious that the unequal battle could only have one outcome.[21]

The standard anti-aircraft gun, the 2-pounder pom-pom, had a slow muzzle velocity and relied on a high volume of fire, so it was normally in a four-barrelled or eight-barrelled mounting. Guns with a faster muzzle velocity, such as the Oerlikon and the Bofors, were scarce in 1940. The navy had gone to great lengths to develop aiming systems against surface ships, but anti-aircraft gunnery posed different problems – the target moved much faster, in three dimensions, and was far more manoeuvrable. A tachymetric system of measuring the aircraft's speed was rejected before the war, and gunners relied on 'eye-shooting'. They used sights with two or three rings, each representing 100 knots of an aircraft's speed.

> The method of using the sight is very simple. Look at the aircraft, note its direction of flight and estimate its aim-off speed. Point the gun so that the aircraft is flying towards the centre of the sight, with its nose the distance from the centre corresponding to your estimate of its aim-off speed. As the attack develops and the aim-off speed increases, bring the nose of the aircraft further and further out from the centre, always adjusting direction of aim-off to keep the aircraft flying towards the centre of the sight.[22]

It was not particularly effective. After watching exercises in the destroyer *Eskimo* in 1940, Joseph Wellings of the United States Navy observed, 'I have met two skippers who claim to have shot down planes with pom-poms. I am convinced that any hits were only due to the volume of fire.'[23]

In attacking an invasion fleet, the British destroyers would have the advantage of surprise, and the enemy would find it difficult to maintain constant and strong air patrols over it, particularly in the case of the numerous supply convoys that would be necessary. Also, perhaps, the destroyers might be in the open sea, which would increase their manoeuvrability, but in general they would be far more successful with fighter cover. Even if it was available, the RAF might be reluctant to take aircraft away from the defence of its airfields. In addition, the navy had a policy of shooting at unidentified aircraft that approached within 1,500 yards of its ships, which did not improve relations with the RAF. Only a programme of training in aircraft recognition would solve that problem in the long term. If cover was not available due the defeat of the RAF or its commitment elsewhere, then they would have to accept the risk of heavy losses in defence of their country, and the issue might hang in the balance.

There was some debate about the best method of low-level attack on an invasion fleet, and orders were issued as the Dunkirk evacuation was completed:

> Experience has shown that when carrying out low bombing attacks it is more difficult to estimate the correct moment of release than to track the aircraft over the target. Thus range errors are greater than line errors, and the resultant pattern is an ellipse, the major axis of which is along the track.

Therefore with a single bomb it was better to fly along the line of the vessel, but with a stick of bombs it should be attacked from an angle, or the stick should be wide enough to cover errors in range.[24]

There were experiments on the best way to sink a barge. Tests were carried out late in August off the gunnery range at Shoeburyness in Essex. A 110-ton steel barge was ballasted to simulate a load of 266 fully armed troops and 40-pound and 250-pound bombs were to be dropped on it, but the results are not recorded. For attacks on small vessels, such as barges and E-boats, the Admiralty favoured setting the bombs to detonate a foot or so above the water, but further tests in April 1941 showed something different. In the case of a 1,000-pound bomb on a steel barge, 'A "near miss" by 15 yards will not sink a barge. Wooden hatch covers will be destroyed, personnel under wooden hatches will probably be killed, and those under deck plating will probably suffer from severe concussion.' But such a miss would sink a wooden barge. For a lighter bomb, 'It is deduced that a 250 lb. G.P. bomb fuzed to burst at about 10 feet below the surface at a distance of about 15 feet, will cause the flooding of at least one compartment of a barge and will probably sink it.' A 100-pound bomb bursting about 10 feet below the water and 12 feet away would have a similar effect.[25]

The navy gave a good deal of thought to attacks on cruisers and larger ships, which might escort an invasion force, though the Germans had very few of these. Bomber pilots were advised that a direct hit was needed in such cases as 'the heavier classes of ship can "take it", therefore 'the "near miss mentality" is a snare and delusion and must be eradicated when considering attacks on heavy ships'. Destroyers and smaller warships, however, were a different case, and a near-miss could put one out of action, though it was far better to get a hit – 'there is often a chance of salvage and repair from near miss damage whereas penetrating hits more frequently result in severe internal damage, fires and total loss.' The navy was keen to destroy a ship totally so that naval force could be deployed elsewhere, but in an invasion situation the most important thing was to disable as many as possible and to disrupt the enemy formation, so that he would be confused and disorganized on landing.

Army–Air Cooperation

The experience in France and Belgium and on the beaches of Dunkirk had shown how an air force and an army could cooperate far more dynamically than the RAF plans allowed. In particular it had demonstrated the role of the Stuka dive-bomber in attacking tanks, troops and even civilians. Corporal Jim Anderson of the Royal Engineers describes his experience:

> Enemy air traffic was heavy at the time and suddenly a Stuka attack swept in. I dived into the roadside ditch next to a small culvert or large drainpipe, and thought my last moment had come as the Stukas straddled the area with their bombs. One was very close and caused casualties amongst the French troops. Half-buried I struggled out of the loose earth and as I stood up in the smoke and dust a Frenchman popped his head out of the culvert near my feet and shouted: 'A bas, il vient avec la mitraileuse'; [get

down, he is coming with the machine gun] as I plunged down again I literally 'felt' the bullets passing above my head.[26]

Dive-bombing created need for inter-service cooperation on several different levels. For the RAF, the simplest solution was to shoot down the enemy. They had clearly failed to do this in France because a large part of their force had been held back in the home country and because they did not have any radar chain or observer system to direct the fighters on to the bombers. At sea the dive-bomber increased its reputation after Dunkirk by attacking convoys in the English Channel and forcing the abandonment of the route. However, when they began to attack ground targets in southern England they suffered disproportionate losses. Göring ordered a strong escort, with three fighter Gruppen to each Stuka Gruppe, but on 18 August two dozen Stukas were shot down in what proved to be their last effort over Britain.[27] When it was able to dispute control of the air, the RAF could defeat the dive-bomber menace, but what would happen if the RAF fighter force itself was defeated, as seemed quite possible for much of the summer of 1940?

One approach was to train the army in how to respond to dive-bomber attack. Air Vice Marshal Whatton, on the staff of GHQ Home Forces, was perhaps relying on experience in colonial warfare when he wrote, 'Sirens and whistling bombs are devices similar to paint, feathers and war cries which savages employed to gain an ascendancy in morale over their enemies. Little material damage is done unless morale is affected.' As a result, a flight of six Fairey Battle aircraft was detailed to tour the area commands and give the troops experience of standing up to attack. In October the King's Shropshire Light Infantry went to Billinghay, where they were split up into groups of about 30 to watch the demonstration, with running commentary. They would also be sprayed with imitation mustard gas, which would smell of aniseed but, they were assured, would not mark their clothes.[28]

Not everyone was happy with the success of such operations, for the Battle had no diving brakes and could only go into a shallow dive, while six aircraft were not nearly enough to reproduce the intensity and length of a real attack, which might feature a hundred aircraft or more.

According to Wing Commander Paul of the Air Ministry, 'the Army themselves say that they are pleased with the shows that have been put on for them. But it is considered that, in actual fact, these demonstrations are leading thousands of inexperienced soldiers to expect a type of attack that they will never see; and that when the actual attack comes, they will be taken by surprise.'[29]

Another possibility was for the RAF to develop its own dive-bombing tactics, or to find another way of supporting the troops on the ground. This was difficult, because its bomber and fighter crews had assumed that they would be taking part in a different kind of war and had no training in observing the battle on the ground, or spotting targets of opportunity.

After Dunkirk there were frequent insults and attacks on men in RAF uniform in pubs and on the streets, for soldiers believed that they had been let down and that the RAF had failed to provide them with cover on the beaches. This was a fallacy, as fighters could often operate better some way forward of the army, where they were out of sight, and the RAF went to some trouble to explain this:

> Fighter aircraft have as their primary object in countering invasion, the attack of enemy aircraft. This necessitates their having a very high rate of climb, great speed and very considerable fire power. To gain these characteristics they must accept short endurance and an allotment of ammunition which lasts only for a few seconds in actual combat. Their tactical employment is essentially offensive.

Fighters did not have the fuel to undertake patrols but were sent out on specific missions to intercept a known enemy raid:

> Naturally troops will be interested in the protection afforded to them by Fighter operations. Those who are being attacked by dive bombers at 'A' ... expect to see fighters over them to act in close defence. It must be made clear to them that any fighter seen over 'A' will be no protection against the bombs though they will provide some 'morale' uplift and may shoot down the enemy bombers after they have dropped their bombs ...[30]

Sir Hugh Dowding, in charge of Fighter Command, continued to maintain that air defence was practically the only role of his force. Its job was to shoot down enemy aircraft, whether fighters, bombers or troop-carrying transports – particular priority was given to destroying any aircraft that might be carrying tanks, reflecting the general concern about a panzer force reaching the United Kingdom. Early in July, GHQ Home Forces was allowed five liaison officers at Fighter Command HQ, but one suspects that their presence was less than welcome, for they had little to offer to the struggle in the air. The duty officer was to 'interfere as little as possible with the other Duty Officers', but to keep a close watch on the operations table and 'realise that it is his duty to seek out information' so that 'information of value does not pass unnoticed'. His role was 'to keep G.H.Q Home Forces informed of any information available at H.Q. Fighter Command which has a bearing on the military situation'.[31]

In Dowding's opinion of 2 July,

the most likely form of attack would be a high level circus of fighter aircraft over a selected area in which attempts would be made to land troop carrying aircraft and bombers. Fighter squadrons would have to occupy the enemy fighters while others were to attack the transport and bombing planes at low level. The present best distribution he considered to be one squadron against the fighters and two squadrons at lower levels.[32]

Fighter aircraft might be used to attack enemy light craft, but only 'if the air situation permits'. The famous legless fighter pilot Douglas Bader was in command of a squadron at Coltishall at this time, and one night he found his pilots in a state of some concern over a report that the enemy had landed:

There was a moment's silence while he digested the news.
'So the bastards are coming. Bloody good show! Think of all those juicy targets on those nice flat beaches. What shooting!'
And he made a rude sound with his lips which was meant to resemble a ripple of machine-gun fire.[33]

But in fact there is no sign that this was Fighter Command policy, and Bader's job was to fight for command of the air above the invasion area.

Bomber command was rather more enthusiastic about direct cooperation with the army, perhaps because its early efforts at the strategic bombing of Germany had soon foundered and it was struggling to find a role. Early in July it agreed that if invasion was imminent seven Blenheim medium bomber squadrons, half of the aircraft in No. 2 Group, would be placed under the authority of GHQ Home Forces along with two Fairey Battle squadrons, half of No. 1 Group. Arrangements were made to affiliate each of the squadrons to an army command. In an emergency even more forces might be drawn on, including basic training schools with their instructors, the half-trained crews of Operational Training Units and aircraft from the Fleet Air Arm.

GHQ Home Forces tried to find out what light bombers, particularly Blenheims, could do in the event of an enemy landing, and a paper of mid-August began by outlining the differences between aerial bombardment and long-range artillery. Bombers could not keep up a sustained attack, though to a certain extent that was contradicted by the experience of Stuka attacks in France. Bombers could not improve on their accuracy by observing the fall of shot, as each bomber had to take independent aim. Unless there was complete air superiority, bombers could not wait over an area for a target to appear; therefore it would take longer to bring bomber 'fire' on to a target. Finally,

> Under normal conditions of battle the bomber has great difficulty in distinguishing between friend and foe, and it is unsafe to rely on its ability to do so. The bomber is not a part of the battle as are the troops on the ground. It comes from and returns to an atmosphere quite different from that on the battlefield, so that precise and up to date information about the relative positions of the opposing forces is even more difficult to obtain than on the battlefield itself.

The great majority of RAF pilots 'possessed ... no background of training or experience that would enable them to take useful independent action of the battlefield ...'. As to tactical employment, the bombers could attack the ships as they crossed the sea, but it was noted that ships were too small and manoeuvrable to be ideal targets. The prospects were better in the vicinity of the beach as the enemy landed, but the report was cautious: 'Bomber attack will cause disorganization and casualties, but it cannot be expected to do more than delay and incommode the landing operations.'

Other tactics were needed once the enemy was ashore. Bombers had attempted to disrupt the heads of armoured formations in France, but that had not been successful. It was useless to block the roads in such open country, as the enemy could go across fields. Then vehicles were too spaced out for more than one or two to be damaged by an individual attack, and attacks on temporary congestion were usually too late because of the time taken to report it from a reconnaissance aircraft. Machine-gunning could be quite effective, but the Blenheim and the Battle were weakly armed in that respect. The best hope was to concentrate attention on beaches and ports as the enemy unloaded his stores, and on defiles, which were more common in southern England than in northern France and Belgium. But there was no suggestion that air attack would destroy the enemy by sea or by land.[34]

Paratroops and gliders posed other problems. Obviously the RAF's first job was to shoot them down if possible, easy if they attacked by day but much harder at night, for the RAF still had no means of counteracting the night bomber until well into 1941, while the Germans could use radio beams to guide their aircraft on to their targets. The next task was to follow the attackers as they crossed the coast and plot their landings. As early as 16 May it was agreed that Observer posts and searchlight stations should be responsible for reporting landings and sending messages to the nearest Fighter Command sector station, which would pass it on to the army command. By 9 July, after many false alarms, the system had become rather more sophisticated. Observers and searchlight units were only to report what they had actually seen themselves, and not just rumours. To avoid incidents involving friendly airmen, only drops of at least six men were to be reported, and army liaison officers were to be attached to the sector stations.[35]

Attention had been drawn to gliders during the invasion of Belgium, but their limitations were not fully understood. One possibility that was considered early in June was that they might be towed to a point about ten miles off the coast and then released to find their way in. They had several advantages over paratroopers – they were silent in the last part of the journey and thus could not be heard by the Observer Corps. In addition, 'if a safe landing is made a formed body of some strength emerges from the aircraft and is thus more dangerous than a number of scattered parachutists.' Would radar be able to detect the largely wooden craft after they parted company with their towing aircraft, and would the plotting services be able to cope with them if they moved inland? Tests at Swanage towards the end of June reassured the authorities that they would, but if the Germans were to develop gliders with no metal parts at all, it might be much more difficult. A procedure was also adopted for the radar stations to follow the gliders inland using the 'backward looking properties' of their sets and sending the information on to the Observer Corps.[36]

Clearly one of the main aims of a parachute or glider attack would be to seize airfields so that more troops could be flown in. This raised the thorny question of airfield defence. According to orders of 24 June, 'the Station Commander is responsible to the Group for the preparation of a Station Defence Scheme', which should, however, be submitted to the army for criticism and suggestions. Most stations earmarked machine-guns for use against paratroops, but they had no defence against armoured fighting vehicles except Molotov cocktails. At a meeting on 3rd June, the Air Officer Commanding No. 1 Group of Bomber Command stated that some of his stations were newly set up and had no defence scheme except a small army detachment with two machine-guns. His colleague in No. 2 Group claimed that there was no coordination between various stations and that the station commanders had to spend an undue amount of time on the matter.[37] The C-in-C agreed that the army had given very little priority, but the army replied that it could not afford to spread its troops too thinly to every point that might be attacked, and that each aerodrome had up to 2,000 men who ought to be trained and organized in the use of weapons. The eventual answer, in 1942, was the formation of the RAF Regiment to defend airfields.

Army cooperation squadrons were much closer to the land battlefield, as their name implies, but they were few in number and limited in equipment and role. They mostly used Lysanders, which had already been found lacking in France. They were directly attached to the army, with three squadrons in Eastern Command, two for Northern Command and one each for Scottish, Southern and Western, and a flight in Northern Ireland, so in principle there were a dozen aircraft for an army corps of perhaps 60,000 men. In action, according to orders of June 1940, they were to be used for tactical reconnaissance by day, and by night in exceptional cases. They were to report on enemy activity on shore. Their responsibility did not extend beyond the beach, though they might 'locate and report immediately the strength, composition, estimated speed and course of any enemy forces seen approaching the beach'. They could drop bombs in exceptional circumstances, for example when the invaders were approaching the beach or actually disembarking.[38]

These squadrons remained a weak feature in the British defences. An Army Cooperation Command was set up at the end of the year, equipped with American Tomahawk aircraft of much higher performance, but General Brooke continued to complain that the RAF obsession with the bombing of Germany made future development impossible: 'the army was being starved of any types suitable for the direct support of the land forces,' he complained in 1942, and he soon decided, 'The situation is hopeless and I see no solution besides the provision of an army air arm' – which, in the event, was not to happen until 1957.[39]

Close air support was clearly more useful in the attack, when the positions of enemy strongpoints were already known. On the defensive, it was impossible to predict the movements of a fast enemy column. An Air Staff paper of August set out some thoughts on how support might be given during a counterattack by allowing tanks and infantry to penetrate where artillery support was not available. Two things were essential – that the ground forces could indicate the targets to the bombers, and that they could be concentrated sufficiently to attack effectively in the short time that might be available. It was easy enough to indicate the targets in a set-piece attack, but in that case artillery would probably be available. Therefore, 'the close support bomber's true role is for giving support on ad hoc targets which could not be foreseen when the attack was planned and when the infantry or A.F.V.s had advanced beyond the power of the artillery to assist them.' To make this effective, a good deal of training would be needed at all levels. On the airfield, the bomber crews would have to adopt Fighter Command standards of instant readiness. A means of rapidly briefing the pilots was needed; they would be given coordinates and learn a much higher standard of map reading; and 'much experiment will be needed to determine the most appropriate method of indicating to the close support bomber pilots the line beyond which they can bomb without endangering our own troops'. They also needed training in the best tactical approach to a target, allowing for a getaway as well. Meanwhile, army commanders would have to learn what it was practicable for a bomber to do. Two squadrons were allocated for experiment in these areas in the third week of August. One exercise that month used a squadron of Blenheims to attack army columns heading for Harwich on the east coast, but it was felt that such attacks had already proved useless in France, and nothing much was learned. [40]

It was suggested that a brigade of infantry or a battalion of tanks should be able to call on bomber support if needed, but this caused many command difficulties. There was no question that the formation in question should communicate directly with the bombers: 'Even if there should be enough close support bombers to permit of definite squadrons being allotted in sufficient strength to each formation which might require them, the principles of parcelling out bombers to lower formations is inherently uneconomic ...' From the air force point of view it would be better to have a three-stage process, in which a ground formation would contact RAF control, which would then pass the message to the bomber stations, which would instruct the aircraft captains. The control centre would have to prioritize requests, and each would need 'a senior Army officer who can interpret a general directive in terms of the amount of support to be given to successive calls for assistance as these come in. This Army officer must be in the mind of the Commander fighting the battle.'[41]

All this pointed towards the setting up of joint operations rooms. The RAF had been familiar with the concept since the late 1920s, for it realized that it could only get the best use of its limited air power by amassing all the information at a central point and directing the aircraft to where they might find targets on land, sea or air. As the paper indicated, the Fighter Command operations room was the best model, as it had to deal with rapidly moving and unpredictable situations.

Such a policy had been agreed on 2 July. One operations room was to be set up immediately in GHQ near London, followed by others in the area commands, and perhaps more in the corps headquarters. The army would find the accommodation in a spacious building reasonably safe from bombing, and the RAF provided most of the staff. The primary purpose was 'maintenance of the most up to date record possible of the movements of enemy forces which land, from the aspect of attack by air bombardment'. It was to allot objectives to the bomber forces, and coordinate reconnaissance. The Central Combined Operations Room at GHQ Home Forces had direct links to the Air Ministry War Room, the headquarters of Bomber Command, Coastal Command and Fighter Command, the Admiralty War Room, the Home Security War Room and the combined operations rooms of the subordinate army commands. An area operations room was in direct telephone contact with the aerodrome, where their affiliated squadron was based, with any army corps operations room under the command, with the Lysander squadron and with Nos. 1 and 2 Bomber Groups in the case of Southern and Eastern Commands.[42]

The main RAF figure in the Central Combined Operations Room was the Air Staff Officer in Charge, a group captain and personal representative of the C-in-C of Bomber Command. Under him were several duty controllers, with one always on watch. As well as running the operations room, he was 'at all times, to be fully conversant with the progress of operations'. He was to make sure that the air operations board was kept up to date, recording the availability and state of readiness of aircraft and the bombing missions ordered. He was to receive requests for bomber assistance and pass them on to the air staff officer. He had a squadron leader under him, 'responsible for the collection and dissemination of air intelligence matters and for passing all such information to the Control Combined Operations Room without delay'. The controller also worked closely with G2(air), an army staff officer who was 'responsible for the initial presentation of the military situation in the key situation map'. He was assisted by the Intelligence Watch Keeper, who also recorded the progress of bomber sorties. Area commands were similar, but the most senior RAF officer was a wing commander.[43]

For attacking the enemy as he landed on the beaches, a schedule was drawn up in the spring of 1941, rather late in the day. According to Charles Carrington, the army liaison officer with Bomber Command,

> I spent the month of February collecting and arranging lists of likely invasion beaches from information supplied by EASTCO and SECO, which I had already visited in October and November. With strong support from [Brigadier Claude] Oxborrow and his staff, we sorted and numbered them, eliminating some as unlikely, and by the end of the month produced a list of 107 points which might be denoted as Invasion Bombing Targets.[44]

There were 25 possible invasion beaches in Norfolk, 19 in Suffolk, 9 in Essex, 29 in Kent, 26 in Sussex, as well as 52 more in the north of England, which was still considered a possible area for invasion. Their locations were to be issued to army and RAF units 'with the object of providing a system of quick reference to a number of tactically important points easily recognizable from the air and likely to provide effective targets for air attack'. It was still implied that the bombers would attack the enemy as he exited from the beach, rather than as he disembarked: 'They are in all cases points on the foreshore opposite the landing exit from a practicable landing place.'[45]

Cooperation between the army, navy and air force made considerable strides in the middle months of 1940, as the necessity for it became blindingly obvious, but it still had a long way to go to make up for years of bitter rivalry. There is no doubt that almost everyone, serviceman or woman, volunteer or civilian, was committed to defeating an enemy invasion to the best of his ability. However, one suspects that the attacks on the enemy forces would have been carried out with a great deal of courage and enthusiasm but with little coordination, and many opportunities would have been wasted.

13

THE THREAT RESOLVED

THE RESOLUTION, 1805

Napoleon Bonaparte had not expected the British to declare war on him in 1803 despite the gradual worsening of relations. The ships fitting out in his ports were intended to restore the French position in the West Indies, not to attack British interests. He had no immediate plan for a war against Britain, except to conquer King George's personal kingdom of Hanover. He already knew something about the possibilities of invading Britain, and in 1798 he had rejected the idea: 'Whatever efforts we make, we will not, within a period of several years, gain the superiority of the sea. To perform a descent on England without being master of the seas is a very daring operation and very difficult to put into effect.'[1] France was even further from the control of the seas by 1803, yet Napoleon revived the idea of invasion, perhaps because he had no active enemies on the continent, and there was no alternative except a long and uncertain war on British trade.

Despite British fears, the invasion was not going to come quickly because it took time to build up a flotilla and even longer to prepare suitable ports. The man in charge of the programme was Pierre-Alexandre-Laurent Forfait, who had been born in 1752 in Rouen and became an engineer-constructor with the navy. He had visited England to study shipbuilding there and first met the rising Napoleon Bonaparte in Venice. His subsequent appointment as Minister of Marine was not successful and he left as the Treaty of Amiens was signed. Now he was appointed Inspector General of the Flotilla against England. He had designed many innovative smaller vessels, including some for the difficult passage up the River Seine to Paris.

There were four main types of vessel in the invasion flotilla, all with a shallow draft for crossing sandbanks and beaching as close in as possible. They could be rowed but would sail, very poorly except with the wind right astern, as there was little below the water to stop them being pushed sideways. The British had an answer to this in Captain Shanck's retractable keel, rather like the ones used on a modern dinghy, while the Dutch had long used lee boards, which could be dropped over one side or another to stop the vessel being blown sideways. But there is no sign that the French paid much attention to these ideas except in the craft they took over from the Dutch.

The largest invasion craft were the *prames*, known as *bateaux de grandes espace* and rather like small warships. Each was 120 feet long with a dozen 24-pounder guns along its sides, with a crew of 38 sailors plus 120 soldiers. These were not very successful, and only a few were built. Next came the vessels of the *premier espace*, or *chaloupes cannonières*, 76 to 80 feet long and armed with three 24-pounders. The *bateaux cannonières* were 60 feet long, with three smaller guns and 100 soldiers. They came in several types, the *Muskin*, *Carline* and Dutch versions, all intended to row more than sail. Then there were the *péniches*, or barges, as long as the *bateaux cannonières* but even lighter in construction, effectively just enlarged rowing boats carrying 60 troops each. Dutch barges and small cargo vessels were also taken over, just as the Germans would do in 1940. The whole building programme cost Napoleon's treasury nearly 30 million Francs, far more than he had expected. Progress was slow, and Napoleon began to suspect that many of the civilian contractors had signed up just for the initial advance, without any intention to press on with the building; the contractors replied that they often had to wait a long time for due payments. In the event, there was no chance of having a suitable fleet ready during 1803, and deadlines for the spring of 1804 were constantly extended. In May 1804, as Napoleon was crowned Emperor, 1,273 out of 2,008 vessels were ready and only 149 of these were fully manned.[2]

Napoleon had decided on the short sea route, with nearly all his invasion craft based in the Boulogne area. Calais was rejected as a port because it was very small and did not have the sandbanks of the Bassure de Bass to protect the anchorage outside. Boulogne needed much work to make it viable as a launching port for the invasion. It was a small river port, much affected by the rise and fall of the tides. Napoleon ordered the channel to be dredged, a very laborious operation in the days before steam power. A semicircular basin 78 metres in diameter, the Bassin Napoléon, was dug out to hold many of the invasion craft, with others moored in the river. Several forts were built to defend the port against attack from the sea, with some on offshore rocks and Fort Rouge on the beach outside the harbour entrance, as well as numerous batteries along the coast. The small ports of Étaples, Ambleteuse and Wimereaux were to be developed from almost nothing to hold hundreds of vessels each. Progress on the works was just as slow as with the flotilla, and in August 1803 British intelligence reported,

> They are making amazing works, upwards of 3,000 hands employed besides the soldiers. ... The fort buildings at low-water mark are to be finished in three months, but five weeks are elapsed and only an eighth finished. The opening for the harbour to admit frigates is an immense undertaking, and it is thought cannot succeed; it is Bonaparte's order and must be attempted.[3]

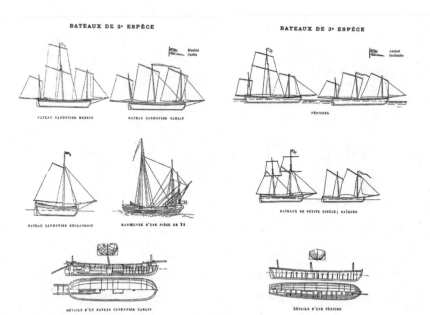

Various types of flotilla craft. (*From Desbrières,* Projets de Tentatives)

Napoleon's Grande Armée, the most formidable land force in the world, was camped on the heights above Boulogne and in surrounding villages. By August 1804 it had 130,000 men and 20,000 horses. Inaction and rumour took their toll, and in November 1804 Forfait complained, 'It seems quite evident that the army no longer plans on invading England. I hear this view expressed every day, indeed expressed in such a way as to make me despair ...'[4] One of its commanders, Marshal Soult, claimed that its spirit was good, desertion was almost nil and discipline was being maintained. But inactivity, within tantalizing sight of the enemy coast,

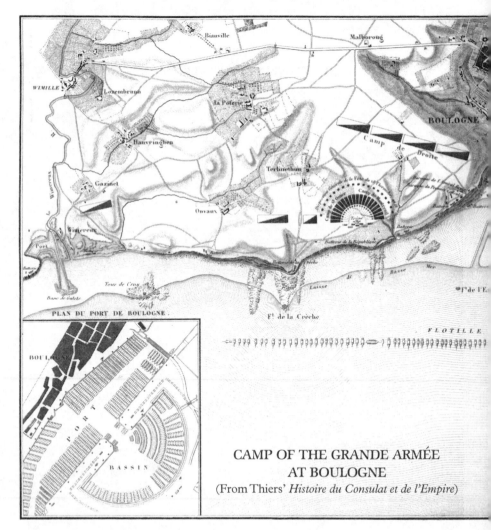

**CAMP OF THE GRANDE ARMÉE
AT BOULOGNE**
(From Thiers' *Histoire du Consulat et de l'Empire*)

was taking its toll after nearly a year and a half, and nearly ten per cent of the force was absent. Seven thousand of these were accounted for by illness, a figure that was down since the winter but which was still high. There were numerous duels, and acts of indiscipline were punished with great severity. In February 1804, for example, one Private Loudière was shot by firing squad for undermining confidence in the army, and orders of the day announced severe penalties for desertion.[5]

In September 1804 the flotilla was organized into seven divisions with 108 vessels each. The first line was to be formed of *péniches*, the second

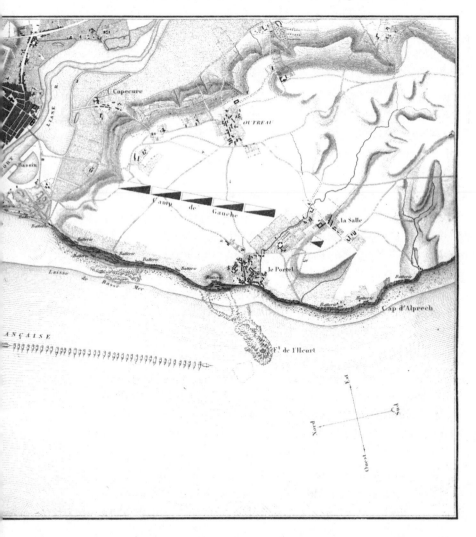

of *chaloupes cannonières*, the third of *bateaux cannonières* and the fourth of transports. *Péniches* and *chaloupes cannonières* were to operate in pairs, carrying 197 troops between them, including three cart drivers and eight surgeons. Each pair also carried 12,000 cartridges, 1,200 flints for muskets, 1,200 biscuits and four sheep. [6]

Records of French plans are rather vague about where the force was to land but there is no sign that they had any intention of attacking the east coast. Craft were moved in large numbers from Ostend and Flushing to Boulogne, and that would not have made any sense for an attack on Essex. They were also intended for as short a voyage as possible, which ruled out anything east of Beachy Head. Almost certainly they would have attacked on what became the 'Martello coast' east of Dover, and in that sense the British defences were well planned, though too late to have any effect. And within that area the short crossing to either side of Romney Marsh was the most attractive. Years later, Napoleon would claim that his forces would simply have looked for an opportunity.

Napoleon spent many days on horseback and in his coach inspecting the works and urging progress. He remained optimistic and in July 1804 wrote to Admiral Latouche Tréville in the Mediterranean, 'If we can be masters of the strait for six hours, we will be masters of the world.'[7] His visits to the ports provided him with an education in nautical affairs, which he was slow and reluctant to accept. On 20 July 1804 he was at Boulogne and ordered Admiral Bruix to send boats into the roads for a review. Bruix refused because he could see that strong winds were on the way, and the furious Napoleon threatened him with a whip then dismissed him. Rear Admiral Magon was given the task, and boats duly went out; thirteen were lost due to the storm and the actions of British warships, which were far more seaworthy in these conditions. Many more fetched up at other ports, and up to 400 men were lost. But in private Napoleon was unrepentant and wrote to his wife, 'I went to bed with all the sensations inspired by a romantic and epic dream.'

He was back in Boulogne on 25–6 August for another review. He went out to inspect his fleet and it was attacked by frigates and gun-brigs, including Captain Owen's famous *Immortalité*. The British suffered some damage, but the French were obliged to retreat into the protection of their shore batteries. The Emperor was silent about this in his correspondence, but within weeks he was planning ways to lure the great British fleets away from the region so that his own ships of the line could concentrate and take control of the Channel. And his estimate of how long would be needed was revised upwards – now he would have to be master of the seas for 45–50 days.

Napoleon's position was strengthened on 12 December when Spain declared war on Britain after an attack on her treasure frigates from Latin America. The Spanish navy gave Napoleon a substantial force of fine ships of the line, though poorly manned. It was a long-standing French policy to fit out expeditions supported by ships of the line and carrying troops to overwhelm an isolated part of the far-flung British Empire. Building on this, Napoleon conceived a series of plans, each of which involved uniting the French and Spanish fleets, while luring the British away from the scene of the action. The initial movements could be coordinated by means of the telegraph, which could send messages to and from Paris in a few minutes. But once out of the harbour each fleet had to use its own initiative without any instructions. By the plan of 29 September (before the Spanish joined the war) Admiral Villeneuve was to escape Nelson at Toulon and land troops at Surinam; Rear Admiral Missiessy would leave Rochefort and head for Martinique to take St Lucia and Dominica from the British, while a smaller expedition went to the Atlantic island of St Helena; the biggest fleet, sailing from Brest under Admiral Ganteaume, would land troops in Ireland. But there were delays due to bad weather, and Admiral Cornwallis's blockade was enough to make it impossible to escape from Brest without a fight, which Napoleon did not want. Villeneuve did leave Toulon on 18 January but was immediately struck by gales and returned. Nelson was watering his ships off Sardinia and heard the news a day later, but not that the French had turned back. Repeating his voyage that had led to the battle of the Nile, he sailed eastward to Egypt. This left a huge gap in the British defences, but the French lacked the intelligence to exploit it, and Nelson was back on station by the end of February. Missiessy was the only French commander who was able to sail successfully. He arrived in the West Indies on 22 February but was ill by this time, as were many of his crews, and they achieved little.

Villeneuve sailed again on 30 March while Nelson was watering. Again the British admiral lacked information, and this time he patrolled off Sardinia until on 18 April he heard that the French were off Gibraltar. He deduced correctly that Villeneuve was heading across the Atlantic and set off in pursuit, a month behind. In the meantime there was political paralysis in Britain, as Melville was impeached and there was a vacuum at the Admiralty until Barham took charge. Off Cadiz, Sir John Orde's squadron was scattered and failed to send frigates to warn Nelson of the enemy movements. Villeneuve picked up one French and six Spanish ships to add to his force and went on his way. But meanwhile the squadrons at Ferrol, Rochefort and Brest were unable to sail. With one large Franco-Spanish fleet at large and with unknown intentions, and with Nelson's fleet out of communication with the rest of the world as it crossed the Atlantic, there was a feeling on both sides that the invasion crisis was at last close to a climax. In London, Benjamin Silliman observed:

> The alarm of invasion is now more active than ever, and the government have contributed to it not a little, by ordering all officers and soldiers absent from their respective corps, and every volunteer to be ready at a moment's warning; should he step out of his own house, he is directed to leave a card specifying where he may be found. The regiments of volunteers muster every morning, and the whole island is in a state of vigilance, activity and solicitude.[8]

Nelson made good time chasing Villeneuve across the Atlantic, and on 4 June he arrived at the British base on Barbados, while Villeneuve was 100 miles away at Martinique. There was every prospect of a great battle in the West Indies, except that Nelson heard a false report that the French were heading for Trinidad. He sailed south, while Villeneuve went north and then headed back to Europe. As soon as he knew this, Nelson sent the fast frigate *Curieux* home with the news, while taking his own fleet back to station in the Mediterranean. Captain Bettesworth of the *Curieux* sighted the French in the distance – crossing the Atlantic by a more northerly route than would be expected if they were heading back to the

Mediterranean. He reported this to Barham when he reached London. There was just time to put together a fleet off Cape Finisterre at the north-west corner of Spain. On 23 July, Admiral Sir Robert Calder sighted Villeneuve's forces in the distance. He had a force of fifteen ships of the line against the enemy's twenty, but British admirals were expected to take on odds like that. For once he was against an enemy who had some experience at sea, though not in battle. There ensued a confused action in fog and darkness during which Calder captured two ships of the line. He thought he had done rather well, hinting that he might be rewarded, perhaps 'deserving of any mark of royal bounty'. Such a victory might have been acclaimed ten years ago, but in the meantime Nelson had raised the standards. Calder was to face the contempt of public opinion for not crushing the enemy, and eventually a court martial. In reality he had put a stop to Napoleon's plan and scored a great strategic victory, if it was only a mediocre tactical one. When Nelson returned to European waters it was clear that Napoleon's plan had failed. Meanwhile, his government faced financial crisis and an accumulation of enemies in Eastern Europe. On 26 August the camp at Boulogne was vacated as the troops marched off to fight Austria and Russia.

On his arrival in Britain, Nelson feared that might face criticism for failing to defeat the French, but he need not have worried, for more than ever he was a popular hero. He spent three weeks of romantic bliss with Lady Hamilton in his home at Merton south of London. This was interrupted when news arrived of a new enemy concentration. After Calder's action, Villeneuve had entered the Spanish port of Ferrol, where he had picked up more Spanish ships. Then he had taken his ships south to Cadiz, joining the ships already there to create a huge Combined Fleet of around 40 ships of the line. This needed to be watched, and Nelson was given command of a new British force building up off the port.

He arrived on station on 28 September in his flagship *Victory*. He kept his ships of the line out of sight of the coast, so that the enemy would not know how many he had, and used frigates to inform him of enemy movements. He might have had to wait for years if the French had decided to stay put as they usually did, but Villeneuve was goaded by Napoleon's aspersions on his character and ability and began to move out on 19 October. Nelson was ready, and around midday on the 21st, the two fleets met in battle.

The Battle of Trafalgar is subject to myths, like any other. It did not settle the issue of an invasion – that had already been decided when Napoleon marched east. The French and Spanish sailed into battle with no hopes of victory, though they had 33 ships of the line to Nelson's 27. Nelson's new and daring tactics were known as the 'Nelson Touch', but in fact he used very little of the plan he had outlined to his captains before the battle. He attacked in two columns, and the one led by his old friend Cuthbert Collingwood entered the action first. There was fierce fighting, and Nelson was mortally wounded by a sniper from *Bucentaure* but lived long enough to know that he had won a great victory – 20 enemy ships were captured or destroyed, but most of the prizes were lost in the storm that followed the battle.

It was not the end of any threat of invasion, but now it seemed very unlikely, even though the French defeated the Austrians and Russians at Austerlitz on 2 December. Pitt died on January 1806, and Europe settled down to a long period of war. Napoleon tried to impose his Continental System on Europe, forbidding all ports to trade with Britain. This caused much resentment and led eventually to revolts in Spain and Portugal. These set in motion the Peninsular War in which British land forces became seriously engaged on the continent again under the supremely competent Arthur Wellesley, later Duke of Wellington. But Napoleon's downfall only came after he invaded Russia in 1812 and lost thousands of troops in the winter snows, triggering a catastrophic war against almost all the crowned heads of Europe. As always, Britain needed allies to fight a continental war but ended on the winning side.

But supposing, somehow, Napoleon had succeeded in landing a viable force in southern England? General Dumouriez informed the British authorities of a plan that had been made in 1779, when the French and Spanish had control of the English Channel during the war with America. Forces would land at Rye and Hythe on either side of Romney Marsh and then take the heights around Appledore, where they would spend up to a week consolidating. They would march on in three main columns, one of 12,000 men heading for Goudhurst and Tonbridge, the main one of 20,000 men for Biddenden and Coxheath, and the third of 8,000 men passing through various villages on the way to Rochester. The army would reunite south of Dartford for its final march on London. It was hoped peace might be made on Blackheath, then on the south-east outskirts of London. If not, the army would form a line four miles long from Forest Hill to Deptford for its march into the city. All this assumed little action by the British forces. Dumouriez had to admit that now 'the English are better prepared to counter attack', but he took no account of the fortifications being built around Romney Marsh or those preventing a Medway crossing at Rochester.

William James imagined the final showdown taking place on Blackheath, this time a battle rather than a surrender.[9] It is difficult to be certain what would have happened there, if the navy had ever allowed the troops to land and the rest of the army had let them get that far. The quality and tactics of the British were rather uneven, between the highly efficient light infantry and the rigid, over-detailed training of some regiments of the line under their dilettante officers, not to mention the effects of the volunteers and irregular troops. Dumouriez had learned something about British preparations since 1779 and wrote 25 years later:

> I refuse to believe that an enemy could ever get near enough to the Metropolis when the whole of England was up in arms; when patriotism was firing one of the bravest nations in Europe; and when that nation was fighting for all it held most dear and most sacred.

THE RESOLUTION, 1940

Hitler was just as surprised as Napoleon when he found it necessary to plan an invasion of Britain. When they found themselves in possession the whole European coastline from the Spanish border to the Arctic Circle, the Germans were not ready to complete the job by invading Britain. They had not expected such an quick and easy victory in

393

France. Even after France fell, they had not expected Britain to resist for long, and some elements in Britain as high as Cabinet level were ready to do a deal in the face of defeat. Indeed, in November 1939, when the Kriegsmarine began planning for an invasion, it had seemed a rather remote contingency.[10]

Britain had enjoyed a certain amount of respite after Dunkirk while the Germans completed the conquest of France, a Franco-German armistice being signed on 22 June conceding all the northern and western coastlines to German occupation. The Royal Navy crippled the French Mediterranean Fleet at Oran to prevent the ships falling into enemy hands – an operation carried out with very heavy hearts and only justified by the gravest necessity. Churchill made it clear that there was no prospect of making any arrangement with Germany by his speech to the House of Commons on 18 June:

> Hitler knows that he will have to break us in this island or lose the war. If we can stand up to him, all Europe may be free, and the life of the world may move forward into broad, sunlit uplands; but if we fail then the whole world, including the United States, and all that we have known and cared for, will sink into the abyss of a new dark age made more sinister, and perhaps more prolonged, by the lights of a perverted science. Let us therefore brace ourselves to our duty and so bear ourselves that if the British Commonwealth and Empire lasts for a thousand years, men will still say, 'This was their finest hour.'[11]

Hitler had no conception of the revulsion and horror that his policies created in the rest of the world and could not believe that the British would resist now that the war seemed lost. The Luftwaffe and the German navy began to turn towards their attack on Britain, and both services believed they could conceivably defeat the country on their own. U-boats were already attacking shipping in the Western Approaches to Britain, though they were very weak in numbers. There were never more than forty of them available for service during that summer, and sometimes as few as twenty, but the British had very few convoy escorts – an average of two per convoy, mostly old destroyers or converted trawlers. During July to October the U-boats sank 73 ships in convoys and 144 outside convoy. This amounted to more than 600,000 tons of shipping, not yet enough to bring Britain to heel, but an indication of what could be done with a larger U-boat force. This could have a long-term effect on the invasion plan, if Hitler was patient enough to wait for Britain to be starved of food and fuel; but patience was not one of Hitler's strengths. The other effect was to divert a large number of destroyers and other vessels for convoy escort in Atlantic waters, so that they would not be available to stop the first wave of an invasion fleet. Those between convoys at their bases in the Clyde or Liverpool could be brought into action in a day or two. It was not policy to escort merchant ships all the way across the Atlantic, but those farthest out might take a week to get back home if called upon.

The Luftwaffe began its air offensive against Britain in rather desultory fashion, with small night raids on towns from South Wales to Aberdeen, followed at the beginning of July with daylight attacks on ports and inland towns. Later the British came to date 10 July as the start of the major attack, though it was a case of a gradual acceleration rather than a sudden change of gear. After that date the German bombers concentrated mostly on shipping and ports on the English Channel, and soon they would greatly reduce the effectiveness of London as a port. On 14 July the BBC Radio commentator Charles Gardner watched a fight over the Strait of Dover:

> There's one going down in flames. Somebody's hit a German and he's coming down with a long streak – coming down completely out of control – a long streak of smoke – and now a man's baled out by parachute. He's a Junkers 87, and he's going slap into the sea – and there he goes. SMASH! A terrific column of water and there was a Junkers 87.[12]

On 7 July, Hitler turned his attention to the invasion of Britain and directed the chiefs of staff of the three services to begin planning. The army was to estimate British land strength and the capacity of German coastal batteries, the navy was to find possible landing places and sea routes and discover what shipping was available throughout Germany and occupied Europe. The Luftwaffe was to work out the chances of attaining air supremacy and to assess the effects of a possible parachute landing. Together the services were to evolve 'a plan for the transport for the maximum number of troops with a minimum of shipping and aircraft space'. But for the moment, 'All preparations must be undertaken on the basis that the invasion is still only a plan, and has not yet been decided upon.' It was still agreed between Hitler and Raeder, the head of the navy, that invasion should be 'a last resort to force Britain to sue for peace'.[13]

Hitler issued slightly more decisive orders in his Directive No. 16 of 16 July 1940:

> As England [sic], in spite of the hopelessness of her military position, has so far shown herself unwilling to come to any compromise, I have decided to begin to prepare for, and if necessary carry out, an invasion of England.[14]

Both the timing and the wording are significant. It was not issued until midway through July, by which time the invasion season of summer was halfway over, and the British had already gone through the first phase of their defensive preparations – it was three days before Ironside was replaced by Brooke and the period of stop lines was over. And the wording was unusually hesitant for a dictator whose style was usually peremptory, to say the least. It was only to be carried out 'if necessary', as a last resort if all else failed. Hitler's bluffs had succeeded so often in the past, from the occupation of the Rhineland to the taking over of Czechoslovakia. The British, he believed, had nothing material to gain by fighting on, and in his view they were racially almost akin to the Germans. They had their great empire overseas and no need for one in Europe. Obviously Churchill was a barrier to this, but he could be overthrown as easily as his predecessor had been from within his party.

Moreover, Hitler was already moving towards an even more momentous and far less ambiguous decision. In August he ordered the planning for Operation 'Barbarossa', the invasion of the Soviet Union. It seemed to have many advantages. It would mostly rely on the army, the most successful of the German armed forces. It would open up vast supplies of food and oil, which Germany desperately needed. And it fitted well with Nazi racial and political theories – that Slavs were inferior and Bolshevism must be eliminated.

Meanwhile the orders to the army, navy and air force commanders for the invasion of Britain were that the RAF must be 'eliminated to such an extent that it will be incapable of putting up any substantial opposition to the invading troops'. Both flanks of the invasion area were to be mined to prevent naval intervention, though that was far easier in the narrow waters of the Strait of Dover than on the much longer line from Alderney to Portland; and heavy coastal guns were to support the front, though it is difficult to see how they would have made much difference.

There was no doubt about the army's ability to defeat Britain on land. It was greatly superior in numbers, training, morale, self-confidence and tactical doctrine. The escape of the British Expeditionary Force from Dunkirk was unfortunate – it meant that Britain now had some kind of army to oppose the invasion – but it had lost practically all its equipment, and its morale was shattered. No one on either side of the Channel doubted that if the Germans could land in equal strength, they would beat the British army. The air force was numerically stronger than the RAF, though not as much as British intelligence and myth tended to believe. It was roughly equal in the quality of its fighters and bombers though, of course, completely dominant in dive-bombers, which might play a crucial role in the war by land and sea. It had an effective paratrooper force, though that had suffered heavy losses during the recent campaign. But paratroopers could never win a campaign on their own. There were not enough of them, they had no heavy weapons and equipment, and they had also lost the advantage of surprise since Belgium.

The bulk of the invasion force would have to come by sea, and this was the weak link in the plan. As always, it was the navy that had to make the greatest changes to support an invasion. The army would face an uncomfortable and dangerous journey across the sea, after which it would fight as usual, perhaps with some limitations on its equipment. The air force would support it with reconnaissance, with fighter defence, with strategic bombing in advance of the landing, with attacks on enemy shipping and military forces, but these were jobs that the air force had always trained for. The navy would have to build or convert a whole new force of landing craft out of nothing, for conventional warships were too deep in draught to operate on the beaches, and in any case they were few in number and desperately needed for their real work, fighting enemy naval forces. The Germans had no tradition of amphibious warfare, except for a raid on the Russian island of Osel in 1917, in the sheltered and tideless waters of the Baltic. They did not have the British experience of countless colonial landings over the years, or the Gallipoli invasion, and their success in Norway was against a totally unprepared nation. They had done almost nothing to develop landing craft and had to find what they could during the remains of the summer and autumn of 1940. Already by 19 July, Raeder was complaining: 'The task allotted to the Navy in operation 'Sea Lion' is out of all proportion to the Navy's strength and bears no relation to the tasks that are set to the army and the Air Force.'[15]

However, there existed a resource in the large numbers of merchant ships captured in Europe, which were largely redundant now that occupied Europe was blockaded. These could be adapted to carry troops and vehicles, though they could not land them on beaches. They might load them into more specialized landing craft just off the beaches, or wait until a port had been captured or constructed. There was no lack of ideas, and floating bunkers, hydrofoils and airscrew-powered vessels were all tested without any success. A total of 174 merchant ships were taken over and converted. Most were cargo ships and were fitted with extra bulkheads, straw sacks for the passengers to sleep on and hatches and horse stalls. There was no time to modify the derricks, so conventional ships' boats would have to land the troops, since they were not designed for beaching. Some could be landed in fast eight-man assault boats, though there were never enough of these. Others would be loaded into the barges, which travelled independently, after each had discharged its own load. The merchant ships were armed by the navy, which mounted anti-aircraft guns, and by the army, which fitted field guns. Fast passenger vessels were also taken over, mainly for the diversionary expedition to the north.

The bulk of the invasion fleet would be carried in the numerous flat-bottomed barges that were to be found in the continental waterways. They were not designed for the open sea, and their withdrawal from normal use for any length of time would disrupt the transport system and therefore the war economy. About half of them were unpowered and would have to be towed. The general plan was for a tug to pull one powered and one unpowered barge on the voyage to the beaches, a journey of perhaps 30 hours at slow speed. They came in a great variety of shapes and sizes, built by a great number of private contractors and often for specialized use in a particular canal. The navy agreed that the invasion fleet would have a 'singular composition ... Large numbers of slow, unwieldy transport units concentrated in a small space, mixed with motor boats of the most varied types, and escorted by light units of the Navy and auxiliary vessels ...'[16]

The biggest snag was that they had no means of landing troops and vehicles on beaches. The British had already developed landing craft with bow ramps integral to the design, which allowed vehicles or a platoon of troops to be discharged in seconds. The Germans did not risk interrupting the integrity of the bow by this system. They tried other systems, including one in which a vehicle would have to go up one ramp to cross the bow, then down another into the water. Some craft used a two-part ramp that folded out flat; in others the ramp had to be constructed by troops in the water after beaching. A long ramp might be extended out from the bows, but it took up a great deal of space on deck. There was also the portal ramp, which was lowered by an overhanging crane. Some barges needed an engineer team of sixteen men just to set up the ramp, in addition to the normal crew. Because of the height of the bow, all the ramps were very long to let the vehicle into the water at a suitable angle. All relied on the craft being firmly aground during the whole process of unloading. Vehicles that were not waterproofed, including most of the motor transport, would have to wait for the tide to go out a little more, so that they could have a dry run ashore.

German forces ashore relied heavily on their tanks, and it was essential to find ways of landing them. Lighter vehicles such as the Panzer II could be converted to float, but their operational value was small. The Panzer III and IV were converted to travel underwater after being lowered by a crane. Tests in June and July showed that it could

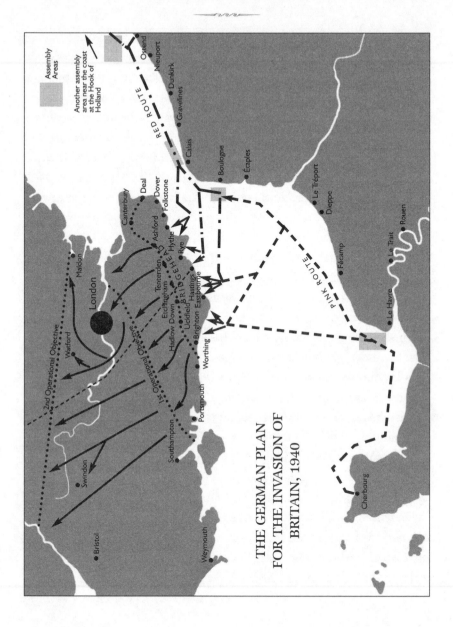

THE GERMAN PLAN
FOR THE INVASION OF
BRITAIN, 1940

work reasonably well in fair weather up to 7 metres deep, but they had to keep moving if they were not to sink into the sand. A tank could not stop to let others to catch up, or if it came against natural or artificial obstructions. Four armoured divisions were set up using these tanks. Later experience, including the loss of many DD swimming tanks during the Allied invasion of Normandy four years later suggest that not many of the submersible panzers would have survived in moderately bad weather; and, unlike the DDs in Normandy, these were to provide a large proportion of the invasion force, not just its first wave.

During the voyage over it had to be accepted that, 'The Army cannot count on keeping the divisions together.'[17] Crews were inexperienced, navigation was likely to be confused, and attacks by ships and aircraft would break it up so that each barge would have to be ready to take the initiative. Even if the formation was intact, it was expected to turn at right-angles off the beach in question, then approach it in as tight a formation as possible. Very few of the barge crews were experienced, and some were sailors from the Baltic or the canals who had never had to deal with cross-tides, which might be about two knots in the conditions to be expected, perhaps with the leeway caused by the wind to be added to that. Such tides caused great difficulties during the Normandy landings in 1944, despite many years of training, and they would have caused the invading forces to be separated, with many landing on the wrong beach.

Great dangers had to be accepted on landing. The ideal time to land was two hours after high tide, with the water level falling.

A landing at low tide has the disadvantage of rising water during the disembarkation, but the advantage that vessels which have run aground will float again. A landing at high tide has the disadvantage that craft are grounded and immobile for about twelve hours until the next high tide, and if the next high tide does not reach the level of the previous one, it may not even float then. Rising water is unfavourable in any case at the time of landing, since it causes transport units which are aground to float again and again, thus altering their position and delaying the disembarkation. The first requirement, therefore, is a time when the water is ebbing, about two hours after high tide.[18]

The transports would need a considerable time to unload. To arrive at two hours after high water would mean that the vessel was grounded for at least eight hours until the tide lifted it off again. During this time it would be highly vulnerable to land, sea and air attack, and it is unfortunate that the British did not realize what an opportunity they would miss here. A naval or aerial bombardment on beached barges could have been devastating. They would have had no chance to evade it – and, unlike at sea, a near-miss was almost as good as a hit.

The first wave allowed for 26,800 troops in the eastern landing, 13,400 between Bexhill and Eastbourne and 21,100 west of Beachy Head, all isolated and unable to support one another. Between them they would have very little artillery and 250 tanks, assuming all of them landed, which was highly unlikely. Planning for the second wave was very sketchy. It would take several days to get the ships and barges back to pick up more troops, with severe delays at both ends. And one major snag of the south-east coast as a landing area was that it had no major ports, either natural or artificial. West of Beachy Head there was Newhaven, a small ferry port. There was nothing east of Beachy Head except the ancient and silted up harbour of Rye. At the very edge of the landing area was Folkestone, a ferry port that was unlikely to be captured intact. If it was, it could perhaps have unloaded 600 tons of supplies a day, barely enough to support one division, not to mention the problem of transporting it along the front just inland from the coast. Of course, Dover was only a few miles away and had more extensive facilities, but it was likely to be fiercely defended, with guns mounted on the heights on both sides dominating the harbour below, and directed by Admiral Ramsay of Dunkirk fame.

Apart from the lack of invasion vessels and experience, the German surface fleet was greatly under strength during the second half of 1940. It was outnumbered locally by about five to one by the British. U-boats were few, but they were expected to protect the flanks of the landing. Minefields were also to be laid. It was possible that one across the twenty miles of the Strait of Dover could have been laid in time, but the other flank was about a hundred miles long and with much deep water where conventional mining was difficult. And the German Navy had no plans to defend the minefields if British minesweepers led their fleet through it, as they inevitably would.

THE END OF INVASION

There was a wide divergence between the initial army and navy plans for the invasion of Britain. The army wanted separate forces to set out from Cherbourg, Le Havre and the Channel Ports. They wanted a landing 'on a broad front extending approximately from Ramsgate to a point West of the Isle of Wight',[19] with landings at Lyme Bay, Selsea Bill to Brighton, and Eastbourne to Dover. The navy objected that this would take up too much shipping and that the landings in the west would be too exposed. Acrimonious debate ensued during the first two weeks of August. On the 7th, General Halder, Chief of the Army General staff, stated: 'I utterly reject the Navy's proposal; from the point of view of the Army I regard their proposal as complete suicide. I might just as well put the troops that have been landed straight through the sausage machine.'[20] A landing west of the Isle of Wight was dropped, but that was not enough for the navy. On the 14th the Chief of Naval Staff asserted that, 'Simultaneous landing operations near Brighton in the west and Deal in the east cannot be carried out. The likelihood that even the first landing will be successful, not to speak of subsequent reinforcements, is so small as to make the attempt unjustifiable.'[21] Eventually a compromise plan was agreed on the 16th. Area 'A', around Deal, was dropped from the plan. Elements of the Sixteenth Army would land on either side of Romney Marsh in areas 'B' and 'C', as Napoleon would have done in 1803–5. Another would land in Area 'D' around Eastbourne, exactly the Martello Tower coast that had been identified as the site of invasion 135 years earlier. There would be a diversionary operation to the north, when four transports and warships would leave Norway and head for the British coast between Aberdeen and Newcastle. But controversially the western and eastern operations remained on the agenda. There was to be a 'simultaneous landing of four to five thousand troops at Brighton by motor-boats and the same number of airborne troops at Deal–Ramsgate'.[22]

Contrary to what the British authorities believed, there was never any plan to invade on the east coast. The Germans preferred the short sea route for the actual assault, and that meant sending large numbers of barges through the Strait of Dover in preparation. Their problems in doing that were greatly overestimated by the British, an issue that was highlighted a year and half later when the Germans were able to get the battlecruisers *Scharnhorst* and *Gneisenau* through against strong air opposition.

The other difference between the army and the navy was over the timing of the landing. Initially the army wanted it to be at dawn, to give the maximum cover to the final approach and allow a full day's operations in daylight. The navy objected to this, for it was possible that the British fleet in the Firth of Forth might come south under cover of darkness, avoiding detection by German patrols and radar – it might be off the Strait of Dover first thing in the morning. On the other hand, 'If the crossing is made by day, air reconnaissance can locate the position of enemy naval forces. The operation would be stopped if necessary.'[23] By 14 September the army's 'stubborn resistance' to this was dropped because 'the front-line generals, like the Navy, are opposed to a night crossing'.[24] Moreover, from the air force's point of view, if there really was air superiority, the dive-bomber could operate in daylight to destroy the enemy fleet.

It was obvious that the plan was only possible with air supremacy over Britain, not just air superiority. According to a noted air historian, 'air superiority was to be measured by the extent of the gap between strategic desirability and tactical feasibility. When the two were separated by the weather alone, a state of air supremacy, or command of the air, existed.'[25] It was necessary for the Luftwaffe to win this before the invasion of Britain could even begin, but it did not have long before winter. Apart from the weather, the plan had to be put into effect before the British could recover from defeat in France. As Ironside and Brooke reorganized and re-equipped the British army and prepared defences in their different ways, the gap between British and German strength on the ground began slowly to narrow.

The air assault on Britain was ordered for 5 August, but there were several delays due to bad weather. 'Adler Tag', or 'Eagle Day', was 13 August, when the Luftwaffe began its campaign to eliminate the RAF. Formations of bombers were escorted by Bf 109s, and the less effective 110s. There was some success, as with attacks on the Kentish aerodromes of Manston, Lympne and Hawkinge. Six radar stations were also bombed. Only the one at Ventnor on the Isle of Wight was put out of action, but that created a ten-day gap. Further attacks on radar stations might have been decisive, but they never came. Later in the day there were attacks on airfields in Essex and south-central England. But the RAF could claim a victory in the air. It believed it had shot down 78 enemy aircraft, but in fact it had destroyed only half that number. On the other hand, it had only lost fifteen of its own aircraft and seven pilots, so the results were definitely in its favour. This was a pattern that was to be repeated over the next month. The fight intensified on 15 August, when the Luftwaffe launched a record 1,786 sorties, including ill-fated raids on the north of England. By the 19th it was clear that raids on aircraft factories were difficult to execute well, and it was decided to send strongly escorted formations of bombers with a view to luring Fighter Command into the skies, while at the same time attacking the sector stations, which had the control facilities.

This was beginning to have some effect, and Fighter Command was under serious pressure when on the 24th one German aircraft bombed London against Hitler's orders. Bomber Command attacked Berlin the following night, with consequences that were more moral than material. As the American journalist William Shirer reported, 'The Berliners are stunned. They did not think this could ever happen. When this war began Göring assured them it couldn't ... they believed him.'[26] Hitler's response, against the advice of Göring, was a sustained attack on London. This was the final stage on what became known as the 'Battle of Britain'. Churchill had first originated the phrase, as he did with so many. But when he said to Parliament on 18 June, 'the "Battle of France" is over. I expect the Battle of Britain is about to begin', he was thinking about a full-scale invasion attempt, not a series of air battles over southern England, which is what the term came to mean.

Meanwhile the German High Command was more indecisive than ever. On the crucial date of 11 September, Hitler postponed his decision for three more days. He apparently wavered on the 13th and planned to call it off. The Chiefs of Staff conferred with him on the 14th, and he decided not to cancel it completely: 'If operation "Sea Lion" were called off now, British morale would be lifted and our air attacks would be easier to bear.'[27] The Luftwaffe had a bad day over Britain on the 15th, and two days later the naval War Diary contained the entry, 'The enemy Air Force is by no means defeated; on the contrary it shows increasing activity. The weather situation as a whole does not permit us to expect a period of calm ... the Führer therefore decides to postpone "Sea Lion" indefinitely.'[28] RAF bombing was beginning to have some effect on the barges in the invasion ports, and their absence from their usual duties was beginning to affect the economy. Finally, on 12 October it was decided to cancel the operation until the following spring at the earliest. Meanwhile, plans for Barbarossa were already advanced, and there is no sign that the army used the winter to do much training in amphibious warfare. When spring did come, large German forces were already committed to the Mediterranean theatre. In May the paratroop arm was devastated during the invasion of Crete. The superb new battleship *Bismarck* was finally ready and might have played a decisive part in covering an invasion. Instead she was expended on a sortie into the Atlantic.

Having suffered unacceptable losses by day, the German bomber offensive was carried out by night – London was a very easy target to find from the north coast of France, and the Germans had radio aids to help with the bombing of cities such as Coventry. It was the beginning of what the British called the 'Blitz', a shortening of 'blitzkrieg', or 'lighting war'. The name was appropriate in that it represented destruction from the sky, but otherwise it had little in common with the original. The blitzkrieg combined the air force with all branches of the army – the Blitz involved the air force alone on the German side. And the Blitz was a rather slow means of attack, far from a lightning war. It was far less effective than the Germans hoped and the British feared.

Before the war they had planned for a quarter of a million casualties in the first week, and 1.2 million over six weeks. In fact, Britain suffered a total of 22,000 killed and 28,000 admitted to hospital as a result of bombing during the second half of 1940. The Blitz did not do serious damage to the British war economy, and it did not break the morale of the people. In fact, it showed that bombing was more likely to increase the determination of the victims than to break their spirit, a lesson that political and military leaders do not seem to have fully learned, even today.

The events of the summer and autumn had great effect in the United States, which Churchill knew was crucial to winning the war. In November, Ambassador Joseph Kennedy's remark that 'democracy is finished in England' ruined his career. His countryman Ed Murrow had already told his radio listeners:

> If the people who rule Britain are made of the same stuff as the little people I have seen today … then the defense of Britain will be something which men speak of with awe and admiration as long as the English language survives.[29]

Before the Battle of Britain was resolved, Churchill and Roosevelt had agreed on the 'destroyers for bases' deal by which Britain gained fifty obsolete and rather ineffective ships. But they had great symbolism, and it was a daring act for a neutral nation. On 5 November, as the Blitz dragged on, Roosevelt was re-elected president with a large majority and soon agreed on the 'lend-lease' scheme of sending huge quantities of supplies to Britain. The bombing of London, covered by Murrow's evocative broadcasts, did much to bring American public opinion behind Britain.

What might have happened next if Hitler had proceeded? When the Western Allies landed in Normandy in June 1944, they had spent four years developing suitable landing craft, which they did with great ingenuity. They had already mounted landings in North Africa and Italy as well as the Pacific. They achieved complete tactical surprise, for the enemy was misled about both the date and the place of the landings, so much so that Rommel took the opportunity to have some leave at exactly the wrong time. The German army was immeasurably more formidable than the British one had been in 1940, but the Allies had the benefit of heavy bombing of the region and a naval bombardment of the beaches. Yet the invasion was no pushover. There were heavy losses on 'Omaha' Beach and much confusion on the other four, which would have been exploited by any counterattack. Invading a country by sea was far more difficult than Hitler and his generals could conceive in 1940, though his admirals had some idea of the problems.

14

COULD IT HAVE HAPPENED?

Did Napoleon and Hitler really mean it? Both were used to quick and startling victories, to kicking on open doors and finding that the whole house came tumbling down. Napoleon had fought some very hard battles, for example at Marengo against the Austrians in 1800, but in general the regimes opposed to him in continental Europe were antiquated and ripe for defeat or overthrow; Hitler had no experience of serious opposition. In both cases their plans for invasion were highly optimistic, but that is partly because neither was familiar with the particular problems (and opportunities) of sea warfare. In both cases there is a good deal of ambiguity about what they really meant, but Napoleon was more committed to the idea than Hitler. He had more than two years with no other major campaign to fight, and only came to realize the difficulties very slowly. He spent huge amounts of money, not just on the craft of the invasion flotilla but on building the ports to launch it. He spent many days travelling round the invasion ports. His Grande Armée was kept unoccupied on the cliff of Boulogne for all that period, a very expensive way to mount a mere threat. Hitler, on the other hand, already had plans for a very different invasion, even before the attempt on Britain reached a climax – a triumphal parade through London in 1940 would have been even more heady than his one through Paris that summer, but his real object was several thousand miles away, in Moscow. He was an opportunist to the core, and any sign of British weakness would have been exploited to the full, but he believed he did not need to defeat Britain for the moment. That does not mean he was not serious. His constant vacillations during September suggest that he was reluctant to let go of the idea, though they tended to reduce his standing in the eyes of his chiefs of staff.

Like Trafalgar, the Battle of Britain is the subject of a great deal of myth. The Luftwaffe was never as strong as British intelligence calculated, or the press reported. German losses were also overstated, though in fact they were considerable. But it was not that which caused the Germans to lose: it was their mistaken decision to switch to the bombing of British cities. This was just the kind of policy that air marshals like Trenchard and Portal approved of, but it was also what removed any possibility that the RAF would be defeated, and effectively it ended the prospect of invasion.

Could they ever have succeeded? Napoleon almost certainly not, for there was never any likelihood of luring enough British forces away to give him superiority in the English Channel, and a major French victory at sea was almost inconceivable. The French plans relied very heavily on good weather in the Channel, but that cannot be relied on even with modern forecasting. At best an invasion at any time in 1803–5 would have been a huge gamble against great odds; at worst it would have been a catastrophe for the French army and navy. There was never any real prospect of the French finding another way to weaken the British seriously enough to make an invasion possible. Unlike the Germans they could not hope to get at them by blockade or air attack.

Could the Germans have succeeded with any plan in existence during the summer and autumn of 1940? Operation 'Sea Lion' was tested during an exercise in the Royal Military College at Sandhurst in 1973, using some of the original participants. There were severe time constraints on the landing. It was planned at high tide, but had to be done after the Luftwaffe had achieved a certain degree of air superiority and a sufficient number of barges had been assembled, but before winter closed in. The first wave was therefore launched on the night of 22 September. They suffered only light losses on the way over, while the Royal Navy lost a cruiser and three destroyers in exchange for three destroyers. The advanced elements of nine divisions landed on beaches between Rottingdean, near Brighton, and Folkestone, while parachutists took the airfield at Lympne in Kent. As there were only three British divisions in Kent, and the Home Guard was not yet fully equipped, resistance was light. The RAF flew a thousand sorties that morning, using bombers, fighters and even trainers fitted with bombs. They had some success, as the Luftwaffe was constrained by the short range of its Bf 109s.

The Germans had still not captured a major port – only the small one of Newhaven – and air attacks made it increasingly difficult to unload ships on the beaches. Their forces headed towards Folkestone against some resistance and the port was only captured after it had largely been immobilized. At sea, a diversionary naval sortie from Norway in the direction of northern Britain was completely destroyed. British cruisers entered the Channel, but two of them were sunk by coastal guns, Stukas and E-boats. Overall the Germans had already lost a quarter of their scarce barges during the first day, partly because they were very unseaworthy.

The RAF lost a quarter of its strength during the morning of the 23rd, while the Home Fleet massed its forces of cruisers and battleships. The Luftwaffe also suffered heavy losses in fighters and bombers but the 22nd Division was air-landed at Lympne to augment the forces in Kent, and fight off a counterattack by New Zealanders. Meanwhile the first counterattacks began, and an advance on Hastings was beaten off by the 42nd Division, while the Australians recaptured Newhaven, increasing the German supply problem.

The air battle continued in the afternoon of the 23rd as the Luftwaffe put up its maximum strength and the RAF concentrated on attacking ships and airfields. The navy still kept the battleships of the Home Fleet out of air range, but within the invasion area it had 17 cruisers and 57 destroyers, far superior to the German strength. The German force at Le Havre put to sea with three of the remaining destroyers and 14 E-boats but was wiped out. There were now elements of ten German divisions ashore in England, but most of them were incomplete and the supply problem became increasingly desperate. That evening the Führer held a conference in which there were bitter disputes between the navy and the army, who wanted more troops sent over despite bad weather and heavy naval losses. It was decided to launch another wave of troops across the Strait of Dover on the night of the 23rd/24th, though with the short notice they could not land before dawn, and the divisions supplied from Le Havre could not be reinforced at all. At daybreak the British 5th Destroyer Flotilla found the invaders ten miles off the coast and attacked them to great effect as a huge air battle developed overhead. Two-thirds of the German barges were sunk; the few ships that reached Folkestone could only unload very slowly.

By this time the British divisions had moved into the area from the north and west, and the landing forces were isolated, with only two to seven days' ammunition left. There was no hope of advance or reinforcement. It was decided to evacuate. With British naval superiority, there was no chance of another Dunkirk and only 15,000 of the 90,000 men who landed were saved. These were not huge numerical losses for the army, but its image of invincibility was severely dented, while the Luftwaffe was shattered. Germany was far from being defeated, but it is doubtful if an invasion of Russia would have been practicable for some years.

The invasion plan was deeply flawed and it is difficult to see how it could have succeeded against any determined resistance. This is not to say that the Germans could never have invaded Britain. Hitler might have had a chance if the attacks on the RAF had continued longer and the U-boat arm had been built up to cause more pressure on resources. That was not likely to happen during 1940, and patience was not a Nazi virtue. By 1941, Hitler had other plans. Both Napoleon and Hitler reacted in the same way to their failure to invade Britain – by implying that it was never a serious plan in the first place, and by turning eastwards. In both cases it was eventually their downfall.

NOTES

1. The Threat

1 *The Churchill War Papers,* ed. Martin Gilbert, vol II, *Never Surrender,* London, 1994, p. 247

2 Quoted in Karol Kulik, *Alexander Korda,* London, 1975, p. 251

3 *The Complete Works of George Orwell,* ed. Peter Davison, vol 12, *A Patriot After All,* London, 1998, pp. 120–1

4 *Churchill War Papers,* vol III, *The Ever-Widening War,* London, 2000, p. 620

5 *The Oxford Dictionary of Quotations,* Oxford, 1996, pp. 489–90

6 Ibid., p. 339

7 George Orwell, *Collected Essays and Journalism,* vol 1, *At an Age Like This,* 1968, p. 491

8 Paul Deichmann, *Luftwaffe Operations in Support of the Army,* London, 1996, p. 28

9 *Conway's All the World's Fighting Ships, 1922–1946,* London, 1980, p. 220. But figures from other German sources vary.

2. The British

1 The History of Parliament, vol III, *The House of Commons 1790–1820,* London, 1986, p. 636

2 Benjamin Silliman, *Journal of Travels in England, Holland and Scotland,* vol 1, Newhaven, Connecticut, 1812, p. 210

3 National Portrait Gallery, London, no 1075

4 Christopher Lloyd, *The British Seaman,* London, 1968, p. 284

5 Silliman, op. cit., vol I, p. 297

6 Jane Austen, *Pride and Prejudice,* 1813, reprinted London, 1995, pp. 315–16

7 Thomas Malthus, *An Essay on the Principle of Population,* 1798 reprinted Mineola, New York, 2007, p. 193

8 Jane Austen, *Mansfield Park,* 1814, reprinted London, 1996, p. 77

9 Silliman, op. cit., vol I, p. 307

10 J. C. Sainty, *Office Holders in Modern Britain,* vol IV, Admiralty Officials, London, 1975, pp. 47, 41

11 William Marshall, *The Review and Abstracts of the County Reports to the Board of Agriculture,* vol 5, reprinted New York, 1968, p. 383

12 Ibid., p. 80

13 Ibid., p. 77

14 Ibid., p. 82

15 Ibid., p. 64

16 Navy Records Society, vol 119, *Manning Pamphlets,* ed. J. S. Bromley, 1974, p. 353

17 Francis Place, *Autobiography,* ed. Mary Thale, Cambridge, 1972, p. 218

18 Ibid., pp. 127–8

19 Malthus, op. cit., 194

20 Silliman, op. cit., vol I, p. 299

21 Patrick Colquhoun, *The Police of the Metropolis, 1806,* reprinted Montclair, New Jersey, 1969, p. 2

22 Silliman, op. cit., vol I, p. 233

23 Ibid., vol II, pp. 210–11

24 Ibid., vol I, p. 265

25 Ibid., vol I, p. 266

26 Ibid., vol I, pp. 264–5

27 *Picture Post, 1938–50,* ed. Tom Hopkinson, London, 1970, p. 49

28 J. B. Priestley, *English Journey,*

London, 1934, p. 401

29 George Orwell, *The Road to Wigan Pier*, London, 1967, p. 98

30 Ibid., p. 79

31 John Mortimer, *Clinging to the Wreckage*, London, 1982, p. 48

32 *The Meynellian Science*, note by Algernon Burnaby, Leicester, 1932, pp. 70–1

33 *English Journey*, p. 117

34 Sir Peter Jeffrey Mackie, *The Keepers Book*, London, 1924, p. 515

35 Frank Green and Sidney Wolf, *London and Suburbs, Old and New*, London, 1933, p. 221

36 Roy Tinsley, *Types and Faces*, Pudsey, 1996, p. 6

37 Monica Dickens, *One Pair of Hands*, London, 1939, pp. 286, 278, 276–7

38 Larry Forrester, *Fly For Your Life*, London, 1958, pp. 32–3

39 Alan Bennett, *Writing Home*, London, 1998, p. 18

40 *English Journey*, p. 3

41 Morris Motors Ltd, *The Manual of the Morris-Oxford Six*, Cowley, 1930, pp. 5–6

42 Sellers and Yeatman, *1066 and All That*, 1930, reprinted London, 1985, p. 86

43 English Journey, op. cit., pp. 250–1

44 Ibid., pp. 22

45 Quoted in David Cannadine, *In Churchill's Shadow*, London, 2002, p. 168

46 *Manchester Guardian*, 25 April 1932

47 *The Road to Wigan Pier*, pp. 19–20

48 Keith Laybourn, *Britain on the Breadline*, Stroud, 1998, p. 10

49 H. V. Morton, *I Saw Two Englands*, ed. Tommy Candler, London, 1989, p. 10

50 Orwell, *Collected Essays*, vol 1, pp. 528–9

51 J. P. W. Mallalieu, *On Larkhill*, London, 1983, p. 198

3. The Civilians

1 A. M. Broadley and H. F. B. Wheeler, *Napoleon and the Invasion of England*,

London, 1908, vol 1, p. 269

2 Silliman, op. cit., vol 1, p. 189

3 Wheeler, op. cit., p. 248

4 Ibid., p. 303

5 Grey, *Parliamentary History*, vol 30, London, 1817, col 175

6 Ibid., col 165

7 Silliman, op. cit., vol I, p. 151

8 43 Geo III Cap 55

9 C. R. Davey, *The Sussex Militia List 1803, Southern Division*, Pevensey Rape, Eastbourne, 1988, p. iii

10 National Archives, WO 30/70

11 Peter Bloomfield, *Kent in the Napoleonic Wars*, Gloucester, 1987, p. 150

12 National Archives, WO 30/30

13 *Dumouriez and the Defence of England*, ed. J. Holland Rose, London, 1909, p. 265

14 Charles Clode, *The Military Forces of the Crown*, vol 1, London, 1889, p. 419

15 National Archives, WO 30/70

16 *Kent in the Napoleonic Wars*, p. 49

17 J. W. Fortescue, *The County Lieutenancies and the Army, 1803–1814*, reprinted Uckfield, nd, pp. 30–2, 92–4

18 *Kent in the Napoleonic Wars*, p. 151

19 National Archives, WO 30/70

20 Orwell, *Collected Essays and Journalism*, vol 2, *My Country Right or Left*, London, 1968, p. 241

21 National Archives, CAB 66/12

22 *Air Raid Precautions, Training Manual No 1, Basic Training in Air Raid Precautions*, London, 1940, p. 7

23 Glasgow and West of Scotland College of Domestic Science, *Some Recipes for Wartime Dishes*, London, 1940, *passim*

24 Orwell, op. cit., p. 356

25 Robert Silvey, *Who's Listening*, London, 1974, pp. 105–7

26 Edmund Ironside, *Diaries, 1937–1940*, ed. Macleod and Kelly, London, 1962, p. 377

27 Peter and Leni Gillman, *Collar the Lot*, London, 1980, *passim*
28 National Archives, CAB 120/62
29 Ibid.
30 Ibid.
31 National Archives, CAB 66/9
32 National Archives, CAB 120/439
33 National Archives, CAB 120/62
34 National Archives, CAB 66/10
35 Harold Nicholson, *Diaries and Letters, 1939–45*, ed. Nigel Nicolson, London, 1967, p. 96
36 George Orwell, *Complete Works*, ed. Davison, vol 12, 1998, *A Patriot After All*, p. 188
37 Joan Ham, *Storrington in Living Memory*, London, 1982, p. 82
38 National Archives, CAB 66/11. HO 186/2884

4. The Leaders
1 Silliman, op. cit., vol I, p. 221
2 John Ehrman, *The Younger Pitt*, vol 3, *The Consuming Struggle*, London, 1996, p. 543
3 See Sidney and Beatrice Webb, *English Local Government from the Revolution to the Municipal Corporations Act*, vol 1, London, 1906, passim
4 Ibid., vol I, p. 287
5 *Kent in the Napoleonic Wars*, pp. 150–1
6 *Navy Records Society*, vol 39, *The Barham Papers*, vol III, ed. Sir John Knox Laughton, 1911, p. 114
7 Silliman, op. cit., vol I, p. 336
8 Ibid., vol II, p. 115
9 *Oxford Dictionary of National Biography*, entry on Sir David Dundas
10 Lord Alanbrooke, *War Diaries*, ed. Danchev and Todman, London, 2001, p. 273
11 *The Churchill War Papers*, vol II, pp. 363, 478, 511, 656, 851
12 Edward R. Murrow, *In Search of Light, The Broadcasts of Edward R. Murrow, 1938–1961*, New York, 1967, p. 237
13 Winston and Clementine Churchill, *Speaking for Themselves*, ed. Mary Soames, London, 1997, p. 454
14 A. F. U. Green, *The British Home Guard Pocket-book, 1942*, reprinted London, 2009, p. 133
15 John Colville, *The Fringes of Power: Downing Street Diaries, 1939–1945*, London, 1985, p. 763
16 Charles Carrington, *Soldier at Bomber Command*, London, 1987, p. 39
17 *Ironside Diaries*, p. 333
18 Ibid., p. 335
19 *Soldier at Bomber Command*, p. 28
20 *Churchill War Papers*, op. cit., vol II, p. 1158
21 Ibid., pp. 531–2
22 Alanbrooke, op. cit., p. 93
23 *Ironside Diaries*, p. 387
24 Alanbrooke, op. cit., p. 93
25 *Soldier at Bomber Command*, p. 28
26 *Churchill War Papers*, vol II, pp. 421–22, 447
27 Sir Brian Horrocks, *A Full Life*, London, 1960, p. 97
28 *Fringes of Power*, pp. 762–3

5. Intelligence
1 National Archives, WO 1/397
2 Ibid.
3 Ibid.
4 Ibid.
5 G. R. Balleine, *The Tragedy of Phillipe d'Auvergne*, London and Chichester, 1973, pp. 112–13
6 National Archives, WO 1/918
7 Ibid.
8 National Archives, WO 1/397
9 National Archives, WO 1/398
10 Ibid.
11 Silliman, op. cit., vol II, pp. 130–2
12 Ibid., vol II, p. 135
13 National Archives, ADM 1/6035
14 Ibid.
15 National Archives, ADM 1/6083
16 National Archives, WO 1/398
17 National Archives, ADM 1/6305
18 Ibid.
19 Ibid.
20 National Archives, WO 1/397

21 National Archives, ADM 1/6038
22 David Reynolds, *In Command of History*, London, 2004, p. 249
23 National Archives, AIR 2/3097
24 Bruce Robertson et al, *Spitfire: the Story of a Famous Fighter*, Letchworth, 1960, p. 33
25 National Archives, AIR 39/293, no 312
26 National Archives, AIR 14/2379
27 National Archives, AIR 34/715
28 Gordon Welchman, *The Hut Six Story*, Cleobury Mortimer, 1997, p. 102
29 Ibid., p. 113
30 National Archives, AIR 19/493
31 Corelli Barnett, *Engage the Enemy More Closely*, London, 1991, p. 105
32 National Archives, WO 199/906
33 National Archives, WO 199/906
34 National Archives, WO 199/141
35 National Archives, HW 48/1
36 National Archives, WO 199.566
37 *Churchill War Papers*, vol 2, p. 495
38 National Archives, WO 199/906
39 National Archives, AIR 16/430
40 National Archives, ADM 116/4480
41 National Archives, ADM 179/151
42 National Archives, ADM 1/10762
43 *Churchill War Papers*, vol 2, p. 352
44 Ibid., p. 496
45 Ibid., p. 720 n1
46 Ibid., p. 799
47 Ibid., p. 851
48 Alanbrooke, op. cit., p. 108

6. Where and How?
1 *Churchill War Papers*, vol 2, p. 297
2 Richard Glover, *Britain at Bay*, London, 1972, p. 75
3 Yolande O'Donoghue, *William Roy, Pioneer of the Ordnance Survey*, London, 1977
4 HMSO, *Notes on Map Reading, 1929*, reissued 1940, pp. 7–8
5 *Dumouriez and the Defence of England*, passim
6 National Archives, ADM 1/538, KP

III 49–52
7 *Oxford Dictionary of National Biography*, entry on Frederick Dreyer
8 National Archives, WO 199/99
9 National Archives, WO 199/99
10 Ian Nairn and Nikolas Pevsner, *Sussex*, Harmondsworth, 1965 p. 578
11 Sir Frederick Dreyer, *The Sea Heritage*, London, 1955, p. 366
12 National Archives, WO 277/37
13 National Archives, AIR 22/59
14 National Archives, AIR 2/4793
15 National Archives, ADM 179/687
16 *Churchill War Papers*, vol 2, p. 343
17 *Dumouriez and the Defence of England*, p. 357
18 Ibid., p. 350
19 National Archives, WO 30/116
20 *Navy Records Society*, vol 96, *The Keith Papers*, ed. Christopher Lloyd, 1955, vol III, p. 48
21 Ibid., p. 49
22 *Dumouriez and the Defence of England*, p. 271
23 *The Keith Papers*, p. 51
24 Ibid., p. 51
25 National Archives, WO 199/99
26 *Soldier at Bomber Command*, op. cit., p. 28
27 *The Keith Papers*, p. 50
28 Ibid.
29 Ibid.
30 *Journals and Correspondence of Sir Harry Calvert*, ed. Sir Harry Verney, London, 1853, pp. 456–7
31 *The Keith Papers*, op. cit., p. 50
32 See, for example, National Archives, ADM 1/2144, 10/8/03
33 Calvert, op. cit., p. 482
34 *Britain at Bay*, p. 83
35 *The Keith Papers*, p. 49
36 Ibid., p. 49
37 National Archives, WO 277/37, p 48
38 *Dumouriez and the Defence of England*, p. 285
39 *The Keith Papers*, p. 49; *Dumouriez and the Defence of England*, p 285
40 Dreyer, *Sea Heritage*, p. 367

41 National Archives, ADM 1/538

42 National Archives, ADM 1/1529, 10/9/03

43 *Calvert*, op. cit., p. 471

44 *Dumouriez and the Defence of England*, p. 310

45 *Calvert*, op. cit., p. 476

46 Hilaire Belloc, *The County of Sussex*, London, 1936, pp. 147–8

7. The Defences

1 Charles James, *New Military Dictionary*, vol 1, 1810, np

2 Ibid., vol 2, 1811, p. 81

3 Whitworth Porter, *History of the Corps of Royal Engineers*, London, 1889, vol 2, p. 170

4 *Eleventh Report of the Commissioners of Military Enquiry, 1809*

5 Major J. T. Hancock, 'The First British Combat Engineers' in *Royal Engineers Journal*, Vol LXXXVIII, No. 4, December 1974, p. 203

6 P. A. L. Vine, *The Royal Military Canal*, Newton Abbott, 1972, p. 69

7 Porter, *Royal Engineers*, pp. 202–4

8 Jonathan Coad, *The English Heritage Book of Dover Castle and the Defences of Dover*, London, 1995, p, 68

9 *Bygone Kent*, vol 10, no 3, 1989, Frank Kitchen, *The Guns of Dungeness*, p. 180

10 *The Royal Military Canal*, p. 38

11 S. G. P. Ward, 'Defence works in Britain, 1803–1805', in *The Journal of the Society for Army Historical Research*, vol 27, 1949, p. 29

12 National Archives, WO1/629

13 *Kent in the Napoleonic Wars*, p. 123

14 National Archives, WO 1/629

15 Ward, *Defence Works in Britain*, p. 30

16 *Kent in the Napoleonic Wars*, pp. 133, 131–2

17 *The Royal Military Canal*, p. 40

18 *Kent in the Napoleonic Wars*, p. 125

20 National Archives, WO 166/57, p. 151

21 Ibid., p. 152

22 Ibid., p. 153

23 Ibid., p. 144

24 Ibid., p. 154

25 National Archives, WO 199/1695

26 National Archives, WO 199/48, p 35

27 National Archives, WO 365/143

28 Henry Wills, *Pillboxes: A Study of UK Defences, 1940*, London, 1985, p. 54

29 Ibid., p. 55

30 Ibid., pp. 46–9

31 William Foot, *Beaches, Fields, Streets and Hills: The Anti-Invasion Landscapes of England, 1940*, York, 2006, pp. 40–5

32 Ibid., pp. 138–45

33 Michael Joseph, *The Sword in the Scabbard*, London, 1942, p. 119

34 National Archives, WO 277/37

35 Alanbrooke, *War Diaries*, p. 94

36 National Archives, WO 166/1

37 National Archives, WO 199/48

38 National Archives, WO 199/48

39 National Archives, WO 166/468

40 *Beaches, Fields, Streets and Hills*, pp. 530–7

41 Wilks, *Worcestershire, passim*

42 National Archives, WO 166/72

43 National Archives, WO 166/57

44 National Archives, ADM 234/436

8. The Navy

1 *The Naval Chronicle*, vol 9, 1805, p. 247

2 Ibid.

3 C. S. Forester, ed., *The Adventures of John Wetherell*, London, 1954, pp. 27–8

4 Ibid., p. 31

5 *Navy Records Society*, vol 14, *The Blockade of Brest*, ed. John Leyland, vol 1, 1898, p. 8

6 Brian Lavery, *Nelson's Fleet at Trafalgar*, London, 2004, p. 13

7 Sir Nicholas Harry Nicolas, *The Dispatches and Letters of Lord Nelson*, vol VII, 1846, reprinted London, 1998, pp. 89–91

8 A. T. Mahan, *The Influence of Sea Power upon the French Revolution and Empire*, vol I, London, 1892, p. 118

9   Ibid., vol I, p. 338

10 *Blockade of Brest*, p. 344

11 A. N. Ryan, 'The Royal Navy and the Bockade of Brest', in Martine Acerra et. Al., ed., *Les Marines de Guerre Europeénnes, XVII–XVIIIe Siècles*, Paris, 1984, pp. 186–7

12 *Blockade of Brest*, pp. 30–1

13 Quoted in Henry Baynham, *From the Lower Deck*, London, 1972, p. 48

14 Ibid.

15 William Richardson, *A Mariner of England*, ed. Spencer Childers, reprinted London 1970, p. 210

16 *The Keith Papers*, vol 3, p. 42

17 Ibid., p. 43

18 *National Maritime Museum manuscripts*, AUS/6

19 *Kent in the Napoleonic Wars*, p. 76

20 *National Maritime Museum manuscripts*, KEI 28/98

21 *Kent in the Napoleonic Wars*, pp. 76–7

22 *National Maritime Museum manuscripts*, KEI 28/98, 2/6/04

23 *The Keith Papers*, vol 3, p. 4

24 Ibid., p. 23

25 Ibid., p. 44

26 *Navy Records Society,* vol 28, *Letters of Admiral Markham*, ed. Sir Clements Markham, 1904, p. 117

27 *National Maritime Museum manuscripts*, KEI 28/96, 10/3/04

28 *National Maritime Museum manuscripts*, KEI 26/8

29 *The Keith Papers*, vol 3, p. 53–4

30 John Marshall, *Royal Naval Biography*, 1823–35, vol 2, part 1, pp. 128–30

31 Charles Owen, *No More Heroes*, London, 1975, p. 131

32 Tristan Jones, *Heart of Oak*, 1984, reprinted Shrewsbury, 1997, pp. 29, 44–5

33 Hannen Swaffer, *What Would Nelson Do?*, London, 1946, p. 89

34 *Heart of Oak*, p. 19

35 *What would Nelson Do?*, pp. 92–3

36 John L. Brown, *Dairy of a Matelot, 1942-45*, Lowesmoor, Worcester, 1991, p. 8

37 Nicholas Monsarrat, *Three Corvettes*, reprinted London, 2000, p. 188

38 J. Lennox Kerr and David James, *Wavy Navy, by Some Who Served*, London, 1950, p. 194

39 Admiralty Fleet Order 882/1941

40 Ewen Montagu, *Beyond Top Secret U*, London, 1977, p. 16

41 J. Lennox Kerr and Wilfred Granville, *The RNVR*, London, 1957, p. 160

42 National Archives, ADM 1/10566

43 Quoted in Oliver Warner, *Cunningham of Hyndhope*, London, 1967, p. 62

44 Sam Lombbard-Hobson, *A Sailor's War*, London, 1983, pp. 100–2

45 National Archives, ADM 199/360

46 National Archives, ADM 199/360

47 National Archives, ADM 199/360

48 National Archives, ADM 199/687

49 National Archives, ADM 199/687

50 National Archives, ADM 199/360

51 National Archives, ADM 199/687

52 National Archives, ADM 199/1200

53 National Archives, ADM 1/18897

54 National Archives, ADM 199/687

55 National Archives, ADM 1/18897

56 National Archives, ADM 199/360

57 National Archives, ADM 199/687

58 National Archives, ADM 3/324/5

59 Sir William James, *The Portsmouth Papers*, London, 1946, p. 69

60 National Archives, ADM 199/680

61 Sir A. P. Herbert, *Independent Member*, London, 1950, p. 159

62 National Archives, ADM 199/375

63 National Archives, ADM 199/360

64 National Archives, ADM 199/375

65 National Archives, ADM 199/360

66 Nicholas Archives, PREM 3/324/5

67 National Archives, ADM 199/1737

68 National Archives, ADM 199/687

9. The Army

1   Charles James, *New Military Dictionary*, op. cit., vol I, no page nos

2   Ibid., vol I, p. 40

3   Adam Smith, *The Wealth of Nations,* 1776, reprinted London, 1925, vol I, p. 111

4   *Parliamentary Papers, 1806–7,* vol IV, p. 175

5   Charles James, *The Regimental Companion,* vol I, London, 1811, p. 23

6   Ibid., p. 452

7   *The Recollections of Rifleman Harris,* ed. Christopher Hibbert, reprinted London, 2006, pp. 1–2

8   Charles James, *The Regimental Companion,* London, 1811, vol II, 1811, p. 247

9   *War Office, Rules and Regulations for the Formation, Field Exercise and Movements of His Majesty's Forces, 1803,* pp. 1–2

10   *The Regimental Companion,* vol I, p. 258

11   Silliman, op. cit., vol I, p. 231

12   *The Regimental Companion,* vol I, p. 199

13   Ibid., pp. 204–5

14   *War Office, Rules and Regulations,* p. 282

15   H. Dickinson. *Instructions for forming a Regiment of Infantry for Parade or Exercise, together with the Manouevres as ordered to be Practised by His Majesty's Infantry Forces ...,* London, 1803, pp. 7–10

16   Ibid., p. 92 *ff*

17   *Kent in the Napoleonic Wars,* op. cit., p. 7

18   *Napoleon, Maxims 47,* Quoted in *The Daily Telegraph Dictionary of Military Quotations,* ed. Tsouras, London, 2005, p. 80

19   *Kent in the Napoleonic Wars,* p. 167,

20   National Archives, WO 12/2787

21   *Kent in the Napoleonic Wars,* pp. 83–5

22   *Dumouriez and the Defence of England,* p. 295

23   Ibid., p. 296

24   Ken Kimberley, *Heavo, Heavo, Lash up and Stow,* Kettering, 1999, p. 10

25   David Niven, *The Moon's a Balloon,*

26   Alan Shepherd, *Sandhurst,* London, 1980, passim

27   L. R. Ellis, *The War in France and Flanders,* London, 1953, p. 326

28   *'Boomerang', Bless 'em All,* London, 1942, pp. 54–5

29   H. M. D. Parker, *Manpower: A Study of Wartime Policy and Administration,* London, 1957, pp. 485, 488

30   National Archives, WO 199/725

31   *Army Training Memorandum, June 1940,* p. 14

32   *Army Training Memorandum, July 1940,* pp. 14–15

33   Jeremy A. Crang, *The British Army and People's War, 1939–1945,* Manchester, 2000, p. 23

34   *Bless 'em All,* p. 52

35   *Army Training Memorandum no 32, May 1940,* pp. 11–2

36   National Archives, WO 216/61

37   *Bless 'em All,* introduction

38   National Archives, WO 365/77

39   National Archives, WO 199/1656

40   National Archives, WO 216/61

41   National Archives, WO 32/9415

42   Ibid.

43   Ibid.

44   *Army Training Memorandum, August 1940,* pp. 8–9

45   Alanbrooke, *War Diaries,* p. 90

46   *Army Training Memorandum, August 1940,* p. 4

47   *Bless 'em All,* p. 26

48   National Archives, WO 199/725

49   *Army Training Memorandum, May 1940,* p. 15

50   *War Office, Infantry Section Leading, 1938,* p. 8

51   *Army Training Memorandum, August 1940,* p. 14

52   *Army Training Memorandum, July 1940,* p. 6

53   *The Sword in the Scabbard,* op. cit., p. 153

54   John Cloake, *Templer, Tiger of Malaya,* London, 1985, p. 83

55   *The Sword in the Scabbard*, op. cit., p. 40
56   *Military Training Pamphlet no 23*, pt I, *Fighting Troops and their Characteristics*, p. 16
57   War Office, *Training in Fieldcraft and Elementary Tactics, Military Training Pamphlet no 33, 1940*, p. 4
58   *The Sword in the Scabbard*, op. cit., p. 74
59   *Bless 'em All*, p. 29
60   *Army Training Memorandum, June 1940*, p. 1
61   *Army Training Memorandum, September 1940*, p. 12
62   *Churchill War Papers*, vol 2, p. 943n
63   Horrocks, *A Full Life*, p. 100
64   *Army Training Memorandum, June 1940*, p. 13
65   Basil Collier, *The Defence of the United Kingdom*, London, 1957, pp. 130, 124n
66   *Churchill War Papers*, vol 2, p. 1035
67   National Archives, WO 166/5
68   *The Defence of the United Kingdom*, op. cit., pp. 125, 127, 219
69   Howard Chaplin, *The Queen's Own Royal West Kent Regiment, 1920–1950*, London, 1954, pp. 152–4
70   *Churchill War Papers*, vol 2, p. 418
71   National Archives, CAB 66/10
72   National Archives, WO 166/4170
73   National Archives, WO 166/4400
74   *The Diaries of Evelyn Waugh*, ed. Michael Davie, London, 1976, p. 472
75   Ibid.
76   *The Sword in the Scabbard*, pp. 112–13
77   Ibid., p. 115
78   Ibid., pp. 163–4
79   National Archives, WO 166/4532
80   National Archives, WO 166/72
81   National Archives, WO 166/72
82   *Army Training Memorandum, June 1940*, p. 12
83   National Archives, WO 166/72
84   *Army Training Memorandum, September 1940*, p. 7
85   National Archives, WO 166/772
86   National Archives, WO 166/5196
87   National Archives, WO 199/1770

88   National Archives, WO 199/141
89   National Archives, WO 166/814
90   National Archives, WO 166/4170
91   National Archives, WO 166/57
92   National Archives, WO 166/57
93   *Army Training Memorandum, July 1940*, p. 5
94   *The Diary of Evelyn Waugh*, p, 473
95   National Archives, WO 166/4532
96   *Army Training Memorandum, October 1941*, p. 9
97   Horrocks, *A Full Life*, p. 93
98   *Churchill War Papers*, vol 2, pp. 458, 461
99   Alanbrooke, op. cit., p. 94
100 National Archives, WO 166/1
101 National Archives, WO 24/937
102 National Archives, WO 166/4170
103 National Archives, WO 199/1619
104 National Archives, WO 212/28
105 B. R. Mitchell, *Abstract of British Historical Statistics*, Cambridge, 1962, p. 230
106 Quotes from National Archives, WO 199/1770
107 *The Sword in the Scabbard*, p. 118
108 National Archives, WO 166/1004

10. The Air Force

1   *Keith Papers*, vol 3, p. 54
2   Navy Records Society, vol 92, *Naval Miscellany IV*, ed. Christopher Lloyd, 1952, pp. 424–68
3   *Keith Papers*, op. cit., vol 3, p. 6
4   David Crook, *Spitfire Pilot*, London, 2008, p. 52
5   Jimmy Corbin, *Last of the Ten Fighter Boys*, Stroud, 2007, p. 67
6   Air Ministry, *The Royal Airforce Builds for War*, 1956, reprinted London, 1957, pp. 84–5, 78
7   Winston G. Ramsey, ed., *The Battle of Britain, Then and Now*, London, 2000, p. 46
8   Winston Churchill, *The Second World War*, vol III, *Their Finest Hour*, London, 1967, pp. 193–4
9   John James, *The Paladins*, London,

1990, p. 108

10   Tim Vigors, *Life's Too Short to Cry*,
London, 2008, p. 54

11   Andrew Boyle, *Trenchard*, London,
1962, p. 517

12   J. E. 'Johnnie' Johnson, *Wing Leader*,
London, 1959, p. 17

13   Crook, *Spitfire Pilot*, op. cit., p. 32

14   *The Last of the Ten Fighter Boys*, pp.
25–6

15   Ibid., pp. 34–5

16   Ibid., p. 23

17   Ibid., p. 28

18   Ibid., p. 31

19   Geoffrey Wellum, *First Light*, London,
2003, p. 11

20   Ibid., p. 18

21   *Life's too Short to Cry*, p. 123

22   Crook, *Spitfire Pilot*, pp. 45–6

23   Johnson, op. cit., p. 125

24   C. G. Jefford, *Observers and
Navigators*, Shrewsbury, 2001, p. 128

25   Max Hastings, *Bomber Command*,
London, 1979, p. 83

26   *Observers and Navigators*, p. 142

27   Spike Milligan, *Adolf Hitler: My Part
in his Downfall*, London, 1972, p. 57

28   *Fly for your Life*, pp. 156–60

29   National Archives, AIR 8/224

30   National Archives, AIR 24/1598

31   National Archives, AIR 2/3065

32   National Archives, AIR 2/3065

33   'Raff', *Behind the Spitfires*, London,
1941, p. 33

34   Frank Muir, *A Kentish Lad*, London,
1997, p. 62

35   *Manpower*, pp. 485, 488

36   Air Ministry Order 433/1940

37   Air Ministry Order 330/1940

38   Air Ministry Order A 692/1940

39   *Fly for your Life*, p. 145

40   Allen Wheeler, *Flying Between the
Wars*, p. 157

41   National Archives, AIR 41/1

42   Sir Charles Webster and Noble
Frankland, *The Strategic Air Offensive
Against Germany, London*, 1961, vol
IV, pp. 115–27

43   Guy Gibson, *Enemy Coast Ahead –
Uncensored*, Manchester, 2003, p. 73

44   Ibid., pp. 104–5

45   Johnson, op. cit., pp. 35–6

46   Ibid., p. 36

47   Ibid., p. 45

11. The Citizen Soldiers

1   National Archives, WO 30/70

2   National Army Museum,
manuscripts, 7805-72

3   J. W. Fortescue, *The County
Lieutenancies and the Army*, p. 102

4   *Journal of the Society for Army
Historical Research*, vol IX, p. 125

5   National Army Museum,
manuscripts, 6911-4-6

6   Austin Gee, *The British Volunteer
Movement, 1794–1814*, Oxford, 2003,
p. 54

7   National Archives, HO 51/109

8   *Journal of the Society for Army
Historical Research*, vol 40, 1962, p.
141

9   *The Diary of Joseph Farington*, ed.
Garlick and Macintyre, New Haven
Connecticut, 1978–98, p. 2115

10   *The British Volunteer Movement, 1794–
1814*, p. 122

11   *The Diary of Joseph Farington*, p. 2143

12   George Hanger, *Reflections on the
Menaced Invasion*, London, 1804,
reprinted 1970, pp. 155–6

13   J. W. Fortescue, *The County
Lieutenancies and the Army*, p. 104

14   Ibid., p. 105–6

15   National Army Museum,
manuscripts, 6807-367

16   *The County Lieutenancies and the
Army*, pp. 134–6

17   Silliman, op. cit., vol I, p. 72

18   Ibid., vol I, p. 172

19   *The Diary of Joseph Farington*, pp.
2402, 2156, 2153

20   *Reflections on the Menaced Invasion*, op.
cit., pp. 147–8

21   Ibid., p. 144 n

22   James, *Regimental Companion*, 1804,

vol I, p. 119

23   National Archives, ADM 1/2147

24   Richard Woodman, 'The Royal Trinity House Volunteer Artillery', in *Mariner's Mirror*, vol 69, 1983, pp. 393–4

25   *Punch, 4 September 1940*, p. 244

26   Imperial War Museum, documents, papers of Captain C. Ingram, 84/7/1

27   *Home Guard Training Instruction No 1*, p. 3, in National Archives, WO 199/872B

28   John Goodwin, *The Military Defence of West Sussex*, Midhurst, 1995, pp. 94, 96

29   Mick Wilks, *The Defence of Worcestershire and the Southern Approaches to Birmingham in World War II*, Almeley, Herefordshire, 2007, pp. 47, 86, 105–8

30   J. B. Priestley, *All England Listened*, pp. 14–18

31   *Training Instruction No 6*, p. 4

32   *The British Home Guard Pocket-Book, 1942*, reprinted London, 2009, p. 27

33   Ibid., p. 12

34   Gilbert, *Churchill*, p. 422

35   National Archives, WO 199/872B

36   Ibid.

37   *Training Instruction No 2*, p. 3

38   Horrocks, *A Full Life*, p. 96

39   National Archives, WO 199/872b

40   *Ironside Diaries*, op. cit., p. 344

41   Alanbrooke, op. cit., pp. 89, 98

42   National Archives, WO 166/1

43   S. P. Mackenzie, *The Home Guard*, Oxford, 1996, pp. 114–15

44   *Punch*, December 4, 1940, p. 456

45   National Archives, WO 199/872B

46   *The Sword in the Scabbard*, p. 72

47   M. D. S. Armour, *Total War Training for Home Guard Officers and NCOs*, 1942

48   *Home Guard Pocket-Book*, p. 25

49   Orwell, *Collected Essays ...*, vol 2, *My Country Right or Left*, p. 368

50   *Home Guard Pocket-Book*, p. 35

51   Mackenzie, *Home Guard*, p. 91

52   Tom Wintringham, *New Ways of War*, London, 1940, pp. 63–5

53   *Training Instruction No 5*, p. 4

54   Mackenzie, *Home Guard*, pp. 63–5

55   *Training Instruction No 3*, p. 4

56   *Training Instruction No 1*, p. 1

57   Tom Wintringham, *The Home Guard Can Fight*, 1940, p. 15

58   Mackenzie, *Home Guard*, p. 7

59   *The Home Guard Can Fight*, pp. 25, 28

60   *Training Instruction No 14*, p. 1

12. Working Together

1   Navy Records Society, vol 138, *Shipboard Life and Organisation*, ed. B. Lavery, 1998, pp. 623–4

2   Quoted in Cyril Field, *Britain's Sea Soldiers*, Liverpool, 1924, pp. 296–7

3   Ibid., p. 288

4   Quoted in D. Spinney, *Rodney*, London, 1969, p. 187

5   Quoted in Field, op. cit., p. 262

6   *Keith Papers*, op. cit., vol 3, p. 41

7   Ibid., p. 47

8   National Archives, ADM 186/329, 1/9804

9   Alanbrooke, op. cit., p. 96

10   Ibid., p. 112

11   *Churchill War Papers*, vol 2, p. 489

12   National Archives, WO 199/1419

13   National Archives, ADM 2234/436, pp. 94–5

14   Air Historical Branch, *The RAF in Maritime War*, vol I, nd, p. 97

15   Ibid., pp. 212–18

16   Ibid., Appendix XI, p. 251

17   Ibid., p. 189

18   Sir Roderick Macdonald, *The Figurehead*, Bishop Auckland, 1993, p. 6

19   *The RAF in Maritime War*, p. 185

20   Ian Hawkins, ed., *Destroyer*, London, 2005, p. 79

21   Ibid.

22   Admiralty, *Gunnery Pocket Book*, BR 224/45, 1945, p. 162

23   Joseph Wellings, ed. Hattendorf, *On His Majesty's Service*, Newport, 1983, p. 76

24 National Archives, AIR 14/242

25 National Archives, AIR 14/976

26 Quoted in A. J. Barker, *Dunkirk, the Great Escape*, London, 1977

27 Winston G. Ramsey, ed., *The Blitz: Then and Now*, London, 1987, p. 197

28 National Archives, WO 166/4400

29 National Archives, AIR 14/563

30 National Archives, AIR 20/2804

31 National Archives, AIR 16/430

32 National Archives, AIR 20/2804

33 Johnson, op. cit., p. 43

34 National Archives, AIR 2/7218

35 National Archives, WO 166/1, 199/901

36 National Archives, AIR 20/2265

37 National Archives, AIR 14/810

38 National Archives, AIR 39/40

39 Alanbrooke, op. cit., pp. 238, 258

40 National Archives, AIR 20/4326

41 National Archives, AIR 20/4326

42 National Archives, WO 166/1

43 National Archives, AIR 20/4326

44 *Soldier at Bomber Command*, p. 27

45 Ibid., pp. 226–8

13. The Resolution

1 Quote in Lavery, *Nelson and the Nile*, London, 1998, p. 9

2 Alan Schom, *Trafalgar: Countdown to Battle*, London, 1990, p. 90

3 *Keith Papers*, vol III, p. 31

4 Schom, op. cit., p. 197

5 Edouard Desbriere, *Projets and Tentatives de Débarquement aux Îles Britannique*, 1900–5, pt II pp. 233–8

6 Ibid., pp. 76, 82; *Trafalgar: Countdown to Battle*, p. 78

7 Desbriere, vol 4iii, p. 11

8 Silliman, op. cit., vol I, pp. 313–4

9 *Regimental Companion*, vol I, 1811, p. 97

10 *The Fuehrer Conferences on Naval Affairs*, ed. Showell, London, 2005, p. 110

11 *Churchill War Papers*, vol 2, p. 268

12 *The Blitz Then and Now*, vol 1, p. 138

13 *Fuehrer Conferences*, pp. 112–13, 114–15

14 Ibid., p. 116

15 Ibid., p. 117

16 Ibid., p. 123

17 Ibid., p. 133

18 Ibid., p. 123

19 *Fuehrer Conferences*, p. 116

20 Ibid., p. 125

21 Ibid., p. 127

22 Ibid., p. 128

23 Ibid., pp. 123–4

24 Ibid., pp. 137–8

25 Noble Frankland, *History at War*, London, 1998, p. 72

26 *The Blitz: Then and Now*, vol 1, p. 247

27 *Fuehrer Conferences*, p. 137

28 Ibid., p. 138

29 Edward R. Murrow, *In Search of Light*,

New York, 1967

BIBLIOGRAPHY

General and Political History

1803–5

A. M. Broadley and H. F. B. Wheeler, *Napoleon and the Invasion of England*, London, 1908

Linda Colley, *Britons*, London, 1994

Richard Glover, *Britain at Bay*, London, 1972

The History of Parliament, vol III, *The House of Commons 1790–1820*, London, 1986

J. C. Sainty, *Office Holders in Modern Britain*, vol IV, *Admiralty Officials*, London, 1975

J. Steven Watson *The Reign of George III*, Oxford, 1960

1940

C. L. Mowat, *Britain between the Wars, 1918–1940*, London, 1968

A. J. P. Taylor, *English History, 1914–1945*, Oxford, 1975

Phillip Zeigler, *London at War*, London, 1996

Social and Economic History

1803–5

Patrick Colquhoun, *The Police of the Metropolis*, 1806, reprinted Montclair, New Jersey, 1969

Thomas Malthus, *An Essay on the Principle of Population*, 1798, reprinted Mineola, New York, 2007

William Marshall, *The Review and Abstracts of the County Reports to the Board of Agriculture*, reprinted New York, 1968

Patrick O'Brien and Roland Quinault, *The Industrial Revolution and British Society*, Cambridge, 1993

Adam Smith, *The Wealth of Nations*, 1776, reprinted London, 1925

Sidney and Beatrice Webb, *English Local Government from the Revolution to the Municipal Corporations Act*, London, 1906

Ben Wilson, *Decency and Disorder, 1789–1837*, London, 2007

1940

Angus Calder, *The People's War*, London, 1971

Keith Laybourn, *Britain on the Breadline*, Stroud, 1998

Norman Longmate, *How We Lived Then*, London, 1971

B. R. Mitchell, *Abstract of British Historical Statistics*, Cambridge, 1962

London School of Economics, *New Survey of London Life and Labour*, London, 1930

Robert Silvey, *Who's Listening*, London, 1974

SOCIAL COMMENTARY

1803–5

Jane Austen, *Pride and Prejudice*, 1813, reprinted London, 1995

— *Mansfield Park*, 1814, London, 1996

Benjamin Silliman, *Journal of Travels in England, Holland and Scotland*, vol I, Newhaven, Connecticut, 1812

1940

H. V. Morton, ed. Tommy Candler, *I Saw Two Englands*, London, 1989

Edward R. Murrow, *In Search of Light: The Broadcasts of Edward R. Murrow, 1938–1961*, New York, 1967

George Orwell, *The Road to Wigan Pier*, London, 1967

— *Collected Essays and Journalism*, vol 1, *At an Age Like This*, 1968

— *Collected Essays and Journalism*, vol 2, *My Country Right or Left*, London, 1968

— *The Complete Works of George Orwell*, ed. Peter Davison, vol 12, *A Patriot After All, 1940–1941*, London, 1998

J. B. Priestley, *English Journey*, London, 1934

— *All England Listened*, New York, 1967

OFFICIAL HISTORIES

Basil Collier, *The Defence of the United Kingdom*, London, 1957

L. R. Ellis, *The War in France and Flanders*, London, 1953

F. H. Hinsley, *British Intelligence in the Second World War*, vol 1, London, 1979

H. M. D. Parker, *Manpower: A Study of Wartime Policy and Administration*, London, 1957

S. W. Roskill, *The War At Sea*, 3 vols, London, 1954–61

Sir Charles Webster and Noble Frankland, *The Strategic Air Offensive Against Germany*, London, 1961

Navy Records Society Publications

Vol 14, *The Blockade of Brest*, vol I, ed. John Leyland, 1898
Vol 39, *The Barham Papers*, vol III, ed. Sir John Knox Laughton, 1911
Vol 92, *Naval Miscellany IV*, ed. Christopher Lloyd, 1952
Vol 96, *The Keith Papers*, Vol III, ed. Christopher Lloyd, 1955
Vol 119, *Manning Pamphlets*, ed J. S. Bromley, 1974
Vol 138, *Shipboard Life and Organisation*, ed. B. Lavery, 1998

Individual Biographies and Personal Accounts

Political 1803–5

John Ehrman, *The Younger Pitt*, vol 2, *The Reluctant Transition*, London, 1983
— *The Younger Pitt*, vol 3, *The Consuming Struggle*, London, 1996

Political 1940

David Cannadine, *In Churchill's Shadow*, London, 2002
Winston S. Churchill, *The Second World War*, vol III, *Their Finest Hour*, London, 1967
— *The Churchill War Papers*, vol II, *Never Surrender*, ed. Martin Gilbert, London, 1994
— *Churchill War Papers*, vol III, *The Ever-Widening War*, ed. Martin Gilbert, London, 2000
— and Clementine Churchill, *Speaking for Themselves*, ed. Mary Soames, London, 1997
John Colville, *The Fringes of Power: Downing Street Diaries, 1939–1945*, London, 1985
Martin Gilbert, *Churchill: A Life*, London, 2000
Roy Jenkins, *Churchill*, London, 2001
David Reynolds, *In Command of History*, London, 2004
Harold Nicholson, *Diaries and Letters, 1939–45*, ed, Nigel Nicolson, London, 1967

Naval 1803–5

G. R. Balleine, *The Tragedy of Phillipe d'Auvergne*, London and Chichester, 1973
Henry Baynham, *From the Lower Deck*, London, 1972
C. S. Forester, ed., *The Adventures of John Wetherell*, London, 1954
Sir Nicholas Harry Nicolas, *The Dispatches and Letters of Lord Nelson*, 1846, reprinted London, 1998
William Richardson, *A Mariner of England*, ed. Spencer Childers, reprinted London 1970

Naval 1940

Sir Frederick Dreyer, *The Sea Heritage*, London, 1955

John L. Brown, *Dairy of a Matelot, 1942–45*, Lowesmoor, Worcester, 1991

Ian Hawkins, ed., *Destroyer*, London, 2005

Sir William James, *The Portsmouth Papers*, London, 1946

Tristan Jones, *Heart of Oak*, 1984, reprinted Shrewsbury, 1997

Sam Lombard-Hobson, *A Sailor's War*, London, 1983

Sir Roderick Macdonald, *The Figurehead*, Bishop Auckland, 1993

Nicholas Monsarrat, *Three Corvettes*, reprinted London, 2000

Charles Owen, *No More Heroes*, London, 1975

Oliver Warner, *Cunningham of Hyndhope*, London, 1967

Joseph Wellings, ed. Hattendorf, *On His Majesty's Service*, Newport, 1983

Military 1803–5

Sir Harry Verney, ed., *Journals and Correspondence of Sir Harry Calvert*, London,
1853

Christopher Hibbert, ed., *The Recollections of Rifleman Harris*, reprinted London,
2006

Military 1940

Lord Alanbrooke, *War Diaries*, ed. A. Danchev and D. Todman, London, 2001

'Boomerang', *Bless 'em All*, London, 1942

John Cloake, *Templer, Tiger of Malaya*, London, 1985

Michael Davie, ed., *The Diaries of Evelyn Waugh*, London, 1976

Sir Brian Horrocks, *A Full Life*, London, 1974

Michael Joseph, *The Sword in the Scabbard*, London, 1942

Spike Milligan, *Adolf Hitler: My Part in his Downfall*, London, 1972

David Niven, *The Moon's a Balloon*, 1971

Air Force

Andrew Boyle, *Trenchard*, London, 1962

Charles Carrington, *Soldier at Bomber Command*, London, 1987

Jimmy Corbin, *Last of the Ten Fighter Boys*, Stroud, 2007

David Crook, *Spitfire Pilot*, London, 2008

Larry Forrester, *Fly For Your Life*, London, 1958

Guy Gibson, *Enemy Coast Ahead – Uncensored*, Manchester, 2003

J. E. ('Johnnie') Johnson, *Wing Leader*, London, 1956

Frank Muir, *A Kentish Lad*, London, 1997

'Raff', *Behind the Spitfires*, London, 1941

Tim Vigors, *Life's too Short to Cry*, London, 2008

Geoffrey Wellum, *First Light*, London, 2003

Allen Wheeler, *Flying Between the Wars*, Henley-on-Thames, 1972

Civilian 1803–5

The Diary of Joseph Farington, ed. Kenneth Garlick and Angus Macintyre, New Haven, Connecticut, 1978–98

Francis Place, *Autobiography*, ed. Mary Thale, Cambridge, 1972

Civilian 1940

Monica Dickens, *One Pair of Hands*, London, 1939

Sir A. P. Herbert, *Independent Member*, London, 1950

John Mortimer, *Clinging to the Wreckage*, London, 1982

NAVAL HISTORY

1803–5

Charles Derrick, *Memoirs of the Rise and Progress of the Royal Navy*, London, 1806

Brian Lavery, *Nelson and the Nile*, London, 1998

— *Nelson's Fleet at Trafalgar*, London, 2004

Christopher Lloyd, *The British Seaman*, London, 1968

A. T. Mahan, *The Influence of Sea Power upon the French Revolution and Empire*, vol I, London, 1892

N. A. M. Rodger, *The Command of the Ocean: A Naval Histoy of Britain, 1649–1815*, London, 2004

A. N. Ryan, 'The Royal Navy and the Bockade of Brest', in *Les Marines de Guerre Europeénnes, XVII–XVIIIe Sièctes,* ed. Martine Acerra et al, Paris, 1984

Alan Schom, *Trafalgar: Countdown to Battle*, London, 1990

1940

Corelli Barnett, *Engage the Enemy More Closely*, London, 1991

J. Lennox Kerr and David James, *Wavy Navy, by Some Who Served,* London, 1950

J. Lennox Kerr and Wilfred Granville, *The RNVR*, London, 1957

Hannen Swaffer, *What Would Nelson Do?*, London, 1946

MILITARY HISTORY

1803–5

Charles Clode, *The Military Forces of the Crown*, London, 1889

Jeremy A. Crang, *The British Army and People's War, 1939–1945*, Manchester, 2000

J. W. Fortescue, *The County Lieutenancies and the Army, 1803–1814*, reprinted Uckfield, nd

George Hanger, *Reflections on the Menaced Invasion*, London, 1804, reprinted 1970

1940

Timothy Harrison Place, *Military Training in the British Army, 1940–1944*, London, 2000

AIR FORCE HISTORY

John Foreman, *Fighter Command War Diaries*, vol 1, September 1939 to September 1940, Walton on Thames, 1996

Winston G. Graham, ed., *The Blitz: Then and Now*, London, 1987

Max Hastings, *Bomber Command*, London, 1979

John James, *The Paladins*, London, 1990

C. G. Jefford, *Observers and Navigators*, Shrewsbury, 2001

Winston G. Ramsey, ed., *The Battle of Britain: Then and Now*, London, 2000

John Ray, *The Battle of Britain, New Perspectives*, London, 1994

VOLUNTEERS

Austin Gee, *The British Volunteer Movement, 1794–1814*, Oxford, 2003

HOME GUARD

M. D. S. Armour, *Total War Training for Home Guard Officers and NCOs*, 1942

A. F. U. Green, *The British Home Guard Pocket-book*, 1942, reprinted London, 2009

P. Mackenzie, *The Home Guard*, Oxford, 1996

Penny Summerfield and Corinna Peniston-Bird, *Contesting Home Defence*, Manchester, 2007

Tom Wintringham, *The Home Guard Can Fight*, 1940

— *New Ways of War*, London, 1940

INTELLIGENCE

Ewen Montagu, *Beyond Top Secret U*, London, 1977

Michael Smith, *Station X*, London, 1998

Gordon Welchman, *The Hut Six Story*, Cleobury Mortimer, 1997

EQUIPMENT, TECHNIQUES ETC

Naval 1803–5

William Falconer, *Universal Dictionary of the Marine,* 1780, reprinted Newton Abbot, 1970

Robert Gardiner, *Frigates of the Napoleonic Wars,* London, 2000

Brian Lavery, *Ship of the Line,* vol 1, 1983

David Lyon, *The Sailing Navy List,* London, 1993

Rif Winfield, *British Warships in the Age of Sail,* Barnsley, 2005

Naval 1940

Admiralty, *Gunnery Pocket Book,* BR 224/45, 1945

John Campbell, *Naval Weapons of World War Two,* London, 1985

Robert Gardiner, ed., *Conway's All the World's Fighting Ships, 1922–46,* London, 1980

D. K. Brown, *Nelson to Vanguard: Warship Development 1923–1945,* London, 2000

— ed., *The Design and Construction of British Warships, 1939–1945,* London, 1995

Army 1803–5

D. W. Bailey, *British Military Longarms, 1715-1865,* London, 1986

H. Dickinson, *Instructions for forming a Regiment of Infantry for Parade or Exercise, together with the Manoeuvres as ordered to be Practised by His Majesty's Infantry Forces ...,* London, 1803

Charles James, *New Military Dictionary,* 2 vols, 1810–11

War Office, *Rules and Regulations for the Formation, Field Exercise and Movements of His Majesty's Forces,* 1803

Army 1940

George Forty, *British Army Handbook, 1939–1945,* Stroud, 1998

Ian V. Hogg, *British and American Artillery of World War 2,* London, 1978

Military Library Research Service publications:

Army Training Memoranda, Part 1, September 1939 to 1941

Operations, Military Training Pamphlet no 23, Operations

Orders of Battle of the British Army, ed. H. F. Joslin

Bart H. Vanderveen, *The Observer's Fighting Vehicles Directory of World War II,* London, 1969

War Office Publications:

Tom Davis and John Bodsworth, ed., *Small Arms Training 1937,* Cambridge, 2004

The Textbook of Small Arms, 1929, reprinted 1999

Infantry Section Leading, 1938

Training in Fieldcraft and Elementary Tactics, Military Training Pamphlet no 33, 1940

The Training of an Infantry Battalion,Military Training Pamphlet no 37, 1940
The German Army in Pictures, 1940

REGIMENTAL AND CORPS HISTORIES

R. Money Barnes, *The Uniforms and History of the Scottish Regiments,* London, 1960
Ian F. W. Becket, *Discovering English County Regiments,* Princes Risborough, 2003
Shelford Bidwell, *Gunners at War,* London, 1970
Howard Chaplin, *The Queen's Own Royal West Kent Regiment, 1920–1950,* London, 1954
Cyril Field, *Britain's Sea Soldiers,* Liverpool, 1924
Sir Basil Liddell-Hart, *The Tanks: The History of the Royal Tank Corps and its Predecessors,* 2 vols, London, 1959
Whitworth Porter, *History of the Corps of Royal Engineers,* London, 1889

AIR FORCE

F. J. Adkin, *RAF Ground Support Equipment since 1918,* Shrewsbury, 1996
Air Ministry, staff histories:
 The Royal Air Force Builds for War, 1956, reprinted London, 1957
 Air Historical Branch, *The RAF in Maritime War,* vol I, nd, vol 2, September 1939 to June 1941
 T. C. G. James, *The Growth of Fighter Command, 1936–1940,* reprinted London, 2002
L. E. F. Coombs, *Control in the Sky,* Barnsley, 2005
Paul Francis, *British Military Airfield Architecture,* Yeovil, 1996
William Green, *Famous Bombers of the Second World War,* London, 1959
Bill Gunston, *Classic World War II Aircraft Cutaways,* London, 1995
Tim Hamilton, *Identification, Friend or Foe,* London, 1994
Robin Higham, *Bases of Air Strategy,* Shrewsbury, 1998
Francis K. Mason, *The Hawker Hurricane,* London, 1962
Gordon Mitchell, *R. J. Mitchell: Schooldays to Spitfire,* Stroud, 1997
Bruce Robertson et al, *Spitfire: the Story of a Famous Fighter,* Letchworth, 1960
Society of British Aircraft Constructors, *The British Aircraft Industry,* London, 1939
Owen Thetford, *Aircraft of the Royal Air Force since 1918,* London, 1995
T. E. Winslow, *Forewarned is Forearmed,* London, 1948

CIVILIAN PAMPHLETS

Air Raid Precautions, *Training Manual No 1: Basic Training in Air Raid Precautions*, London, 1940

S. Evelyn Thomas, *ARP – A Concise, Fully Illustrated and Practical Guide*, St Albans, c.1940

V. J. Wilmoth, *The Auxiliary Fireman*, London, 1939

TOPOGRAPHY

J. Holland Rose, ed, *Dumouriez and the Defence of England*, London, 1908

Edmund Vale, *Seas and Shores of England*, London, 1936

FIXED DEFENCES

William Foot, *Beaches, Fields, Streets and Hills: The Anti-Invasion Landscapes of England, 1940*, York, 2006

Andrew Saunders, *Fortress Britain*, Liphook, 1989

Henry Wills, *Pillboxes: A Study of UK Defences, 1940*, London, 1985

FRANCE

David Chandler, *The Campaigns of Napoleon*, London, 1967

Vincent Cronin, *Napoleon*, London, 1971

Edouard Desbrières, *Projets de Tentatives de Débarquement aux Îles Britannique*, Paris, 1900–5

E. H. Jenkins, *A History of the French Navy*, London, 1973

George Nafziger, *Imperial Bayonets*, London, 1996

Robert S. Quimby, *The Background of Napoleonic Warfare*, New York, 1957

GERMANY

The Fuehrer Conferences on Naval Affairs, ed J. P. M. Showell, London, 2005

Paul Deichmann, *Luftwaffe Operations in Support of the Army*, London, 1996

Ian Kershaw, *Hitler*, vol 1, *1889–1936*, London, 1998; vol 2, *1936–45*, 2000

Peter Schenk, *The Invasion of England, 1940,* London, 1990

J. R. Smith and Anthony Kay, *German Aircraft of the Second World War,* London, 1972

Adam Tooze, *The Wages of Destruction,* London, 2006

LOCAL HISTORIES

Peter Bloomfield, *Kent in the Napoleonic Wars,* Gloucester, 1987

Jonathan Coad, *The English Heritage Book of Dover Castle and the Defences of Dover,* London, 1995

C. R. Davey, *The Sussex Militia List 1803, Southern Division, Pevensey Rape,* Eastbourne, 1988

John Goodwin, *The Military Defence of West Sussex,* Midhurst, 1995

Joan Ham, *Storrington in Living Memory,* London, 1982

P. A. L. Vine, *The Royal Military Canal,* Newton Abbott, 1972

Mick Wilks, *The Defence of Worcestershire and the Southern Approaches to Birmingham in World War II,* Almeley, Herefordshire, 2007

JOURNALS

Bygone Kent

Journal of the Society for Army Historical Research

Mariner's Mirror

MANUSCRIPTS, NATIONAL ARCHIVES

See the Notes for individual citations. The following series were found to be the most useful:

Admiralty (ADM)

ADM 1 is the general series. In 1803–5 it consists of letters from individuals and bodies, such as fleet commanders, captains and government bodies. There are several volumes, e.g., 1/6035-8, specifically on intelligence. By 1940 the series has developed into files on individual cases, for example 1/18997 on coastal forces and 1/10762 on the CHL radar chain. For that period it is better to do a keyword search, as the subject may be found in many different series. ADM 116 is a series of individual cases, for example 116/4480 on methods of attacking invasion forces. ADM 179 includes the correspondence of the Portsmouth Command. ADM 199 consists of war history cases and papers, including the War Diaries of Dover (199/360) and the Nore (199/365). As with many war diaries, they include far more than the title suggests, including patrol routines, training programmes, etc. Admiralty Fleet Orders can be consulted in ADM 182, or more conveniently in the Royal Naval Museum at Portsmouth.

Air Ministry (AIR)

AIR 2 series is the general one for the Air Ministry. It includes 2/3065 on maintenance personnel, 2/4793 on meteorological services and 2/7218 on the use of bombers in army cooperation. AIR 14 comprises the registered files of Bomber Command, including some on the defence against invasion, airfield defence and photo reconnaissance. AIR has the files of Fighter Command, including some on intelligence organization. AIR 20 is of papers collected by the Air Historical Branch for the production of official and staff histories, including anti-invasion plans and action against gliders. AIR 22 is intelligence summaries and weather charts, and AIR 24 has the operational records of various commands. Air Ministry orders can be found in AIR 72, with an index in 72/90.

Cabinet Papers (CAB)

CAB 66 includes the papers and memoranda produced for the War Cabinet. CAB 120 has the records of the Ministry of Defence Secretariat, both in 1940.

Home Office (HO)

For the 1803–5 period, HO 50 has the correspondence between the office and the military commander-in-chief. HO 51 includes the military correspondence of the Home Office, including the establishment books of the volunteer corps.

Government Communication Headquarters (HW)

HW 48/1 has intelligence reports on German invasion preparations.

Prime Minister's Papers (PREM)

PREM 3 has his operational correspondence and papers, including many miscellaneous matters.

War Office (WO)

WO 1 has the correspondence of the Secretary at War, the Secretary for War and the Commander-in-Chief for 1803–5, including letters and intelligence reports. WO 166 is war diaries of World War II for various formations, starting with General Headquarters (166/1) and through corps and divisions to individual battalions. Again they include many more documents than the titles might suggest. WO 199 is headquarters papers, including many matters such as defence works, RASC supply depots and the Dreyer Report on the beaches. WO 212 includes orders of battle and organization tables. WO 216 is the papers of the Chief of the Imperial General Staff.

INDEX

A map of South-Eastern England and the Strait of Dover, taken from the Times Survey Atlas of the World, 1920. The French port of Boulogne is also shown.